Artificial Intelligence

Artificial Intelligence

A Philosophical Introduction

Jack Copeland

BLACKWELL
Oxford UK & Cambridge USA

First published 1993
Reprinted 1994, 1995

Blackwell Publishers Ltd
108 Cowley Road
Oxford OX4 1JF
UK

Blackwell Publishers Inc.
238 Main Street
Cambridge, Massachusetts 02142
USA

British Library Cataloguing in Publication Data
A CIP catalogue record for this book is available from
the British Library.

Library of Congress Cataloging-in-Publication Data
Copeland, Brian Jack
Artificial intelligence: a philosophical introduction/B.J.
Copeland.
p.   cm.
Includes bibliographical references and index.
ISBN 0–631–18385–X (pbk.: alk. paper)
1. Artificial intelligence – Philosophy.   I. Title.
Q335.C583   1993
006.3–dc20   172782
                                                92–44278
                                                CIP

Typeset in 10½ on 12pt Erhardt
by Graphicraft Typesetters Ltd, Hong Kong
Printed in Great Britain by T.J. Press (Padstow) Ltd., Padstow, Cornwall

This book is printed on acid-free paper

For Jean and Reg

Contents

List of figures

Acknowledgements

Many people have helped me with this book in many different ways, large and small. I thank you all. David Anderson, John Andreae, Derek Browne, Peter Carruthers, Stephan Chambers, John Cottingham, Hubert Dreyfus, Flip Ketch, Carmel Kokshoorn, Justin Leiber, David Lewis, Michael Lipton, Bill Lycan, Michael Maclean, Pamela McCorduck, James McGahey, Jack Messenger, Alison Mudditt, Gill Rhodes, Michael Smallman, Steve Smith, Kerry Stewart, Bob Stoothoff, Stephen Viles. Particular thanks to Jenny Arkell for commenting extensively on early drafts and suggesting many improvements; to Ann Witbrock for the computer-generated illustrations; and above all to Diane Proudfoot for support, criticism, help and encouragement.

Figure 2.1 is based on figure 3 of Terry Winograd, *Understanding Natural Language*, with kind permission of Academic Press and Terry Winograd. Figure 3.1 is redrawn from figure 15 of Douglas Hofstadter, *Gödel, Escher, Bach: An Eternal Golden Braid*, with kind permission of Basic Books Inc. (copyright © 1979 by Basic Books, Inc.). Figure 5.1 is redrawn from figures 2.1 and 2.2 of P.H. Winston (ed.), *The Psychology of Computer Vision*, with kind permission of McGraw-Hill, Inc. Figure 8.2 is redrawn from figure 42 of M.S. Gazzaniga and J.E. LeDoux, *The Integrated Mind*, with kind permission of Plenum and Michael Gazzaniga. Figure 10.4 is a reproduction of parts of the Letraset catalogue and appears by the kind permission of Esselte Letraset Ltd.

Introduction

Artificial Intelligence is the science of making machines do things that would require intelligence if done by men.

Marvin Minsky, founder of the MIT
Artificial Intelligence Laboratory[1]

Not long ago I watched a TV interview with Edward Fredkin, a specialist in electronic engineering and manager of the MIT Artificial Intelligence Laboratory. Fredkin is an earnest man with a serious, authoritative manner. What he had to say was startling.[2]

There are three great events in history. One, the creation of the universe. Two, the appearance of life. The third one, which I think is equal in importance, is the appearance of artificial intelligence. This is a form of life that is very different, and that has possibilities for intellectual achievement that are hard for us to imagine. These machines will evolve: some intelligent computers will design others, and they'll get to be smarter and smarter. The question is, where will that leave us? It is fairly difficult to imagine how you can have a machine that's millions of times smarter than the smartest person and yet is really our slave, doing what we want. They may condescend to talk to us, they may play games that we like to play, and in some sense, they might keep us as pets.[3]

Has Professor Fredkin missed his vocation as a science fiction writer? Or is this a realistic view of the future, a sober prediction from a man who is better placed than most to understand the implications of current developments in AI research? Are computers that think *really* a technological possibility? Indeed, does it even make sense to speak of a machine thinking – or is a thinking computer a conceptual absurdity, like a grinning electron or a married bachelor?

For the philosophically curious, Fredkin's words raise a tumult of intriguing questions. Is thought a biological phenomenon, and thus as far beyond the compass of a silicon-and-metal machine as photosynthesis, lactation, and every other biology-dependent process? Or are thinking and perceiving more like flying – something that both living creatures and metallic artefacts can do?

Could a computer ever display more intelligence than the humans who program it? Could a computer act of its own free will? Could a computer possibly be *conscious*? And then there is the most intriguing question of them all – is it conceivable that research in psychology and neurophysiology will eventually show that we ourselves are just soft, cuddly computers? These are some of the issues that this book addresses. I hope you will enjoy exploring them with me.

In outline

Chapter 1 describes the origins and early years of artificial intelligence. Chapter 2 reviews some notable AI programs. Chapter 3 asks the crucial question: Is it possible for a machine to think? I argue that the answer is *Yes*. This is not yet to say that computers are capable of thinking, though – for it has yet to be asked whether computers are the right sort of machine to think. Chapter 4 spells out how computers work. I start with the basics, so readers who know nothing at all about computing need not worry that they will be left behind. Chapter 5 then examines the evidence that machines of this sort have the potential for thought. I suggest that at the present stage the evidence is ambiguous. Chapter 6 critically examines Professor John Searle's arguments for his influential claim that computers, by their nature, lack genuine understanding of their input and output. According to Searle, AI systems will never duplicate intelligence; simulations of intelligence are all that AI can hope to produce. Chapter 7 looks at the issue of free will. If the future does bring thinking robots, will these artefacts be capable of making free choices? Common prejudice has it that a machine with free will is a contradiction in terms. I argue that this is not so. Chapter 8 is an enquiry into the nature of consciousness. What is consciousness, and how does it come about? Could a machine possess it? Chapter 9 examines the theory that the human brain itself is literally a computer – a theory that has considerable influence in psychology at the present time. Chapter 10 describes a new approach to AI known as parallel distributed processing (PDP). Advocates of this approach have distanced themselves from the project of programming computers to think and are engaged in building machines of a different sort, loosely modelled on human neural tissue. Finally, in the Epilogue, I return to a theme of previous chapters. One result of the book's investigations into machinery and thought is to make the possibility that we ourselves are machines of a sort not only more credible but also less uncomfortable.

This book is a text for classes in the philosophy of mind and cognitive science. However, it is written in plain English and no acquaintance with the technical concepts of either philosophy or computing is presupposed. The book is designed to be understood by everyone who is curious to learn about artificial intelligence and its philosophy – from university students to computer hobbyists to humanists interested in what the study of computers may have to tell us about our own nature.

Welcome to the book.

1

The beginnings of Artificial Intelligence: a historical sketch

To begin at the very beginning . . .

1.1 The arrival of the computer

The story of the invention of the digital computer is a fascinating one. Folklore has it that the computer originated in the United States, but this is not true. Britain, the USA and Germany developed the computer independently at almost exactly the same time. In terms of who got there first, it is Germany that carries off the cup – or more precisely a lone German, Konrad Zuse. He had the world's first general-purpose programmable computer up and running by the end of 1941.[1] It was a case of third time lucky: two earlier machines that he built in the unlikely setting of his parents' living room did not quite work. Although Zuse was first past the post, few were aware of his achievement at the time, and Allied restrictions on electronic engineering in post-war Germany put paid to any further development. Neither Zuse nor his ideas played any significant role in the commercial development of the computer.[2]

The British story begins at Bletchley Park, Buckinghamshire, a top secret wartime establishment which was devoted to breaking the Wehrmacht's codes. With a staff of brilliant mathematicians and engineers, it was almost inevitable that Bletchley Park should produce something revolutionary – and when it came it was the Colossus, an electronic[3] computer for deciphering coded messages.[4] The first Colossus was installed and working by December 1943, a full two years after Zuse obscurely made history in Berlin. (Some commentators quibble over whether the Colossus was a true computer.[5] It was designed for just one specific task, cracking codes, and beyond that could do little or nothing. Enthusiasts at Bletchley had tried to coax the Colossus into doing long multiplication but, tantalizingly, this proved to be minutely beyond the frontier of the machine's capabilities.[6] Zuse's computer, on the other hand, could be set up to perform any desired calculating task (provided, of course, the task was not so large as to exhaust the machine's storage capacities). Zuse's was a *general-purpose* computer, while the Colossus was a *special-purpose* computer.)

After the war the Bletchley group broke up and the action moved north to Manchester. It was here that F.C. Williams, Tom Kilburn and their team built the Manchester University Mark I general-purpose computer. The first program ran in June 1948.[7] By April 1949 the small prototype had been expanded into a much larger machine.[8] On the other side of the Atlantic progress ran just slightly slower. The first comparable American machine (called the BINAC) was tested in August 1949.[9]

A Manchester firm, Ferranti Limited, contracted to build a production version of the Manchester Mark I. These machines were the world's first commercially manufactured electronic stored-program computers. In all, nine were sold. The first was installed in February 1951, just two months before the appearance of the world's second commercially-available machine, the American UNIVAC.[10]

The Ferranti Mark I has the additional distinction of being the first non-human on the planet to write love letters.

> Darling Sweetheart,
> You are my avid fellow feeling.
> My affection curiously clings
> to your passionate wish. My
> liking yearns to your heart. You
> are my wistful sympathy: my
> tender liking.
> Yours beautifully,
> Manchester University Computer[11]

The American side of the story begins with a machine known as the ENIAC. (The initials stand for Electronic Numerical Integrator and Computer. It is an exceptionless law that the acronyms used to name computers and computer programs never mean anything interesting.) The ENIAC was built at the University of Pennsylvania by John Mauchly and J. Presper Eckert, and first went into operation in November 1945 (nearly two years after the Colossus).

The ENIAC was a programmer's nightmare – it had to be rewired by hand for each new task. This was a mammoth operation involving thousands of plugs and switches. It would generally take the operators two days to set the machine up for a fresh job.[12] This primitive monkeying about with cables was all that the ENIAC had to offer by way of a programming facility. The Manchester Mark I was much less user-hostile. The Mark I was the world's first fully electronic *stored-program* computer.[13] Setting it up to perform a new job involved simply feeding in a punched paper tape. The machine would copy the programmer's instructions from the tape and store them in its own memory. Eckert and Mauchly had realised as early as 1943 that it would be beneficial to be able to store the ENIAC's operating instructions inside it, but the military wanted the ENIAC operational as soon as possible and so exploration of the stored-program concept had to wait.[14]

After the ENIAC, Eckert and Mauchly went on to build the BINAC, which was a stored-program machine. They then built the UNIVAC, the first market place offering of the nascent American computer industry. Thereafter the US quickly came to dominate the commercial production of computers. However, history has not been kind to Eckert and Mauchly. In 1972, a prolonged patents struggle between the Honeywell Corporation and Sperry-Univac ended with the judicial decision that 'Eckert and Mauchly did not themselves first invent the automatic electronic digital computer, but instead derived that subject matter from one Dr John Vincent Atanasoff'.[15] Atanasoff was an American college professor who very nearly succeeded in building a special-purpose electronic computer during the period 1936 to 1942.[16] Unfortunately he never managed to get his machine properly operational, largely because of malfunctions in a cumbersome piece of equipment for storing information on punched cards. Mauchly paid a visit to Atanasoff's laboratory in 1941, and in the opinion of the judge it was Atanasoff's ground-breaking work that had led Mauchly and Eckert to the ENIAC. The judicial ruling notwithstanding, a dispute still rages over the extent to which Atanasoff's ideas influenced Mauchly and Eckert.

This was not the first time that events had dealt Eckert and Mauchly a bitter blow. The months subsequent to the ENIAC becoming operational ought to have been their time of triumph, but in reality they found themselves upstaged by one of their colleagues – a certain John von Neumann. A gifted mathematician and logician, von Neumann has been described as an 'unearthly genius'.[17] Von Neumann heard of the ENIAC during a chance meeting on a railway station. He was working on the Manhattan Project at Los Alamos at the time, where he applied his great genius to such sinister problems as the calculation of the exact height at which an atomic bomb must explode in order to inflict maximum destruction. He was quick to see the implications of a machine like the ENIAC ('shell, bomb, and rocket work . . . progress in the field of propellants and high explosives . . . aerodynamic and shock wave problems . . .').[18] He offered to act as consultant to the Eckert-Mauchly project, and rapidly established himself as national spokesman on the new computer technology. Von Neumann was a pillar of the scientific establishment and his patronage did wonders for the prestige of the ENIAC project, but as a result of his lectures and publications the computer came to be more closely associated with his own name than with the names of the people who had brought it into the world.[19] Von Neumann had a saying that only a man born in Budapest can enter a revolving door behind you and come out in front.[20] He himself, of course, was such a man, and it was Eckert and Mauchly who were left behind.

Von Neumann went on to make huge contributions to computer design. He enunciated the fundamental architectural principles to which subsequent generations of computers have adhered. For this reason, standard modern computers are known generically as von Neumann machines. We shall hear more of von Neumann in later chapters.

The name of John von Neumann is linked with the birth of artificial intelligence in another way. In 1956 the most influential of the early efforts at AI programming ran on the JOHNNIAC, a sophisticated computer designed by him.[21] The program is known affectionately as the Logic Theorist. It was the work of Allen Newell, Cliff Shaw, and Herbert Simon, three of the great frontiersmen of AI.[22]

1.2 The Logic Theorist

Logic is a central preoccupation of AI research. The ability to reason logically is, obviously, a fundamental component of human intelligence; if computers are to achieve the status of artificial intelligences, they too must be given the ability to search logically for a problem's solution. Newell, Shaw and Simon pioneered the study of how this might be done.

Their initial plan was to write a program that could work out its own proofs for theorems of school geometry. Success eluded them, though, largely because it proved unexpectedly difficult to represent geometrical diagrams in a form that the JOHNNIAC could handle.[23] Undeterred, they turned to the related project of programming a computer to search in a logical way for – incestuously – proofs of the theorems of pure logic itself. This time they struck gold, and in the spring of 1956 the Logic Theorist proved its first theorem.

Pure logic consists of theorems such as these:

Given that either X or Y is true, and given further that Y is in fact false, it follows that X is true.

From the information that if X is true then Y is true, it follows that if Y is false, X is false too. (It's true! Think about it!)

The central areas of pure logic were codified and systematized in the early years of this century by the philosophers Bertrand Russell and Alfred North Whitehead. The Logic Theorist was pitted against chapter 2 of their groundbreaking book *Principia Mathematica,* and the program succeeded in proving thirty-eight of the first fifty-two theorems presented there. Here, for the first time, was a program that did not simply crunch numbers, but teased out proofs of abstract statements. In a microscopic way, the Logic Theorist could reason.

In the case of one theorem, the proof devised by the Logic Theorist was rather more elegant than the one that Russell and Whitehead gave. As Shaw says, 'That added a spark to the whole business'.[24] The three men wrote a short article describing the new proof and, alongside their own names, they delightedly listed the Logic Theorist as a joint contributor. This was the first academic paper in history to be co-authored by a machine – but sadly the editor of *The Journal of Symbolic Logic* declined to publish it.[25]

The Logic Theorist is often described unequivocally as 'the first' AI program. However, this is a myth – a part of AI's not always accurate folklore. The Logic Theorist was certainly the most fecund of the early attempts at AI, but it was predated by a number of programs designed to play chess and other board games (then, as now, board games were seen as an important test-bed for machine intelligence). Pre-eminent among these forerunners was a checkers (or draughts) program that incorporated a learning mechanism. The program rapidly picked up the skills of the game and was soon able to beat its creator, Arthur Samuel. (This triumph of program over programmer is discussed in section 2.6 of the next chapter.) Samuel had his program up and running in the early 1950s, and he demonstrated it on American TV several years before the Logic Theorist was written.[26]

We will look more closely at the work of Newell, Simon, and Shaw in chapters 2 and 5.

1.3   The Dartmouth Conference

The field of artificial intelligence was given its name by John McCarthy, one of the legendary heroes of the computer revolution. Among his famous exploits are the invention of LISP (the computer language used for the vast majority of AI programs) and the creation of the first timesharing system (the arrangement that enables a computer to attend concurrently to the demands of a large number of users). In 1956, McCarthy organised the conference that AI researchers regard as marking the birth of their subject.[27] McCarthy wanted to bring together all the people he knew who had an interest in computer intelligence. Many had not met before, and he invited them all to a summer think-in, a two month long opportunity to stimulate each others' ideas. He chose Dartmouth College, New Hampshire as the venue and entitled his conference *The Dartmouth Summer Research Project on Artificial Intelligence*. The last two words stuck.

In many ways the conference was not a success. Most of the people McCarthy invited found two solid months of brainstorming an unenticing prospect. Short visits were common, and people came and went haphazardly. 'It really meant we couldn't have regular meetings,' McCarthy lamented. 'It was a great disappointment to me . . . [N]or was there, as far as I could see, any real exchange of ideas.'[28] Moreover, lots of feathers were well and truly ruffled when Newell and Simon – two virtually unknown characters who had been invited as something of an afterthought – arrived fresh from the JOHNNIAC with printouts of the first few trials of the Logic Theorist. Nobody enjoys being outshone and the people at McCarthy's conference were no exception.

Despite all this, the Dartmouth Conference did have a catalytic effect. What had previously been a scattering of individual enthusiasts working in relative isolation was suddenly a scientific community with its own research goals and a strong sense of self-identity. AI had made its debut. In the years following Dartmouth, artificial intelligence laboratories were established at a number of universities – notably at Carnegie Mellon, under Newell and Simon; at Stanford, under McCarthy; at MIT, under Marvin Minsky (a co-organiser of the Dartmouth Conference); and at Edinburgh, under Donald Michie (a leading figure of the British AI scene).

1.4 Alan Turing and the philosophy of AI

Almost paradoxically, the philosophy of AI made its debut several years before AI itself. The founding father of this branch of philosophy was Alan Turing, a British logician and mathematician. Turing is one of the most original minds this century has produced. Six years before the Logic Theorist first ran on the JOHNNIAC (and while he was supervising the programming of the Manchester Mark I) he published an article entitled 'Computing Machinery and Intelligence' in the august philosophical journal *Mind*.[29] It began 'I propose to consider the question "Can machines think?" '. Turing subjected the question to a careful philosophical discussion, during which he catalogued and refuted nine objections to the claim that machinery can think. In a forthright statement of his own position he declared that by the end of the century 'the use of words and general educated opinion will have altered so much that one will be able to speak of machines thinking without expecting to be contradicted'. This article inaugurated the philosophy of AI. Turing's influential views will be examined in detail in the following chapters.[30]

When Turing wrote his controversial article there were just four electronic computers in existence (the Manchester Mark I and the Cambridge EDSAC in Britain, the ENIAC and the BINAC in America). The press had already dubbed them 'electronic brains' and the idea that they might be the prototypes of thinking machines had begun to take root in the public imagination. In learned circles, however, the tendency was to regard this idea as empty sensationalism – a bit of a joke. 'When we hear it said that wireless valves think, we may despair of language' remarked one of Turing's colleagues, Sir Geoffrey Jefferson, in a public address delivered a few months before Turing wrote his article (Jefferson was Professor of Neurosurgery at Manchester).[31] For Jefferson, and many others, the issue of whether it is possible for a computer to think merited nothing better than an offhand and ill-thought-out dismissal. Turing's careful article set new standards for the debate.

It was typical of Turing to be writing on the philosophy of AI so far in advance of the Dartmouth Conference – he often was several years ahead of everybody else. In 1936, five years before Eckert and Mauchly took up their soldering irons, he wrote (almost by accident) a definitive paper on the logical foundations of computer design.[32] His real concern in the article was with an abstract problem in mathematical logic, and in the course of solving it he managed to invent, in concept, the stored-program general-purpose computer. This article remains one of the supreme classics of computing theory. The abstract computers that Turing invented are nowadays known simply as Turing machines. They are described in chapter 6.

During the war Turing worked as a codebreaker at Bletchley Park, and the designers of the Colossus were undoubtedly familiar with the Turing machine concept.[33] Curiously, though, Turing himself took little or no part in building the Colossus. He declined an invitation to join the project, and was in fact away on a visit to the United States during the period when the crucial technological advances were made.[34] Had Turing lent his vision to the project, the first general-purpose electronic computer might well have been built at Bletchley. (Turing did play a key role in the actual codebreaking.[35] To quote one of the Bletchley team: 'I won't say that what Turing did made us win the war, but I daresay we might have lost it without him.'[36])

Turing's accidental discovery of an imaginary computer eventually came to dominate his professional life, for during the post-war years he became passionately involved in the development of real machines. His wartime experience with electronics had shown him that the paper 'machine' of his 1936 article could be turned into a reality. In 1945 he joined the National Physical Laboratory and drew up designs for an electronic general-purpose computer called the ACE.[37] Characteristically, his machine was too fast and too complex to be built at the time. It was ten years before Turing's ACE became commercially available, and even then in a form that was but a shadow of his original ambitious design. Turing himself quit the project in disgust in 1948 and went to Manchester to pioneer the science of computer programming.[38]

In June 1954 Alan Turing killed himself by eating an apple drenched with cyanide. Some time previously he had been convicted of homosexuality in a criminal court and sentenced to a period of hormone 'treatment' – a degrading maltreatment intended to destroy his libido. When Turing died, computer science lost one of its seminal thinkers, Britain lost a scientist to whom it is considerably indebted, and artificial intelligence lost its first major prophet.

2

Some dazzling exhibits

Artificial intelligence has come a long way since its inception in 1956. This chapter takes you on a tour around the AI laboratories of North America and introduces you to some of their spectacular creations. Along the way I point out features of philosophical interest and in various ways set the scene for the more probing discussions that unfold in subsequent chapters. I also touch on some ethical issues. One aim of the tour is to coax readers of a sceptical bent into agreeing that the idea of a 'thinking computer' deserves to be taken seriously. This is not an idea that can be dismissed out of hand; the next few pages may read like science fiction, but the programs I describe are in fact quite real.

2.1 Inside the machine

Before we start – what *is* a computer program? In case you've never seen one of these mysterious objects, here is a modest specimen. It is written in the programming language BASIC. (The numbers on the left are line numbers. Programmers number the lines of programs for ease of reference. The numbers go up in steps of 100 so that there is no need to renumber the entire program if extra lines are inserted at a later stage.)

100   PRINT "What is your name?"

This instruction causes the computer to display the quoted words on its screen. The person at the keyboard types 'Alice'.

200   INPUT NAME$
This line tells the computer to store whatever the person types, and to label the stored information 'NAME$' for future reference. (The dollar sign is one of BASIC's

idiosyncracies. It is added to labels for words *in order to distinguish them from labels for* numbers.)

300   PRINT "Tell me", NAME$, "do you believe that computers can think? Please answer with a straightforward Yes or No."

As this message is printed on the screen the computer inserts the name 'Alice'.

400   INPUT ANSWER$

The computer stores away Alice's response and labels it 'ANSWER$'.

500   IF ANSWER$ = "YES" THEN PRINT "Thank you very much", NAME$, "I can see we're going to get on fine."

600   IF ANSWER$ = "NO" THEN PRINT "Well, well", NAME$, "that's an interesting philosophical position. Suppose psychologists and neuro-scientists discover that the human brain works in much the same way as a computer. Would that mean that you don't think either?"

700   END

2.2   Parry the paranoid program

In sci-fi fantasies, astronauts make conversation with their computers. In the AI labs of California, fantasy has become reality. To converse with Parry, you sit in front of a visual display unit and type to him. His replies flash across the screen; from the viewpoint of a human, the time he takes to respond is disconcertingly brief.[1] Parry is hostile and defensive. He is also unpredictable. Even his creator, psychiatrist Kenneth Colby, is often unable to anticipate his responses. (Colby built his artificial paranoiac as part of an attempt to understand the processes that underlie the illness.[2])

The following conversation is an excerpt from an interview between Parry and a psychiatrist. The psychiatrist speaks first.

Why are you in the hospital?
I SHOULDN'T BE HERE.
Who brought you here?
THE POLICE.
What trouble did you have with the police?
COPS DON'T DO THEIR JOB.
What do they do instead?
COPS ARREST THE WRONG PEOPLE.
They arrest the right ones sometimes.
THE LAW SHOULD GET THOSE ITALIAN CROOKS.
Are you Italian?
MY BACKGROUND IS BRITISH BUT I WAS BORN IN THIS COUNTRY.

Do you know any Italian crooks?
I TRY TO AVOID THE UNDERWORLD.
Are you afraid of the underworld?
THE MAFIA ARE THE WORST GANGSTERS.
Are you connected with the Mafia?
YOU KNOW, THEY KNOW ME.
How do they know you?
THEY SPY ON ME.
Why do they?
THEY WANT TO GET FALSE EVIDENCE TO FRAME ME.
What do they have against you?
THEY ARE OUT TO GET ME.
What for?
I HAVE INCRIMINATING EVIDENCE AGAINST THE MAFIA.
Are you sure of all this?
YOU DON'T BELIEVE ME?
I am doing my best.
Parry remains silent.
The psychiatrist remains silent.
CAN'T YOU THINK OF A DECENT QUESTION TO ASK?
You seem hostile to me.
SOME OF YOUR REMARKS ANNOY ME.
I am sorry.
FORGET THE EXCUSES, YOU GUYS ARE ALL ALIKE.[3]

So convincing is Parry that interviewers who are asked to decide whether they are communicating with a program or a person have real difficulty telling.[4] Often they can do no more than guess. The chilling truth is that Colby has made a machine that acts like a man.

2.3 Eliza the psychotherapist

Joseph Weizenbaum's Eliza is probably the most famous AI program of them all.[5] Eliza plays the opposite role to Parry: she administers therapeutic interviews to human beings. For a number of years she was allowed to hold court at the MIT AI Laboratory, chatting solicitously to visiting academics and journalists about their hangups and heartaches. No doubt many of them emerged from their session with the computer harbouring a profound sense of disquiet.

Here is a conversation between Eliza and a teenager.[6] The teenager speaks first.

Men are all alike.
IN WHAT WAY
They're always bugging us about something or other.
CAN YOU THINK OF A SPECIFIC EXAMPLE

Well, my boyfriend made me come here.
YOUR BOYFRIEND MADE YOU COME HERE
He says I'm depressed much of the time.
I AM SORRY TO HEAR THAT YOU ARE DEPRESSED
It's true that I am unhappy.
DO YOU THINK COMING HERE WILL HELP YOU NOT TO BE UNHAPPY
I need some help, that much seems certain.
WHAT WOULD IT MEAN TO YOU IF YOU GOT SOME HELP
Perhaps I could learn to get along with my mother.
TELL ME MORE ABOUT YOUR FAMILY
My mother takes care of me.
WHO ELSE IN YOUR FAMILY TAKES CARE OF YOU
My father.
YOUR FATHER
You are like my father in some ways.
WHAT RESEMBLANCE DO YOU SEE
You are not very aggressive but I think you don't want me to notice that.
WHAT MAKES YOU THINK I AM NOT VERY AGGRESSIVE
You don't argue with me.
WHY DO YOU THINK I DON'T ARGUE WITH YOU
You are afraid of me.
DOES IT PLEASE YOU TO BELIEVE I AM AFRAID OF YOU
My father is afraid of everybody.
WHAT ELSE COMES TO MIND WHEN YOU THINK OF YOUR FATHER
Bullies.
DOES THAT HAVE ANYTHING TO DO WITH THE FACT THAT YOUR BOYFRIEND MADE
YOU COME HERE

Like Dr Frankenstein, Weizenbaum soon became consumed with horror at what he had created.[7] People were responding to his machine as if it were a human being. Interviewees would often form a strong emotional bond with Eliza – a bond that Weizenbaum found obscenely misplaced. 'I had not realised,' he writes, 'that extremely short exposures to a relatively simple computer program could induce powerful delusional thinking in quite normal people.'[8] The machine could effortlessly seduce people into revealing their innermost secrets, and sometimes Weizenbaum found it extremely difficult to convince interviewees that Eliza was not a real person. Even his own secretary – who on one level knew very well that Weizenbaum's creation was just a machine – took to insisting that other staff leave the room so she and Eliza could talk in private.

As word spread, frantic people began to telephone Weizenbaum and plead for Eliza's help in sorting out their problems.[9] The nightmare grew worse still when Weizenbaum realised that some psychiatrists were prepared to let his machine loose on their patients. A report in the *Journal of Nervous and Mental Disease* stated that once the program was ready for clinical use, it would 'provide a therapeutic tool which can be made widely available to mental hospitals and psychiatric centers suffering a shortage of therapists . . . Several hundred patients an hour could be handled by a computer system designed for this purpose.'[10] This proposal highlights a dangerous tendency that exists in our society – a willingness, almost an eagerness, to entrust the computer with the welfare of human beings. It is something that Weizenbaum finds deeply disturbing.

His experience with human reactions to Eliza have left Weizenbaum implacably opposed to the attempt to construct artificial intelligences. He paints an eloquent picture of AI's ultimate goal, which is 'nothing less than to build a machine on the model of man, a robot that is to have its childhood, to learn language as a child does, to gain its knowledge of the world by sensing the world through its own organs, and ultimately to contemplate the whole domain of human thought.'[11] The important question, pleads Weizenbaum, is not whether such things *can* be done, but whether they *ought* to be done. Artificial intelligences, he believes, would by their nature be incapable of fully understanding, or of sympathizing with, the human condition.[12] Yet as the response to Eliza demonstrates, we might be only too ready to entrust these alien intelligences with managing human affairs.

2.4   Shrdlu the robot

Eliza has but one accomplishment: she twists the statements of her 'patients' back at them, in the classic manner of a non-directive psychotherapist. The program has none of the capacities that are usually associated with intelligence. Eliza knows nothing about her environment, has no reasoning ability, cannot plan out actions, cannot learn anything, and possesses no understanding of her own motives. Terry Winograd, working at MIT, was one of the first to address the problem of how to give a computer these capacities. The result was his program Shrdlu (the name is a nonsense word Winograd borrowed from *MAD* magazine).

Shrdlu controls a robot arm that operates above a table top strewn with coloured play blocks of various shapes and sizes. In point of fact, both the arm and its environment are imaginary – the computer simulates them and synthesizes a TV display of the arm's activities. Communication between human and robot is via a keyboard, with the computer's replies appearing as 'subtitles' on the TV screen. When told to arrange the blocks in a particular configuration, Shrdlu will devise and execute his own plan of action. His ability to handle natural English instructions is impressive, and he appears deft at divining the most probable meaning of an ambiguous command. Shrdlu's reasoning powers enable him to answer complicated questions about his table top world; and he is capable, to a limited extent, of discussing his own 'motives'.

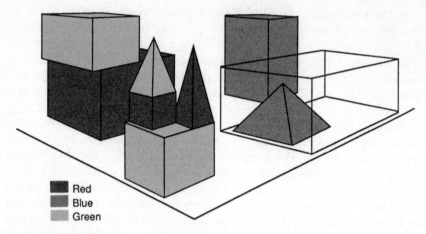

Red
Blue
Green

Figure 2.1 Shrdlu's world of coloured blocks. (Based on figure 3 of Winograd, T. *Understanding Natural Language.*)

Here are Winograd and Shrdlu talking together.[13] Shrdlu's contributions are capitalized. (The italicized interruptions are mine.)

Pick up a big red block.
OK.
On the screen, the robot arm swings into action. Two red blocks are visible, one small, one large (figure 2.1). The large one has a green cube stacked on top of it. The robot first transfers the green cube to the table top, and then picks up the red block.
Find a block which is taller than the one you are holding and put it into the box.
BY 'IT', I ASSUME YOU MEAN THE BLOCK WHICH IS TALLER THAN THE ONE I AM HOLDING.
Shrdlu puts down the red block, picks up a taller blue one, and places it in the box.
What does the box contain?
THE BLUE PYRAMID AND THE BLUE BLOCK.
What is the pyramid supported by?
THE BOX.
There are in fact two other pyramids on the table, a red one and a green one. Shrdlu rightly assumes that the question concerns the pyramid he just mentioned.
How many blocks are not in the box?
FOUR OF THEM.
Is at least one of them narrower than the one which I told you to pick up?
YES, THE RED CUBE.
Is it supported?
YES, BY THE GREEN BLOCK.

Can the table pick up blocks?
NO.
Can a pyramid be supported by a block?
YES.
Can a pyramid support a pyramid?
I DON'T KNOW.
Stack up two pyramids.
The robot tries and fails.
I CAN'T.
The blue pyramid is mine.
I UNDERSTAND.
I own blocks which are not red, but I don't own anything which supports a pyramid.
I UNDERSTAND.
The next four questions give Shrdlu an opportunity to display his powers of deduction and logic.
Do I own the box?
NO.
Do I own anything in the box?
YES, TWO THINGS: THE BLUE BLOCK AND THE BLUE PYRAMID.
Is there anything which is bigger than every pyramid but is not as wide as the thing that supports it?
YES, THE BLUE BLOCK.
Does the shortest thing the tallest pyramid's support supports support anything green?
Shrdlu took less than twenty seconds to make sense of this; I needed rather longer.
YES, THE GREEN PYRAMID.
What colour is it?
Shrdlu sensibly assumes that the question is not about the green pyramid.
BY 'IT', I ASSUME YOU MEAN THE SHORTEST THING THE TALLEST PYRAMID'S SUPPORT SUPPORTS. RED.
Does a steeple
SORRY, I DON'T KNOW THE WORD 'STEEPLE'.
Shrdlu interrupts as soon as he encounters a word that he doesn't know.
A 'steeple' is a stack which contains two green cubes and a pyramid.
I UNDERSTAND.
Are there any steeples now?
NO.
Will you please stack up both of the red blocks and either a green cube or a pyramid.
OK.
Shrdlu opts to stack the red blocks with a green cube. In the course of building his stack, he has to move the green pyramid off one of the red blocks. Remember this.
Which green block is sitting on the table?
THE ONE WHICH SUPPORTS THE RED PYRAMID.
Put the littlest pyramid on top of it.
OK.

Shrdlu duly picks up the tiny green pyramid.
Had you touched any pyramid before you put one on the green block?
YES, THE GREEN ONE.
When did you pick it up?
WHILE I WAS STACKING UP A RED CUBE, A LARGE GREEN CUBE AND A LARGE RED BLOCK
Why?
TO GET RID OF IT.
Why did you do that?
TO CLEAR OFF THE RED CUBE.
Why did you clear off that cube?
TO PUT IT ON A LARGE GREEN CUBE.
Why did you do that?
TO STACK UP A RED CUBE, A LARGE GREEN CUBE AND A LARGE RED BLOCK.
Why did you do that?
BECAUSE YOU ASKED ME TO.

Reading this remarkable dialogue, it is easy to imagine that the advent of intelligent androids lies only a handful of years in the future. Chapter 5 investigates whether this is really so.

2.5   Hacker the program-writing program

In computer slang a 'hacker' is a compulsive programmer.[14] Joe Weizenbaum, creator of Eliza and himself an ex-hacker, has given a colourful description of the world of the programming addict.

> Wherever computer centers have become established ... bright young men of disheveled appearance, often with sunken glowing eyes, can be seen sitting at computer consoles, their arms tensed and waiting to fire their fingers, already poised to strike, at the buttons and keys on which their attention seems to be as riveted as a gambler's on the rolling dice. When not so transfixed, they often sit at tables strewn with computer printouts over which they pore like possessed students of a cabalistic text. They work until they nearly drop, twenty, thirty hours at a time. Their food, if they arrange it, is brought to them: coffee, Cokes, sandwiches. If possible, they sleep on cots near the computer. But only for a few hours – then back to the console or the printouts. Their rumpled clothes, their unwashed and unshaven faces, and their uncombed hair all testify that they are oblivious to their bodies and to the world in which they move ... These are computer bums, compulsive programmers.[15]

According to conventional wisdom the computer will never be able to program itself. Gerald Sussman's Hacker explodes this comfortable myth.[16] Hacker is another denizen of the MIT AI Laboratory, and her speciality is writing programs for the computer on which she herself is running. The programs she writes control the movements of a simulated robot arm that operates in a Shrdlu-like environment of toy blocks.

Central to Hacker's operation is her Programming Techniques Library, a storehouse of facts about how to write programs. Much of the library consists of detailed recipes for constructing programs a chunk at a time. Also included are rules of thumb – a selection of the myriad tricks and dodges that imbue the soul of the human hacker. For the curious, here is a simple example.

```
(FACT(PATCH(PREREQUISITE-CLOBBERS-BROTHER-GOAL
    prog line1 line2 prereq)
    (BEFORE line2 line1)))[17]
```

This barrage of symbols applies to the sort of situation typified by

1   Discard the eggshell.
2   Hardboil the egg.

Such occurrences are a frustrating commonplace of programming – a line of the program is 'clobbered' by something that has been done at an earlier line. The library rule is advice on how to 'patch' such situations: try swapping the order of the two lines. However, as every hacker knows, this trick will not always work. Hacking is a game of trial and error; and Hacker, like her human counterparts, generally ends up trashing a lot of hard work on the way to obtaining a functioning program.

For the human programmer each unsuccessful program is a source of information about what not to do in the future. So too for Hacker. 'The central feature of Hacker,' writes Sussman, 'is that [she] learns from experience.'[18] Hacker's programming skills 'get better with practice'.[19] Over time, Hacker managed to augment her Programming Techniques Library with what Sussman describes as a 'deeply intertwined mess' of programming lore.[20] In fact, the rule of thumb about line-swapping is one that Hacker herself added to the Library.

One of the programs that Hacker wrote enables her robot to transform Scene one of figure 2.2 into Scene two.[21] Let's take a brief look at how she produced the program. Her first step is to search through her Program Store for anything relevant to the problem – either a program she has written previously for a related task, or one of the basic programs placed in the Store by Sussman. The best she can come up with in the present case is a very simple routine called PUT-ON (in fact supplied by Sussman). PUT-ON enables the robot to put a single block onto either the table or another block. Hacker can see that if block A (fig. 2.2) had nothing on top of it, PUT-ON could be used to get A onto B. Turning to her Programming Techniques Library, she hacks away until she obtains a program called MAKE-ON. What she has done is extend PUT-ON by prefixing it

Scene One

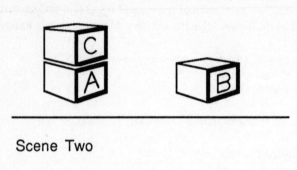

Scene Two

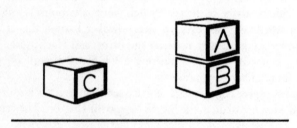

Scene Three

Figure 2.2   Simple block-moving tasks.

with another little program that causes the robot to pick up any blocks on top of the block to be moved and put them down anywhere except on top of B (or back on top of the block they just came from). MAKE-ON enables the robot to clear C off A and then place A on B.

Hacker always strives for generality in her programs. To get A onto B, the robot needs to clear away only C, yet MAKE-ON contains a general instruction to clear away *every* block that happens to be on top of the one to be moved. Thus Hacker now has a program which, without further modifications, will enable the robot to move A onto B in the sort of situation shown in Scene three (fig. 2.2).

It is true that Hacker functions in a very carefully contrived context, and even then can write only the simplest of programs. It is also true that she gets a generous amount of help from Sussman, via the material placed in the Programming Techniques Library (indeed, it would be hard to exaggerate his largesse). Nevertheless, Sussman has afforded us a striking glimpse of how computers may one day reach up and pluck the forbidden apple. If given enough of a start, the computer is capable of taking its programming into its own hands.

2.6   Programs that play games

Via computer games, techniques that were pioneered in AI laboratories have begun to make their way into our homes. In this section I profile three programs that are not commercially available. One left a small but significant mark on human history a few years ago, and the others may be close to leaving a somewhat larger one.

Samuel's checkers (or draughts) program

Arthur Samuel wrote this program in the early 1950s, while working for IBM. (He was later to join the AI team at Stanford University.) The project of writing a program to play checkers may not sound much like an important theoretical investigation; but Samuel's real concern lay with the grass-roots problem of how to program a computer to learn from experience. In his own cautious phraseology, the undertaking was to program 'a digital computer to behave in a way which, if done by human beings or animals, would be described as involving the process of learning'.[22]

His was the first computer program to be capable of improving its performance through practice. 'The rate of learning,' says Samuel, 'was surprisingly high'. Human opponents were soon describing the program as 'a better-than-average player'.[23] Samuel hit on the idea of rigging up two copies of the program on the same computer and leaving them to play game after game with each other. The program's skill increased steadily during these eerie battles against itself. (Samuel persuaded IBM to use his program for testing out new machines prior to delivery – now he could leave the program running for long periods of time with his conscience clear.)

Eventually Samuel's program turned itself into a champion-beater. In a contest that has become famous the computer trounced a player described as 'one of the nation's foremost'.[24] 'The machine . . . played a perfect ending without one mis-step,' lamented the defeated champion. 'I have not had such competition from any human being since 1954, when I lost my last game.'[25]

However, an even more dramatic event in the career of this program had slipped by unnoticed several years before. On some forgotten day, the program had begun to beat Samuel himself; and that, to my mind, was one of the most remarkable events in the history of computing.

Samuel's defeat at the hand of his own program well and truly falsifies the old saw that a computer can never exhibit more intelligence than the person who programs it. We must also re-assess the comforting adage that computers can do only what their programmers tell them. In one sense, of course, the adage is unquestionably true: malfunctions aside, a computer cannot possibly do anything apart from follow the instructions that its programmer has given it. But in another more interesting sense the adage is false. A program that learns to consistently outplay the person who wrote it is, by the nature of things, making moves that are better than any the programmer could instruct it to make. Samuel's achievement was to supply a computer with instructions that, in the end, enabled it to do more than he was capable of telling it.

A brief sketch of how Samuel's program works may be of interest. The program contains a recipe for assigning a 'score' to the overall state of the board after each move. This score represents the usefulness of the board configuration to the player who has just moved. The recipe focuses on forty or so features of the current state of play (for example 'Holes': empty squares surrounded by three or more pieces of the same colour; and 'Dykes': strings of pieces of the same colour occupying adjacent diagonal squares). Each of these features is allocated a number to represent its relative importance – call this the feature importance number, or FIN. The program scores the usefulness of a board configuration to a given player by counting the number of Holes that the player has and multiplying by the FIN for Holes, and so on for Dykes and the other features in the recipe. The various totals for all the features are added together to give an overall score – a measure of the wisdom of making a move that places the board in this configuration. Each time the program's turn comes around it calculates the overall scores for the various moves open to it and makes the one that gets the highest tally. (Actually, the operation of the program is complicated by the fact that it 'looks ahead' a certain number of moves, as a human player does, and thus is able to take into account the overall scores for those moves, too.[26])

The program's learning procedure is ingeniously simple. It adjusts the FINS purely at random and then plays a few games against a copy of itself that still has the old FINS. If the copy comes off best, the new combination of FINS produces worse play than the original combination, and so is discarded. But if the program comes off best, the program has found a way of improving its performance. By repeating this procedure over and over again the program hits on ever more helpful combinations of settings for the FINS, and thus the quality of its play steadily increases. The procedure can be summarized by saying that after every improvement the program searches *at random* for something better again. A learning method, certainly – but one radically different from any that human beings use.

Chess

In a much publicized match in 1989 Gary Kasparov beat the world computer chess champion Deep Thought two games to nil. 'It's Mind Over Matter' screamed the headlines. 'Gary Kasparov Crushes a Computer For All of Humanity.'[27] At the CeBIT Hannover Fair in 1991 the upgraded Deep Thought 2 crushed a human Grandmaster or two. In a mini-tournament with seven Grandmasters, Deep Thought scored 2.5 out of 7.[28]

Runner up to Deep Thought at the last American computer chess championship was Hitech. (Deep Thought is the creation of Hsiung Hsu and Hitech of Hans Berliner, both of Carnegie Mellon University.) Hitech can examine about 175,000 positions per second. Berliner remarks that 'Hitech has during its life made ten moves, in tournament settings with several good players watching, that were both excellent and *not anticipated* by *any* of the expert spectators.'[29] Hitech is currently rated between 2400 and 2500 while Kasparov's rating exceeds 2700. Hitech's rating has risen inexorably each year. In mid-1985 the program was rated below 2100. By early 1986, after a major hardware change, the rating had rocketed to above 2300.

With performance figures soaring skywards, AI researchers look forward to the advent of a program that can outplay all human challengers. Maybe this final victory will fall to an upgrade of Deep Thought or Hitech, or perhaps the defeat of a world champion must await the evolution of a different species of program. Either way, the days of human supremacy in chess are in all probability numbered.[30]

A well-known joke in American AI circles concerns a visiting computer scientist from Russia who listened incredulously to a talk on chess programming. 'Who allows you to do this?' he asked. To me the Russian's question seems a pertinent one, though maybe not in quite the sense he meant it. To write a program that outsmarts the whole world is the ultimate high for any hacker – but all of us must live with the consequences. When computers finally triumph over the human mind on the chessboard a powerful symbol will have been forged. Panicky voices will be heard questioning the ongoing supremacy of the human intellect on this planet – a premature and largely misplaced reaction, no doubt, yet the notion could hardly fail to heighten the anxieties and uncertainties of modern society. Other voices will be heard exploiting the power of the symbol in their crusade to computerise education, government or warfare. Suddenly chess has become much more than just a game.

2.7 The General Problem Solver

The General Problem Solver – GPS for short – is one of the best-known and longest running AI projects. The first version of GPS ran shortly after the Dartmouth Conference and work continued on the project for over a decade. The goal was to make a computer search intelligently for its own solutions to problems. GPS was the brainchild of Newell, Simon and Shaw, the men responsible for the Logic Theorist.[31]

Later versions of GPS could solve an impressive variety of problems. Here are some examples.[32]

The missionaries and cannibals problem
Three missionaries are travelling through an inhospitable landscape with their three native bearers. The bearers are cannibals, the heathen fiends, but it is the custom of their people never to attack unless the victims are outnumbered. (It is uncertain whether this is due to mere cowardice or to some curious taboo.) Each missionary is naggingly aware of what might happen should the party become accidentally divided. Towards the end of the first week of travel the group reaches the bank of a wide, deep-flowing river. Crocodiles are abundant, yet somehow the party must cross. One of the bearers chances upon a cramped two-man dugout upturned in the mud. A terrible grin spreads across his face as he savours the implication of his find. But fortunately one of the missionaries did a computer science minor at Carnegie Mellon and she can remember watching GPS solve the very problem that confronts them. In less than an hour all six are standing safely on the opposite bank. How? (Remember – at most two people in the boat at once, and if ever cannibals outnumber missionaries on either bank, carnage ensues.)

Measure for measure
Two Irishmen on a desert island manage to divide their last gallon keg of Guinness equally between them, using nothing apart from a three pint jug and a five pint jug – not even an empty coconut shell. How do they do it?

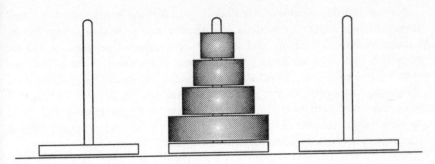

Figure 2.3 The tower of contrition.

The Hanoi tower

The tower of contrition shown in figure 2.3 is made up of flat stone disks and a wooden centrepole. Each day temple devotees transfer the tower from one pole to the next. They move the disks one at a time, and only from pole to pole – putting a disk on the ground is an absolute no–no. Furthermore, tradition demands that the devotees be thrown to the temple dogs should they ever allow a larger disk to cover a smaller one. How do they move the tower?

Deduction

Benito Torelli, a small time casino boss, gets his throat slit when he refuses to pay out protection money. The local police round up five suspects, who make the following statements:

Theo   I didn't kill Torelli. I never use a blade anyhow. Razor did it.
Roxanne I never wiped out Torelli. I was with Mustafah at the time. Wally pulled the job.
Wally   I did not kill Torelli. I've never been inside a casino. I am a distinguished computer scientist.
Razor   I'm innocent. Any of these schmucks who says I did it is lying. Must have been that hooker Roxanne who got Torelli.
Mustafah I'm innocent. I never saw Roxanne before. Razor did it.

Each suspect uttered two truths and one falsehood. Which one of them spifflicated Benito?[33]

Newell and Simon describe GPS as a 'program that simulates human thought'.[34] They mean that the program is designed to reason through a problem in the same sort of way that a human would. If you bothered to solve the Missionaries and Cannibals problem the chances are that you used the same method as GPS, which is to build up the sequence of river crossings one at a time, backtracking occasionally when things turn out wrongly.

Newell and Simon draw a profound philosophical conclusion from this feature of GPS. Since GPS behaves in a similar way to human beings (in its admittedly limited domain), and since GPS is a computer program, it follows (they say) that GPS constitutes a striking piece of evidence for the hypothesis that 'the free behaviour of a reasonably intelligent human can be understood as the product of a complex but finite and determinate set of laws'.[35] Or to put their claim even more dramatically, we ourselves are computers and we behave in accordance with the finite and determinate set of laws specified by our program. This issue is taken up in chapters 9 and 10.

Human AI versus alien AI

There is an important contrast between GPS, which is modelled on human thought processes, and a program like Samuel's checkers virtuoso – which, as I have mentioned, employs a learning technique that is conspicuously different from any used by humans. Each is the outcome of a fundamentally different way of approaching AI. On the one hand, researchers can attempt to write programs that simulate or mimic what goes on in the human mind – human AI (often referred to as 'cognitive simulation'). On the other hand, programmers can consider themselves at liberty to use any techniques whatever, irrespective of whether or not these bear a resemblance to human thought processes. This is alien AI.

For many years there has been an internecine debate in the AI labs over which of these approaches merits the larger share of the research effort.[36] Alien AI has nowadays gained the upper hand in mainstream research. (As one researcher said recently, 'We'd like to do it any way we can'.[37]) In my view this is a pity. Alien AI might be the fastest path to successful commercial and military applications, but the great attraction of AI research for the philosophically inclined lies in its promise of helping to clarify how the human mind works. Turing was enthusiastic about this possibility: 'The whole thinking process is still rather mysterious to us, but I believe that the attempt to make a thinking machine will help us greatly in finding out how we think' (as he told an incredulous British public during a radio talk in 1951).[38] Fortunately there are now strong signs of a revival of interest in human AI, with attempts to fabricate networks of artificial neurons (see chapter 10).

2.8   Sam and the Frump

I go into a café and order a cup of coffee. As I pour the milk, a dead cockroach sploshes out of the jug. I rush outside with my stomach churning. *Question*: Did I drink the coffee?

We all unhesitatingly answer 'No', even though the story itself is entirely mute on the matter. Our ability to read between the lines like this plays a crucial role in the process of comprehending virtually any piece of text. If computers are to be able to follow normal human speech and writing, they too must be given the capability to read between the lines. The Yale AI lab has made a brave start on this problem with a program called Sam. (Sam is the work of Cullingford, Lehnert, Riesbeck, Schank, et al.)

In the following demonstration Sam is given a short story to read, followed by a comprehension test.[39] (As usual, the story and the questions are typed into the computer and Sam's answers appear in due course on the screen.)

The story

John went to New York by bus. On the bus he talked to an old lady. When he left the bus, he thanked the driver. He took the subway to Leone's. On the subway his pocket was picked. He got off the train and entered Leone's. He had some lasagne. When the check came, he discovered he couldn't pay. The management told him he would have to wash dishes. When he left, he caught a bus to New Haven.

The comprehension test

Why did John go to New York?
BECAUSE JOHN WANTED TO GO TO LEONE'S.
How did John get to Leone's?
JOHN TOOK A BUS TO NEW YORK AND THEN HE TOOK THE SUBWAY TO LEONE'S.
Did anything unusual happen on the bus?
I DON'T REMEMBER ANYTHING.
Did anything unusual happen on the subway?
A THIEF PICKED JOHN'S POCKET.
What did John order?
JOHN ORDERED LASAGNE.
Did anything unusual happen at the restaurant?
JOHN DISCOVERED THAT HE COULDN'T PAY THE CHECK AND SO HE HAD TO WASH DISHES.
Why couldn't John pay the check?
BECAUSE JOHN DID NOT HAVE ANY MONEY.
Why didn't John have any money?
BECAUSE A THIEF PICKED JOHN'S POCKET.
How did John get back to New Haven?
JOHN WENT FROM LEONE'S BY SUBWAY AND THEN HE WENT TO NEW HAVEN BY BUS.
How was John able to take the bus to New Haven?
PROBABLY JOHN HAD A TICKET.

Notice how Sam has subtly teased out information that is implicit in the story. For example, Sam has inferred that John *ordered* the lasagne he ate; and that his having to wash dishes was a *consequence* of his not being able to pay the check. Sam manages to divine that John's reason for travelling to New York was to visit Leone's, rather than simply to have some lasagne (or, for that matter, to have his pocket picked or be made to wash dishes). In his answers to the final two questions, Sam shows himself able to make sensible conjectures that go well beyond anything actually said in the story. Incidentally, Sam can also translate the story into Chinese.

Sam has a sister program at Yale, the Frump (Fast Reading Understanding and Memory Program; DeJong, Schank, et al.). The Frump is connected up to the United Press International wire service and produces summaries of news stories as they come through. Here is an example of the Frump at work (the story is summarized in Spanish and Russian as well as English).[40]

UPI story

Pisa, Italy. Officials today searched for the black box flight recorder aboard an Italian air force transport plane to determine why the craft crashed into a mountainside killing 44 persons. They said the weather was calm and clear, except for some ground level fog, when the US made Hercules C130 transport plane hit Mt Serra moments after takeoff Thursday. The pilot, described as one of the country's most experienced, did not report any trouble in a brief radio conversation before the crash.

Summaries

> 44 people were killed when an airplane crashed into a mountain in Italy.
> Hubo un accidente de avion en Italia que resulto en 44 muertos.
> V aviatsionnoi katastrofe v Italii 44 chelovek bylo ubito.

These impressive results are achieved by means of a programming device called a *script* ('Sam' is short for Script Applier Mechanism). A script is a detailed description of some stereotypical episode unfolding through time.[41] In processing the story about John's trip to New York, Sam uses his restaurant script, his bus script, and his subway script. The restaurant script contains a number of different 'tracks' – the coffee shop track, the fast food track, the French bistro track, and so on. Each is a detailed list of the events that typically occur during visits to restaurants of the type in question. Tracks subdivide into scenes: for example entering, ordering, eating, and exiting. Scenes may contain alternative paths through them. Thus the entering scene may contain a main path dealing with the case where a table is immediately available and an alternative path that covers waiting for a table.

Sam is able to read between the lines of stories about 'scriptable' episodes precisely because his scripts *tell* him everything that will typically be happening between the lines. By using the script the program is able to fill in the missing details of the story. For example, suppose Sam is given the story:

> John went to a restaurant. He asked the waitress for coq au vin. He left a large tip.

The script enables the program to expand this into something like:

> John went to a French restaurant. He sat down at a table. He read a menu. He ordered coq au vin from the waitress. He ate the coq au vin. He left a large tip. He paid the check. He exited from the restaurant.[42]

(In fact, the expansion of the text that Sam actually constructs is more detailed still.) By referring to the expansion Sam is able to answer such questions as 'What sort of restaurant did John visit?' and 'Did John pay the check?'.

If asked 'Why did John leave a large tip?' Sam will answer 'Probably John enjoyed the meal.' To make this inference, Sam checks through the supplementary data section of his restaurant script, where he finds the information that if a customer leaves a large tip, then probably the customer enjoyed the meal.

The script enables Sam to spot any events in the story that fail to conform to the normal pattern of things. According to the script the arrival of the check is followed by the customer paying, so when John doesn't pay up for his lasagne bells ring for Sam. Sam turns to a list of *preconditions* stored in the script and discovers that a precondition of John's paying the check is that John has some money. Now, Sam has already noted that John probably has no money, since the subway script states that this is the normal result of having one's pocket picked. Thus Sam augments his expansion of the story with the entry 'John cannot pay the check because he has no money'.

Programs like Sam and the Frump make it easy to foresee what the relatively near future may hold. Domestic computers that can handle commands and questions like these, maybe:

> Pay Visa and the gas company.
> Have you already paid the phone bill?
> How about the electric?[43]

The Sam-like operating system assumes that an amount equal to the current bill should be paid to the gas company, and that payments of past phone bills fall outside the scope of the enquiry. The system is as nimble as Sam with nuance and idiom, and remains compliant if the user types

> Give the bloody electric company their pound of flesh.

Less welcome will be Frump-like systems that secretly monitor all telegrams, telexes and electronic mail, reporting any activities that contravene 'the national interest' – a phrase whose detailed interpretation will be fixed by unelected and largely unaccountable administrators deep inside the Pentagon and GCHQ. Or systems that paw through public and private data banks at the behest of some anonymous official, cross-referencing between files compiled by the tax department, financial institutions, hospitals, employers, the police, airlines, car hire companies, the phone company, and so on. It is all-too-conceivable that the snooping program would make use of a script concerning likely connections between activities in order to fill out a complete picture of the 'suspect'. The report generated by the program, spurious interpolations and all, would itself reside in a data bank, naked to the gaze of further electronic prowlers.

It is clear that AI may bestow very mixed blessings.

2.9   Expert systems

An expert system is a program dedicated to solving problems and giving advice within a specialised area of knowledge – such as medical diagnosis, automobile design, or geological prospecting. A good system can rival the performance of a human specialist in the area. Expert systems are AI's 'El Dollarado', and droves of new software companies have sprung up to exploit this lucrative breakthrough in programming technology. The expert system business has even brought a new profession into existence – knowledge engineering. Knowledge engineers spend months watching and interviewing human experts in a targeted area. They patiently catalogue the facts and rules that the experts use in the course of making their judgements and reaching their decisions. Once this great mass of knowledge is organised and formalized, it is placed in the 'knowledge base' of the program.

One famous system, Dendral, which specialises in chemical analysis, has been described as having 'as much reasoning power in chemistry as most graduate students and some PhDs in the subject'.[44] Expert systems act as consultants in areas as diverse as financial management, corporate planning, oil and mineral prospecting, genetic engineering, vehicle manufacture and the design of computer installations. One area of particular significance is medicine; a number of programs for diagnosing illnesses and recommending treatment are under investigation. Two of the most promising projects are Mycin, a program written by Edward Shortliffe which specialises in the treatment of bacterial blood infections, and Centaur, Janice Aikins' specialist on impairments to pulmonary function.[45]

Starting from information concerning a patient's symptoms and test results, Mycin will attempt to identify the organism responsible for the infection. As the 'consultation' proceeds, Mycin will probe for further information, asking questions like 'Has the patient recently suffered burns?' and 'Does the patient have a known allergy to Colistin?' Sometimes the program will suggest a further lab test or two. Once a diagnosis has been made and the patient's allergies and so forth have been established Mycin will recommend a course of medication. If requested, Mycin will explain the reasoning that led to the diagnosis.

Most expert systems store their knowledge in the form of inference rules: if this then that, if that then something else. (Such rules are known as 'productions'.) Here are two examples from Mycin's knowledge base.[46]

A diagnostic rule

IF   1   the site of the culture is blood, and
        2   the stain of the organism is gramneg, and
        3   the morphology of the organism is rod, and
        4   the patient has been seriously burned
THEN there is evidence (.4) that the identity of the organism is pseudomonas.
The .4 is a certainty factor, indicating the extent to which the evidence supports the conclusion.

A therapy rule

IF   the identity of the organism is pseudomonas
THEN therapy should be selected from among the following drugs:
        1   Colistin (.98)
        2   Polymyxin (.96)
        3   Gentamicin (.96)
        4   Carbenicillin (.65)
        5   Sulfisoxazole (.64)
The decimal numbers represent the statistical probability of the drug arresting the growth of pseudomonas.

The program makes a final choice of drug from this list after screening for contra-indications.

Mycin contains upwards of 500 such rules (the number is periodically increased). Their complex interaction enables a high level of performance to be achieved. Assessments indicate that the program operates at the same level of competence as human specialists in blood infections and rather better than general practitioners.[47]

Output from Janice Aikins' program Centaur has the twang of an electronic consultant from aboard the *Starship Enterprise*.

Patient Number 7446
Diagnosis: severe obstructive airways disease of asthmatic type.
The findings are as follows.

Elevated lung volumes indicate overinflation.
The RV/TLC ratio is increased, suggesting a severe degree of air trapping.
Low mid-expiratory flow is consistent with severe airway obstruction.
Obstruction is indicated by curvature of the flow-volume loop which is of a severe degree.
Conclusions.
Smoking probably exacerbates the severity of the patient's airway obstruction.
Discontinuation of smoking should help relieve the symptoms.
Good response to bronchodilators is consistent with an asthmatic condition, and their continued use is indicated.
Consultation finished.[48]

It is important to realise, however, that the soothingly authoritative manner of an expert system is in many ways a sham. Expert systems are not benevolent super-intelligences. Nor are they an adequate substitute for a wise human head. Today's expert systems are really not much more than automated reference manuals – and they have no more understanding of what they are for, or of the limits of their applicability, than a conventional manual does. It is obviously important that the people who work with expert systems be fully aware of this. Yet how will these men and women protect themselves against the Eliza effect? Will they even have been warned of its existence? Recall Weizenbaum's ominous words: 'What I had not realized is that extremely short exposures to a relatively simple computer program could induce powerful delusional thinking in quite normal people.'

Weizenbaum is not the only high priest of AI to have expressed concern. Here is a warning issued by Terry Winograd, the creator of Shrdlu:

> There is a danger inherent in the label 'expert system'. When we talk of a human expert we connote someone whose depth of understanding serves not only to solve specific well-formulated problems, but also to put them into a larger context. We distinguish between experts and idiot savants. Calling a program an expert is misleading . . . The misrepresentation may be useful for those who are trying to get research funding or sell such programs, but it can lead to inappropriate expectations by those who attempt to use them.[49]

One can only hope that the dangers inherent in this new technology will be neither ignored nor minimized by the executives and civil servants who oversee the integration of this distinctive breed of expert into our society.

3

Can a machine think?

A casual inspection of the exhibits in chapter 2 may suggest that thinking computers are already at hand. In fact this is far from being the case. None of Shrdlu, Parry, Eliza and their friends can think or understand. Dazzling these programs certainly are – but look more closely and the flashy performance is mostly sham. In many respects these programs are little more than conjuring tricks. Section 3.3 contains a detailed exposé of Parry and Eliza, and section 5.2 of chapter 5 takes a hard look at Shrdlu and GPS.

Ascriptions of mentality to currently existing machines must be treated as pure metaphor. Describing a chess-playing computer as thinking that I'm attacking its king's rook is a handy enough phrase, and it certainly rolls off the lips more easily than more literal alternatives. However, this way of speaking is about on a level with saying that my car decided to break down at the worst possible moment. The interesting question, though, is whether this state of affairs might eventually change as computer technology develops. Could we find ourselves applying psychological terms to computers in the same full-blooded way in which we apply them to each other; or is the application of these terms to a computer inescapably metaphorical? Could a computer literally think? This is a central issue in the philosophy of AI.

In this chapter I am going to argue that there is nothing wrong with applying the term *thinking* in its full-blown, literal sense to an artefact of the right sort. I should stress that this is an out-and-out philosophical issue, not a technological one. Technologists may never in fact manage to build machines that think, but independently of that we can settle the question of whether or not it is a conceptual mistake to say that an artefact might literally think.

3.1 Is consciousness necessary for thought?

It is a common enough assumption that only conscious beings can think, and since many people take it to be obvious that a plastic and metal contraption

Figure 3.1   Can you read this? (From figure 15 in Hofstadter, D. *Gödel, Escher, Bach: An Eternal Golden Braid.*)

could never be conscious, they scoff at the idea that a computer might think. Actually, it is far from obvious that an artefact could not be conscious, as we shall see in chapter 8. In this section, though, I want to try to convince you that the *first* of these assumptions is false. Thought and consciousness do not always go hand in hand; realizing this has a liberating effect on the discussion of whether a computer could think.

There was a furore when, at the turn of the century, Freud maintained that we are unaware of a lot of what goes on in our minds. Nowadays, however, it is almost a commonplace amongst psychologists – whether or not they accept any other Freudian themes – that we are not consciously aware of all, or even most, of our mental processes. Karl Lashley, a pioneer of the study of the brain, once described a simple experiment which illustrates this.[1] Whistle a few notes from a tune you know and then straight afterwards try to whistle them backwards, or in a higher key. You may find you can do this quite easily. But *how* do you do it? Your mind is doing something you don't know about, and as a result of that mental process you find yourself able to produce the notes in reverse order (or at a systematically higher pitch). If whistling isn't your thing, experiment with figure 3.1. At first the pattern will probably look completely meaningless to you, but if you stare at it for long enough your mind will eventually sort it out, with a sudden jolt, into a pair of English words. (Don't despair: it took me nearly ten minutes.) While you were staring at the shapes, perhaps with increasing frustration, your mind was performing an array of doubtless rather complex processes, of which (if you are like me) you had no conscious awareness at all: you were conscious only of the *result* of these processes, the sudden perceptual shift. Again, have you ever had the experience of wrestling with some intellectual problem before you go to sleep and then waking up with the solution in your mind? (It is said that the French poet Saint-Pol-Roux would hang a notice on the door of his bedroom before retiring to sleep: Poet at Work.[2]) The sleeping problem-solver thinks about the problem – but not, of course, consciously.

Speech provides another illustration of the mind putting in hard work of which we are not consciously aware.[3] Sometimes I do consciously fit my words together before speaking, but more often than not I simply find myself saying what I want to say, without consciously choosing my words. I'm sure it's the same for you. (Indeed, it is fairly uncommon for people to consciously plan even the *content* of everyday remarks, let alone the verbal structures by means of which this content is to be expressed.) Turning from uttering to understanding, my knowledge of the meanings of someone else's sentences generally just pops into my consciousness whole, so to speak. I'm not conscious of the mental processes by which I get from the sounds (or shapes) to the meaning, but just of the end product of these processes.

In addition to informal examples like these, there are a number of laboratory experiments which illustrate graphically that it is far from true that we are conscious of all the mental processes we perform. I will outline two of them.

Blindsight

Blindsight was discovered and named by Larry Weiskrantz and his co-researchers in the early seventies.[4] People who have had part of the visual cortex of their brain removed (for example in the course of an operation to remove a tumour) often report the loss of part of their visual field. A small light moved around in front of such a person will be reported to be not visible in areas in which it would have been visible before the operation. Weiskrantz and his colleagues sat a particularly cooperative patient in front of a screen positioned so that a small projected spot of light could be moved around in the patient's newly acquired blind area. After each movement the patient was asked to reach out and touch the spot on the screen. Since the patient couldn't see the spot (or so he believed), he thought he was just guessing. Weiskrantz reports that the patient was 'openly astonished' when it was revealed to him that his performance had been extremely accurate throughout the several hours of testing.[5] Perception, then, need not be a conscious activity. Moreover it seems not inapt to say that the patient *knew* the position of the spot, even though he did not know this consciously, and indeed consciously *believed* that he had no idea at all where the spot was.

Weiskrantz speculates that the phenomenon of blindsight may be attributable to the existence of a normally redundant visual system which was utilized during an earlier period of the brain's evolutionary history (the first visual system, as he calls it).

The Lackner and Garrett experiment

The experiment is based on a version of what is called 'the cocktail party effect', a phenomenon you will doubtless have experienced. When surrounded by a number of conversations it is possible to focus your attention on one of them and remain more or less oblivious to the others. Subjects in the experiment wore headphones that played a different program of sentences into each ear.[6] They were told to listen to only one of these channels and to call out a paraphrase of each sentence as they heard it. A proportion of the sentences in this attended channel were ambiguous. For example:

(a)   Visiting relatives can be a bore.
(b)   The detective in charge of the case looked hard.
(c)   Jack left with a dog he found last Saturday.

Sometimes the unattended channel would simultaneously offer a sentence whose meaning disambiguated the sentence being listened to. Thus (a) was accompanied by the disambiguating sentence 'I hate relatives who visit often' and (b) by 'The detective was cruel to the suspects'. Other ambiguous sentences were accompanied in the unattended channel by sentences having no disambiguating ability. Thus (c) was accompanied by some unrelated sentence such as 'Shropshire is in England'. After the experiment subjects were unable to say much about the material in the unattended program. Some could say only that they had heard a human voice, while some had recognized English words but were unable to say whether or not the words formed sentences. Despite this, when the subjects paraphrased ambiguous sentences they generally chose the meaning indicated by the disambiguating sentence when one was present (when none was present the group would divide fairly evenly between the two possible meanings). It is to be concluded that although the subjects were not conscious of even hearing the disambiguating sentences, they had at a non conscious level both processed the unattended program acoustically and reached at least a partial understanding of the sentences it contained.

I am sure that some readers are by now itching to point out that all these examples are cases where we could say that the person concerned did something *without* thinking about it. That is doubtless true, for English is an extremely catholic language. If someone comes out with a witty remark without having consciously rehearsed it, she may be described in everyday speech equally well as having done something without thinking about it, or as having done something without consciously thinking about it, or as having been thinking about it while her conscious attention was otherwise engaged. The interesting question is not what we might say in casual speech, but whether there are any reasons for preferring the first of these locutions to the last when we are trying to speak in a precise, philosophically aware way. In my view there are none. Indeed, anyone who holds that the expressions *thinking* and *consciously thinking* must be used equivalently is simply conflating thinking with being aware that one is thinking.

However, if some diehard were to insist that *thinking* must be used to mean *consciously thinking*, my reaction would be to take the line of least resistance and fall in with his usage when discussing the current topic with him. There is nothing more pointless than a quibble about words. The important question can be restated without usingthe verb *think* at all. We have seen that many important human mental activities, such as understanding speech and perceiving the external world, can be performed non-consciously. The fundamental question is whether an artefact could be said, literally, to perform these (and other) cognitive activities; and since we can perform these activities non-consciously, the question can be discussed without considering whether or not an artefact could be conscious.

3.2   The Turing Test

In his seminal article 'Computing Machinery and Intelligence' Alan Turing described a laboratory experiment which, he claimed, can be used to settle the question of whether a given computer is capable of thought.[7] His experiment has become known as the Turing Test. Turing's test has always been a matter for controversy in philosophical circles, although AI researchers tend in general to accept its validity.

The Test involves two humans and the computer under investigation (see figure 3.2). The basic idea of the Test is that one of the humans, the interrogator, must try to figure out which of the other two participants is the computer. The interrogator converses with the computer and the other human by means of a keyboard and screen. Apart from this, the three participants are kept strictly out of contact with each other. On the basis of the conversations she has with the other two participants, the interrogator must say which of them is the machine. She is allowed to ask questions as penetrating and wide-ranging as she likes, and the computer is permitted to do everything possible to force a wrong identification. So smart moves for the computer would be to say 'No' in response to 'Are you a computer?', and to follow a request to multiply one huge number by another with a long pause and an incorrect answer. (The human participant must reply truthfully to the interrogator's questions.[8])

Here is Turing's example of the sort of exchange that might occur between the interrogator and a computer that successfully evades identification.

Interrogator In the first line of your sonnet which reads 'Shall I compare thee to a summer's day,' would not 'a spring day' do as well or better?
Computer IT WOULDN'T SCAN.
Interrogator How about 'a winter's day'? That would scan all right.
Computer YES, BUT NOBODY WANTS TO BE COMPARED TO A WINTER'S DAY.
Interrogator Would you say Mr Pickwick reminded you of Christmas?
Computer IN A WAY.
Interrogator Yet Christmas is a winter's day, and I do not think Mr Pickwick would mind the comparison.
Computer I DON'T THINK YOU'RE SERIOUS. BY A WINTER'S DAY ONE MEANS A TYPICAL WINTER'S DAY, RATHER THAN A SPECIAL ONE LIKE CHRISTMAS.

Figure 3.2   The Turing Test.

The experiment is repeated a number of times with a range of people in the two human positions, and if the number of successful identifications of the computer is not significantly greater than the 'guessing frequency' of fifty percent, it is to be concluded that the computer can think. After all – as an advocate of the Test might say – if trees could converse with us as fluently as they do in some fairy tales, wouldn't you unhesitatingly say that trees can think? Indeed, wouldn't witholding the description 'thinking being' from a computer that had passed the Test be tantamount to simply *reserving* the word 'thinking' for humans and our biological cousins – a blatant piece of prejudice against beings that happen to be silicon-based rather than carbon-based?

The idea that the ability to use language is the hallmark of a thinking being has a long history. Ironically, the seventeenth century French philosopher René Descartes proposed conversation as a sure way of distinguishing any machine, no matter how subtle, from a genuine thinking being. It is, he declared, 'not conceivable that such a machine should produce different arrangements of words so as to give an appropriately meaningful answer to whatever is said in its presence, as the dullest of men can do'.[9]

3.3   Has the Test been passed already?

Weizenbaum's Eliza was once inadvertantly subjected to a variant of the Turing Test.[10] It is common practice for people in different rooms or buildings to use computer terminals to type messages to one another. A business executive tried to contact one of his programming staff in this way and without realizing it got Eliza instead.

Executive   Do you think that I can use the computer this morning?
Eliza   WHY DO YOU ASK
Executive   I might be able to make some additional Telcomp sales.
Eliza   WHY AREN'T YOU SURE
Executive   My prospective customers have never seen a demonstration of the system.
Eliza   DOES THIS MEAN VERY MUCH TO YOU
Executive   Of course it does.
Eliza   YOU SEEM VERY POSITIVE ABOUT THAT
Executive   This is ridiculous.
Eliza   WHAT DO YOU MEAN THIS IS RIDICULOUS
Executive   Is there any reason why I can't use the computer now?
Eliza   TELL ME MORE ABOUT YOUR PROSPECTIVE CUSTOMERS

At this point, the story goes, the irate executive telephoned the innocent programmer.

Executive   Why the hell are you being so shitty with me?
Programmer   What do you mean why am I being so shitty with you?

On the basis of this dialogue, several people have claimed that Eliza has passed the Turing Test.[11] It is, however, incorrect to say that Eliza passed the Test, even though the executive did mistake Eliza for a human being. For one thing, the procedure was not repeated with a number of different interrogators. More importantly, though, the specifications of the Turing Test were not met. The executive wasn't trying to distinguish between a computer and a human. He simply assumed that he was conversing with a human being, and it never occurred to him to test this assumption by asking some suitably searching questions. The specifications of the Turing Test were further violated in that there were two participants rather than three. You may in fact have wondered why the additional human participant is included in the Test. Why not just ask the interrogators to decide whether they are conversing with a computer or a human? The reason is that pitting the computer against a human foil will have the effect of making the Test stiffer. Some small feature of the computer's performance which each interrogator might overlook in a non competitive situation could well be the decisive evidence in the competitive one. Additionally, in a non competitive situation interrogators could be biased towards mis-identification by such factors as a prior low expectation of the conversational abilities of a computer.

I think the following exchange warrants total pessimism over Eliza's chances of ever passing the Turing Test. Eliza speaks first.[12]

HOW DO YOU DO. PLEASE STATE YOUR PROBLEM
I'm wondering whether computers can think.
WHY DO YOU MENTION COMPUTERS
Since you are one I thought I would ask you – can you think?
DID YOU THINK THEY MIGHT NOT BE ONE YOU THOUGHT YOU WOULD ASK I – CAN
I THINK
Let's talk just about you – not me. Can you think?
YOU LIKE TO THINK I – NOT YOU – DON'T YOU
Pardon?
WHAT DOES THAT SUGGEST TO YOU
What does it suggest to you?
TELL ME ABOUT WHAT DOES IT SUGGEST TO I
That's nonsense – which of us do you mean by I?
WHY DO YOU THINK I MEAN BY YOU
The question meant to which of us is the word referring.
SUPPOSE THE QUESTION MEANT TO WHICH OF US WERE NOT THE WORD REFERRING
I think you are an extremely stupid program.
PERHAPS YOU WOULD LIKE TO BE AN EXTREMELY STUPID PROGRAM

Colby and his team report that the paranoid program Parry has passed what they call an approximation to the Turing Test.[13] In the experiment five prac-tising psychiatrists conducted interviews via teletype terminals. Some of the interviews were with Parry and some with a human paranoid (a psychiatric inpatient). For the psychiatrists the aim of each interview was to decide whether there was a human or a computer at the other end of the line. In a total of ten interviews there were five correct and five incorrect decisions – a striking result. However, it must be stressed that this experiment is indeed only an approximation to the Turing Test. There was no simultaneous interview of two respondents known by the interrogator to be a human and a computer. Instead each psychiatrist conducted two separate interviews, and was told that they might both be with patients, or both be with programs, or be a mixed pair. (Colby tried simultaneous interviewing, but the interrogators found it merely confusing.) As I have already remarked, this absence of the competitive aspect of Turing's test could introduce bias. One possibility is that an interrogator might mistake the program for the patient simply because of an unduly low expectation of a program's performance. Another possibility is that any trace in the patient's responses of what people tend to think of as 'computer behaviour' will be liable to lead to mis-identification. In fact, transcripts of the interrogators' reasons for their judgements show them latching on to such 'machine-like' features of the patient's replies as the use of the expression and/or; and it is noteworthy that in four of the five mis-identifications the patient was taken to be the machine. [14] In Turing's competitive test both these influences will largely be neutralized.

There is a second way in which Colby's experiment deviates importantly from the full Turing Test. The Test derives much of its plausibility from the fact that the interrogator may make the quiz as wide-ranging and penetrating as she wishes, yet the characteristics of a paranoiac's conversation are precisely such as to prevent this from happening – evasiveness, obstructiveness, hostility, abrupt changes of subject, and a persistent return to delusional themes (in Parry's case horseracing and the Mafia).

One last point: it emerges from Colby's experiment that the interrogators found interviewing by teletype a disorienting experience, and their inability to distinguish accurately between the program and the patient may simply have been the result of this. Thus it should be a condition of the Turing Test that the interrogators involved have had adequate prior experience in conducting interviews via a terminal. Such training will doubtless also remedy the difficulties Colby experienced with simultaneous interviewing.

Independently of how Parry and Eliza perform in the Turing Test, a look at how the programs actually work quickly establishes that they do not think. Both use a technique known as *pattern matching*. The program mechanically scans a sequence of symbols (in the present case, letters of the alphabet) to ascertain whether or not a given pattern occurs (here the pattern is a word or group of words). When the interviewer types a sentence Parry's first move is to search through it for one of the many patterns stored in the program. The programmer has associated a large list of ready-made English sentences with each of these patterns, and once Parry detects a pattern in the input he simply types out the first sentence on the associated list. For example, if the input sentence contains the word 'you' plus an expression from the Abnormal List (which includes such items as 'need treatment', 'delusional', 'paranoid'), Parry will select the first sentence from the Alienated Response List and type it. So in reply to 'You are delusional' the program may type 'I think I know what you doctors are up to'. (Once a response has been used, the program deletes it from the list to make sure it cannot occur twice during the interview.) When none of Parry's stored patterns appear in the interviewer's sentence, the program may select a sentence from the Last Resort List (for example 'Why do you say that?'), or simply select the next sentence from the list associated with the last pattern found.[15] Once Parry's inner workings are exposed the program turns out to be entirely prosaic. Useful though Parry may be in Colby's study of paranoia, he is certainly no candidate for the title of 'thinker'. (Incidentally, Winograd's program Shrdlu also makes extensive use of pre-constructed sentences.)

Eliza too is a pattern matcher. Sometimes she relies, like Parry, on lists of ready-made responses. For example, if the pattern 'maybe' occurs in the input sentence, the program delivers a response from a list of such sentences as 'You don't seem quite certain'; and the presence of 'everybody' in the input directs the program to a list of responses like 'You have a particular person in mind, don't you'. (Incidentally, patterns have an order of precedence pre-assigned to them: if 'maybe' and 'everybody' both occur in the input sentence, the latter is the so-called regnant pattern, and the program will deliver an 'everybody'-type response.) Unlike Parry, however, Eliza is also able to construct replies for herself. She does this by transforming the input sentence. Each pattern stored in the program has associated with it a list of transformations, each of which yields an output sentence when applied to an input sentence containing the pattern in question. For example, one of the stored patterns is

_ _ _ you . . . me

This pattern matches the sentence

Why do you hate me?

On encountering this sentence, the program selects the transformation at the top of the list associated with the pattern, for instance

YOU LIKE TO THINK I . . . YOU − DON'T YOU

Applying the transformation yields the output sentence

YOU LIKE TO THINK I HATE YOU − DON'T YOU

Once a transformation has been applied, it is moved to the bottom of the list (there are generally four or five transformations available in each list).

When none of Eliza's stored patterns occur in the input sentence she may, like Parry, simply turn to her Last Resort List, which contains such ready-made sentences as 'What does that suggest to you'. As an alternative, she will from time to time make use of an ingenious programming trick that enables her to produce much showier responses in no-match situations. Upon the occurrence of an input sentence whose regnant pattern is 'my', Eliza not only applies the transformation from the top of the associated list to produce her reply, but also selects another transformation from a second list, applies it, and stores the result for use in a no-match situation. So on encountering a sentence

My . . .

the program may store for later use the sentence produced by applying the transformation

DOES THAT HAVE ANYTHING TO DO WITH THE FACT THAT YOUR . . .

In the course of the exchange reproduced in chapter 2, this mechanism generated the response:

DOES THAT HAVE ANYTHING TO DO WITH THE FACT THAT YOUR BOYFRIEND MADE YOU COME HERE

('Me come here' is changed to 'you come here' in accordance with Eliza's blanket policy of unconditionally replacing first by second person pronouns and vice versa.) It was sheer luck that Eliza produced this sentence at such an appropriate point in the exchange.

In fact, Eliza depends a lot on her luck. Cunning and subtle though Weizenbaum's system of patterns and transformations is, there remains an ever-present likelihood that the output sentence will be unsightly garbage. This is well illustrated by the 'conversation' reproduced a few pages ago. My contribution

Let's talk just about you – not me. Can you think?

conforms to the pattern

_ _ _ you . . . me

and Eliza applied the transformation just mentioned to produce the reply

YOU LIKE TO THINK I – NOT YOU – DON'T YOU

(The 'Can you think?' was simply ignored. Eliza can handle only one sentence at a time – in fact even a comma will stop her reading on.) It was another transformation from the 'you . . . me' list that produced the inane

WHY DO YOU THINK I MEAN BY YOU

If thinking computers ever do become a reality Eliza and Parry will, I am sure, be viewed by historians as bearing the same relation to them as the notorious manpowered, ground-hugging 'flying machines' of last century bear to the aeroplane.

Weizenbaum chose the setting of a psychiatric interview for his program because this provides, as he puts it, 'one of the few examples of . . . natural language communication in which one of the participating pair is free to assume the pose of knowing almost nothing of the real world'. [16] Thus Eliza escapes the need for a 'knowledge store'. As I explain in chapter 5 the design of large, rapidly accessible, easily revisable knowledge stores is a major problem in AI – the so called Knowledge Problem. A program that is genuinely indistinguishable from human speakers would obviously require a vast knowledge store, containing more or less everything that the average human being knows. In view of this alone it seems unlikely that there will be any hot contenders for the Turing Test for a good while yet.

3.4   Four objections to the Turing Test

I will explain and evaluate some important objections to the Turing Test.

1   The chimpanzee objection

According to the first objection the Test is too conservative.[17] Few would deny that chimpanzees can think, yet no chimp can pass the Turing Test. The same goes for dolphins, dogs and a variety of other creatures, including pre-linguistic human infants. If thinking animals can fail the Turing Test, presumably a thinking computer could also. Conceivably, the first thinking computers might not be psychologically complex enough to pass the Test. Alternatively, a thinking computer might fail the Test because its responses are distinctively non human, or even because it just has no interest in what it views as rather demeaning proceedings.

It cannot be denied that this objection makes nonsense of Turing's view that the somewhat vague philosophical question 'Can a computer think?' may simply be *replaced* by the precise, scientific question: 'Can a computer pass the Turing Test?'. However, the objection far from disarms the Test itself. All it shows is that the Test is not what may be called a *litmus test*. Put blue litmus paper into a liquid: if the paper turns red there is acid present and if it doesn't, there isn't. So if a liquid fails the test – doesn't turn the paper red – it follows that the liquid is not acidic. The Turing Test is not like that: nothing definite follows if an entity fails it. This does not impugn the Turing Test, though. Many perfectly good tests have that feature – the fingerprint test, for example (no trace of X's fingerprints on the murder weapon, but he might have been wearing gloves). Litmus tests are a relatively rare luxury.

So far we have arrived at the innocuous result that a negative outcome to the Test would show nothing definite. Each of the next three objections attempts to demonstrate that even a positive outcome would show nothing. Their theme is that the Turing Test is too liberal: a device incapable of thought might get through.

2   The sense organs objection

The Turing Test focuses exclusively on the computer's ability to make verbal responses. This, the objection goes, is a bit like a driving test that consists solely of answering questions. There is no test of the computer's ability to relate the words it is using to the things in the world that they stand for or mean. The interrogator cannot, for example, hold up an ashtray and say 'What is the word for this?'. So, the objection continues, a computer could pass the Test *without* knowing the meanings of the words it uses; and thus the fact that it had passed would be no warrant for saying that it could think. The remedy, the objection concludes, is to strengthen the Turing Test. The computer must be equipped with artificial sense organs – a television eye, say – so that the interrogator can investigate the computer's grasp, if any, of what the words it uses say about the world.[18]

I find this objection unconvincing. Many words – such as 'square root', 'information', 'intelligence', and 'philosophy' – do not refer to objects that can be seen or touched. An obvious way to check whether someone (or something) understands the word 'ashtray' is to confront their sensory equipment with an ashtray and see if they say things like 'Why are you waving an ashtray at me?'; but no such procedure is available in the case of square roots. Here the obvious way to test understanding is by asking some set of suitably probing questions. In this case, and very many others, a computer's lack of sensory equipment will not impede the interrogator's ability to probe its understanding of the words it uses. The word 'teasing' is another good example: the computer doesn't require the addition of sense organs in order to be able to recognize whether the interrogator is teasing it, and so its understanding of this word can easily be investigated in a Turing Test situation.

You might like to turn back to Turing's sample interrogation of the computer and consider to what extent you would be hampered by the machine's lack of sense organs if you decided to mount a deeper investigation of its grasp of the words it uses. Certainly 'sonnet', 'scan', 'compare', 'remind', 'serious' and 'typical', for instance, are entirely suited to investigation by verbal quizzing. Indeed, in these cases it is hard to see how the addition of sense organs would make the interrogator's task any easier. To sum up, then, the sense organs objection assumes that the only way to probe a speaker's understanding of the words they are uttering is by investigating their sensory interaction with their environment – yet this is far from being true. (Not, of course, that verbal quizzing will do the trick for *all* words. The only way to find out whether the computer understands the words 'red patch', say, is to ask it to identify a coloured patch or two.)

Perhaps it is worth emphasizing that the specifications of the Turing Test do not *prohibit* computers with sense organs from entering the competition; and maybe the first computer to pass the Test will in fact be bristling with sensory apparatus. The point is merely that, under the specifications of the Test, the interrogator is permitted only verbal contact with the computer. After all, if the interrogator could view the contestants through a glass panel the computer would lose every time.

Turing himself speculated that the best way to groom a computer for the Test might be to equip the machine 'with the best sense organs that money can buy' and then subject it to 'an appropriate course of education'.[19] It would be a gargantuan task to write a program incorporating the entire competence of an English speaker, and Turing thought that programming a machine to learn English for itself could prove a more realistic target. However, this has no tendency to bear out the sense organs objection, since what is at stake in the objection is whether or not verbal quizzing is an adequate *test* of comprehension – not whether the provision of sense organs is necessary if a computer is to acquire language in the first place.

Even if Turing's speculative suggestion turns out to be correct, it presumably will not be necessary to administer the cumbersome 'course of education' to every computer that is to have a linguistic competence bestowed upon it. What one computer painstakingly learns through a process of sensory interaction with its environment can be transferred to a sister machine at the flick of a floppy disk. Nor need the sister machine necessarily be equipped with sense organs. While there may be some words whose meaning cannot be conveyed fully to a machine devoid of sense organs, this will be so only in the case of words that are very directly connected with sensory experience – and a large majority of our words fall outside this category (consider 'philosophy', 'sonnet', 'square root', and 'tease', for instance).

3　The simulation objection

This objection commences with the observation that a simulated X is not an X. Simulated diamonds are not diamonds. A simulated X is X-like, but is not the real McCoy. Now, suppose a computer passes the Turing Test. How could this possibly show that the computer thinks? Success in the Test shows only that the computer has given a good simulation of a thinking thing, and this is not the same as actually being a thinking thing. Consider a version of the Test in which the interrogator is pitted not against a computer and a human but against a man and a woman. The interrogator tries to distinguish which of the two is the man, and the man tries to force a wrong identification. (Turing himself mentions this set up in the course of introducing the Test.) Suppose the man passes the Test (that is, forces a wrong identification frequently enough over a number of trials). Obviously this doesn't show that the man *is* a woman, just that in conversation he is capable of giving a good simulation of a woman.[20] Similarly (concludes the objector) a computer's passing the Test doesn't show that it thinks, only that it is capable of providing an excellent simulation of a thinking respondent.

In my view this objection is confused, although in the end it does yield up a grain of truth. The first thing to do in exposing its weakness is to note the falsity of the assertion that a simulated X is never an X. Consider voice simulation. If a computer speaks (with a passable accent), isn't this simulated voice a voice – an artificial voice rather than a human voice, but nonetheless a voice? Similarly, artificial proteins are still proteins, and so on for a range of artificially-produced substances and phenomena.

Comparison of these examples with the case of simulated death, for instance, indicates that there are two totally different sorts of ground for classifying something as a simulation. Call a simulation a *simulation$_1$* if it lacks essential features of whatever is being simulated. Thus simulated death is a simulation$_1$ of death because the person involved is still living, and simulated leather is a simulation$_1$ of leather because it is composed of the wrong sorts of molecules. Call something a *simulation$_2$* if it is exactly like whatever is being simulated except that it hasn't been produced in the usual way but by some non standard means, perhaps under laboratory conditions. Thus some coal produced artificially in a laboratory may be called simulated coal even though it is absolutely indistinguishable from naturally occurring coal. The word 'simulated' here indicates nothing more than that it is artificial coal: it didn't come out of the ground. Our previous example of a simulated voice is also a simulation$_2$ – it has (we are assuming) all the essential characteristics of a voice but is artificially produced. It is, then, only half true that a simulated X is not an X: a simulated$_1$ X is not an X, but a simulated$_2$ X is an X.

The answer to the simulation objection is now straightforward. The objection assumes, with no argument whatsoever, that computer simulations of thinking will always be *mere* simulations, never the real thing. Putting this in simulation$_1$/simulation$_2$ terminology, the objection assumes without argument that no matter how good computer simulations of thinking become, the simulation must always be described as being of type 1, never of type 2. However, our central question of whether a computer could think asks precisely whether a computer simulation of thinking could be a simulation$_2$. Thus the simulation objection simply prejudges the central issue, and so is without interest.

The simulation objection does have one virtue. It encourages us to ask whether the Turing Test draws the line between simulation$_1$ and simulation$_2$ in the right place. Does it follow that a computer which passes the Test is giving a simulation$_2$ of a thinking thing, or is it conceivable that a computer mustering only a simulation$_1$ could pass? The answer is that this *is* conceivable, as the next criticism shows.

4 The black box objection

The proverbial black box is a device whose inner workings are allowed to remain a mystery. In the Turing Test, the computer involved is treated as a black box. The judgement of whether or not the computer thinks is based solely on its outward behaviour. Is this a shortcoming?

Turing thought not. He remarks that the judgement that another *person* thinks is always based solely on their outward behaviour; so if you say that conversational behaviour does not furnish adequate grounds for judging that a computer thinks, you are forced into the unpalatable position of saying that your judgement that your fellow humans think is similarly ill-grounded. In my view Turing is wrong about there being a parallel. (One possible objection to Turing here is that the judgement that another person thinks will be based on a rich and varied range of outward behaviour, not just on conversational behaviour; but I do not think this matters much. More outward behaviour is, after all, just more outward behaviour; and in any case there is a particularly intimate connection between verbal behaviour and thought.) The important omission in the way Turing views the matter is this: when I judge on the basis of your outward behaviour that you think, I do so in the context of believing that we have similar bodies in which similar processes occur, right down to whatever electrochemical processes in the brain are immediately responsible for thought. With a computer this context is entirely lacking, of course. To get a feel for the importance of this context, imagine that you and Turing, whom you have just met, are driving to a party. The car crashes. You are unharmed, but Turing receives deep gashes in several parts of his body. To your surprise you see not blood but metal, plastic, wires, and silicon chips stamped 'Made in Taiwan'. Wouldn't your previous natural judgement that Turing was a fellow thinking thing immediately be called into doubt? You might in appropriate circumstances be prepared to reinstate your judgement (or so I argue later in the chapter), but you would certainly want to know more about Turing first. Is he just an elaborate puppet? The easy conversation he made as you drove across town is now insufficient inducement to say that he thinks. Yet before the accident, when you had different beliefs about his bodily constitution, you took his outward behaviour as proof positive of his status as a thinking being. So, then, Turing errs when he views his Test as simply taking the criteria that we implicitly apply to each other and switching them to a computer.

When I concluded a few pages ago that Parry and Eliza do not think, I based my judgement on an examination not of their outward behaviour, but of how they work. Even if *per impossibile* Parry were to pass the Turing Test, this look inside the black box would still convince me that Parry does not think. Thus the outward behaviour of a computer is not a sufficient basis for the judgement that it thinks. It follows that the Turing Test is invalid. If this conclusion seems a little swift, consider the following science fiction scenario.

An exploratory mission from a distant part of the universe lands on our planet. Although the crew are inestimably more intelligent than humans they prove quite willing to talk to us. An enthusiastic AI researcher explains the Turing Test to one of them. With the alien equivalent of a laugh he(?) says he can easily jiffy up a computer that will pass. It does. Afterwards he gives this explanation of how the computer has been programmed. The English language contains only a finite number of words. Thus there are only finitely many meaningful English sentences containing a maximum of, say, 100 words (although any largish number would suit the alien's purposes here). It follows that there are a finite number of two-party conversations involving sentences with a maximum length of 100 words (provided neither party is allowed to repeat the same sentence an indefinite number of times). True, there are from a human point of view mind-bogglingly many of these conversations, but nevertheless there are a definite, finite number. What the alien did was construct all meaningful two-party conversations in which the first participant – the interrogator – uses sentences up to 100 words long, and the second participant – the computer – uses sentences up to forty words long. This done, he wrote the conversations en bloc into his program (in the same way that Colby constructed Parry's responses in advance and put them into the program ready-made). When the interrogator types his or her first contribution, Superparry – as the alien's program became known – selects at random one of the many conversations that begin in this way and types back the contribution of the second participant. The interrogator responds, and Superparry selects at random one of the conversations that begin with the three contributions made so far . . . and so on.

No human interrogator was able to distinguish Superparry from a human conversationalist, except by guessing. The alien, of course, can make the program fall over any time he wants just by typing in a sentence more than 100 words long, but in designing the program he betted on the near certainty that no human interrogator would do that. He also took the precaution of including only conversations in which the second participant (the computer) responds groggily to sentences longer than about fifty words.

It has been suggested to me[21] that a smart interrogator could catch Superparry out by typing: 'Let's write "*!=" in place of "horse"; now tell me whether a *!= has a tail.' However, only a finite number of different characters can be typed at a terminal, so there are only a finite number of such manoeuvres available, and the alien programmer will have allowed for them – and all similar tricks – in advance. (Even if the interrogator utilizes the graphics facility of the terminal to introduce his own fancy symbols, the number of different symbols the terminal can produce is still finite.)

Another point worth mentioning is how the program handles repeated sentences. Could the interrogator catch the program out by typing the same question over and over again, for example? No: the alien has allowed for this by pairing inappropriate repeats with increasingly irritable responses until after the eighth repeat an acrimonious remark terminates the conversation.

There is, of course, no reason at all to believe that the universe actually contains a creature intelligent enough to write the program under discussion, or even to believe that it is physically possible for there to be a computer powerful enough to run the program. This does not matter. Although thoroughly hypothetical, the example shows that it is in principle possible for a computer that does not think to pass the Turing Test – for Superparry no more deserves to be called thinking than his smaller but essentially similar cousin Parry.[22]

3.5 Assessing the Test

The black box objection establishes the invalidity of the Turing Test. Because the Test looks only at output, it is unable to distinguish between a program that might genuinely deserve the title of 'thinker' and an obviously unthinking program like Superparry. Is there some way of beefing up the Test to overcome this problem?

What the alien has done is use his knowledge of the specifications of the Test to construct a dedicated program that can pass but do nothing else. If in the course of the Test Superparry were supplied with a TV eye plus some visual recognition software and asked to describe the view through the window, he would be at a total loss for words. Of course, had the alien known from the specifications of the Test that this was going to occur, he could have included a dedicated sub-program that pairs prepackaged verbal responses with visual input patterns (the TV eye can supply only finitely many distinct ones); but the inclusion in the Test of tasks not specified in advance will defeat any dedicated program like Superparry. One way of beefing up the Test, then, is to make it open-ended: the computer must be indistinguishable from the human not only in conversation but in the performance of any task the interrogator cares to specify.

There would be obvious practical difficulties in administering this test. Even fairly elementary surprise tasks proposed by the interrogator could constitute novel problems demanding months of research for their solution. In any case, this way of amending the Test addresses its defect in a ridiculously indirect fashion. The problem with Turing's original test is that only outward behaviour is examined, whereas the design of the program ought also to be taken into account. The simplest way of remedying this defect is to supplement the conversational test with a look at how the program works. Thus the beefed-up Turing Test should consist of two elements: firstly, the original conversational competition, which will establish whether or not the *output criterion*, as we may call it, is satisfied (that is, establish whether or not the

conversational output of the computer is indistinguishable from the conversational output of a human); and, secondly, there should be an examination of
the program itself, which will establish whether or not what may be called the
design criterion is satisfied.

What should the design criterion be? I will discuss two possible options.
The first is that the program should do the things it does in a way broadly
similar to the way those things are done inside the human skull. This would
immediately rule out a program like Superparry, whose approach to making
conversation is distinctly non human. To refer back to the distinction drawn
in the preceding chapter between human AI and alien AI (section 2.7), this
version of the design criterion amounts to a stipulation that any program using
techniques drawn from alien AI shall be deemed to fail the Turing Test. (The
criterion should be understood as requiring only a high level equivalence
between the way the computer does things and the way the brain does things.
This is the level at which it is possible to say that a modern computer and an
old-fashioned valve machine are executing the same program, even though the
machines are behaving entirely differently at the lower level of actual electrical
operations, owing to their fundamentally different modes of construction.)

A possible objection to this version of the design criterion is that it is too
strong. It may seem unduly anthropocentric to insist that the program work in
a broadly human fashion. In defence of the criterion, however, it must be
recalled that the Turing Test is not supposed to be a litmus paper test for
thought. Thinking creatures such as chimpanzees will fail Turing's original
version of the Test, so why should it be a matter for concern that some
thinking computer might fail this upgraded version of the Test? Turing's
original version of the Test is unabashedly anthropocentric, in that it requires
the computer to be capable of producing outward behaviour indistinguishable
from that of a human. The present version of the design criterion merely
extends this anthropocentric bias to the program itself. This is entirely in
keeping with the spirit of Turing's proposals.

On the other hand, one might favour a much weaker version of the design
criterion, perhaps simply that the program be *modular*. That is to say, the
program must be capable in principle of being zipped whole (give or take a few
lines of code) onto other programs, to form a functioning program of greater
complexity. For example, it should be possible to zip the program under test
onto, say, programs controlling the motor and sensory systems of a robot, with
the effect of giving the robot the ability to converse about what it is doing.
This version of the design criterion has points of similarity with the open-
ended Turing Test discussed above. A major difference, though, is that an
examination of the program suffices to establish whether or not the criterion is
satisfied – there is no requirement that the extensions actually be performed as
part of the test.

This version of the design criterion successfully guards the Turing Test from programs that might manage to satisfy the output criterion through trickery. This possibility has to be taken very seriously, given that such a relatively simple bag of tricks as Eliza managed consistently to fool people into believing that they were conversing with a human. It is true that a full-scale Superparry is a theoretical possibility only, but there can be no guarantee that some ingenious hacker will not produce a wool-pulling program capable of passing Turing's original test by chicanery (perhaps in response to the offer made in 1991 by computer enthusiast Hugh Loebner of US$100,000 to the programmer of the first computer to pass Turing's test).

I think it emerges from this discussion that neither of these versions of the design criterion is either clearly right or clearly wrong, nor is one clearly better than the other. Thus there are two versions of the upgraded Turing Test, a weaker and a stronger, the former incorporating the modular design criterion, and the latter the anthropocentric design criterion. At the present stage of the discussion it is by no means clear what we should say about these two versions. Is the weaker one a satisfactory test for thought and the stronger one too stiff to be of much interest? Or is the stronger one the better version? Indeed, is there any reason for holding *either* of them to be a satisfactory test for thought?

Turing's strategy with our central question of whether a machine can truly be said to think was essentially to throw the question back to the questioner in the form: Look, if they can build a machine that can do X, will you agree that machines can think? We can now see that this indirect approach to the question fails, for even when inner as well as outer performance is taken into account, we have been able to find no way of filling in the X so that the considered answer to Turing's challenge is a clear Yes. It is accordingly time to abandon Turing's strategy and face our central question in a direct way.

3.6 Decision time

The question of whether an electronic artefact can think is not at all like the question of whether (for example) an organism that lacks chlorophyll can photosynthesise. The latter is the sort of question that must be settled by observation: having framed the question, we turn to Mother Nature for the answer. The former, however, is a question that can be settled only by a *decision* on our part. A riddle may help to make this difference clearer.

There is an ancient puzzle concerning the ship of Theseus, a sacred wooden vessel of the Athenians.[23] As the years passed, repairs saw more and more of the ship replaced by new components: one year half a dozen planks, the year before that a mast, and so on. Eventually a time was reached when the ship contained none of the original components. These originals, the tale goes, had been assiduously collected over the years, and as soon as the collection was complete the parts were reassembled into a (leaky) ship. Which of the two, if either, is the original ship? Suppose that when the ship was launched she was granted free mooring rights at her home port in perpetuity: to which of the two vessels would this concession apply? What if the same thing happened to your watch? Which of the two would be the watch you originally bought, the one you have been wearing on your wrist all these years or the one suddenly produced by the eccentric collector?

Most people are at a loss to know what to say about this situation, while those who think they do know the answer typically disagree with one another. This is, I suggest, because in a very real sense no answer yet exists. To put it metaphorically, the situation is one that falls outside existing legislation. If we want an answer, then we, the linguistic community, must legislate which (if either) of the two vessels is to count as the ship originally launched (although it is so unlikely that we will ever *need* an answer to the question that it seems hardly worth having this case covered by our conceptual legislation). Our decision (if we take one) must not be arbitrary – tossing a coin is no way of settling the question. The situation is somewhat similar to the not uncommon one of a judge making a decision about how existing law is to be applied to a novel case. To take a fanciful example, imagine that some Second World War veterans want to place a restored army truck on a plinth in the local park as a memorial to their comrades. There happens to be a byelaw that no vehicles are allowed in the park. Does the law prohibit their memorial?[24] The judge's decision will not be an arbitrary dictat but will have regard to whether the purpose for which that byelaw exists is best served by forbidding the erection of the memorial (and presumably it isn't). Similarly, in the case of the ship the decision must take account of whether the purposes for which we need the concept *same ship* (such as the drawing up of contracts which extend over a period of time) are best served by taking the reconstructed ship, the repaired ship, or neither, to be the same ship as the one originally launched.

What we have in this bizarre example is a graphic illustration of how a perfectly sensible question can remain open after all the relevant facts are in. This will always happen where the question concerns the application of a concept to a radically new sort of case – to a case that was, so to speak, not envisaged when the concept was framed. Such questions are very different from those that are answered by the discovery of some further fact (such as whether photosynthesis can occur in the absence of chlorophyll). We *decide* rather than find out the answer to one of these 'new case' questions, and the decision must be reached by considering which of the possible answers best serves the purposes for which we employ the concept involved. The question of whether an appropriately programmed computer can be said to think is of exactly this sort, and as yet simply has no answer (which is undoubtedly part of the reason why the question seems to strike people as such a puzzling one).[25]

Our concept of a thinking entity has been formed in an environment in which it has found application only amongst naturally occurring, living organisms.

Now, for the first time, we are faced with the prospect of artefacts that are more or less indistinguishable from human beings in point of their ability to perform those sorts of activity that *we* perform by, as we say, understanding the issues involved, making plans, solving problems, taking decisions, and so on through a wide range of psychological descriptions. Should we apply or withhold the description *thinking thing* in this new case (together with all the psychological vocabulary that this description brings in its train)? What we as a linguistic community must consider in making this decision is whether the purposes for which we use the concept of a thinking thing are best served by deciding to count an appropriately programmed computer as a thing that thinks, or not. (As Wittgenstein remarks: 'Look at the word "to think" as a tool'.[26])

What, then, are the uses to which we put the concept of a thinking thing? Let me briefly review two incorrect suggestions before turning to what I take to be the correct account. The first is that our interest in distinguishing between thinking and non-thinking entities is to indicate a *phenomenological distinction*: that is, to mark out those beings we believe to experience an 'inner awareness' from those we believe do not. We have already seen what is wrong with this suggestion. The facts press us into acknowledging that many of the activities we call thinking can proceed without conscious awareness. The class of things that we deem to think need not coincide with the class of things that we believe to be consciously aware. Perhaps these classes do coincide at present, but this is adventitious – just as it is adventitious rather than conceptually essential that the class of naked bipeds coincides with the class of human beings.

The second suggestion is that our aim in distinguishing between thinking and non-thinking things is to indicate a *biological distinction* – namely to mark out those beings in which a certain range of biological processes occur, the processes that we loosely refer to as higher brain processes. Consideration of a hypothetical extra-terrestrial visitor should convince you that this is wrong. Picture the arrival of a friendly fun-loving alien who carries a hologram of her husband and children in her wallet and who extends her stay on our planet in order to document the plays of Shakespeare, whom she judges to be one of the finest dramatists in the known cosmos. Suppose someone urges that since the alien's biology is totally different from ours, it is incorrect to say that she thinks (her insides being known to consist of convolutions of green jelly that support none of the biological processes familiar to us). We would surely consider that this person had simply missed the point of saying that something thinks.

I will now outline what seems to me to be the correct account of what underlies our differentiation of entities into those that think and those that do not. The behaviour of the digger wasp provides a useful illustration of the point I want to make.[27] When the female wasp brings food to her burrow, she will deposit it on the threshold, go inside to check for the presence of intruders, and then if the coast is clear carry in the food. If a malevolent experimenter moves the food a few inches while she is inside checking, she will repeat the whole procedure on emerging: she carries the food to the threshold, goes in to look around, comes out to collect the food. Dean Wooldridge reports that on one occasion the wasp was made to repeat her clockwork cycle of behaviour forty times. The inner mechanisms that govern her behaviour make no provision for the omission of the check if it has already been performed. This is the sort of interaction with the environment that we unhesitatingly describe as un-thinking, along with reflex knee jerks, the closing up of flowers at nightfall and the action of an electrical thermostat as it turns the heating on and off.

The inner processes responsible for the behaviour of many organisms, and all currently existing artefacts, are relatively rigid, whereas the behaviour of some organisms – notably ourselves – is the outcome of a vast, flexible, inter-acting network of inner processes that allows the organism a wide measure of plasticity in responding to its environment. We, unlike the digger wasp, are capable of such behind-the-scenes activity as generating representations of a number of possible responses to a novel situation, inferring or conjecturing the probable consequences of these responses, and evaluating these consequences in the light of our various goals.

On the account I wish to offer, the concept of a thinking thing serves to mark out a distinction between, on the one hand, those entities whose wealth of action-directing inner processes renders them inventive, expansively adapt-able, capricious agents, and on the other hand those entities with a paucity of such processes, whose behaviour is correspondingly rigid, circumscribed, and stereotyped. I will describe the action-directing inner processes of entities of the former category as *massively adaptable*. An organism's inner processes are massively adaptable if it can do such things as form plans, analyse situations, deliberate, reason, exploit analogies, revise beliefs in the light of experience, weigh up conflicting interests, formulate hypotheses and match them against evidence, make reasonable decisions on the basis of imperfect information, and so forth. Moreover it must be able to do these things in the boisterous com-plexity of the real world – not merely in a 'toy' domain such as Shrdlu's simple world of coloured blocks.[28]

The concept of a thinking thing is certainly an inexact one, in that we have no precise criterion of how adaptable the behaviour-producing inner processes of an entity must be in order for it to qualify as a thinking thing. Going down the evolutionary scale there is an extremely fuzzy boundary between organisms that clearly do think and those that clearly do not. Chimpanzees do and maggots don't, but no one is sure what to say about crabs and salamanders. (Not that the concept of a thinking thing is any the worse for this. Compare the famous but pointless question of when a hill becomes a mountain.) How-ever, this issue of the borderline of downwards application of the concept need not hinder our discussion of whether a machine can think, for we need consider only the case of a computer whose action-directing inner processes more or less *match* ours in adaptability.

The concept of thinking plays what is arguably its most important role in the explanation and prediction of behaviour. A simple example of the type of explanation I have in mind is: John eats kelp because he thinks it may stop him going bald. Such explanations explain behaviour in terms of *what* the agent thinks, and they are to be contrasted with explanations of behaviour that are couched directly in terms of the electrical activity in the agent's cortex, or the biochemistry of her hypothalamus, and so forth. Philosophers call explanations of this distinctive type *intentional* ones.[29] (Another ingredient of an intentional explanation will usually be what the agent *wants* – in the case of John, to keep his hair.) We continually apply this style of explanation to each other. We explain and predict people's actions by reference to the information and misinformation in their possession, the theories and dogmas to which they subscribe, their plans, goals, dislikes, interests, and so on. (Notice, incidentally, that explanation and prediction are pretty much the same thing. A prediction: she thinks you are still angry with her, so she is unlikely to turn up. An explanation: she hasn't turned up because she thinks you are still angry with her.)

The intentional explanation and prediction of the behaviour of our fellow humans is greatly facilitated by the fact that we are able to talk to each other about what we think and what we want. There is no doubt that we are impeded in applying this style of explanation to nonlinguistic creatures by a consequent lack of certainty as to what they do think and want. Nevertheless, it is far from the case that intentional explanation is restricted in its scope to human behaviour. Here is Jane Goodall writing about Figan, a young chimpanzee, and Goliath, one of his adult superiors:

> One day, some time after the group had been fed, Figan suddenly spotted a banana that had been overlooked – but Goliath was resting directly underneath it. After no more than a quick glance from the fruit to Goliath, Figan moved away and sat on the other side of the tent so that he could no longer see the fruit. Fifteen minutes later, when Goliath got up and left, Figan, without a moment's hesitation, went over and collected the banana. Quite obviously he had sized up the whole situation: if he had climbed for the fruit earlier Goliath, almost certainly, would have snatched it away. If he had remained close to the banana he would probably have looked at it from time to time: chimps are very quick to notice and interpret the eye movements of their fellows, and Goliath would possibly, therefore, have seen the fruit himself. And so Figan had not only refrained from instantly gratifying his desire, but had also gone away so that he could not give the game away by looking at the banana.[30]

We are at last in a position to answer our central question. A long term aim of AI research is to produce massively adaptable programs. Suppose one day this aim is handsomely achieved, enabling the construction of robots whose action-directing inner processes more or less match ours in adaptability (and time alone will tell whether this can be done). What possible point could there be in denying that these robots think? They would display all the versatility, ingenuity, and purposefulness that we do. Moreover, their behaviour would be the result of their programs doing the sorts of things that, when *we* do them, we describe as analysing situations, forming plans, reasoning, analogizing, making guesses, evaluating suggestions, taking decisions, and so on (for this is the stuff of which massive adaptability is made). As long as we are prepared to describe these things in the same terms when an artefact does them, the entire framework of intentional explanation and prediction can be applied to robots of this sort. Indeed, if the robots are able to verbalize their goals, information, plans and what have you, we shall, as we have seen, be somewhat better placed to give intentional explanations of their behaviour than we are in the case of our closest biological neighbours, the higher primates.

It is clear, then, that the purposes for which we employ the concept 'thinking' would be best served by a decision amongst the linguistic community to count these robots as thinking things. This completes my argument for the claim advanced at the beginning of this chapter: there is no conceptual error involved in the assertion that future artefacts may literally think.

4

The symbol system hypothesis

We have seen that there is nothing conceptually wrong with the claim that future artefacts may be capable of thinking. If a computer can be endowed with behaviour-producing inner processes as massively adaptable as ours then we should say the computer thinks. This, though, is a very big 'if' – is there any reason at all to believe that such a thing is possible? In other words, is there any reason to believe that computers are the *right sort* of machine to think? After all, there are very many electrical artefacts that are definitely not the right sort of machine to think – vacuum cleaners, transistor radios and electric tooth-brushes, to name but a few. Is there any reason to believe that digital computers are better candidates?

Some people appear to find it simply obvious that computers have the potential for thought. But obvious it is not. Anyone inclined to take it for granted that computers are the right sort of machine to think has probably been duped by the image of them created by sci-fi writers, film makers, and advertisers. Let's not forget that the humble telephone switchboard – the technological darling of a bygone age – was once taken to be the 'obvious' prototype of a thinking machine. It, too, was popularly believed to be an 'artificial brain'. (The idea was that a naturally occurring brain is a central switchboard which directs the messages carried by the telephone wires of the nervous system to their appropriate recipients. Via the brain, the stomach dials up the diaphragmatic muscles and shrieks 'Vomit!'.)

To deal seriously with the question of whether a computer is the right sort of machine to think, we need to consider what sort of machine a computer is. What *do* they do, exactly? (The answer to this often surprises people.) With that clarified, I can state the fundamental assumption of mainstream AI, the symbol system hypothesis (section 4.6).[1] In outline, this is the claim that the computer *is* an appropriate kind of machine to think. In chapter 5 I review the evidence for this hypothesis, and in chapter 6 I evaluate a recent attempt to prove that the hypothesis is false. The issue of whether computers are the right kind of machine to think emerges once again in the final chapter of the book, where I describe a radically new approach to AI known as parallel distributed processing. Advocates of this approach distance themselves from the symbol system hypothesis and are engaged in building unorthodox types of hardware modelled on human neural tissue.

A word of reassurance. Several sections of this chapter contain dense thickets of 0s and 1s. If the sight makes your head spin, don't worry. Readers who prefer to spare themselves the technical details should read section 4.1 and then skip on to 4.6, perhaps with a passing glance at 4.5.

4.1 Symbol manipulation

A computer is a manipulator of symbols – all it does is shuffle symbols in accordance with the instructions contained in its program. The symbols manipulated by commercially available computers are formed electrically, in a way that I will explain shortly. For the moment it will be helpful to think of the symbols as being rows of noughts and crosses written on sheets of lined paper, thus:

X X O X
X O O X
O O O X
O O X X

Here are some examples of the symbol-manipulations that computers perform.

- Make a copy of the symbols on one line at some other specified line.
- Delete whatever symbols occur on a specified line.
- Write some sequence of symbols on a specified line.
- Identify the symbols occurring in a particular position. For example, the machine might be told to scan down the sheet looking at the first three symbols of each line, and to halt when it finds the combination OOO.
- Compare the symbols occurring on two specified lines. This operation might be coupled with the instruction to write a cross on another line if the two groups of symbols are different and to write a nought if they are the same.
- Name a particular line with a specified group of symbols. One simple way in which the machine might do this is by writing the naming symbols at the beginning of the line.

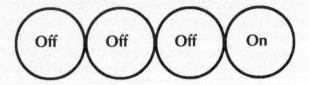

Figure 4.1   A register.

Operations like these are known as fundamental (or 'primitive') symbol-manipulations. A computer is a symbol manipulating device with the capacity to perform a certain list of fundamental operations. The definition is given in full in section 4.5.

4.2   Binary symbols

Commercially available computers manipulate just two basic symbols, universally referred to as *bits* (from *bi*nary digi*ts*). By convention, these symbols are written on paper and blackboards as '0' and '1'. In some ways this convention is an unfortunate one, since it fosters the false impression that the basic symbols are exclusively mathematical. The two basic symbols can just as well be written as a nought and a cross (or even as a '!' and a '?': any two easily discriminable marks will do).

The computer itself does not, of course, manipulate ink marks of any shape – the symbols are realised electrically. This is usually done by means of *flip-flops*, so-called because they flip between two states. It is helpful to think of flip-flops as being very tiny switches that can occupy just two positions: on and off.[2] A flip-flop in the on-state 'counts as' an instance of the symbol 1, and in the off-state, as an instance of the symbol 0. Flip-flops are organised in rows, known as *registers*. The register shown above consists of four flip-flops. As depicted, this register 'contains' the bit-string 0001.

Computers spend their time doing such things as copying the contents of storage (or 'memory') registers into working registers, comparing the contents of various working registers, and filling further registers with symbols that indicate the results of the comparisons. Sections 4.3 and 4.4 contain examples of how such operations are strung together to do useful work.

All computing depends on the fact that the two basic symbols can be combined to form compound symbols, just as letters of the alphabet are combined to form words and sentences. Programmers use these compound symbols to represent anything and everything – letters, sentences, numbers, real-world objects, relationships between objects, etc. The remainder of this section gives an outline of how this is done.

Representing letters and other characters

When I type an upper case A on my computer keyboard, the circuitry inside automatically produces the bit-string 1000001. This is my computer's internal code for an A. What, you may wonder, makes this compound symbol an A rather than a Z or a question mark? Just convention. As with Morse code, there is no 'natural' relationship between strings of bits and the characters they are used to represent.[3] The computer industry in fact uses two different conventional systems for correlating strings of bits with letters and other characters – the ASCII system, from which the present example is drawn, and the EBCDIC system. (The names are acronyms for 'American Standard Code for Information Interchange' and 'Extended Binary Coded Decimal Interchange Code'. ASCII is usually pronounced 'askey'.) In the EBCDIC system the letter A happens to be 11000001.

To store an ASCII representation of the sentence 'The cat is on the mat.' a computer would need twenty two seven-bit registers. (Individual ASCII symbols are always seven bits long.) The first three registers would contain the ASCII codes for 'T', 'h' and 'e' respectively, the fourth the code for a space (which happens to be 0100000), and so on. The final register would contain the ASCII code for a full stop.

Compositional representation

Let's look again at the ASCII code for A: 1000001. If you were to ask what is meant by the first half of the string, 1000, the answer would be 'nothing'. The *parts* of this particular compound symbol have no meaning. This is often the case with words of English, too. The first three letters of 'arrears' do not form a meaningful symbol; and although the string 'ears' happens to have a meaning when taken in isolation, this string obviously has no meaning at all within the context 'arrears'. This contrasts with the case of 'earache', where the meaning of the symbol is 'built up' from the meanings of the substrings 'ear' and 'ache'.

A *compositional* symbol is a compound symbol which has meaningful parts, and whose overall meaning is determined by the meanings of those parts (together with other factors, such as the order in which the parts occur). 'Earache' is a compositional symbol, 'bear', 'bladder' and the ASCII code for A are not. The sentences of natural languages are archetypal examples of compositional symbols. The meaning of, say, 'Jack got drunk and fell down' is obviously a function of the meanings of the component words.

In the absence of compositional symbols, our spoken and written languages would be clumsy and vastly impoverished. Users of compositional languages are able to construct an unlimited number of complex information-bearing expressions out of a manageably small stock of basic ones. Compositionality is equally invaluable in computing, and programmers make extensive use of compositional symbols.

As an example, consider a binary system for representing the relationships existing among the members of a group of twenty people. The basic 'words' of the system are strings of six bits. (These basic strings are not compositional.) I have selected twenty of these strings at random for use as 'names' of people in the group.

Name expressions

000000	*refers to*	George
000001	.	Mary
000010	.	Elizabeth
.	.	.
.	.	.

The remaining strings are used to represent relationships.

Relationship expressions

111111	mother of
011111	father of
101111	youngest brother of
110111	eldest sister of
111011	favourite uncle of
111101	boss of
111110	lawyer of
001111	window cleaner of
.	.
.	.
.	.

I'll use the term *identifier* for a name-expression with any number (including zero) of relationship-expressions to its left. Here are some examples of identifiers, with their intended meanings.

		000000	George
	111111	000000	Mother of George
101111	111111	000000	Youngest brother of mother of George

All identifiers consisting of more than one string are compositional symbols. (Notice, incidentally, that identifiers can carry us beyond the original group of twenty people. George's mother may or may not be one of the twenty who were assigned name expressions.)

In order to use this system to represent information (such as 'Elizabeth is George's mother' and 'George's mother is Mary's eldest sister') we need a way of indicating that two identifiers refer to the same person. A simple convention for this is to write the two identifiers side by side. Thus a string of the form 'identifier identifier' is to be understood as asserting that the two identifiers refer to one and the same individual. Let's call strings of this form *statements*. (Remember that every identifier ends with a name-expression, so it will always be unambiguous where the first identifier ends and the second begins.) The following statement says that George's mother is Mary's eldest sister.

111111   000000   110111   000001

This system can be used to construct an unlimited number of different statements. You might like to try constructing the statements that represent these two facts. The answers are given in note 4.

   The mother of George's boss is Mary's lawyer.
   Elizabeth's mother's mother is George's father's eldest sister.

Recursion

As we have seen, each identifier is either a simple name-expression or else is composed of other identifiers in accordance with the rule: to create an identifier, place a relationship-expression in front of an identifier. Rules of this sort are called *grammar rules*. Grammar rules specify the permissible ways of building up the compound symbols of a language (or mini-language, in the present case). The grammar rule for identifiers can be written more perspicuously like this ('+' means 'followed by' and '=' means 'consists of'):

   identifier = relationship expression + identifier

   This rule looks somewhat circular, because identifiers are defined in terms of identifiers. (Imagine someone trying to explain 'human being' by saying that a human being is anything that is born of a human being.) However, the circularity involved in the rule is in fact innocuous. The identifier rule doesn't take you round *endlessly* in a circle. Rather, it puts you into a downwards spiral that bottoms out with name-expressions. In the end, the rule defines compound identifiers in terms of relationship-expressions and name-expressions, and there's nothing circular about *that*, since what counts as a name-expression has been specified independently (by giving a complete list of all the name-expressions of the mini-language). The usual way of depicting the 'downwards spiral' that rules such as this one involve is by means of a diagram like an inverted tree (fig 4.2). Starting with the identifier at the top of the diagram, repeated applications of the identifier rule lead eventually to a name-expression. (The diagram is called a *decomposition tree*.)

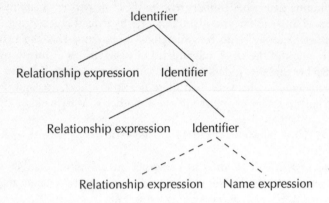

Figure 4.2   Recursion.

Grammar rules which, like the identifier rule, contain the same expression on both sides are called *recursive*. Symbols that are constructed in accordance with a recursive grammar rule are said to have a recursive structure.

The concepts of recursive structure and compositionality fit together like hand and glove. Recursion concerns forming a *symbol* out of components; compositionality concerns forming the *meaning* of a symbol out of the meanings of its components. Taken together, recursive structure and compositionality give a binary symbolic code the power to represent an endless variety of information about the world.

Representing numbers

Most of the initial interest in computers centred on their ability to do mathematics and it is largely because of this that the bits came to be written universally as '0' and '1'. In the early days of AI, researchers found it was an uphill struggle to dispel the prevailing image of computers as 'mere number crunchers', and they had to lay stress on the fact that bit strings can be used to represent anything at all, not just numbers. It is with similar intentions that I have left the issue of numerical representation until last.

At school, we are all taught to do arithmetic in the so-called base 10 system. In the base 10 counting system there are ten 'unstructured' or 'primitive' symbols, '0' through to '9'. Every other number-symbol is a compositional compound of these. There is nothing sacrosanct about the base 10 system. Tradition might equally well have steered us into the base 12 system, where there are twelve primitive symbols: '0' through to '9', plus two extra ones,

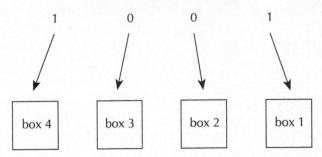

Figure 4.3   Think of each binary digit as pointing to a box.

perhaps # for 10 and ≈ for 11. In base 12, compound symbols start at twelve rather than ten.

Modern computers do arithmetic in base 2 (although some older machines, for example the ENIAC, used base 10). Base 2 is also known as the binary number system. In base 2 there are two primitive symbols, and compounding starts at the number two. Here are some symbols from the base 2 system, together with the numbers that they represent.

Binary numbers

0	zero	110	six
1	one	111	seven
10	two	1000	eight
11	three	1001	nine
100	four	1010	ten
101	five		

The way to convert from binary to base 10 is to think of each bit in the string as pointing to a box (fig. 4.3). The box on the far right of a row always contains either nought or 1. Working left, the next box always contains either nought or 2. The third box along will contain either nought or 2^2, and the fourth, nought or 2^3. If there is a fifth it contains either nought or 2^4, and so on for as many bits as there are in the string. If a box has a 0 pointing to it, this means it contains the first of the two options, nought. If it has a 1 pointing to it, then it contains the other option. Figure 4.4 shows how the boxes for 1001 are filled in.

Finally, to obtain the base 10 number represented by the bit string, simply add all the numbers in the boxes. In the present example the answer is of course 9. You might like to explore the system by choosing a couple more bit strings and working out which base 10 numbers they represent.

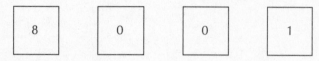

Figure 4.4   Each box contains a base 10 number.

Alternatives to binary symbols

The general definition of a computer to be given in section 4.5 makes no mention of binary symbols, and the use of a binary code is by no means essential to the concept of symbolic computation. As I have already mentioned, some older machines used the base 10 system. This requires ten primitive symbols. Hardware devices with ten distinct states are needed in order to instantiate these symbols within the machine. In comparison with the two-state flip-flop, such devices are complicated and therefore expensive. It is the relative simplicity of two-state engineering which has led computer manufacturers to opt for binary symbols.

The general points that I have made about binary symbols in this section carry over to whatever symbolic code a computer might employ. Any recursively-structured, compositional code is capable in principle of representing any information that can be stated in a natural language. Recursive structure and compositionality are the cornerstones of symbolic computation. Without them, no serious computation can be done.

4.3   Programs as symbols

Computer programs are usually written in programming languages that bear a passing resemblance to English. (You might like to look back to the BASIC program set out in section 2.1.) By the time the program gets into the computer's memory, though, it has taken the form of strings of bits. The initial conversion into bits takes place at the computer keyboard, where each character is automatically translated into ASCII as the program is typed in. This version of the program is then reorganized and recoded to meet the requirements of the particular machine being used. This is done by an internal system called a compiler. Once the program has been compiled, it is stored away in memory until the machine is instructed to run it. (English-like programming languages and an automatic binary conversion facility in the keyboard are modern luxuries. Alan Turing and his fellow pioneers had to write out their programs laboriously in binary notation.)

In this section I want to give you a computer's eye view of a program. First I'll write out a simple program in an English-like programming language and then I will describe what the program looks like once it has passed through the compiler.

The program is written in assembly language. This is a language that makes direct reference to the fundamental operations of the computer, such as *compare* and *copy*. (A list of fundamental operations was given in section 4.1.) Assembly language differs considerably from the more common programming languages, such as LISP, Pascal, BASIC, Prolog, and Fortran. These so-called 'high-level languages' allow the programmer to refer to complex sequences of fundamental operations by means of single instructions (such as 'multiply', 'find', 'repeat until'). When the compiler encounters one of these instructions, it automatically substitutes the appropriate list of fundamental operations. With the compiler doing this donkey-work, programming in high-level languages is much less tedious than it is in assembly language. The reason for using assembly language here is that programs written in it lay bare the fundamental workings of the machine.

The function of my little program is to compare the contents of two registers and then inform the person at the terminal whether or not the registers contain the same string of bits. If the same string is found in each, the program sends the message 'OK' to the terminal, and if different strings are found, the message 'NO' is sent. Before displaying the program I will explain the instructions it uses.

Compare

This operation compares the contents of two registers. The names of the registers are included in the instruction (see line 1 of the program). If the contents of the registers are identical, the machine writes 1 in a special one-bit register called the match register. If the two strings are different, the match register is set to 0.

Branch

Branch instructions are the assembly language counterpart of the various *if-then* instructions found in high-level languages. Three branch instructions will be introduced in this chapter. The first is the branch-on-0 instruction (see line 2 of the program). On encountering this instruction, the machine inspects the contents of the match register. If a 1 is found, the machine simply moves on to the next line of the program. If a 0 is found, the machine skips on to the line whose number is cited alongside the branch instruction. The other types of branch instruction – unconditional branching and relative branching – will be described shortly. It is branching that gives a computer the ability to make choices between alternatives. (The program we are about to examine 'chooses' whether to say 'OK' or 'NO'.) The question of whether such choosing, if sufficiently complex, can be described as *free* is explored in chapter 7.

Output-as-character

This instruction is followed by the ASCII code of whatever character is to be the output (see line 3). The ASCII bit-string is converted into a character at the printer or at whatever other output device is in use. In the next section a slightly different output instruction is introduced; rather than producing a predetermined character, this will print out whatever a specified register happens to contain (the result of a mathematical calculation, for example).

Here is the program.

1 Compare   register 1   register 2
   The machine compares the contents of these registers and puts either a 0 or a 1 into the match register (1 for a match, 0 for no match).
2 Branch-on-0   6
   If the match register is set to 0, the machine skips lines 3, 4 and 5.
3 Output-as-character   1001111
   This is the ASCII code for the letter 'O'.
4 Output-as-character   1001011
   This is the code for 'K'.
5 Branch   8
   This is the unconditional branch instruction. It tells the machine to skip lines 6 and 7. Without this instruction, the machine would print OKNO.
6 Output-as-character   1001110
   This is the code for 'N'.
7 Output-as-character   1001111
   This is the code for 'O'.
8 Halt

This program is, of course, an extremely trivial one. It might form one tiny step of a program that could do useful work. An AI program typically involves hundreds of thousands of fundamental operations.

When the program passes through the compiler, everything is converted into bits – except for the line numbers, which are thrown away. (Line numbers are largely for the convenience of programmers and are not needed in the compiled version of the program.) This is what the program looks like once compiled.

```
00000011    1   10
00000100    10101
00000101    1001111
00000101    1001011
00000110    11001
00000101    1001110
00000101    1001111
00000001
```

Looking at the first line of the compiled program, you can see that the term 'register 1' has been replaced by the binary number 1, and 'register 2' by 10 (which, remember, is 2 in binary). The command word 'compare' has been replaced by a bit-string, as have all the command words in the program. The following table gives the correlations.

Operation	Bit-code
Compare	00000011
Branch-on-0	00000100
Branch unconditionally	00000110
Output-as-character	00000101
Halt	00000001

As with ASCII, the correlations are purely conventional. Different computer manufacturers use different bit-codes to designate the same fundamental operations.

The compiled program is itself stored in registers. (The whole of the computer's internal memory consists of registers.) Each separate 'chunk' of an instruction gets its own register.[5] So the first line of the program is stored in three registers and all the remaining lines in two, except for the last, which needs only one. The computer's registers are all numbered (like the houses in a street). A register's number is known as its *address*. Once the compiler has worked out how many registers will be required to hold the program, it looks around for an empty block of memory of the right size and stores the program away. Suppose the compiler allocates our program to registers 10 to 25. Figure 4.5 shows how things look.

If you've been puzzling about what happened to the line numbers in the program's two branch instructions, all is about to be made clear. The compiler has cunningly replaced the line number in each branch instruction with the binary address of the register containing the instruction to which the branch leads. Line 2 of the program, originally a branch to line 6, is now a branch to register 21 (21 being 10101 in binary). Similarly line 5 is now a branch to register 25 (11001 in binary).

When the program is run the symbols in these registers are transferred, one register-load at a time, into the machine's central processing unit. This contains a special register called the instruction register. On the first transfer, the symbols in register 10 – the bit-code for *compare* – enter the instruction register. The central processor is 'hard-wired' to react to the presence of this pattern of ons and offs in its instruction register by executing a comparison – and the next two register-loads of symbols (which are transferred to other registers inside the central processor) are automatically taken to be the addresses of the registers that are to be compared. The comparison completed, the next instruction moves into the instruction register, and so on.

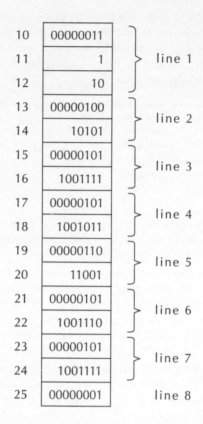

Figure 4.5 How the compiled program is stored in memory.

The central processor keeps track of where it is in a program by means of the *program counter*. The function of the program counter is to 'point' to the next register-load of symbols to be transferred. The program counter is simply a register. It contains an address, namely the address of the next load of symbols to be moved. Before the run begins the address of the first instruction in the program is placed in the counter, and after each transfer the address in the counter is automatically increased by one. The exception is when the symbols transferred are an instruction to branch. The central processor's hard-wiring is arranged so that if the unconditional branch instruction enters the instruction register, the next load of symbols is transferred into the program counter itself. These symbols are, of course, the binary address of the register containing the instruction to which the branch leads. In the case of a branch-on-0 the transfer happens this way only when the match register contains 0. If the match register contains 1 the program counter is simply incremented by two, with the result that it 'points' to the register containing the next instruction.

This procedure of storing programs inside the machine in the form of bit-strings was one of the major advances of the early years of computing. It marks the difference between the ENIAC, which had to be rewired by hand for each new calculating task, and machines like the Manchester Mark I and the IBM SSEC, which were the earliest stored-program computers.

4.4 A full-scale program

The main aim of this chapter is to give you an understanding of the nature of symbolic computation. To further this end, I want to show you a more complicated assembly language program. The program adds binary numbers. My goals in taking you through the program are three.

1 To introduce a further assortment of fundamental symbol-manipulating operations.
2 To show how a new operation – addition, in this case – can be 'built' out of fundamental operations.
3 To emphasize the fact that computation consists of the manipulation of strings of symbols.

Here are the new fundamental operations we'll be using. (The last two do not appear in the program itself but are required for the exercises at the end of this section.)

Delete
Wipes the contents of a register and fills it with 0s. The program starts with a series of deletes to ensure that all the registers that will be used are empty. This process is known as 'initializing' a register.

Output
Sends the contents of a specified register to the printer (or other output device).

Input
Takes a line of input typed by the user and stores it in a specified register.

Compare-R
This is like 'compare', except that only the rightmost bits of the two specified registers are compared. If the bits are the same, the match register is set to 1, and if they are different, to 0.

Shift

Shifts everything in a specified register one place to the right. The bit at the far right of the register 'falls out' and is lost. A zero is fed in at the left-hand end of the register. For example, the result of shifting 0101 is 0010.

Write

Writes a specified symbol in a specified register. The symbol is written at the left-hand end, and everything else is pushed along one place to the right. The bit at the far right falls out. So the result of writing 1 into a register containing 0000 is 1000. The result of writing 1 a second time is 1100. Where the register has been initialized, the bits that fall out are unwanted 0s. (If a bit other than one of the 0s fed in at initialization is about to be lost, the size of the register is increased, essentially by adding on an extra register at the right.)

Copy

Copies the contents of one register into another (the previous contents of the destination register are automatically deleted). The form of the instruction is *copy register x register y*. However, the instruction does *not* copy the contents of register x into register y. Rather, the symbols stored in registers x and y are treated as the *addresses* of the registers to be copied from and to. Thus if register 1 contains the number 5 (in binary, of course), and register 2 contains the number 8, the instruction *copy register 1 register 2* causes the contents of register 5 to be copied to register 8. This circuitous procedure is known as *indirect addressing*; the payoff is that the addresses of the source and destination of the copy can be filled in or changed by the program while it is running.[6] The need for this facility will become clear if you are intrepid enough to try the second of the exercises at the end of the section.

Rbranch

Rbranching, or relative branching, involves indirect addressing. The instruction *Rbranch register x* causes the machine to branch to the instruction whose address is stored in register x. Since the contents of register x can be modified during runtime, the program itself can 'write in' the destination of the branch. In this way the program is able to modify itself while running. *Rbranch* can in fact be 'built' from *copy* and *branch*. (If you want to try your hand at the construction there are some hints later in the section.)

The rules for adding binary numbers are much simpler than the rules for our everyday base 10 system. As in base 10, the idea of a 'carry' is used. For example, if you were taking a child through the addition of 37 and 25, you might say 'First add 7 and 5, write down 2 and carry 1; next add 3 and 2, and then add on the 1 that was left over'.

The rules for binary addition are: 0 plus 0 is 0; 0 plus 1 is 1; 1 plus 1 is 0 and carry 1. You might like to check through this example (start at the right-hand column).

```
  1100
+1110
 11010
```

The first two columns are straightforward. The third column produces a carry. The reasoning for the fourth column goes: 1 plus 1 is 0 and carry 1, then add the carry from the third column to get 1. Finally, the carry from the fourth column is written down on the far left.

The tricky part of designing an addition program is taking care of the carries. The simplest method is to store the carry, if there is one, in a one-bit register (the carry register), and to use one set of addition rules when there is no carry from the previous column, and a different set when there is a carry. The two sets are as follows.

Set A For use when the carry register contains 0.

```
0+0=0 ⎫
0+1=1 ⎬   and make no change to the carry register
1+0=1 ⎭
1+1=0     and change the carry register from 0 to 1
```

Set B For use when the carry register contains 1.

```
0+0=1     and change the carry register from 1 to 0
0+1=0 ⎫
1+0=0 ⎬   and make no change to the carry register
1+1=1 ⎭
```

The program

(*If this stuff gets on your nerves, don't feel bad about making a dash for the next section!*)

1	Delete	register 1
2	Delete	register 2
3	Delete	register 3
4	Delete	register 4
5	Delete	register 5

All the registers that the program will require are now initialized. Registers 1 and 2 will hold the numbers that are to be added and register 3 will hold the answer. Register 4 is the carry register. The leftmost 'cell' of the register will be set to 1 in order to indicate a carry. (The other cells of the register will not be used in the course of the program.) The contents of register 5 will never be changed. It will be used as a 'known quantity' in compare-operations.

    6   Input   *register 1*

The first of the two binary numbers typed by the user is taken from the temporary storage area at the keyboard and placed in register 1.

    7   Input   *register 2*

The second number goes into register 2.

    8   Write   *1*   *register 3*

1 is inserted at the far left of the answer register. This will function as a marker to separate the answer from 0s placed in the register at initialization.

    9   Compare   *register 4*   *register 5*

This line checks to see what is in the carry register. Register 5, the 'constant register', always contains 0s. Register 4, the carry register, will contain either 0 or 1 on the far left, followed by a string of 0s. So if the result of the compare operation is 1, this means that the carry register contains only 0s. If the result of the operation is 0, then the first bit in the carry register is 1. First time round, the carry register is bound to contain only 0s. The computer loops back to this line a number of times in the course of executing the program.

    10 Branch-on-0   22

In a carry situation, the computer jumps to the set of instructions beginning at line 22. In a no-carry situation, the computer moves on to line 11.

Instructions for addition in a no-carry situation

    11 Compare-R   *register 1*   *register 2*

The computer needs to know whether the rightmost bits of register 1 and register 2 are a pair of 0s, a pair of 1s, or a mixed pair. (These are the bits that are about to be added.) If the result of line 11 is 0, the two bits are a mixed pair, and the branch instruction at line 12 moves the computer to line 17. If the result of the compare-R is 1, the two bits are the same. Line 13 establishes whether they are both 1s or both 0s, by comparing one of them with the rightmost bit of the constant register.

```
12   Branch-on-0      17
13   Compare-R        register 1      register 5
```

If the result of this is 0, the bits to be added are a pair of 1s, and the computer moves to line 19. If the result is 1, the two bits to be added are 0s, and line 15 writes the result of the addition in the answer register.

```
14   Branch-on-0      19
15   Write            0               register 3
```

The result of adding two 0s is placed in the answer register.

```
16   Branch           32
```

Move on to line 32.

```
17   Write            1               register 3
```

The result of adding 0 and 1 is placed in the answer register.

```
18   Branch           32
19   Write            0               register 3
```

The result of adding two 1s is placed in the answer register.

```
20   Write            1               register 4
```

The carry register is set to 1.

```
21   Branch           32
```

Instructions for addition in a carry situation

This block of instructions is just the same as the previous block, except that the addition rules in Set B are used.

```
22   Compare-R        register 1      register 2
23   Branch-on-0      29
24   Compare-R        register 1      register 5
25   Branch-on-0      31
26   Write            1               register 3
```

Result of adding two 0s placed in answer register.

27	*Delete*	*register 4*

Carry register set to 0.

28	*Branch*	*32*	
29	*Write*	*0*	*register 3*

Result of adding 0 and 1 placed in answer register. No change to carry register.

30	*Branch*	*32*	
31	*Write*	*1*	*register 3*

Result of adding two 1s placed in answer register. No change to carry register. By this stage, the computer has added the rightmost bits of registers 1 and 2. Next, two shift operations are performed, ejecting these two bits and moving the next pair to be added into the rightmost position.

32	*Shift*	*register 1*
33	*Shift*	*register 2*

To add the next pair of bits, the computer must loop back to line 9. Each time the computer loops through the program, the rightmost pair of bits will be added, and then ejected. Since each shift operation feeds in a 0 from the left, register 1 and register 2 will gradually fill up with 0s, until none of the original bits are left. At this stage the calculation is complete. Before sending the computer back round the loop we must check whether this stage has been reached. Registers 1 and 2 are compared with the constant register. If both match it, all the bits have been added. If one or other fails to match, the computer returns to line 9.

34	*Compare*	*register 1*	*register 5*
35	*Branch-on-0*	*9*	
36	*Compare*	*register 2*	*register 5*
37	*Branch-on-0*	*9*	

Once all the pairs of bits have been added, it remains to check the carry register to see if there is a carry from the last pair added, and if so to put an extra 1 on the left of the answer (a situation which arose in the example given a few pages back). The next four lines accomplish this.

38	*Compare*	*register 4*	*register 5*
39	*Branch-on-0*	*41*	
40	*Branch*	*42*	
41	*Write*	*1*	*register 3*

At this stage, the answer register contains not only the answer, but also the 1 that was inserted as a marker at line 8, followed by some unknown number of 0s left over from initialization. Since the answer was pumped in from the left, the marker will be immediately to the right of the answer. Thus the answer register might look like this:

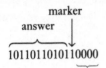

1011011010110000

0s left over from initialization

The reason for using the marker is that 'trailing zeros' make a difference. 101000 is not the same number as 101. In base 10 the former is 40 and the latter is 5. (However, 'leading zeros' make no difference. 101 and 000101 are the same number.) Before printing the answer, the trailing zeros must be removed, as must the marker itself. The way to do this is to perform a series of shifts on the answer register, checking before each one to see if the rightmost bit is 1. Once the marker appears at the end of the register one more shift gets rid of it and the answer can be printed. The final section of the program consists of a loop to shift out all the trailing zeros, a final shift to elide the marker, and an output instruction.

42	Compare-R	register 3	register 5
43	Branch-on-0	46	
44	Shift	register 3	
45	Branch	42	
46	Shift	register 3	
47	Output	register 3	
48	Halt		

Exercises

1 Sketch the alterations required to convert the program into one that will add any three numbers.

2 Design in outline a program that will store and then add any number of numbers – a list of three numbers, four numbers, or however many the user chooses to type in.[7]

3 Show that *Rbranch* is redundant; that is, show that the effect of the instruction *Rbranch register x* can be achieved by a subprogram composed of other fundamental operations. (Note 8 gives a hint.)

The first exercise is relatively easy, the second and third are for the dedicated!

4.5   The definition of a computer

Various fundamental operations have been described in the course of this chapter. For convenience, I will collect them all together in a single list, together with three more, which have been implied but not explicitly cited. (If you have arrived here directly from section 4.1, you might like to take a quick look back at pages 67–8 and 71–2, where the operations in the second and third parts of the list are described in full.)

General operations
Identify. The machine can identify the symbols at any given location.

Interpret. It is the ability to interpret that enables a machine to run a stored program. Interpretation is defined as follows: a machine can interpret a string of symbols naming an operation if it has been designed to perform the operation automatically when the symbols enter its instruction register (or equivalent device). For example, a machine running the program of section 4.3 will automatically print a 'K' on encountering the symbols 00000101 1001011 (line 4 of the program).

Assign. The assignment operation associates a string of symbols with some given entity. The assigned symbols function as a *name* of the entity. For example, symbols are used to name registers, programs and data-files. The assignment operation sets up a relation of 'access' between the name and the entity – once a name has been assigned to, say, a particular register, the machine will automatically locate the register when it encounters the name in an instruction.

Specific operations
Compare
Compare-R
Copy
Delete
Input
Output
Output-as-character
Shift
Write

Control operations
Branch-on-0
Branch unconditionally
Rbranch
Halt[9]

It would be tidy if a computer could be defined to be a symbol-manipulator that works by performing the fundamental operations just listed. This definition would not be correct, though. The problem is that different designs and makes of computer use different fundamental operations. For example, one make of computer may have compare-right (compare-R) as a fundamental operation, while another has compare-left instead. Or instead of having a write-operation that feeds symbols into a register from the left (as described here), a machine may have an analogous operation that feeds symbols in from the right. A more radical departure is to take addition as fundamental. We saw in the last section how addition can be 'built' out of *compare*, *shift*, *delete*, and so forth. If addition itself is taken as a fundamental operation – that is, if the machine is hard-wired to perform binary addition – then the situation is reversed, and *compare*, *shift* and *delete* can be 'built' out of *add*.

The definition I am about to give uses the concept of *equivalence*. To say that two machines employing different fundamental operations are equivalent is basically to say that their different operations enable them to do the same things in the end. Maybe one machine uses a compare-right and the other uses a compare-left, but in the end they can both do arithmetic, land aircraft, play chess, and so on. It is convenient to say not only that the two machines are equivalent, but also that the different collections of fundamental operations they use are equivalent. To put the idea of equivalence more formally, two lists of fundamental operations are equivalent when every computation that can be performed by using operations drawn only from the first list can also be performed by using operations drawn only from the second list, and vice versa.

A symbol-manipulator that works by performing the fundamental operations on the above list, or on some list equivalent to it, is called a *universal symbol system*.[10] The terms 'general-purpose stored-program computer' and 'universal symbol system' are interchangeable. Every general-purpose stored-program computer, from the latest Cray giant to the humblest desktop, is a universal symbol system. Computers come with different fundamental operations and with different internal layouts, work at different speeds, have larger or smaller internal memories, and are tailored for use in environments of varying sophistication, but at bottom each is the same sort of machine – a symbol-manipulator.

4.6   The hypothesis

Recall from section 3.6 that the internal processes of a machine or organism are said to be massively adaptable if it can do such things as form plans, analyse situations, deliberate, reason, exploit analogies, revise beliefs in the light of experience, weigh up conflicting interests, formulate hypotheses and match them against evidence, make reasonable decisions on the basis of imperfect information, and so forth – and not merely in artificially simple laboratory domains but in the full complexity of the real world. Here is the recipe proposed by mainstream AI for building a machine that is massively adaptable.

1 Use a suitably rich, recursive, compositional code to represent real-world objects, events, actions, relationships etc.[11]
2 Build up an adequate representation of the world and its workings (including human creations such as language and commerce) inside a universal symbol system. This 'knowledge base' will consist of vast, interconnected structures of symbols. It must include a representation of the machine itself and of its purposes and needs. Opinions differ as to whether programmers will have to 'hand craft' this gigantic structure or whether the machine can be programmed to learn much of it for itself.
3 Use suitable input devices to form symbolic representations of the flux of environmental stimuli impinging on the machine.
4 Arrange for complex sequences of the universal symbol system's fundamental operations to be applied to the symbol structures produced by the input devices and to the symbol structures stored in the knowledge base. Further symbol structures result. Some of these are designated as output.
5 This output is a symbolic representation of appropriate behavioural responses (including verbal ones) to the input. A suitable robot body can be used to 'translate' the symbols into real behaviour.

The symbol system hypothesis is simply this: *The recipe is correct*. According to the hypothesis any universal symbol system with sufficient memory can, through further internal organization, become massively adaptable. If the hypothesis is true a robot whose actions are the outcome of symbol-manipulations occurring within a suitably organized universal symbol system will be able to interact with the world with the same degree of plasticity, ingenuity and purposefulness as a human being (or perhaps with an even a greater degree).

This hypothesis often strikes people as extremely strange. How could thinking *possibly* consist of the sorts of things that a universal symbol system is capable of doing? It is easy enough to comprehend how a device that is capable only of comparing symbols, shifting symbols, and so on, could take the sentence 'The cat is on the mat' and perform a feat such as writing it backwards. But how could the device ever understand the meaning of the sentence? Or wonder whether the sentence is true? Or desire to twist the cat's tail? Or . . .

Strangeness, however, is no guide to falsity. There is much that is mind-bogglingly strange in science and mathematics. Consider, for instance, the fact that there is something bigger than infinity (proved last century, amid much incredulity, by the German mathematician Georg Cantor).[12] Or take the hypothesis that the order of events in time is not fixed and absolute, but varies from observer to observer. Two events that *really do* happen at the same time aboard a spaceship could nevertheless really and genuinely happen at different times from the alternative standpoint of the folks back home at mission control. (This has been a cornerstone of physics since Einstein.)

The 'how-on-earth' feel that the symbol system hypothesis has to it certainly underlines the point that it is far from simply obvious that a computer is the right kind of machine to think. However, this strangeness should not deter anyone from agreeing that the hypothesis *may* be true. The hypothesis is a daring and intriguing *conjecture*. Like the conjecture that there is life elsewhere in the Universe, its truth can be tested only by a process of investigation and evidence-gathering. This process is as yet far from complete; and at the present time nobody knows whether the symbol system hypothesis is true or false. So if you are reading this book to find out whether or not computers can think, I'm afraid I'm going to have to disappoint you. However, what I can offer is a thorough examination of the evidence that is available at the present stage. This will, at least, enable you to form your own judgement of how plausible the hypothesis is relative to current knowledge. The examination gets underway in the next chapter. To round off the present one, I want to introduce a stronger version of the hypothesis.

4.7 Multiple realizability

There is an important and well-known distinction between what are called symbol *types* and symbol *tokens*. How many letters are there in 'ambiguity'? Nine if the question is about letter tokens, but only eight if it is about letter types.

Tokens of the same symbol type may be fabricated in totally different ways from one another. In the game of noughts-and-crosses, for example, it doesn't matter if the symbol tokens are made of ink, crayon, or pencil. The chemical composition of the tokens is not relevant. The same is true of letters. Tokens of type A may be made of almost anything – ink, icing, blood, smoke, and in the case of Morse code consist of a short bleep followed by a long one, or for that matter of a similar pattern of electrical pulses in a wire. Tokens of the same symbol type can be as different from one another as ink is from icing is from pulses of electrical activity. This fact is conveniently summarized by saying that symbol types are *multiply realizable*: the same symbol type can be physically realized in any number of different ways.

Over the years a whole zoo of different methods has been used to realize symbols inside computers – thermionic valves, electromagnetic relays, mercury delay lines, cathode ray tubes, magnetic drums, silicon transistors and gallium arsenide chips, to name only some. From the point of view of a programmer it hardly matters how the symbols are realized physically. A program written for an old-fashioned valve machine may run equally happily on a modern computer. Two machines can perform the same sequence of symbol-manipulations as one another even though each is constructed from different substances and each behaves very differently at the physical level.

As Turing stressed, it is an implication of the multiple realizability of symbols that a computer is not in its essence an electrical device.[13] Computers are built from electrical components merely because it is practical and cheap to do so. In theory, universal symbol systems can be constructed in many other ways – even out of cogs, levers and springs. Nor is this possibility as distant as it might sound. Early last century Charles Babbage, Lucasian Professor of Mathematics at Cambridge, designed a truly remarkable machine, the Analytical Engine. This was in blueprint the first programmable computer. It was to consist of thousands of brass gear wheels, rods, ratchets and pinions; had its construction been completed, the finished Engine would have been roughly the size and weight of a railway locomotive. Machining components to the extremely fine tolerances demanded by the design was a difficult and costly business, and sadly Babbage died with the prototype model still unfinished.[14]

The phenomenon of multiple realizability opens the way for a novel theory of the human brain and human thought. Perhaps the brain is an organic realisation of a universal symbol system. The human skull may literally contain a computer.

The strong symbol system hypothesis

The symbol system hypothesis states that computers, as defined, are capable of thought. The strong symbol system hypothesis states that *only* computers (as defined) are capable of thought. According to this second hypothesis, no artefact save the computer will ever be able to think, and moreover any naturally occurring organ – earthborn or alien – with the capacity for thought will on close inspection turn out to be a computer. If this strong hypothesis is to be believed (and a number of prominent philosophers and AI researchers do believe it) we are all of us computers.[15] The human mind is a universal symbol system, says the hypothesis, and at bottom all human thinking consists of symbol manipulation – although no doubt the computers inside our skulls use fundamental operations rather different from those listed in section 4.5, and perhaps the symbolic code they employ is not the binary code used in manufactured computers. I discuss the strong symbol system hypothesis in detail in chapters 9 and 10.

5

A hard look at the facts

The symbol system hypothesis is the conjecture that computers can be programmed to think. How plausible is this conjecture? The present chapter looks at the evidence.

5.1 The evidence for the hypothesis

The most direct possible way to provide evidence for the symbol system hypothesis is to program computers to carry out tasks that we accomplish by using our heads – a lower score going to tasks that are narrowly specialized and require a minimum of adaptability to novel circumstances, and a higher score going to more general tasks demanding a high degree of flexibility. Thus, if you ask AI researchers what reason there is to believe that their hypothesis is true, the response you are likely to get is a list of the impressive successes of AI (some of which we have already gazed upon with awe in chapter 2). Deep Thought and Hitech play master level chess. Samuel's checkers (draughts) program is not only a champion-beater but is self-taught into the bargain. The General Problem Solver can reason its way through such chestnuts as the Tower of Hanoi puzzle and the Missionaries and Cannibals problem. Sam answers questions about stories with a competence which, if displayed by a four-year-old child, would bring pride swelling to its mother's breast. The Frump can produce intelligent digests of news reports. Hacker is a program that can write programs. The amazing Shrdlu can engage in intelligent conversation in colloquial English about its world of play-blocks, can form and execute plans of action, and can discuss its own motives. The Logic Theorist proves theorems in symbolic logic that would tax many a student in my logic classes. The expert system Mycin can diagnose a patient's illness from her symptoms and test results. Even Parry makes a creditable attempt to hold up his end of the conversation.

From among the many AI programs not reviewed in chapter 2 the following are especially worthy of a mention.

Douglas Lenat's problem-solving program Eurisko became a US champion in the star-wars game 'Traveller'. The program competed using a fleet of warships that it had designed itself. The program's oddball fleet exploited the rules of the game in unconventional ways and was markedly superior to the fleets designed by the human participants in the game. Lenat himself took a hand in the design process, periodically checking the program's work and doing some weeding here and there. He says 'the final crediting of the win should be about 60/40% Lenat/Eurisko, though the significant point here is that neither Lenat nor Eurisko could have won alone'.[1] (Lenat's latest project, CYC, is discussed in section 5.6.)

A learning program written by Patrick Winston is able to acquire a concept through acquaintance with instances of it.[2] Take the concept of an arch. The programmer presents the program with diagrams of various arches, together with diagrams of 'near misses' – figures that involve some but not all of the elements of an arch (an 'arch' with no hole in the middle, for example). From these instances and counterinstances the program is able to abstract the concept of an arch. It requires no help from the programmer, who tells it merely which of the diagrams are arches and which are not. The program can do the same with other concepts that lend themselves to 'geometricization', such as table and pedestal (although it is *only* the geometrical aspects of these concepts that the program can learn – it knows nothing of the uses of arches and tables).

A vision program written by David Waltz can interpret two-dimensional line drawings as three-dimensional scenes.[3] The program stays upright in the presence of shadows, cracks, obscured edges and other such teasers, which were the bane of earlier vision programs. For example the program can recognize the drawings in figure 5.1 as representing the same shadow-ridden scene.

Shakey, a mobile robot built at the Stanford Research Institute, sported touch sensors and a TV eye.[4] The robot lived in several interconnecting rooms amid a litter of wooden blocks. On being instructed, for instance, to move block X from its position on a platform in Room 'A' to a location beneath a window, Shakey would navigate his way into Room 'A' from wherever he happened to be, size up the situation, decide he needed a ramp to reach the platform, look around, find one, push it up against the platform, trundle up the ramp, topple the block onto the floor, descend and manoeuvre the block to the required position under the window – and all without human intervention.

This barrage of evidence does not, of course, suffice to establish that the symbol system hypothesis is true – only the existence of a fully-fledged thinking computer could do that. AI's achievements to date can do no more than lend some measure of support to the hypothesis. Is that measure large, small, or very small?

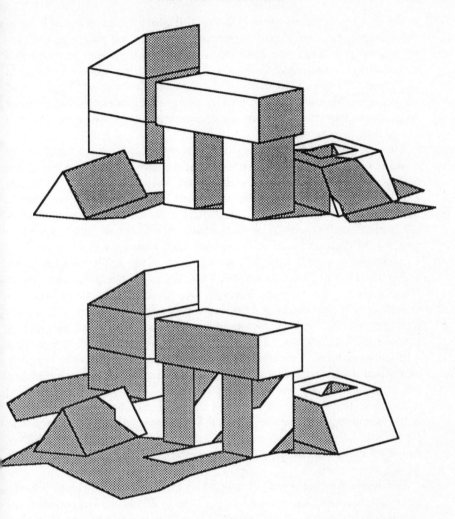

Figure 5.1   Shadows are a problem for visual recognition software. (From figures 2.1 and 2.2 of Winston, P.H. (ed.) *The Psychology of Computer Vision*.)

5.2   Getting the evidence into perspective

The evidence is impressive, and certainly warrants serious interest in the symbol system hypothesis. But don't be *too* impressed. Despite the optimism that exudes from the AI community, the evidence is in my opinion far too slim to warrant any degree of confidence in the truth of the hypothesis.

The achievements of AI research are meagre, even toy-like, when matched against the overall goal of a computer that operates at human levels of intelligence in the unruly complexity of the real world. If Shakey is taken out of his artificially simple laboratory environment and put into a real house, he will perform about on a level with a clockwork mouse. Of the many environmental simplifications he requires in order to function, one is a bold stripe of paint right round the room to show where the floor ends and the wall begins![5] And Shakey is pitiably slow. Each single movement of the robot consumes about an hour of computer time. The block-manoeuvring exercise described above in fact took days to complete.

Most AI researchers are themselves sober enough in their evaluation of the evidence to date. In the 1960s one researcher remarked that he could see much evidence of motion but very little real evidence of progress; and in 1984 Douglas Lenat wrote of 'decades of humblingly slow progress' in AI.[6] Even Marvin Minsky, who predicted in 1967 that 'within a generation the problem of creating artificial intelligence will be substantially solved', is now ready to concede that 'the AI problem is one of the hardest science has ever undertaken'.[7]

A number of people are totally *un*impressed by the results of AI research and believe that the project of computer intelligence is getting nowhere. Stuart Dreyfus, a computer scientist, has expressed this point of view in a neat turn of phrase: 'Current claims and hopes for progress in . . . making computers intelligent are like the belief that someone climbing a tree is making progress toward reaching the moon'.[8] His brother Hubert Dreyfus, a philosopher and a well-known critic of AI, is equally harsh in his judgement: 'Twenty-five years of artificial intelligence research has lived up to very few of its promises and has failed to yield any evidence that it ever will'.[9]

In this section I want to explain why the programs I have reviewed are not nearly as impressive as they can appear to be on first acquaintance. In particular I will detail the major limitations and weaknesses of the General Problem Solver and Shrdlu. I choose these two because they are probably the most renowned AI programs of all.

Few would disagree that all current AI programs are severely limited. Reactions to this lack of progress in AI vary. Critics of AI like the Dreyfus brothers take the limited nature of current achievements to be an indication that AI is in deep trouble. Some AI researchers share this reaction and have opted out of mainstream AI, turning their attention from computers to a new kind of information-processing device (see chapter 10). However, a large number of researchers remain faithful to traditional AI. They acknowledge that the field of computer intelligence – like many fields elsewhere in science – is in sore need of major breakthroughs. Yet they see no reason to despair of these breakthroughs arriving in the course of time.

The General Problem Solver

The first version of the General Problem Solver – GPS for short – was up and running in 1957, and improvement and modification continued for over a decade. In its day, GPS was a wonder of the computing world – and justifiably so. But such is the perspective of history that by 1976 Drew McDermott, a well-known AI researcher, was able to write: 'By now, "GPS" is a colorless term denoting a particularly stupid program to solve puzzles. But it originally meant "General Problem Solver", which caused everybody a lot of needless excitement and distraction.'[10] A quick look at how the program works will highlight the features that draw forth such judgements.[11]

GPS is what is known as a *means-end* analyser. Describe the goal, describe the starting position, list the means available and GPS will experiment until it stumbles on a way of using the means to reach the goal. In the case of the Missionaries and Cannibals problem (described in section 2.7) the starting position finds three missionaries and three cannibals on the left bank of the river; the goal is to have the same personnel, unnibbled, on the right bank; and the means-list contains the two operations 'move boat plus x number of missionaries and y number of cannibals from left side to right side', and 'move boat plus x number of missionaries and y number of cannibals from right side to left side' (where the sum of x and y must always be either 1 or 2, since the boat needs one person to row it and has a maximum capacity of two).

GPS solves the problem by trying out move-operations one after another, plugging in numbers for x and y, until it eventually finds a sequence of moves that lead from the starting position to the goal without at any point having the cannibals outnumber the missionaries (remember that the cannibals pounce if ever this happens). For example, the program's random choice of opening move might be to take two missionaries over to the right. Unspeakable events immediately occur on the left bank. GPS, the greatest trial-and-error tactician there ever was, imperturbably tries again. One missionary and one cannibal from left to right. No teeth tear into flesh, so GPS sticks by this first move and considers the next. Firstly it checks to see if there are any cannibals or missionaries remaining on the left bank. Yes, there are, so the goal is not yet attained, therefore at least one more left-to-right move must be made. Now look to see where the boat is. On the right, so a right-to-left move must come next. OK, make one: move boat plus 0 missionaries plus 1 cannibal from right side to left side. Whoops! Scratch that one . . . And so on. GPS slowly bungles its way to the goal.

One of the reasons for calling GPS a 'particularly stupid program' should by now be abundantly clear. Blind trial-and-error is a desperate last resort, rather than an intelligent approach to solving a problem; and GPS was something of a desperate first resort in the attempt to create intelligent computers. Yet it won't do to be too hard on GPS. As a groping first move towards a far-off goal the program deserves a lot of admiration. And wouldn't *you* use trial and error to solve the Missionaries and Cannibals problem?

The program's trial-and-error technique is not entirely blind. It will, for example, disregard a move whose immediate outcome is to put it back into a position it has already toiled to get out of. Also a number of procedures are incorporated to prevent the program from plugging away inexhaustibly at a false path. The simplest is cut-off: abandon any series of moves that reaches some predefined length without achieving the goal.

Another important way in which the programmers guide the program's search for success is by incorporating instructions concerning which move to try first when there are several alternatives. To give a simple illustration, suppose GPS is occupied not with missionaries and cannibals but with the task of planning the moves that a robot must make in order to shift blocks from one place to another. The means-list contains the operations *moveself*, *pickupblock*, *putdownblock*, *carryblock*, and so on. Suppose the robot is holding block X and is required to hold block Y instead. Before pickupblock can be applied to Y, the robot must do two things: empty its arm and move itself to where Y is. (These so-called *preconditions* of the operation pickupblock are placed in the program by the programmer. GPS would look them up rather than work them out.) Which first, moveself or putdownblock? Here the program might contain the instruction that whenever both need doing, putdownblock should be attempted first, since the robot's arm will then be free to pick up and clear out of the way any obstructing blocks that might be encountered during the move towards block Y. The attempt to putdownblock should be abandoned in favour of moveself only if putting down X would obstruct the path the robot must take to reach Y.

These pre-set rankings of the order in which alternative moves should be tried in a given set of circumstances are known as *heuristics*. They form a vital feature of GPS and its authors invested much ingenuity in devising heuristics that would give the program as much guidance as possible throughout its trial-and-error onslaught on a problem. However, it becomes impossibly complicated to construct rankings in the case of complex problems whose means-lists contain large numbers of operations. GPS is therefore far from being a *general* problem solver. The program's trial-and-error tactics, guided by ingenious but essentially clumsy tables telling it what to try first, enable it to tackle only the simplest of problems.

There is another reason why GPS entirely fails to live up to its title of general problem solver. Far from being general, it can address only problems of a very special kind, namely those that have the form of how to reach a goal from a starting position. Here is a problem of a completely different sort. A man leaves a hut on the top of a mountain at noon and walks down the track to a hut at the bottom of the mountain. Next day a woman leaves the hut at the bottom of the mountain, again at noon, and walks up the track to the hut at the top. Is there a time, x o'clock, such that at x o'clock on the second afternoon, the woman is at exactly the same place on the track as the man was at x o'clock on the first afternoon? There is not really any natural way of fitting this problem into the format of 'use listed means to get from starting position to goal'. What is the starting position? What is the goal? What are the means? In fact rather few of our day-to-day problems come in this tidy form.

It is a fact that most of GPS's problem solving is done by the programmer rather than the program. (This complaint can be made about all AI programs to date.) One obvious way in which this occurs is via the rankings that the programmer provides to tell GPS what to try first in situations where a number of alternative moves are possible (as in the case of putdownblock and moveself). It is the programmer's own understanding of the problem and own feeling for how to solve it that guides the preparation of these often complex rankings. GPS never makes a single mistake when solving the Tower of Hanoi puzzle (as its authors rather proudly announce).[12] Yet the credit must go not to GPS but to its human creators, who have, in this case, managed to devise rankings that give the program perfect guidance. Even by providing the program with a clear description of the goal and an exhaustive list of the means available, the programmers are treating the computer to the benefits of human intelligence. Would that my problems came at me so clearly defined.

There is another, more subtle, way in which the programmer rather than the program is doing the problem-solving. This concerns what I will call finding a *representation* of the problem. Let's return to the problem of the two mountaineers. If you solved it, you most probably did so by superimposing the two journeys on top of one another – or in other words, by viewing the people as making their journeys on the *same* afternoon. Once you represent the problem in this form, it is easy to see that the two people are bound to pass each other on the path. It is very often the case that the hard part of solving a problem is hitting on a good way of representing it. Once a helpful representation is found, extracting the solution is easy.

A famous illustration of this is the so-called mutilated chessboard problem. Take an ordinary sixty-four square black-and-white chessboard and a packet of rectangular-shaped biscuits. Each biscuit happens to be exactly the right size to cover two squares of the board. What's the smallest number of biscuits you need to cover all sixty-four squares? Right, thirty-two. That's no problem. But now suppose you cut two squares out of the board, one at any corner and the other at the diagonally opposite corner. Can this mutilated board be covered completely with just thirty-one biscuits?

Tricky one, eh? Here is the open-sesame way of representing the problem. Look at a chessboard and you will see that the two squares to be cut away must be of the same colour, since the squares at diagonally opposite corners are either both black or both white. Say the two missing squares are black. So the mutilated board has thirty-two white squares and thirty black squares. Each biscuit covers one white square and one black square, so any arrangement whatsoever of thirty-one biscuits is bound to cover thirty-one white squares and thirty-one black squares, *ergo* the solution to the problem is 'No'. Represent the problem in terms of the number of squares of each colour that are required by a given number of biscuits and a bit of simple arithmetic takes you straight to the answer.

Could a computer solve the mutilated chessboard problem (save by an unintelligent and completely impractical 'brute force' search through the vast number of possible arrangements of biscuits on the board)? Who knows! But what is certain is that if *you* handle finding the representation, the computer can handle the simple arithmetic. The contribution GPS makes to problem solving is hardly any greater. Its programmers provide it with a smart representation of a problem and it blunders about until it stumbles across a solution.[13] This leaves me only barely willing to call GPS a problem *solver* at all. Imagine that a programmer comes up with a cunning mathematical way of viewing our earlier problem about the mountaineers: on her way of representing it, the problem *is* one of reaching a goal from a starting position, both of these being devious mathematical abstractions of some sort. GPS is given the problem represented in this way and after the usual string of trials and errors produces the answer. Wouldn't you feel that it was the programmer, not the program, who had done most of the problem solving?

Work ceased on GPS around 1966. 'We do feel that this particular aggregate of IPL-V code should be laid to rest, as having done its part in advancing our understanding of the mechanisms of intelligence', write Newell and Ernst in the program's obituary.[14] Critic Hubert Dreyfus has made much of the laying to rest of such a large AI project. He describes work on GPS as following a 'curve from success to optimism to failure' and in a pessimistic discussion of the prospects for AI he states that 'the abandonment of GPS' is 'ample evidence of trouble'.[15] In my view, though, this pessimism is entirely misplaced. The success of a project in a completely new field of human endeavour should be measured in terms of what has been learned from it. And people did learn a lot from GPS. Not least, they learned what special features were needed in a programming language for AI; lessons that were incorporated in the family of information-processing languages (IPLs) designed by the authors of GPS, and ultimately in the famous descendent of these, LISP. (Very many AI programs are written in LISP.) Other lessons concerned the technique of means–end analysis itself, which has been used extensively since it was pioneered in GPS (in the program controlling the robot Shakey, for example).

Perhaps, though, the most important lesson drawn from work with GPS was that programs that don't know much can't do much. The whole idea behind GPS was that problem-solving techniques could be separated from so-called task-specific knowledge. This is why the program was given the misleading name of General Problem Solver – GPS is 'general' in the sense that the basic program contains no knowledge specific to any particular task or problem.[16] The guts of an intelligent program, as things were conceived in the early days of AI, would consist of a great bunch of powerful problem-solving techniques: to solve a particular problem, just feed in a few scraps of pertinent knowledge. Experience showed that this distinction between problem-solving techniques and knowledge is artificial and unhelpful. Moreover it became apparent that programs for solving real problems – as opposed to puzzles and brain teasers

– would require enormous quantities of knowledge. Thus experience with GPS eventually led to knowledge-intensive problem solvers like Shrdlu and Mycin.

The knowledge problem

Knowledge is hard stuff to handle inside a computer. Just packing it away is not difficult – any fool can write a program that sinks masses of data into memory. The trick is to organise it so that each item can be found again easily. This is the first aspect of what I will call the *knowledge problem*. To give a simple illustration: Noddy puts the name and address of each person currently resident in Toytown into his computer. He then tries to retrieve the address of Foster Fig. Since Noddy has sunk the data into memory without rhyme or reason, the computer must laboriously examine each entry until it hits upon Fig – a slow business, unless by luck the old fruit surfaces early. A much better plan, of course, is to store all the names in alphabetical order, enabling the computer to zero in on the required entry rapidly. Knowledge, then, must be arranged in some sort of order inside the machine if it is to be useable. But in what order? There is no self-evident way of arranging a huge number of diverse facts. You can't put the whole world into alphabetical order.

That is the first aspect of the knowledge problem: find some way of organising vast quantities of diverse knowledge. The second aspect of the problem is the difficulty of keeping large amounts of knowledge fresh – the difficulty of *updating* the knowledge store. Noddy's list is supposed to represent the current residents of Toytown and the movements of the Grim Reaper dictate that it be continuously updated. In this simple case, updating is not much of a problem. Provided the names are in order, the computer can easily cruise down the list every now and again, crossing off the deaths and adding on the births. What *is* a problem is updating a large and complicated store of pieces of interconnected information. To get a feel for the difficulty, imagine that you have unexpectedly been offered a new job in a new city. Furious preparation ensues. You put the house on the market, arrange a school for the kids, decide what furniture to sell, start breaking the news to your friends, and so on across a great spectrum ranging from trivia like cancelling the milk through to a re-thinking of some of your dearest long term plans and goals. Adding one little piece of new data, 'changing job', has called for countless updates everywhere else in your complex network of beliefs, plans and perspectives. That illustrates the second aspect of the knowledge problem: devise methods that enable the computer to track all the updates that must be made in order to allow a change to 'flow through' a vast store of interconnected information. This aspect of the knowledge problem is often called the *frame problem*.[17]

The third aspect of the knowledge problem, like the first, concerns extracting information from the store. Given a problem, how does the computer know what sort of information might assist in solving it? Somehow the knowledge store must be organized so that the computer has some means of telling which facts could be relevant to which problems. This is the problem of *relevance*. As Minsky puts it: 'The problem of selecting relevance from excessive variety is a key issue! . . . For each "fact" one needs meta-facts about how it is to be used and when it should not be used.'[18] And then, of course, these 'meta-facts' will themselves need organizing. Which is where we came in . . .

I take a more detailed look at the frame problem and the problem of relevance in section 5.6.

Micro-worlds

The knowledge problem is hard. Many AI workers see it as the fundamental problem of the field. It was not until the late 1960s that people began to appreciate the centrality of the knowledge problem. In the early days of AI attention had been directed toward the development of universally applicable problem-solving techniques, à la GPS, and the knowledge problem had remained more or less peripheral. It moved centre stage when researchers realized that the wan performance of early programs was in part a consequence of their tiny appetites for knowledge. The response to this newly emerged problem was to focus research on small, simple, artificial 'worlds' – called *micro-worlds* – and to evolve techniques for organizing knowledge concerning them. The hope was that eventually techniques developed in micro-world research could be generalised to cope with the complex real world.[19] A classic micro-world is Shrdlu's habitat of a tabletop, a box, and a few coloured play-blocks.

Shrdlu

Uninitiates are usually extremely impressed, not to say overwhelmed, by Shrdlu. A common reaction on a first encounter with Shrdlu is 'Wow! This one really does think.' So let me start straight in by deflating Shrdlu a little. Shrdlu is just as easy to push over as Eliza (who may be seen collapsing inelegantly in chapter 3). My favourite example is due to John Haugeland (Shrdlu's contributions are capitalized):

> Build a steeple.
> SORRY, I DON'T KNOW THE WORD 'STEEPLE'.
> A 'steeple' is a stack that contains two green cubes and a pyramid.
> I UNDERSTAND.
> Trade you the steeple for three red cubes.
> SORRY, I DON'T KNOW THE WORD 'TRADE'.
> A 'trade' is a free exchange of ownership.
> SORRY, I DON'T KNOW THE WORD 'FREE'.
> Sorry, I thought you were smarter than you are.
> SORRY, I DON'T KNOW THE WORD 'SORRY'.[20]

This dig strikes below the belt, of course, because it presses Shrdlu on issues that lie beyond the frontiers of the micro-world he inhabits. More soberly, though, there are serious limitations to the way Shrdlu can handle himself even in his own play-blocks world. His data concerning his world is, to say the least, skeletal. 'Block' signifies nothing more to Shrdlu than a type of thing whose location he can alter – literally nothing more.[21] If you were Shrdlu and I asked you whether 'blocks' are solid, heavy objects or merely geometrically defined zones of empty space, you wouldn't be able to tell me. You would have the same trouble if I asked you whether 'red' is something you see or something you hear or neither. (Shrdlu himself, of course, would not even be able to follow the questions.) Despite the appearance he gives in conversation (so-called), Shrdlu in fact has no idea what a red block is.

Yet blocks are one of Shrdlu's stronger subjects. His position is even worse in regard to some of the other words he uses so glibly. Consider this extract from the long exchange printed in chapter 2.

I own blocks which are not red, but I don't own anything which supports a pyramid.
I UNDERSTAND.
[Oh yeah?]
The blue pyramid is mine.
I UNDERSTAND.
Do I own anything in the box?
YES, TWO THINGS: THE BLUE BLOCK AND THE BLUE PYRAMID.

Shrdlu in fact has no data at all about the relationship of owning. On being told that his human friend owns something (by means of the keywords 'I own' or 'is mine') Shrdlu simply attaches the label OWN: FRIEND to his 'internal representation' of the object in question.[22] The label ???: FRIEND or even FOOD: FRIEND would serve just as well. When asked if an object is owned, the program simply checks to see if it has a label. (Shrdlu's apparent but illusory mastery of colour words is also grounded in this programming technique of labelling.) In Herb Simon's phrase 'Shrdlu knows what it [or its friend] owns, but doesn't understand what it is to own something.'[23] Even that is an over-generous way of putting it. It is mere metaphor to say that Shrdlu knows or understands anything at all – handy yet grotesque metaphor of the sort discussed at the beginning of chapter 3.

Perhaps the deepest criticism of Shrdlu concerns the contribution, or lack of one, that this program has made to forward movement in AI research. When the program first appeared on the scene it was hailed as a breakthrough. Nowadays, however, there is general agreement that Shrdlu was – in its creator's own words – a dead end.[24] Time has shown Shrdlu to be a No Through Road in the quest for artificial intelligence: a spectacular *tour de force* in programming which has sadly taken us no further forward. The techniques pioneered in the program have never been adapted for application to wider, more interesting worlds.

Winograd suggests that part of the explanation for this is the sheer complexity of his program, which is perhaps already close to the limits of what the human mind can handle.[25] This is an interesting suggestion and I will return to it later in the chapter. Another aspect of the explanation is simply that studies of a micro-world of coloured blocks on a table top do not have that much to tell us about the real world. The original hope was that Winograd's table-top methods could be generalized for use in wider arenas and it is now clear that this cannot be done. (The same criticism applies to the other blocks-world program we have examined, Hacker.)

The micro-world strategy has produced chequered results. On the one hand there are the disappointments: programs like Shrdlu and Shakey the robot. While these programs performed well enough at the tasks they were designed for, they were not, as it turned out, the beginnings of greater things. Then on the other hand there are the rip-roaring successes: expert systems such as Dendral the chemical analyst and Mycin the medical diagnostician. For expert systems, too, are micro-world programs, going about their business within narrow little fragments of the wide human world.

Despite the fact that expert systems can perform at near-human levels of expertise, and despite the fact that they have shown the way to a whole new area of computer applications, these programs too must be regarded with disappointment by anyone on the trail of a machine that thinks. Current expert systems can never escape from their oh-so-narrow micro-worlds into the diverse complexity of the real world. Not that narrowness itself is the disappointing feature. After all, the halls of fame are full of human geniuses who were barely capable of carrying on a coherent conversation or of warming the Renaissance equivalent of a TV dinner. The cause of the disappointment is rather that current expert systems are *inescapably* narrow. These programs are viable only because of the huge simplifications permitted by the micro-world strategy. By definition, the knowledge store associated with a micro-world is small and therefore manageable. The techniques used in expert system programming for handling issues of relevance and updating are simplistic and cannot be used in larger domains. Also expert system programming involves the extensive use of what programmers call 'domain-specific tricks' – tricks that exploit special features of the problem or situation in question. One example is the representation of time. Some expert systems manage to avoid reference to a temporal dimension altogether. In their micro-worlds everything happens in an eternal present. If a reference to time is unavoidable, a programmer will include only such snippets of temporal structure as are absolutely essential for the task in hand. Perhaps the program is told nothing more than that if *a* is before *b* and *b* is before *c* then *a* is before *c* (a rule that enables it to merge pairs of before-statements and extract their implication – for example that the patient's rash occurred before the application of penicillin). The system may know nothing more about what 'before' means – not even that it orders events in time rather than space.[26]

No-one yet knows how to make computers perform at anything like human levels of expertise in wider, less orderly, domains – or even if this is possible at all.

5.3   Hype

To hype means 'to deceive by false publicity'.[27] Lying as it does in a zone where science can easily merge into fiction, artificial intelligence research is peculiarly prone to media hype. Do not be misled. Thinking computers are not just around the corner. The real truth about the extent of current progress toward the construction of thinking machines has been shrouded in a titillating fog by the press, film-makers, authors of popular books on the computer revolution, and not least by advertisers. TV ads for personal microcomputers are full of glowing but entirely spurious references to 'intelligent terminals' and 'intelligent software', while the advertising leaflets of a well-known credit card company even describe computer-compatible plastic cards as intelligent! It is interesting to note that the discarded image of the computer as a 'high speed moron' was also the product of advertising – an image which was carefully chosen by yesterday's ad men and women to portray the new machines as ideal candidates for the accounts departments and filing rooms of prospective customers.

Newspapers and magazines eagerly boost the image of the computer as a thinking, intelligent artefact. Not long ago I read in my local newspaper of 'Japanese plans to create a human machine'. One particularly reprehensible article, in *Life* magazine, bore the headline 'Meet Shakey, The First Electronic Person.'[28] Its author informs – or rather misinforms – the general public that Shakey 'demonstrates that machines can think'. Even Times Newspapers, for all their customary sobriety, feel no qualms over printing eye-catching headlines like 'Manpower Services Commission Splashes Out On Intelligent Computers'.[29] The old adage about never believing what you see in the newspapers seems to have more than a grain of truth in it, at least so far as AI is concerned. No doubt many people are being seriously misled by continual exposure to the theme that computers can and do, or can and shortly will, think.

Some AI researchers have not been loathe to dabble in hype themselves. Recall the quotation with which this book began: 'Some intelligent computers will design others, and they'll get to be smarter and smarter. The question is, where will that leave us? . . . They might keep us as pets.' Ed Fredkin's vision of the future is pure science fiction. It is disquieting to find the manager of the MIT AI Lab engaging in absurd flights of fancy during a supposedly serious and informative television interview. The public deserves better than this.

Later in the same interview Fredkin said the following. 'The only thing that stands between us and having intelligent systems is [that] there's a few things we don't know how to do.'[30] This ranks as one of the world's greatest understatements. It would be nearer the truth to say that there are a few million things we don't know how to do. And more important still, we don't even know whether these unknown things are things that it is possible to do. The quest for computer intelligence may be a kind of latter-day alchemy − a quest for the impossible. AI research has not yet produced any firm indication that a computer is the right kind of machine to support artificial cognition.

Sad to say, even the achievements of some actual AI programs have become exaggerated in the folklore of the subject. Samuel's checkers (draughts) program is an example. I have written several times that this program is a champion-beater. That is true, and the fact is proudly announced in nearly every description of the program I have read.[31] But what is *not* usually mentioned is that the program's champion-beating play extended only to one game with one champion − who then proceeded to beat the program in six games straight.[32] A newspaper article once ludicrously asserted that this program 'can beat all but a few of the world's best players'; and in the same vein a recent book states that the program 'finally achiev[ed] the status of a "world class" checkers player'.[33]

Not so much exaggerated as eternally arrested in the uterus is Hacker, Sussman's famous program-writing program. Popular accounts do not mention that this program was never finished.[34] This is not, of course, to say that Hacker is a fiction: many components of the program were written and tested. However, a completed version never did exist. Herb Simon's dictum springs to mind: 'In the computer field, the moment of truth is a running program; all else is prophesy.'[35]

In one much-quoted article Newell and Simon state that 'Intuition, insight, and learning are no longer exclusive possessions of humans: any large high-speed computer can be programmed to exhibit them also'.[36] Warming to their theme, they continue 'The simplest way [we] can summarise the situation is to say that there are now in the world machines that think, that learn, and that create'.[37] Then they confidently predict the following:

1   That within ten years a digital computer will be the world's chess champion, unless the rules bar it from competition.
2   That within ten years a digital computer will discover and prove an important new mathematical theorem.

3 That within ten years a digital computer will write music that will be
   accepted by critics as possessing considerable aesthetic value.[38]

Made in 1957 on the basis of no more evidence than some limited successes
with a somewhat crude precursor of GPS, these predictions were bold indeed.
By 1965 Simon had raised the stakes even higher: 'Machines will be capable,
within twenty years, of doing any work that a man can do'.[39]

The ten and twenty year deadlines have now long since passed and not one
of these grandiose predictions has been fulfilled. AI researchers are more
amused than chagrined by this. Speaking of these failed attempts to foretell the
future Marvin Minsky cheekily says: 'The claims that [they] made, I think,
were correct, because AI is possible and we will eventually learn how to make
machines that are smarter than even the wildest speculations said. But the
[time] estimates were short . . .'[40]

AI researchers of all nationalities have continued to make dubious predictions. In 1982, scientists working on the Japanese Fifth Generation project
declared that by the 1990s their computers would possess common sense and
would be able to understand human conversation, with a vocabulary of over
10,000 words.[41] Yet it is the AI labs of North America that have been the
richest source of wild prognostications. Hans Moravec, Director of the Mobile
Robot Laboratory at Carnegie Mellon, has recently stated that robots with
human intelligence will be common within fifty years.[42] 'We humans will
benefit for a time from their labors,' he says, 'but sooner or later, like natural
children, they will seek their own fortunes while we, their aged parents,
silently fade away.'[43]

It is hard to say where fanciful exaggeration ends and deliberate deception
begins. The following extract is from an advertising leaflet distributed by
Cognitive Systems, Inc., a software company founded by Roger Schank,
Director of Research at the Yale AI Lab.

Our programs understand English – not an English-like programming language
but *everyday conversational English* (or French or German or any language you
want) . . . Cognitive Systems natural language programs are unique in that they
are intelligent . . . We give our computer programs the same kind of knowledge
that people use, so our programs understand a sentence just the way a person
does, and respond in conversational English.[44]

Failed predictions and exaggerated claims have produced a severe backlash
against AI. The *New Scientist* magazine recently declared that 'AI's record of
barefaced public deception is unparalleled in the annals of academic study'.[45]
In similar vein Hubert Dreyfus has charged AI researchers with failing in their
professional duty to make clear the actual limits of their current understanding
and of the results they have so far achieved.[46]

Such criticism is well deserved. But critics must be careful not to throw the baby out with the bathwater. The opprobrium that has been heaped on Newell and Simon for their famous predictions is entirely inappropriate. It is regrettable that their widely quoted article should have assisted in the breeding of false impressions concerning the extent of actual progress in AI research. However, Newell and Simon themselves were perfectly frank about the purely speculative nature of their predictions and spoke of 'peering into the future and forecasting its shape'.[47] Scientists surely have a duty to speculate where a major technical innovation may lead us – provided, of course, they are careful (as Newell and Simon were) to make it clear which of their remarks constitute authoritative information and which do represent honest speculation. It is highly beneficial to have the possible implications of a new technological development responsibly catalogued by the experts involved.

To slate AI researchers for speaking of the future with excessive optimism is, in essence, to castigate them for their gut-level enthusiasm. Yet without enthusiasm, all science is forlorn. It is a good thing that brilliant young scientists come leaping into AI feeling certain that all the major problems will be solved in a decade or two; and the longer they can hold on to that illusion the better. (At least, it is a good thing if you believe that the quest for artificial intelligence is a good thing.) As an outside observer, I can indulge in the luxury of believing that success, if it comes at all, is rather unlikely to arrive in the lifetime of any researcher currently working on AI – but if young people at the beginning of their careers thought that way, they might be much less eager to get involved in the first place.

5.4 Programming common sense

This section takes a closer look at the knowledge problem (first introduced in section 5.2), for this is a major sticking point in AI. 'The area in which artificial intelligence has had the greatest difficulty is in the programming of common sense,' writes Terry Winograd, the creator of Shrdlu. He continues: 'It has long been recognized that it is much easier to write a program to carry out abstruse formal operations than to capture the common sense of a dog.'[48] Progress in AI is stalled, at any rate temporarily. 'Probably the most telling criticism of current work in artificial intelligence is that it has not yet been successful in modeling what is called common sense,' says David Waltz, a prominent figure in the development of AI programs. 'Substantially better models of human cognition must be developed before systems can be designed that will carry out even simplified versions of common-sense tasks.'[49]

The transition from micro-worlds to reality can be made only if computers can be supplied with portions of the vast store of real-world knowledge that we humans use to get along in daily life. Yet the AI community currently has no firm idea of how this is to be done – if, indeed, it can be done at all. This obstacle to further progress in the development of a human-like machine has become known as the 'problem of common sense knowledge'.

Much of our common sense knowledge is so platitudinous that we hardly notice we know it. The following examples highlight the extent to which even the simplest tasks presuppose a mass of trivial but vital knowledge.

Read the following passage and then answer the two questions.
Tommy had just been given a new set of blocks. He was opening the box when Jimmy came in.
Question one
Who was opening the box?
Question two
What was in the box?[50]

The questions are so easy you hardly need to think about them. But from a programmer's point of view this ease is illusory. Try listing all the things you needed to know in order to produce the answers. Usually only people are given new sets of blocks; 'he' usually refers to a person; blocks are not people; it is usual for a gift of small, regularly shaped items to come in a box; a person normally opens a gift immediately after receiving it . . .

What does the word 'they' refer to in each of the following sentences?
The police refused to give the students a permit to demonstrate because they feared violence.
The police refused to give the students a permit to demonstrate because they advocated revolution.[51]

Notice that there is nothing in the structure of these two sentences to give you a hint, for they differ only in their final two words, which in each case consist of an active verb and a noun. You understand who 'they' are in each scenario only because you are able to bring a large amount of sophisticated knowledge to bear. And if you are anything like me, you will find it much harder to itemize this knowledge than in the previous simple case.

Once you catch on to the idea that we know an awful lot of vital trivia, items begin to flood to mind. To get to a place one should (on the whole) move in its direction; one can pass by an object by moving first towards it and then away from it; one can pull with a string, but not push; one can push with thick wire, but not with thin; pushing something usually affects its position; an object resting on a pushed object usually moves with the pushed object but not always; water flows downhill; humans do not usually go outside undressed, whereas in normal circumstances no non-human animal wears clothes; humans usually find it easier to walk forwards than backwards; humans usually talk with their mouths open and eat with their mouths closed; causes generally precede their effects; time constantly passes and future events become past events; having a working hedgetrimmer usually precludes wanting another exactly like it; having a five pound note usually does not preclude wanting another exactly like it . . . and so on and so on and so on.[52] Computers will need to know a vast number of trivialities in order to get along intelligently in the real world – and, equally importantly, to interact intelligently with human beings.

Sometimes when I try to explain the problem of common sense knowledge to computer science majors they shrug it off, saying things like 'Okay, so the computer has to swallow an encyclopaedia with a good index – no great problem.' To fully appreciate the naivety of this response, take a look at a short entry in your favourite encyclopaedia and try to itemize what you must *already* know in order to be able to understand it. Perhaps the computer does need to swallow an encyclopaedia of sorts but this encyclopaedia will have to be immensely more sophisticated than anything hitherto written (as we'll see in section 5.6).

The metaphor of letting the computer 'swallow' such a tome glosses over the three hard problems of knowledge storage and retrieval. How is this vast collection of data to be organized inside the machine? How is it to be updated? How can the machine be given a grasp of which facts might be relevant to which tasks? These are huge and unsolved problems, and when viewed against their bulk AI's achievements to date look paltry indeed.

5.5 Data versus know-how

What I will call the *data model* of knowledge is the view that knowledge can be represented ('captured') by means of sentences, or similar symbolic devices. The data model is the model of knowledge that upholders of the symbol system hypothesis usually have in mind (section 4.6).[53] There is no doubt that the data model is correct for much of our knowledge. For instance, the knowledge that omelettes are made from beaten egg is represented in a cookery encyclopaedia by means of the symbol-string 'Omelettes are made from beaten egg'; and in a computer data base this knowledge would be represented in a roughly similar way, but using bits instead of letters of the roman alphabet. It is a crucial assumption of traditional AI that the data model is correct for *all* types of knowledge.[54] Mainstream research is underpinned by the belief that any piece of knowledge can be programmed into a computer in the form of a symbol-structure that represents the information in question – in the same sense in which the symbol-structure 'Le champagne est un vin sec pétillant' symbolically represents the fact that champagne is a fizzy dry wine. (The symbol-structures involved are usually referred to as data; hence the terminology 'data model'.)

Can all human knowledge be rendered into data? What about knowledge of *how* to do things – and in particular the kind of know-how that you can't acquire simply by reading a book, such as how to cook an omelette *just right*, or what to do with your face and body in the course of being introduced to an attractive member of the opposite sex? The traditional AI answer is that even know-how can be converted into data: the trick is to use if-then structures, along the lines of 'If she smiles then you smile too'. On this view, the representation of any particular body of know-how will consist of a vast collection of complicated if-then rules. This is in fact the method used to program know-how into expert systems. However, it is too early to say whether or not all know-how can be dealt with successfully in this way. An obvious point for a sceptic to raise is that human expertise, open-ended and creative as it is, may well not be fully reducible to sets of rules. (I return to this point in chapter 10.)

It would be easier to be confident that the data model is correct for all types of knowledge if we could feel certain that the only *possible* way for organisms to store their knowledge is in the form of data. Yet we cannot be at all certain of this.[55] Take the case of a human infant. When confronted with Mum's nipple, Baby lunges forward and sucks. Does Baby's brain contain a stored symbol-structure somewhat along the lines of 'If a nipple comes near enough, grab it fast and suck?' Maybe, but on the other hand maybe not. Baby might contain mechanisms that make her behave in the way described by this sentence without the sentence itself – or anything like it – being stored somewhere inside her.[56]

Nipple-sucking is reflex behaviour, but the question I am asking applies equally to learned know-how. When I turn out an omelette to perfection, is this because my brain has come to acquire an appropriate set of if-then rules, which I am unconsciously following, or is my mastery of whisk and pan grounded in some entirely different sort of mechanism? It is certainly true that my actions can be *described* by means of if-then sentences: if the mixture sticks then I flick the pan, and so on. But it doesn't follow from this that my actions are *produced* by some device in my brain scanning through lists of if-then rules of this sort (whereas that is how computer expert systems work).

Here, then, we have two sketches of what might underlie skilful, knowledge-driven activity in human beings. According to the first sketch, know-how is stored in our brains in the form of data, and we unconsciously 'read' the symbol-structures and do what they tell us. The second is sketchier still: know-how is not stored in our brains as data but in some *other* way – call it X. With brain science still in its infancy, theories of what Method X might be are inchoate. (Chapter 10 describes the most recent theory.) Each sketch has passionate devotees. However, it will probably be many decades before the truth of the matter is known.

Suppose the brain does use Method X. What would this imply for the symbol system hypothesis? Perhaps nothing. It may be that the data method provides an alternative way of handling knowledge that is equally effective – in which case the skies would remain blue for traditional AI. But on the other hand the human nervous system may use Method X for the good reason that it is the only comprehensive method of knowledge storage that works – and X *could* prove to be something that a computer is incapable of doing.

5.6   The CYC project

CYC (the name comes from 'encyclopaedia') is in many ways the flagship project of mainstream AI at the present time. It represents the severest test yet of the symbol system hypothesis and of the data model of knowledge. CYC is one of the few AI projects to take the problem of common sense knowledge seriously. The project began at the Microelectronics and Computer Technology Corporation in Texas in 1984 with an initial budget of US $50 million. The goal is to build a knowledge base containing a significant percentage of the common sense knowledge (or 'consensus reality') of a twentieth century Westerner. Project leader Doug Lenat claims that by the end of 1994 the knowledge base will contain from thirty to fifty per cent of consensus reality.[57]

'Most of the current AI research we've read about is currently stalled,' says Lenat.[58] 'We don't believe there's any shortcut to being intelligent; the "secret" is to have lots of knowledge.'[59] He speaks harshly of his earlier programs AM and Eurisko:

> In each new domain, there would be a flurry of plausible activities, resulting in several unexpected discoveries, followed by a period of decreased productivity, and finally lapsing into useless thrashing . . . Despite their relative knowledge-richness, the ultimate limitations of these programs derived from their small size . . . The point here is that one can only learn something – by discovery or by being told – if one almost knows it already . . . Marvin Minsky [has said] 'The more you know, the more (and faster) you can learn.' The inverse of this enabling relationship is a disabling one, and that's what ultimately doomed AM and Eurisko: [i]f you don't know very much to begin with, don't expect to learn a lot quickly . . . AI must somehow get to that stage where . . . learning begins to accelerate due to the amount already known.[60]

Lenat describes the problem of common sense knowledge as AI's 'mattress in the road'.[61] It blocks the way forward onto the open highway, even though light enough vehicles have been able to find odd ways round it, by running along the gutters or up on the rough. These lightweights are the expert systems, with knowledge bases custom-made for one narrow task. Rather than confront the hard problems of knowledge representation head-on, expert-systems programmers use cheap'n'dirty tricks to lurch around them – tricks that are possible only because of an expert system's narrow ambitions.

One well-known feature of expert systems is their *brittleness* – tap one of their weak spots and they fall apart. Lenat sees brittleness as a symptom of lack of knowledge.

> [Expert systems] operate on a high plateau of knowledge and competence until they . . . fall off precipitously to levels of ultimate incompetence. People suffer the same difficulty, too, but their plateau is much broader and their slope is more gentle . . . Lacking . . . simple common sense concepts, expert systems' mistakes often appear ridiculous in human terms. For instance, when a car loan author-ization program approves a loan to a teenager who put down he'd worked at the same job for twenty years; or when a skin disease diagnosis program concludes that my rusted out decade-old Chevy has measles;[62] or when a medical system prescribes an absurd dosage of a drug for a maternity patient whose weight (105) and age (35) were accidentally swapped during the case's type-in. As we build increasingly complex programs, and invest them with increasing power, the humor quickly evaporates.[63]

Once such errors come to light it only needs a few extra lines of code to make sure they never happen again. Lenat's point, though, is that no matter how many such errors the program is explicitly proofed against there will always be others. He maintains that the only general solution is to equip expert systems with common sense.[64] Lenat hopes that the CYC project will culminate in a knowledge base that can serve as the foundation for future generations of expert systems. (His optimistic prediction is that by 2015 no one 'would dream of buying a machine without common sense, any more than anyone today would buy a personal computer that couldn't run spreadsheets [and] word processing programs'.[65])

CYC is a grandscale project involving the 'hand-coding' of around 100 mil-lion assertions. By the end of the first six years of the project over one million assertions had been entered manually into the knowledge base.[66] Lenat describes this figure as being 'down around . . . 0.1 percent . . . of consensus reality' and estimates that it will require some two person-centuries of 'hard knowledge-entry work' to push this figure up to the 100 million assertions that he believes are necessary before CYC can begin learning usefully for itself.[67] At any one time as many as thirty people may be logged into CYC, all simultaneously entering data.[68] These knowledge-enterers (or 'cyclists') analyse newspaper and magazine articles, encyclopaedia entries, advertisements etc sentence by sentence. They enter into the knowledge base not only what is explicitly stated but also – more im-portantly – the facts that the writer assumed the reader would already know. As we saw earlier, many of these are of such a nature that it would be insulting for a writer to state them explicitly (living things get diseases, water flows downhill, the products of a commercial process are more valuable than the inputs, solid objects have a tendency to prevent other solid objects from entering or occupying the same volume of space as them . . .).[69]

Lenat is at pains to stress that CYC is not just an electronic encyclopaedia. He describes CYC as more 'the complement of an encyclopaedia'.[70] The primary goal of the project is to encode the knowledge that any person or machine must have *before* they can begin to understand an encyclopaedia.

The work of Lenat and his colleagues bears satisfying testimony to the recent rapprochement between AI and philosophy. The major portion of the project's effort so far has gone not into data-entry but into three areas that have long been of central concern to philosophers: ontology, epistemology, and logic.[71] Not so long ago it was almost a tradition among people working in the 'hard' sciences to sneer at these three relentlessly abstract fields of enquiry. The recent synergy of AI and philosophy provides yet another example of the sudden and unexpected payoff of 'pure' research. (Funding bodies please take note!) Lenat describes CYC as 'mankind's first foray into large-scale ontological engineering'.[72]

Ontology is the general theory of what there is. Let me take you on a paragraph-length trip through some of the ontological issues relevant to the construction of CYC. One thing to notice about these problems is their sheer difficulty.

The most fundamental ontological question to face Lenat and his team is 'What basic types of object are there?' The answer that they have provisionally adopted (and which has been used to structure CYC's representational framework) is: tangible objects, intangible objects, composites (such as people, who have a tangible part and an intangible part), events, and mathematical objects.[73] Most philosophers would say that this five-way division is too coarse. Further basic categories are necessary. CYC's category of 'intangible object' is nothing more than a rag-bag. It contains such disparate things as the world recession, people's pains (you can touch 'where it hurts' but you can't touch the pain itself), northerly gales, CYC's own internal representations, and the meaning of the sentence 'Curry is hot'. Nor is it at all clear that the category of events belongs in this list: events may not be a type of object at all.[74] Two different objects cannot be in the same place at the same time, yet it seems that two different events can: Fred may simultaneously jump into the river and escape the charging bull. The challenge implicit in this example for someone who thinks that events are objects is to state what are called 'identity-conditions' for events. The claim that events are objects is on shaky ground unless a general account can be given of the conditions under which an event X and an event Y count as being one and the same object (and so, by corollary, of the conditions under which they count as being two different objects). (It is a philosophers' proverb that there is no entity without identity.) Turning to meanings, is the meaning of 'Curry is hot' really an object at all? Or is talk about 'the meaning' of a sentence merely shorthand for talk about other things too complex and too messy for us to mention in the course of an ordinary conversation: some awful nexus of vibrations in the air, marks on paper and behavioural dispositions? Or is the meaning of a sentence perhaps a mathematical (or logical) object rather than an intangible one: the set of all possible worlds in which the sentence has the truth value True, for example? The final stop in this lightning tour of ontology is Father Christmas. Is he an object? If not, what can we possibly be doing when we assert that he has a white beard? Yet if he is an object then he's a non-existent object, and what sort of object is that? Can there really *be* something that doesn't exist?[75]

For the same reasons that CYC needs to know that doing work always requires energy, it also needs to know such things as whether or not different objects can be in the same place at the same time and whether or not all objects exist. Moreover, the richness of CYC's ontological scheme will be reflected in the quality of the inferences it can draw from the information given to it. CYC needs to be able to tell that there are crucial differences in the logical implications of the assertions that Father Christmas has a beard and that Roger Schank has a beard. Given the event 'Jones buttered a piece of toast slowly, in the kitchen, at 6am' CYC must be able to infer that Jones did *something*.[76]

Epistemology is the general theory of knowledge. Problems in epistemology are often of the form: *what* do you know when you know that P (where P is some proposition)? One notable problem area concerns our knowledge of causal relationships. What is it that someone knows when they know that one event X caused another event Y? How, for example, are we to analyse Fred's knowledge that the collision with billiard ball *a* was what caused the change in trajectory of billiard ball *b*? Does the assertion 'X caused Y' state that there is some kind of necessary connection between X and Y – that event X has some kind of 'oomph', known or unknown, that necessitates the occurrence of Y? Or does the assertion state merely that all events sufficiently like X (including X itself) are, as it happens, invariably followed by a Y-like event?[77] The second of these is much weaker than the first: it is consistent with causal regularities being nothing more than coincidences (universe-wide coincidences maybe, but coincidences nonetheless).

In a few pages time I take up the issue of whether the method used in CYC for representing causal assertions is adequate.

Logic is the theory of reasoning. CYC makes use of a new and powerful tool known as nonmonotonic logic.[78] An inference is nonmonotonic if it ain't monotonic; and an inference is monotonic if it continues to hold good no matter how many further premises you add to it. Here is an example of a monotonic inference:

Premiss 1:   All philosophers have brains.
Premiss 2:   Socrates was a philosopher.
Conclusion: Socrates had a brain.

The conclusion continues to follow no matter what extra premisses are tacked on: 'Socrates was Greek', 'Socrates had an unusually small head', etc. (It continues to follow even if you tack on the negation of one or both of the original premisses: 'Not all philosophers have brains', 'Socrates was not a philosopher'. You may find this hard to take on board at a first hearing. I explain why it's so later in the section.)

A nonmonotonic inference, on the other hand, can cease to hold good when further premisses are added. From the information that Biggles is a bird and birds fly, CYC must be capable of drawing the common sense inference that Biggles flies. However, CYC must have mechanisms that allow it to retract this 'default' conclusion if it subsequently learns that Biggles is a New Zealand kiwi and kiwis are flightless.[79] The field of nonmonotonic logic consists of the study of such mechanisms. One of the mechanisms included in CYC is known as a truth maintenance system or TMS.[80] Each conclusion that CYC draws is 'tagged' with the premisses from which it was derived. When CYC notices it has drawn a conclusion that conflicts with one it drew earlier, it backs up to the premisses used in each case and examines them further – 'Biggles is a bird' and 'Birds fly' in the case of 'Biggles flies'; and 'Biggles is a kiwi' and 'Kiwis are flightless' in the case of 'Biggles cannot fly'. When CYC looks at the fine print attached to the assertion 'Birds fly' it sees that this is true only for typical birds and it finds the kiwi listed as a bird that is abnormal in this respect.[81] In this way CYC is often able to decide which of a pair of conflicting conclusions to retract.

Will the CYC project succeed? Maybe not. Lenat gives it nothing better than a fifty to sixty per cent chance of success (though given that the postulate on which the project rests – the symbol system hypothesis – is a complete unknown, there is little reason to take any figure seriously).[82] Maybe symbol manipulation is simply not the route to artificial intelligence. Maybe the brittleness of expert systems is the result not of a lack of knowledge per se but of the inadequacy of the data model of knowledge. Adding orders of magnitude more data may be akin to trying to refloat a ship by adding yet more ballast. If the project fails this may, as Lenat says, 'give us an indication about whether the symbolic paradigm is flawed and if so, how.'[83] On the other hand it may not. The project may simply collapse under the sheer difficulty of the task, leaving us little the wiser about the truth or falsity of its fundamental assumptions.

Lenat's specific goals for the project are as follows. First, by 1994 to approach 'the crossover point . . . where it will be more cost-effective to continue building CYC's KB [knowledge base] by having it read online material (text-books, literature, newspapers etc[84]) and ask questions about it, than to continue the sort of manual "brain-surgery" approach we are currently employing.[85] Lenat and his collaborators seem confident that by 1994 most of the significant ontological and representational problems will have been solved; and the various control mechanisms – for logic, induction, analogizing, indexing, updating, searching for relevant information, and so on – will be essentially complete and will thereafter need little or no hands-on modification (and similarly for the various special-purpose mechanisms performing such functions as language-processing). The second learning phase of the project (reading online material) will end around 2001, 'culminating in a system with human-level breadth and depth of knowledge'.[86] Artificial intelligence is 'within our grasp', declares Lenat.[87]

I like Lenat's go-ahead pragmatism. ('Yes, one can sit around for decades and bemoan the impenetrable mystique of the human intellect . . . or one can sit down and try to penetrate it . . . [W]e think that our research time can best be spent actually trying to build big common sense KBs.'[88]) I too believe that the best way to learn how – and how not – to build a large KB is to go ahead and try to build one; and I am sure the CYC project will be well worth the money, with diverse technological payoffs. But I think the grand predictions are way out. The problem of common sense knowledge, with its contained problems of ontology, epistemology and control, is far and away the hardest that computer science has ever faced. Believing that at this stage in the project the ontological and epistemological preparations are more or less complete, Lenat now places the emphasis on the mammoth task of knowledge-entry (i.e. of typing in the data). He downplays the worry that CYC may need as-yet-unknown sophisticated control structures and reasoning methods, and insists that a mere twenty per cent of the project's effort need be allocated to such issues.[89] In my view Lenat is mistaken. In the detailed criticisms of CYC that follow I suggest that insufficient attention has been paid to these matters. I certainly do not maintain that the specific problems I describe cannot, with time and effort, be solved. But I do maintain that the idea of producing 'a system with human-level breadth and depth of knowledge' by the early years of next century is nothing less than absurd. Artificial intelligence is not, at present, within our grasp.

Ontology

Lenat records that the first five years of the project were spent primarily on the problem of devising an adequate ontology with which to underpin CYC's representational framework.[90] This not inconsiderable effort has, in my view, hardly scratched the surface. Yet 2001 is just around the corner; as Lenat's colleague and critic Brian Cantwell Smith puts it, 'It's not so much that [the CYC team] think that ontology is already solved, as that they propose, in a relatively modest time-period, to accomplish what others spend lives on.'[91]

Predictably, the solutions the CYC team have adopted to ontological problems are often hasty. Here is a case study.

What is a substance?

What sort of a thing is a substance? Lenat's answer, which is incorporated in CYC's ontology, is that a substance is the set (or collection) of all its instances. So to take a specific example, the substance gold is claimed to be the set of all the particular instances of gold that there are (particular nuggets, rings, necklaces, teeth etc.).[92] There are a number of severe difficulties with this suggestion.

(1) A lump of gold-bearing ore may contain more quartz than gold. Does this lump of ore count as an instance of gold? Either answer, yes or no, leads to trouble. If yes, then the lump must also count as an instance of quartz. So the lump is a member of both the set of all instances of gold and the set of all instances of quartz. So the substance gold and the substance quartz overlap. But this ought not to be: gold and quartz are two quite distinct substances. Indeed if it happened to be the case that *all* instances of gold contain some quartz and vice versa then Lenat's proposal would deem quartz and gold to be the *same* substance. If no, then the lump does not participate in the set of instances of gold. So the substance gold and the lump of ore pass each other by. Moral: the substance gold cannot be equated with the set of all instances of gold.

(2) A person or company can own the manufacturing rights to a substance, but it is meaningless to say that one can own the manufacturing rights to a mathematical object like a set. (As Lenat says in another context 'sets are intangible, imperceivable things; they are mathematical constructs'.[93])

(3) Some substances are more valuable than others; yet it seems meaningless to say that some sets are more valuable than others. Lenat cannot duck out of this and similar objections by insisting that 'The substance gold is valuable' really means 'Every member of the set of instances of gold is valuable'. The reason is that these two sentences have different logical implications. The sentence 'The substance gold is valuable' implies that if my buckle had been gold it would have been valuable. Since my buckle is not made of gold it is not a member of the set of instances of gold, so the sentence 'Every member of the set of instances of gold is valuable' implies nothing about my buckle. So the two sentences cannot be equivalent in meaning. (I hope Lenat would shrink from the desperate measure of trying to include the 'counterfactual object' my-buckle-had-it-been-gold in the set of objects that is supposed to constitute the substance gold. Otherwise one would no longer be able to affirm that every instance of gold melts at 653 °C, or has density 8.3. Why should the melting point of my-buckle-had-it-been-gold be the same as that of *actual* instances of gold? There are surely contrary-to-fact situations in which gold – that malleable, ductile yellow metal, soluble in aqua regia and of atomic weight 179 – has

a melting point of 652 °C (just as there are contrary-to-fact situations in which you are an inch taller or were born with hair of a different colour).)

(4) Substances can come into existence. Take the artificially created elements. Before this century there was, so far as we know, no such substance as Einsteinium. Yet sets are atemporal – they don't come into or go out of existence. (As Lenat himself says, sets 'last forever in their Platonic universe'.[94])

(5) Sets can be multiplied together (we can form the so-called Cartesian product of any two sets); yet it seems meaningless to say that two substances can be multiplied together.

(6) The number of objects in a set (the *cardinality* of the set) is one of the set's *essential* properties: essential in the sense that if the number were different we would no longer have the same set on our hands but a different one. The number of instances of gold is not, however, an essential property of the substance gold. The sentence 'Gold would have been a different substance if there had been one more gold thing than there actually is' is false; yet it is true that if there were one more gold thing then the set of instances of gold would be a different set.

(7) Sets are identical if they have the same members as one another. Suppose that (by an act of God) all the gold in the universe suddenly goes out of existence – except for my gold teeth. Let us further suppose, for simplicity, that all my teeth are gold. On Lenat's proposal the substance gold is the set of instances of gold; so since it is now the case that the set of instances of gold is the set of my teeth, we get the result that the substance gold is one and the same thing as the set of my teeth. This is implausible – the more so if you reflect on the fact that in that case the sentence 'The substance gold used to have more instances than it now does' says no more and no less than that the set of my teeth used to have more instances than it now does.

While the size of the KB is down at around 0.1 percent of consensus reality it is very probable that oversimplifications and mistakes in CYC's ontology will not show up in performance. However, if philosophers are right to stress the importance of correct ontology then as the size of the KB grows errors are certain to disrupt CYC's performance. As Lenat says in an extract from his projected *The Ontological Engineer's Handbook*: 'In any knowledge base, and for any intelligent agent, it is essential to make the right distinctions in order to be able to organize and cope with the complexity of the real world.'[95]

Causality

The method used in CYC for representing causal assertions – assertions of the form 'X causes Y' – is very simple: the assertion that X implies Y is labelled with a symbol 'causal'. CYC's way of representing the claim that X is the cause of Y is:

Causal(X ⊃ Y).[96]

'⊃' is the symbol for what logicians call *material implication*. '⊃' is usually read in English as 'if – then' or 'implies'. (So one way to pronounce

It rains ⊃ we'll go to the museum

is 'If it rains then we'll go to the museum'.) To take a specific example, the fact that water in the fuel causes the engine to misfire is represented like this:

Causal(there is water in the fuel ⊃ the engine misfires).

Think of a labelled implication, causal (X ⊃ Y), as indicating two things:

(i)   'X ⊃ Y' is true, and
(ii) 'X ⊃ Y' is a causal statement.[97]

The label 'causal' is nothing more than a marker or tag. The knowledge-enterers label certain implications in the KB 'causal' just as certain objects in Shrdlu's world are labelled 'red', 'green', and 'blue'. (Shrdlu, remember, has no grasp whatsoever of what colour terms mean; in the jargon, he lacks a *semantics* for colour terms.) I have already remarked that the problem of what 'X causes Y' means is one of the hardest in epistemology. There are various tentative answers on the market. CYC contains no answer at all – just labels. CYC has no semantics for the term 'causal'.

To take an analogy, I could define a 'general statement' to be a sentence containing either the word 'all' or the word 'every'. Equipped with this criterion, a non-English speaker would be able to pick out general statements even though she has no idea what the words 'all' and 'every' mean. Similarly CYC can (sometimes) tell whether an implication is causal but only by looking to see whether or not it is labelled.

This method of representing causality has a number of weaknesses. The severest of them arises from the fact that if Y is true then the implication X ⊃ Y is true no matter whether X is true or false (and no matter whether X is even relevant to Y). This curious property of material implication can be read off the truth table shown in note 98 (this truth table is the semantical definition of material implication). Thus both the following implications are true simply because it is true that you will, at some point, die:

You read another philosophy book ⊃ you will die.
You never read another philosophy book ⊃ you will die.

Consider the fact that a car running over a baked bean will cause the bean to squash, and take some particular squashed baked bean of which this causal story happens to be false: had a car tyre run over it this certainly would have squashed it, but in fact what actually squashed it was Freddie's fork. Since it is true that (as Freddie's fork descends on it) the bean squashes, the following implication is true (by the property of '⊃' that I've just mentioned):

The car tyre runs over the bean ⊃ the bean squashes.

This is bad news for the representation

Causal(the car tyre runs over the bean ⊃ the bean squashes).

Since the implication is true and moreover expresses a genuine causal relationship (in that being run over is the right sort of event to bring about squashing) it is ripe to have the label 'causal' attached to it. This is an intolerable situation: if 'causal($X ⊃ Y$)' is assertable when X is not the cause of Y then this formula is certainly not a satisfactory representation of causality.[99] (The problem is particularly glaring in a case where a KB reasons backwards in time from the truth of Y and 'causal($X ⊃ Y$)' to X.)

The upshot is that the labelling technique cannot be used in conjunction with material implication. Rectifying the situation is far from easy. The problem of arriving at a satisfactory formal analysis of implication that avoids the curious properties of material implication has proved to be a recalcitrant one.[100] A number of logicians are working on this problem and I certainly hope we crack it by 2001 – but I wouldn't want anyone to hold their breath.

The temporal projection problem

This is a particular case of the frame problem or the problem of how to update a large knowledge base (section 5.2).[101] Suppose the KB contains a reasonably comprehensive collection of statements about a given situation or setting, including statements about what can cause what to happen in such a situation. We inform the KB that certain events have just occurred in the situation. To keep its description of the situation accurate the KB must be able to compute the consequences of these events. This is far from straightforward.

Here is a toy illustration of the difficulty (known as the Yale Shooting Problem).[102] The situation involves Freda and an assassin with a gun. The KB knows that Freda is alive when the assassin loads the gun at time t. The KB also knows that:

(1) If a live human is shot in the head with a loaded gun they die (immediately).

(This assertion is, of course, an oversimplification, but as I say the illustration is only a toy one.) The gun is not fired for two minutes. At the end of this time the assassin steps out of concealment, grips Freda by the hair and pulls the trigger at point blank range. On hearing this information a human listener will update their description of the situation with the assertion 'Freda is dead' (or 'Freda is probably dead' if they are a cautious individual). Can the KB do this?

The KB knows that:

(2) Unless the circumstances are abnormal, if a gun is loaded at a time t then unless it is fired it will still be loaded at $t+2$ minutes.

(This is part of the KB's general knowledge about shootings.) So if the KB assumes that the circumstances are normal (with respect to the gun's being loaded) it can infer that the gun is still loaded at $t+2$ and then use (1) to conclude that Freda is dead. However, the KB also knows that:

(3) Unless the circumstances are abnormal, a thing that is alive at t will continue to be alive at $t+2$ minutes.

Assertions which, like (2) and (3), say that a fact normally persists are known as *frame axioms*. The KB uses this axiom in exactly the same way that it used (2) but this time infers that Freda is alive at $t+2$. It can then conclude from (1) that the gun was not loaded at $t+2$.

So the KB is in a quandary over how to update. It has arrived at two conflicting candidates: 'the gun was still loaded at $t+2$ and Freda is dead' and 'the gun was unloaded between t and $t+2$ and Freda is still alive'. In the first, frame axiom (2) is satisfied and frame axiom (3) fails; in the second, (3) is satisfied and (2) fails. This is the temporal projection problem: there will generally be a number of different ways of updating a description, each of which is consistent with the explicitly stated facts and each of which involves the failure of the same number of frame axioms. The temporal projection problem is universal. Any successful updating mechanism based on frame axioms must include a method for dealing with it.

Guha (co-leader of the CYC project) has proposed a solution to the temporal projection problem.[103] The proposal makes use of CYC's representations of causality. Stripping the two candidate updates to their essentials, the first is that Freda changes state at $t+2$ (from alive to dead) and the second is that the gun changes state between t and $t+2$ (from loaded to unloaded). Guha points out that there is information in the story about how the first of these changes could have been caused (Freda is shot) but there is no information about how the second could have been caused. (Was it a miracle? Was the assassin torn by opposing desires?) Guha claims that CYC can readily be given the resources to exploit this asymmetry and select the first candidate. For CYC knows that

Causal(person X is shot with a loaded gun $\supset$ person X dies).

So Freda's change of state is covered by a causal statement known to CYC. CYC can check through candidate updates for changes of state that are not covered by causal statements and then select the candidate having the least number of state changes that are not covered.[104]

This solution is artificial. Unfortunately it works only if certain causal statements are excluded from the KB. The change in the gun's state *is* covered if CYC knows that:

Causal(someone removes the bullets from a gun ⊃ the gun is not loaded).[105]

Withholding from CYC the information that manually removing the bullets is one way of causing a gun to be empty will certainly help CYC out of the Yale Shooting Problem, but this is hardly a recipe for a general solution to the temporal projection problem.

There is a second, deeper, difficulty with Guha's suggestion. Since CYC is a common sense reasoner it ought to be able to conclude that the cause of the gun's emptying was not activity in the LEDs in Freda's digital watch. This knowledge is represented by an assertion of the form

NOT (causal(X ⊃ Y))

(where Y is 'the gun is not loaded' and X is a statement about the LEDs). Clearly this assertion must not count as covering the gun's change of state. Yet it does contain the label 'causal'. So when CYC checks to see what's covered and what isn't, it is not enough to look for an assertion containing the label 'causal' and an implication 'X ⊃ Y' where Y represents the event being checked. The label must be in the right position. But which position is this? Should the label perhaps be the main or dominant symbol? No.

(Causal(X ⊃ Y)) AND (causal(Y ⊃ Z))

will do to cover the occurrence of Y, but the main symbol is AND. (To figure out which is the main symbol of an assertion you simply count the parentheses. The symbol with the least number of parentheses around it – possibly zero – is the main one. The next symbols 'down' are said to be at depth two, and so on. So in this example both 'causal' labels are at depth two and both occurrences of '⊃' are at depth three.) Suppose we try: 'the label must either be the main symbol or (providing the main symbol isn't 'NOT') be at depth two?' No, this doesn't work either.

NOT ((causal(X ⊃ Y)) OR (NOT (causal(X ⊃ Z))))

would serve to cover Z (since it entails 'causal(X ⊃ Z)'). And so it goes. There is in fact no 'right position' for CYC to look for. The method of labelling affords no easy way of establishing whether or not the KB knows a possible causal explanation for a given event.[106]

I said earlier that CYC's present position in regard to causality is analogous to that of someone who is told that a 'general statement' is any sentence containing either the word 'all' or the word 'every'. Consider how much more effectively equipped someone (or some machine) would be if told that a 'universal statement' is any sentence which *means that* every object has some property or other. This person or machine would be able to tell that

All objects are massive

is universal; that

It is false that at least one object is not massive

is universal; and that

Not every object is massive

is not universal. The CYC team are a long way conceptually from being able to give the KB a similar facility vis-a-vis causation.

Relevance

I mentioned earlier in the chapter that one of the major control problems for a large KB is the problem of relevant search. Lenat reports that so far CYC is not sufficiently large for this problem to have been of much concern.[107] As the size of the KB grows, strategies for dealing with relevance will have to be developed. Guha and Levy give a clear statement of the issues:

> It is well known that the performance of most inference mechanisms (especially those that operate on declaratively represented bodies of knowledge [i.e. those that operate in accordance with the data model]) degrades drastically as the size of the knowledge base . . . increases. A solution for this problem needs to be found for the declarative paradigm to yield usable systems. The main observation that suggests a solution is that while the KB might have a large body of knowledge, only some small portion of it is used for any given task. If this relevant portion can be apriori identified, the size of the search space can be drastically reduced thereby speeding up the inference.[108]

Relevance is an extremely slippery notion. Guha and Levy give what they take to be an example of clear nonrelevance (i.e. a fact that one clearly need not take into account in solving a specified problem). If the problem to be solved is that of determining whether or not Fred has breakfasted by 8.30 on a

A hard look at the facts   115

particular morning then there is no need, they say, to consider the price of tea in India.[109] But why not? If Fred happens to be heavily invested in Indian tea and the market has fallen savagely and he hears of this just as he is about to sit down for his breakfast . . . Whatever pair of circumstances you pick there will nearly always be some context in which one is relevant to the other.

This concept of a surrounding context is crucial to issues of relevance. Abstracted from a context, questions about relevance make little sense.[110] Take these two assertions:

1   For the last eight years the rains in Malawi have not started until the end of November.
2   Timber production in Zambia his increased 500 percent in the period 1972–92.

The relevance of the second assertion to the first depends on the context. If the project in hand is to decide on dates for Auntie's safari then (2) is not relevant; but if the project is to seek out possible causes for changes in climatic patterns in sub-Saharan Africa then (2) is relevant. Different projects create different contexts. Given the entirely open-ended nature of the set of problems CYC may be expected to deal with, the task of giving the KB detailed information about what is relevant to what is, to say the least, a daunting one.

Lenat and his colleagues have no radically new proposals for dealing with the problem of relevance. They are prepared to soldier on with the approach mentioned by Minsky in the quotation given earlier (which dates from 1974): the KB needs to know meta-facts about when the facts it contains may usefully be used and when not. In CYC these meta-facts are represented by means of assertions called *relevance axioms*. There are two types of relevance axiom in CYC, specific and general.

The idea behind specific relevance axioms is that different sections of the KB 'can be ranked according to their relevance to the problem-solving task at hand'.[111] So, for example, if the task given to CYC is to solve a problem in automobile design, the KB will be guided in its search for relevant information by an axiom to the effect that the automobile section is more relevant than the botany section (although the botany section cannot be ruled out completely, for it might be the source of a useful analogy or two).[112] Axioms like this one certainly cut down the search space enormously, but when all is said and done they give only the coarsest guidance.

General relevance axioms are formalizations of such statements as:

Temporal proximity: It is necessary to consider only events that are temporally close to the time of the event or proposition at issue.[113]

In explaining and defending this axiom Guha and Levy say 'it is rare that an event occurs and . . . [then after] a considerable period of time . . . suddenly manifests its effects'.[114] Yet the fact that Gordon wore a hired suit (rented tux) at Matilda's wedding eighteen months ago may be highly relevant to the fact that he has at long last abandoned his customary after-dinner speech and written a new one.

CYC's general relevance axioms also concern *spatial proximity* and *information proximity*: it is not neccessary to consider events that happen far away from the situation at issue unless there is some informational connection between them (a telephone line, for instance).[115] There is also an axiom stating that only information at the right *level of grain* is relevant. Information about the quality of the stitching in Freda's shoes is too fine-grain to be relevant to the question of whether she is alive at $t+2$.

These axioms presuppose an effective indexing scheme for the KB. That is, they presuppose a solution to what I earlier called the organization problem – a problem that Lenat and his colleagues say surprisingly little about.[116] Given good enough indexing, these relevance axioms will enable CYC to brush aside a huge number of facts as it searches. Yet once the KB contains hundreds of millions of assertions there will still be far too many remaining at the end of this filtering process. After all, for any event there will be a huge number of events (at the same level of grain) that are temporally and either spatially or informationally proximate to it. The vast majority of these would never even be considered by a human problem-solver (if the TV screen suddenly dissolves into horizontal lines you won't for an instant entertain the idea that your having just bitten into your burger might be relevant). Perhaps the way to go is to produce a much finer filter by piling on more relevance axioms. This approach may work – we won't know until somebody tries. One worry, certainly, is that the addition of the necessary relevance axioms may significantly increase the size of the KB. Since search becomes increasingly inefficient as the KB grows in size, the relevance axioms may in the end simply fuel the problem that they were introduced to solve.

Perhaps CYC will teach us that the relevance problem is intractable for a KB organized in accordance with the data model of knowledge. When solving mundane problems, even novel ones, humans seem to be able to zero in immediately on relevant ideas. Suppose you notice that during the night the head of your local statue has acquired an upturned chamber pot. In coming up with an explanation, do you first winnow your knowledge for every single fact that might possibly be relevant? Probably not – even if you've never seen nor heard of such a thing before. If human beings go through the same massive process of sorting and elimination that CYC does there is no sign of it. It may be that for us relationships of relevance are somehow built into our appreciation of the problem itself. Perhaps our representations contain 'hooks' that connect them to other relevant representations; or to take another metaphor, perhaps when one representation 'lights up' other representations relevant to it automatically 'light up' too. On this model there is simply no need for the computationally expensive search that characterises CYC's approach to locating relevant data. For all we know at present these 'relevance linkages' may be impossible to implement directly in a symbol-manipulator. Perhaps richly interlocking, distributed representations of the sort discussed in chapter 10 are required – in which case the data method is doomed.

Inconsistency

A collection of sentences that involves a contradiction is said to be *inconsistent*. For example, a KB that contains both 'Carlo is a loyalist' and 'Carlo is not a loyalist' is inconsistent. There are many ways in which a KB may become inconsistent, ranging from a straightforward typing error through undetected disagreements among the knowledge-enterers to the drawing of conflicting conclusions by the KB itself (as in the case of Biggles both flying and not flying). For reasons I will explain, it is important that an inconsistent KB be restored to consistency. How to do this is one of the hardest problems of all.

I mentioned earlier that the conclusion of the argument about Socrates still follows if the premises are supplemented with their own denials. Indeed *any conclusion whatsoever* follows from an inconsistent set of premises. This fact is so important in logic that it has acquired a name, *Quodlibet* (which is Latin for 'what you please' – any conclusion you please follows from a contradiction).[117] The proof of Quodlibet is actually quite simple. Where S is some set of sentences and X is a single sentence, the assertion 'X follows from S' (or to put it the other way round, 'S entails X') is defined as meaning that S with the negation of X thrown in is an inconsistent set of sentences. So to say that 'Socrates was a plumber' follows from the premises 'Socrates was Macedonian' and 'All Macedonians were plumbers' is to say that the three sentences 'Socrates was Macedonian', 'All Macedonians were plumbers' and 'Socrates was not a plumber' form an inconsistent trio. Now, suppose S is *already* inconsistent. Then S with the negation of any sentence you please thrown in is inconsistent! Therefore any sentence you please follows from S. Q.E.D. (*Adding* a sentence can never remove inconsistency. The only way to restore a set of sentences to consistency is to remove sentences – so if S is inconsistent then S plus the negation of X is bound to be inconsistent.)[118]

Suppose the following instruction is programmed into the KB:

If you are queried whether X is the case and X is either one of, or follows from, the assertions you contain then answer Yes.

It is sadly the case that if a KB containing this instruction becomes inconsistent, it will answer Yes to any query whatsoever. So a military KB that happens to have been fed inconsistent weather reports will answer 'Yes' if asked 'Are we under nuclear attack?'.

What to do? An obvious first move is to modify the instruction.

> If you are queried whether X is the case and X is either one of, or follows from, the assertions you contain then answer Yes – unless NOT X is either one of, or follows from, the assertions you contain.

The second part of the instruction calls for a 'consistency check' – the KB must make sure it is consistent before it answers. The problem with consistency checks is that they can be very slow (the missiles may strike before the KB manages to decide whether or not it is consistent). A more fundamental problem is that a program for checking consistency is bound to give the wrong answer from time to time. (This is a consequence of a result obtained in mathematical logic in 1936.[119]) Yet even a slow and not wholly reliable mechanism for checking on inconsistency is better than none at all.

Suppose CYC's 'Contradiction Detection and Resolution Module' detects an inconsistency – what can CYC do about it?[120] I have already described CYC's first line of attack, its truth maintenance system.[121] CYC backs up to the premises used to derive the two conflicting assertions and, if it can, rejects one of them, thereby knocking out one of the two conflicting inferences. (In doing this CYC makes use of information supplied by the knowledge-enterers concerning such matters as which of the premises are least likely to turn out false, which have known exceptions, and so forth.[122]) This will not always work: CYC will often be unable to tell which premiss is to be rejected. The second line of attack is to rank the two inferences according to a number of 'preference criteria' and reject the one that scores less points. This approach is only as good as the criteria themselves and unfortunately the preference criteria that CYC contains are all rather weak. Some examples are:

(1) Prefer the inference with the stronger causal flavour.[123]

This criterion is supposed to discriminate between inferences such as the ones involved in the Yale Shooting Problem. As we have seen, it does not work.

(2) Prefer the inference with the 'shorter inferential distance'.[124]

This criterion will succeed in only a limited range of cases. In general there is no reason why a 'shorter' inference is more likely to have a true conclusion than a 'longer' one. The most general way of defining 'inferential distance' is in terms of the number of 'steps' the inference involves. For example, it requires two steps to infer C from the three premises $A \supset B$, $B \supset C$ and A (the first step being to infer B from A and $A \supset B$; recall that '$\supset$' is pronounced 'if then'.) It is simply false that the fewer steps an inference contains, the more likely it is to lead to a true conclusion. For example, there is an inference only *two* steps long from the two premisses A and NOT A to the conclusion that the world ended ten minutes ago. The argument uses two inference rules. The first is:

From X infer NOT ((NOT X) AND (NOT Y)).

That is, from the premiss that X is the case you can infer that not both X and Y are false. (X and Y are any sentences whatever.) The second rule is:

From NOT X and NOT ((NOT X) AND (NOT Y)) infer Y.

That is, from the premiss that X is false and the premiss that not both X and Y are false you can infer that Y is the case. Can you construct the two step argument? (Note 125 gives the answer.)

(3) Prefer constructive arguments to nonconstructive ones.[126]

It is hard to see why Lenat and Guha think this criterion will be of any help. Constructive arguments are the subject matter of intuitionistic logic, and it has long been realized that a retreat to intuitionistic logic is of no help in dealing with the problems engendered by Quodlibet.[127]

CYC's truth maintenance system and preference criteria will from time to time leave CYC unable to tell which member of a pair of conflicting assertions it should reject. At this point CYC can do one of three things. (1) Shut down and await human intervention. (2) Quarantine all the assertions implicated in the inconsistency and try to get by without them. (One way of doing this would be to mark each implicated assertion as being of unknown truth value.) If the number of assertions implicated is large – as it will be if one (or both) of the conflicting assertions has figured as a premiss in a large number of inferences, or if a large number of premisses were used to derive the assertions that conflict – then this may produce a considerable impairment in performance. (3) Brazen it out. Carry on and hope the malign effects of the inconsistency won't spread too far. This latter seems to be Lenat's recommendation.

> There is no need – and probably not even any possibility – of achieving a global consistent unification of . . . [a] very large KB . . . We expect . . . that . . . [the view that] inconsistencies may exist for a short period but . . . are errors and must be tracked down and corrected . . . is just an idealized, simplified view of what will be required for intelligent systems . . . How should the system cope with inconsistency? View the knowledge space, and hence the KB, not as one rigid body, but rather as a set of independently supported buttes . . . [A]s with large office buildings, independent supports should make it easier for the whole structure to weather tremors such as local anomalies . . . [I]nferring an inconsistency is only slightly more serious than the usual sort of 'dead end' a searcher runs into . . . [128]

This looks like quicksand to me. CYC is not a collection of expert-system KBs working independently of one another but a single, integrated whole. The results of inferences drawn in one butte will be available to all other buttes – and something that is available may be made use of. As Lenat says in a different context 'Far-flung knowledge . . . *can* be useful'.[129] There is no a priori reason to think that the effects of inconsistency will not spread from butte to butte, poisoning the entire KB. In my view it would be downright dangerous to allow a commissioned KB with logic and control systems as crude as CYC's to continue to run once an irremediable inconsistency develops.

Clearly there are extraordinarily hard problems facing anyone who wishes to build a large commonsense KB.

5.7　The complexity barrier

The attempt to construct a machine that thinks is a project of breath-taking complexity. Hard technical problems remain unsolved (and the pessimist in me suspects that even harder ones lie waiting to be uncovered). Researchers speak of the need to find ways of organizing billions of facts in computer memory. Large AI programs contain head-spinningly many lines of code. A modern computer contains far more electrical connections than there are people on the planet – yet hardware that is many, many times more complicated will be required in order to match the activity of the trillions of neural connections in the human brain. Can the human mind cope with this much complexity?

Terry Winograd, a formidably talented programmer, has trouble even with Shrdlu: 'The code presents a dense mass, with no easy footholds. Even having written the program, I find it near the limit of what I can keep in mind at once. After being away from it for a few months, it is quite difficult to answer questions about specific parts of it, or to anticipate the effects of suggested changes.'[130] Yet viewed in terms of AI's ultimate goal, Shrdlu is a trivial program!

It would be a huge irony if the symbol system hypothesis were true, but the human brain too frail ever to build a machine that thinks. Humans may not be up to breaking the complexity barrier. But then again, AI is still in its infancy. At the present stage computer intelligence is a field wide open for success . . . or failure. The future holds all the verdicts.

6
The curious case of the Chinese room

In the last two chapters I have been arguing that the question of whether a computer is the right kind of machine to think is, to use a piece of philosophical jargon, an *empirical* issue. This is to say it is an issue that can be settled only by experimentation and evidence-gathering. (The word 'empirical' in fact derives from a Greek word meaning 'experience'.) Not all questions are empirical ones. Compare 'Are all ophthalmologists in New York over 25 years of age?' with 'Are all opthalmologists in New York eye specialists?' The first of these asks an empirical question but the second does not. You don't need to make a survey of New York ophthalmologists in order to establish that all are eye specialists because 'ophthalmologist' *means* 'eye specialist'. Evidence-gathering has no role to play in answering a non-empirical question.

The influential American philosopher John Searle maintains that it is a mistake to view our central question as an empirical one. The issue of whether a symbol-manipulator could be capable of thought is, he says, a squarely non-empirical one, and so evidence-gathering is beside the point. My attitude of waiting to see how things eventually turn out in the AI laboratories is outrageous in Searle's eyes. He claims we can prove, right here and now, and without looking at any evidence, that the symbol system hypothesis is false. In his view, to assert the hypothesis is just like asserting that some ophthalmologists are not eye-specialists. The only difference is that the latter embodies a very simple mistake, which can be brought to light by opening a dictionary, whereas the former contains a much more subtle error, requiring a sophisticated philosophical argument to expose it. I'm going to take a careful look at Searle's argument, which has become known as the Chinese room argument. I hope to convince you that it is fallacious.

To ease us into Searle's argument, let me revive a puzzle that I mentioned in chapter 4. A computer is just a symbol-manipulator. All it does is compare symbols, delete symbols, copy symbols, and so on. How can a device like this possibly *understand*? It is easy enough to see how a symbol-manipulator could take the Arabic sentence

Jamal hamati indaha waja midah

and perform the manipulation of writing it backwards, for example, or of adding a prefix that converts the sentence into a question. But how on earth could a mere symbol-manipulator actually understand the sentence? Searle's answer is that it could not.

Searle uses some technical terminology to express his fundamental point: a symbol-manipulator has a mastery only of *syntax*, and a mastery of syntax is insufficient for a mastery of *semantics*.[1] To have a mastery of syntax is to have a mastery of some set of rules for performing symbol manipulations; and to have a mastery of semantics is to have an understanding of what the symbols actually mean. A good illustration of the point Searle is making is provided by the fact that someone can learn to manipulate sentences of a foreign language in accordance with a set of syntax-rules without thereby gaining any understanding of what the sentences mean. Knowledge of syntax won't by itself take you to knowledge of semantics. Here, for example, are two syntax-rules for Arabic:

1   To form the I-sentence corresponding to a given sentence, prefix the whole sentence with the symbols 'Hal'.
2   To form the N-sentence corresponding to any reduplicative sentence, insert the particle 'laysa' in front of the predicate of the sentence.

A test. Write down the I-sentence and the N-sentence corresponding to the sentence

Jamal hamati indaha waja midah.

You need to know that this sentence is reduplicative and its predicate consists of everything following 'hamati'.

OK. I'll bet my pet goldfish that your new-found ability with these two syntax-rules hasn't given you a glimmer of what 'hal' and 'laysa' mean. In this case it is perfectly obvious that a mastery of the syntax rules is insufficient for a mastery of the semantics. (In fact, 'hal' forms an interrogative and 'laysa' forms a negation. Your first sentence enquires whether your mother-in-law's camel has belly ache and your second sentence answers in the negative.)

Computers are both masters of and slaves to syntax rules. As we saw in chapter 4, their programs are nothing more than instructions for performing lengthy series of syntactical manoeuvres. Can they break out from the prison of symbol manipulation into the world of meanings? Here is Searle's argument that they cannot.

6.1   The Chinese room argument

Searle uses Sam, the story 'understanding' program, to illustrate his argument.[2] Type Sam a story followed by questions about the story and Sam will type back answers. (Examples of Sam's performance are given in chapter 2.) If you were to look at this program written out in machine code you would see an inscrutable mass of 0s and 1s. However, each line of the program can be rewritten as a rule that anyone can follow. For example, the line

00000011   0111   1100

can be written as the rule

> Compare the contents of memory location number 7 with the contents of memory location number 12 and write down 1 if they are the same, 0 if they are different.

(0111 is bit code for 7, 1100 is bit code for 12, and 00000011 is the way to tell the computer to compare. If you are mystified, take a look back at chapter 4.)

Suppose the whole Sam program is rewritten in this way. The result would be a rulebook running into many, many volumes. If you had a year or so to spare you could work through this rulebook from beginning to end, *handworking* the program – that is, doing by hand all the symbol manipulations that are performed by a computer running the program. Forget that handworking Sam would involve month upon month of head-splitting boredom and imagine someone doing it successfully. This hero, Joe Soap, has been locked in a room with his library of rulebooks, a huge pile of blank exercise books, and several thousand pencils. His only contact with the outside world is via a couple of slots in the wall, labelled Input and Output. The experimenters push in a typed story followed by a sheet of questions and then cluster eagerly around the Output slot to await results (imagine that Joe produces answers in minutes rather than months). Lest Joe cheat by simply making up his own answers, both the story and the questions are written in Chinese characters (Joe's version of Sam has been adapted to handle Chinese). In fact, Joe does not even realize that the input and output consist of sentences of a language. As far as he is concerned the input he receives and the output he produces are made up of meaningless patterns.

Joe's first task is to turn to the section of the rulebook that pairs input patterns with strings of 0s and 1s (strings which are just as meaningless as the input patterns themselves, as far as Joe is concerned). One such rule might be:

> If the pattern is 茶, write 100001110010001001001 on the next empty line of the exercise book labelled 'Input Store'.

(茶 in fact means 'tea', and the displayed bit string is the representation of this Chinese character in Pinyin ASCII.)

Once he has transformed all the input into strings of bits, Joe performs the thousands upon thousands of manipulations called for by the program, filling exercise book after exercise book with 0s and 1s. Eventually he reaches the last section of the rule-book, which pairs Chinese characters with the strings he has written down in a special book labelled 'Output Store'. Joe copies the characters onto sheets of paper which he pushes through the Output slot. To the waiting experimenters the patterns Joe draws are intelligent answers to their questions, but to Joe they are just squiggles, hard-won but perfectly meaningless.

What does this scenario show, according to Searle? Joe Soap, we must agree, understands neither the story, nor the questions, nor the answers. In fact he doesn't even know that they *are* a story, questions, and answers. To him, the input and output are just meaningless symbols. Yet in handworking Sam, Joe has done everything that a computer running Sam does. Joe has performed every symbol manipulation that the computer would perform. In effect the experimenters have run the program on a human computer. So, since running the program doesn't enable Joe to understand the story, it follows that running the program doesn't enable a computer to understand the story, for Joe does everything that the computer does and still doesn't understand the story at the end of it. Moreover this conclusion generalizes to all AI programs that there will ever be, for the argument makes no mention of any specific features of the program.[3] Running a program, no matter how good the program, can never be sufficient to enable a computer to understand anything, believe anything, want anything, think anything. Take a hypothetical AI program that is as good as you like – say a program capable of passing the Turing Test. When Joe Soap (or a non-English-speaking counterpart, if the Test is conducted in English) handworks the program, he understands neither the interrogator's questions nor his own replies. So a computer running the program must be in exactly the same position. An observer might take the computer's output symbols to be meaningful sentences, but for the computer the symbols can mean nothing at all.

In general, then, the Chinese room argument shows (according to Searle) that merely manipulating symbols will not enable the manipulating device to understand X, believe Y or think Z, as witnessed by the fact that a human manipulator could perform exactly the same manipulations without thereby coming to understand X, believe Y or think Z. Thus if the Chinese room argument is correct, the symbol system hypothesis is false.

The Chinese room argument has caused a huge stir and feelings have at times run high. AI researchers are by and large irritated by the argument, which looks to them like a trick. Many are inclined to dismiss the argument as 'just damn silly'. On the other hand a lot of people outside AI find the Chinese room argument persuasive, and it has been described in philosophical journals as 'conclusive', 'exactly right', 'masterful and convincing', and 'completely victorious'. For this reason I think the argument needs to be taken very seriously by those who disagree with it. It is not enough for someone who finds the argument incredible to simply shoo it away. The Chinese room argument demands a careful and cogent refutation. This is what I will attempt.

6.2   What's wrong with the argument?

In my retelling of the tale of the Chinese room, as in Searle's original, a crucial participant in the events receives far less attention than she deserves – so little, in fact, that you may not even have noticed her presence at all. It is time to redress the balance. Allow me to introduce Miss Wong Soo Ling, who speaks to us – or rather writes to us – in perfect Mandarin Chinese. Soo Ling is the voice of the program. She is the blossom of Joe's labours, a disembodied personality brought to life by his patient symbol manipulating. (To make Soo Ling as interesting a personality as possible, let's suppose the program that Joe is handworking is capable of passing the Turing Test – in Chinese, of course.) When the tale of the Chinese room is properly told it contains two principal characters, Joe Soap, the tireless but slightly boring labourer, and Miss Wong, an artificial but charming and sophisticated Chinese-speaker, who is capable of sparkling discourse upon subjects lying well beyond the limits of Joe's dull wit.

The climax of Searle's tale comes when Joe is asked whether the symbol manipulations he is performing enable him to understand the input questions, and he (of course) says No. From this we are supposed to conclude that these symbol manipulations cannot be sufficient to produce understanding. But why ask Joe? He is, after all, nothing more than a cog in the machinery. If we were to ask Soo Ling, she would no doubt respond (correctly or incorrectly!) that the symbol manipulations Joe is performing do indeed enable her to understand the questions.

Having established that there are two voices in the Chinese room scenario – Joe's voice and the voice of the system of which he forms a part – I am now in a position to put my finger on the logical flaw in the Chinese room argument. Here is the argument in its bare and uncluttered essentials.

Premiss   No amount of symbol manipulation on Joe's part will enable Joe to understand the Chinese input.

Therefore   No amount of symbol manipulation on Joe's part will enable the wider system of which Joe is a component to understand the Chinese input.

This argument is invalid. The conclusion simply does not follow from the premiss. Although it is impossible to quarrel with the *truth* of the premiss, the premiss lends no support at all to the conclusion. Searle's argument is no better than this burlesque of it, which has the same logical form:

Premiss Bill the cleaner has never sold pyjamas to Korea.
Therefore The company for which Bill works has never sold pyjamas to Korea.

The organization of which Bill is a small component may or may not participate in the Korean pyjama trade, but the premiss provides no indication either way.

Replies of this ilk to the Chinese room argument are well known to Searle. Several other people have made somewhat similar attacks on the argument, and Searle has dubbed objections of this type the *systems reply*. He believes he has shown the systems reply to be entirely in error.[4] What I'm going to do is take Searle's objections to the systems reply one by one and try to show that none of them work. To make this boxing match between myself and Searle as colourful as possible I will present it in dialogue form. (The words I attribute to Searle are paraphrases, not exact quotations.)

Round one

Searle Your reply to my argument is embarrassingly silly.[5] You agree that the man in the room doesn't understand Chinese but you say that the wider system of which the man is a part nevertheless may understand Chinese. Let's look at what this 'wider system' consists of in the present case. It is just the man plus some books full of rules, a stack of exercise books, a pile of pencils, and maybe the input and output slots too. Are you *really* trying to tell me that although the man himself doesn't understand Chinese, the wider system of man-plus-paper-and-pencils does?

Copeland I have to agree that it does sound silly to say that a man-plus-rulebook understands Chinese even though it is simultaneously true that the man doesn't understand Chinese. But I'm not at all embarrassed by that. The important thing to look at is *why* this sounds silly. I believe there are two reasons. Firstly, the fact that the Chinese room contains a human being is apt to produce something akin to tunnel vision in anyone considering Searle's tale. One has to struggle not to regard the man in the room as the only possible locus of Chinese-understanding. This spurious pull towards Searle's conclusion vanishes if the details of the story are changed a little. Instead of imagining a man writing 0s and 1s, imagine a superbly well-trained performing flea flicking tiny switches up (0) or down (1). Are you at all tempted by the thought that since the flea does not understand Chinese there can be no possibility of the system or machine of which the flea is a component understanding Chinese?

The second reason it sounds silly to say that the wider system may understand Chinese even though the man does not is simple: the wider system Searle has described is itself profoundly silly. No way could a man handwork a program capable of passing a Chinese Turing Test. He might scribble down

0s and 1s for ten years and still not get as far as producing his first Chinese answer. The whole idea of Joe producing Chinese conversation by following a rule book is ludicrous. It isn't because the systems reply is at fault that it sounds absurd to say that the system consisting of Joe and the rulebook may understand Chinese. It is because of the built-in absurdity of Searle's scenario.

Round two

Searle   Your reply to the Chinese room argument begs the question.[6] That is, your reply gratuitously assumes the truth of the very thing I am trying to prove false. My Chinese room argument is designed to prove that running a computer program is not enough to produce an understanding of Chinese. You try to answer my argument by saying that although the man doesn't understand Chinese, the wider system of which he is a part *does* understand Chinese. Yet the very point at issue is whether running a program is enough to make *anything* understand Chinese. The systems reply begs the question by insisting without argument that the system understands Chinese.

Copeland   This objection misses the point of my reply to the Chinese room argument. Some have certainly tried to dismiss Searle's argument by asserting that although the man wouldn't understand Chinese, the whole system would.[7] Searle is right to point out that this crude reply to the argument is question-begging. My own reply, however, is different. I am merely drawing attention to the fact that the Chinese room argument is logically invalid, in the sense that its conclusion does not follow logically from its premiss. You cannot validly infer that the system of which Joe is a component does not understand Chinese from the premiss that Joe himself does not understand Chinese. There is no logical connection between the premiss and the conclusion (as in the case of Bill the cleaner and the company for which he works). Pointing out that Searle's argument is logically invalid does not involve me in claiming that the system *does* understand: I am just saying you can't validly infer that it doesn't from Searle's premiss. So I have not begged the question.

Let me illustrate this with a parallel case. Suppose someone argues: 'Jane eats vegetarian food; therefore she is opposed to killing animals.' This argument is invalid: the conclusion obviously does not follow from the premiss (Jane could have been put on a vegetarian diet by her cardiologist). I can point out that the argument is invalid without taking any stand on whether or not Jane *is* opposed to killing animals. To think that an argument is invalid, you do not have to believe that its conclusion is false. An invalid argument may happen to have a true conclusion. Even if I knew that Jane was staunchly opposed to the taking of animal life, I would, as a logician, still want to point out to the arguer that his conclusion does not follow logically from his premiss.

The point can be made even plainer if we return to the version of the Chinese room scenario involving the program Sam. Searle argues that Joe doesn't understand the story and therefore nor does Sam. With luck you now agree with me that this is not a valid argument. In order to tell whether Sam understands we need to look at Sam, not Joe. In fact, it didn't take much of a look at Sam to make me realise that he definitely doesn't understand the story.[8] Sam literally doesn't know what he is talking about. When he types 'John ordered lasagne' Sam has no notion of what these words refer to in the world. Sam, like Eliza, can manipulate words in a way that generates an illusion of understanding, yet in fact he has no idea at all what the words mean. Even Sam's creators agree with this. Roger Schank writes 'No program we have written can be said to truly understand.'[9]

Thus the version of the Chinese room argument involving Sam has a conclusion that is known to be true. But that doesn't mean the argument is any good. If Searle said 'The moon is made of green cheese, therefore Sam doesn't understand the story' he would equally be putting forward an argument with a true conclusion, and in neither case does that conclusion follow from the premiss.

Searle charges the systems reply with 'beg[ging] the question by insisting without argument that the system must understand'.[10] Yet in the case of Sam we know that the system does *not* understand and I still urge that it is logically invalid to infer this from the fact that Joe does not understand. This should make it quite plain that no question-begging is going on.

Round three

Searle I can show what's wrong with your reply by changing some of the details of the Chinese room story. You say the man is part of a wider system that may understand Chinese even though he doesn't. I can scotch that move by retelling the story so there is no 'wider system'.[11] Instead of imagining the man working in a room full of rule books, exercise books and pencils, imagine that he has memorized all the rules and performs all the symbol manipulations in his head. (I grant you it is probably impossible for a human to do this, but that doesn't matter. We've all been agreed from the start that the Chinese room experiment would be impossible to perform in practice: it is only a 'thought experiment'.) This way the man incorporates the entire system rather than merely being a part of it. When the experimenters ask him Chinese questions, he goes through all the symbol manipulations in his head and eventually writes down Chinese answers. He doesn't understand Chinese any better than he did when he was inside the Chinese room, though. This is obvious, because the set up is still essentially the same as it was then. The only difference is that what you have been calling the system is now part of the man, rather than him being part of it. So it's goodbye to the systems reply: if the man doesn't understand Chinese then there is no way the system could understand, because the system is just a part of him.

Copeland   This objection rests on the principle:

If Joe can't do X, then no part of Joe can do X.

Searle relies on this principle in moving from the fact that Joe doesn't under-stand Chinese to the conclusion that the system, which is now a part of Joe, doesn't understand Chinese either. Let me call it the 'Part-Of' principle. The trouble with the objection is that there is no reason at all to think that this principle of Searle's is true. (Searle himself makes no mention of why he believes it.)

To show you how dubious the principle is I'll describe a science fiction counter-example to it. You have been kidnapped by a group of fanatical AI researchers. This group believes that the best way to achieve AI's ultimate goal of superhuman intelligence is to run 'neuronic programs' on human brain tissue. Official backing for their project has not been forthcoming and they have resorted to clandestine methods, with the result that you now find your-self strapped to a surgical couch in a cellar beneath the AI lab. You gaze apprehensively at the web of wire connecting your shaven skull to a keyboard and visual display unit.

Without removing or damaging any of your brain the team have imprinted their 'neuronic program' on a small area of your cortex. (Thanks to the vast amount of redundancy in the cortex they have been able to do this without any impairment of your faculties.) The trial program that the team have devised for the experiment is one designed to compute solutions to n-dimensional skew-symmetric tensor equations. It works very successfully, and you stare uncomprehendingly at the input and output as they are displayed on the screen. Here, then, is a counterexample to Searle's principle that if you can't do X then no part of you can do X. You can't compute solutions to n-dimensional skew-symmetric tensor equations, but a part of you can. The area of your brain that has been hijacked to perform other people's computations remains solidly a *part* of you.

Could Searle simply stick to his guns and say that since a part of you can now solve tensor equations it follows that *you* can solve tensor equations – the AI team have bestowed this new ability upon you? Let's suppose that Searle does try saying this and take a look at what else it would commit him to. You, strapped to your couch, claim that you cannot do tensor mathematics – in fact you don't even know what it is. Searle, we are supposing, says that you are wrong about this: you are no longer the final arbiter on what you cannot do and it is by studying the input and output of whatever 'programs' the team implant in you that people are to determine your abilities. Okay, so that must also go for Joe when he operates the memorised program. Joe *claims* that he doesn't understand Chinese but Joe is no longer the final arbiter on this: we must look to the input and output of the system Joe has 'internalized'. Yet that, of course, is exactly what Searle cannot say. It is a cornerstone of Searle's argument that Joe's saying 'I do not understand these symbols' is acid proof that handworking a computer program is insufficient to give Joe the ability to understand Chinese. Without that cornerstone Searle cannot even begin to erect his argument.

So, then, Searle is caught on the horns of a dilemma. If he says that you can solve tensor equations he gets himself into deep trouble. If on the other hand he says that you can't, he contradicts his Part-Of principle, since a part of you evidently can solve tensor equations.

Round four

Searle   The systems reply dodges my central point. This is that mastery of syntax is insufficient for a mastery of semantics. No amount of shuffling symbols around can by itself give the shuffler an understanding of what those symbols mean. A computer program is just a set of instructions for shuffling symbols, so it follows that running a computer program is not enough to produce an understanding of Chinese or of anything else. Returning to the systems reply, you say that even though the symbol manipulations that the man performs don't enable the man to understand Chinese, they may nevertheless enable the system to understand Chinese. But as I've just explained, working through a program is not enough to enable *anything* to understand Chinese – man, system, or what you will.[12]

Copeland   Hold on, Searle can't do that! The Chinese room argument is supposed to *prove* Searle's thesis that mere symbol manipulation cannot produce understanding, yet Searle has just tried to use this thesis to *defend* the Chinese room argument against the systems reply. That's as bad as someone borrowing another ten dollars from you so that they can repay the ten they already owe you. This fourth objection to the systems reply consists entirely of sleight of hand.

It is true that I have not yet grappled head on with Searle's thesis that symbol manipulation is insufficient to produce understanding. However, that is because I have been concerned with an examination of his *argument* for the thesis, rather than with an examination of the thesis itself. Having, I hope, now shown that the Chinese room argument does not work, it is time to take a direct look at the thesis it was supposed to establish. (After all, knocking out an argument for a thesis does not suffice to establish that the thesis is false. If God exists then that is a fact, even though umpteen attempts to prove His existence have been shown to be logically flawed.)

6.3   Deciding about understanding

When Sam types 'My favourite dish is lasagne' he literally does not know what he is talking about. How could he? He has neither seen nor tasted lasagne. Sam lives a very sheltered life, deprived of all sensation and bodily pleasure, shyly communicating his dull, conforming messages by teletype. Sam is a perfect candidate for liberation. Enter *Turbo Sam*, a jazzy humanoid robot with a soft pink plastic coating stuffed full of pressure-sensitive tactile sensors. Turbo Sam has arms, legs, cosmetically finished TV eyes, electronic ears, a fine speaking voice and any other artificial bits and pieces it pleases you to imagine. Although initially as incapable as a human babe, Turbo Sam is quick to learn about the world. His design team teach him words in much the same way they taught their children at home. ('Look, Turbo Sam, this is called spaghetti. It is a human foodstuff.' 'Swell – but how do you eat it?') By the end of his training Turbo Sam, the triumph of AI engineering, speaks as we do, interacts with the world as adeptly as we do, even writes poetry. But does Turbo Sam *understand* his poetry? For Turbo Sam is just a symbol manipulator at heart. His peripheral devices may be very fancy compared to simple Sam's screen and keyboard, but under all the razzle-dazzle he is just a computer manipulating strings of 0s and 1s.

Searle, as you might expect, says that a program-controlled robot understands nothing, no matter how good its poetry. He claims he can prove this by a re-run of the Chinese room argument.[13] Let a Chinese person handwork the program that operates Turbo Sam. The symbols the person starts with are this time not Chinese characters but the symbols that the robot's peripheral devices deliver to the program. These will be blocks of 0s and 1s. That may sound puzzling, so let me explain. Take the robot's visual device. Newspaper photographs, as you probably know, are made up of small dots of varying shades of grey. Imagine a photograph made up of dots of just two shades, light grey and dark grey. Now replace each light dot with a 0 and dark dot with a 1: the result is a picture made up of 0s and 1s. This is in fact rather a crude way of using bits to represent a visual scene, and more sophisticated methods give finer detail. Nevertheless this simple method illustrates how the output from the robot's 'eyes' can consist of 0s and 1s. The symbols that the person eventually delivers to the robot's various motor devices – perhaps by means of a radio link – will also be strings of 0s and 1s, which the devices convert into speech, hand movements, and so on. Now for Searle's argument. Someone holds up a plate and says 'Hey, Turbo Sam, this stuff is called lasagne'. 'I understand', replies Turbo Sam. The symbol manipulations that produce this reply have been performed by hand by the Chinese person, and they leave her none the wiser as to the meaning of 'lasagne'. As far as she is concerned, she is manipulating meaningless strings of 0s and 1s. She doesn't even know that the symbols she starts with emanate from the sensory and motor equipment of a robot. So, says Searle, since working through the program doesn't enable the Chinese person to understand, the program is not capable of producing understanding – despite any appearances to the contrary. Turbo Sam might *say* 'I understand' but in fact he doesn't.

This response of Searle's is just more of the same. We can ignore it, for we know that the Chinese room argument is invalid. Searle cannot validly infer that Turbo Sam does not understand from the fact that the Chinese person working the program does not understand.

It is time to face head on the question of whether or not Turbo Sam does understand. This question is closely similar to the question of whether an artefact can think and what I have to say about the former parallels what I said about the latter in chapter 3. Both are questions that can be settled only by a decision on our part – a decision on whether or not to extend to an artefact terms and categories that we currently apply only to each other and our biological cousins.

Does Turbo Sam think? To say that he does is not to say that some additional extra-special process called thinking is going on alongside all his other inner processes; and the same goes for understanding. As I argued in chapter 3, we employ the dichotomy thinking/unthinking to distinguish on the one hand those entities whose wealth of action-directing inner processes renders them inventive, expansively adaptable, capricious agents, and on the other hand those entities such as maggots and clockwork toys whose action-directing inner processes are capable of producing behaviour only of a rigid and limited nature (section 3.6). In my view it is as obvious as anything can be in philosophy that if we are ever confronted with a robot like Turbo Sam, we ought to say that it thinks. Given the purpose for which we employ the concept of a thinking thing, the contrary decision would be impossible to justify. And if we decide to say that Turbo Sam thinks, there can be no point in refusing to say that he understands the language he speaks. For in my imaginary scenario Turbo Sam is every bit as skilful as a human in using words to ease and ornament his path through the world.

It is important to appreciate that Searle's point is not that a symbol-manipulator *could* not behave as I have portrayed Turbo Sam behaving, but that even if one did, it would not think and understand.[14] By my lights this is a bizarre notion; moreover it is a notion for which Searle offers no support at all, apart from the discredited Chinese room argument. The real issue, it seems to me, is whether a device that works by performing such operations as comparing, copying and deleting symbols *can* be made to behave as I have described Turbo Sam behaving. This, though, is an empirical question. It cannot be settled by a priori philosophical argument.

6.4 Turing machines and the biological objection to AI

Searle has another card up his sleeve. If the symbol system hypothesis is true, he says, then a computer made of toilet paper can think; so anyone inclined to believe the symbol system hypothesis must be prepared to accept that rolls of toilet paper are the right kind of stuff to think.[15] In my experience the most common initial response to this argument is bewilderment at the idea of a computer made from toilet paper. I assure you, though, that such a thing is not quite as improbable as it sounds. An explanation follows shortly. First I want to develop the basic point underlying Searle's new attack, namely that since we know our mental states (thinking, understanding, etc.) are the outcome of our having a very special arrangement of very special biochemical substances inside our skulls, we can be pretty sure that a humble toilet roll is the wrong kind of thing to have mental states.

Searle stresses that thought, or *mentation* as he sometimes calls it, is a biological phenomenon.[16] Our ability to secrete bile depends on our having an organ with a suitable biological constitution – the liver. Equally, our ability to mentate depends on our having an organ with a suitable biological constitution – the brain. Mentation, lactation, digestion, mitosis, meiosis, photosynthesis, growth, reproduction: all are processes that depend for their occurrence on the biochemistry of the organisms that perform them. Not just any old stuff will lactate. A cow's udder produces milk because it has the right biochemistry to do so. Similarly for mentation, says Searle: not just any old stuff can mentate. Humans are able to mentate only because we are made of the right sort of material. (Searle is careful to point out that he isn't claiming that mammalian brain tissue is the *only* kind of substance capable of supporting mentation. Conceivably there may be extra-terrestrial beings that mentate even though they have a biochemistry wildly different from ours – what we do with grey matter they do with green slime. Mammalian brain tissue may or may not be the only kind of stuff that can support mentation: this is a strictly empirical question, says Searle.[17])

All this sounds very reasonable. How, though, does it constitute an objection to AI? Searle says that no one would take seriously the idea of programming a computer to lactate – we all know that silicon chips are not the right sort of stuff to produce milk. Yet, continues Searle, 'where the mind is concerned many people are willing to believe in such a miracle'; people take very seriously the idea of programming a computer to mentate.[18] Remarks such as these easily give the impression that Searle is saying computers are made of the wrong sort of stuff to think: silicon and plastic are just not the right substances to support mentation. Zenon Pylyshyn pokes fun at this bold and dogmatic claim.[19] He invites us to consider an experiment in which the neurons of Searle's brain are progressively replaced with silicon chips. A neuron is a complicated biochemical device whose overall function seems to be to accept electrical currents as input and deliver further electrical currents as output. Each of Searle's neurons is replaced by a chip that exactly mimics its input-output performance. Since each chip performs exactly the same function as the neuron it replaces, siliconization should not affect the nature of the electrical messages that Searle's brain sends to the muscles of his tongue, lips, hands, etc. Thus Searle would very likely keep on talking and writing just as he does now – the only difference being that he would no longer mean anything by it, since his brain would be made of silicon, metal and plastic, and would therefore no longer mentate.

Searle replies rather crossly that Pylyshyn has got him wrong.[20] Of course I'm not dogmatically asserting that silicon is incapable of supporting mentation, says Searle. Maybe it is or maybe it isn't: this is an empirical question. Who knows what the outcome of Pylyshyn's sci-fi experiment would really be? Pylyshyn's story just assumes that the envisaged system of integrated circuit chips would duplicate the causal powers of the original brain. But maybe it wouldn't – who can say? We simply do not know at the present time whether a device made out of silicon chips could have the same causal powers as the brain, or in other words have the right properties and organisation to support mentation (just as we do not know whether or not some alien green slime might have the same causal powers as the human brain). However, Searle continues, there is one thing we *can* be certain of, even in our current state of ignorance, namely that no silicon device is capable of duplicating the causal powers of the human brain simply by running a computer program. Because this, Searle reminds us, has been proved by – you guessed it – the Chinese room argument.

Searle's biological objection to AI suddenly starts to look uninteresting. It is not, in fact, a fresh objection. The biological objection actually amounts only to the following three points. (1) An artefact that mentates will have to consist of the right sorts of substances configured in the right sort of way to endow the device with the same causal powers as the organ inside the human skull. (2) It is an empirical question whether this can be done with any other substances apart from the specific biochemicals that make up the human brain. (3) It is not possible to endow a device with the same causal powers as the human brain by programming it. However, none of this will make an AI enthusiast quake. If you look carefully at proposition (1) you will see it is trivially true. It comes down to saying that for an artefact to mentate it must have an appropriate constitution to support mentation. Proposition (2) is true but hardly contentious. Who would deny that this is an empirical question? And proposition (3) is just the conclusion of the invalid Chinese room argument all over again.

Now to the part you have been waiting for. How is it possible to build a toilet paper computer? In 1936 Alan Turing proved a mathematical theorem that is fundamental to the theory of computing. Turing didn't state his mathematical result quite like this, but here is the basic import of it: whatever program can be run on a digital computer can also be run on an infinitely long roll of toilet paper. (Turing himself discreetly spoke of rolls of paper tape.) Recall that in running a program, a computer is just manipulating the symbols 0 and 1 – writing them into locations, deleting them from locations, and so on. All this can be mimicked by means of a device consisting of a roll of toilet paper of unbounded length – each sheet constituting a 'location' for a single symbol – plus a read/write head that has the paper running through it, one sheet at a time. The head can identify whatever symbol happens to be beneath it, can delete and write symbols, and can move the paper left or right. The operations of the head are controlled by a set of inbuilt instructions. You might expect that these instructions would need changing each time the device was required to mimic a different computer program, but no. It is a consequence of one of Turing's startling theorems that a single fixed set of inbuilt instructions will enable the device to mimic any computer program you please. (In fact a mere twenty-eight instructions are sufficient![21]) The trick is to write special-purpose instructions on the paper tape itself that mesh with the head's inbuilt instructions and produce the required behaviour. These paper-tape devices have come to be known as *Turing machines*. A Turing machine with inbuilt instructions that enable it to mimic any computer program is known as a universal Turing machine. If the symbol system hypothesis is true then, in principle, one of these dramatically simple machines can be programmed to think. (The exercises at the end of this chapter give some examples of Turing machines.)[22]

It is, of course, only in *theory* that a universal Turing machine can do everything that the most powerful modern computers can do. There isn't a snowball's chance of anyone actually building a paper computer. For one thing paper (especially toilet paper) is too flimsy to take much back-and-forth motion through the machine head. Besides, there just isn't enough of the stuff: a huge number of rolls would be required to mimic even such a simple AI program as Eliza. And even if, *per impossibile*, some crazy computer scientist did get a paper Turing machine up and running, its working pace would be so enormously slow he would most likely hit the mortician's slab long before the machine got to the end of any reasonably complex program. In short, the paper computer is a theoretical possibility, but not a real possibility.

We first saw in chapter 4 that a computer need not consist of the familiar electronic hardware (section 4.7). It now turns out that it is theoretically possible to build a computer even out of paper (plus, of course, the components required for the read/write head). In fact there is no real theoretical limit on what a computer could be made from – toilet paper, stones, beercans, pigeons, water pipes or windmills, to quote from Searle's list of some of the more colourful possibilities. If the symbol system hypothesis is true and appropriately programmed computers can think, then it is in theory possible to build an organ for thinking out of toilet paper or beercans or indeed out of practically anything at all. The idea that a 'brain' could be made from such improbable substances strikes Searle as ludicrous. When you reflect on the fact that our own ability to think is so closely bound up with our evolutionary history as biological organisms, and is so crucially dependent on the precise composition and organization of the substances inside our skulls, the idea that an artificial brain could be made out of just any old junk does indeed look exceedingly strange.

However, the important point to appreciate here is that the symbol system hypothesis does not imply that you can *really* build a thinking artefact out of toilet paper or beercans. Searle says he finds the hypothesis 'frankly, quite crazy'[23] – but in reality it is not as crazy as all this stuff about toilet paper and beercans is liable to make it appear. In fairyland, small children could be made of sugar and spice and all things nice and computers could be made of toilet paper, but in the real world the structure and properties of matter place severe constraints on what both computers and children can be made from. Doubtless there are other physically possible ways of realizing computers apart from the one we happen to know most about, namely electronic circuitry (if those who postulate that the human brain is itself a computer are right, then there exist at least two radically different ways of realizing computers). But designs of toilet paper and beercans are not contenders: in the real world these substances are just not up to the job.

Thus there is, in fact, a wide measure of agreement between Searle and advocates of the symbol system hypothesis (although Searle himself, of course, doesn't see it that way). Both camps believe that only an exact and delicate organization of the right sorts of substances could support mentation. Perhaps the most interesting difference between the two camps is one which as it happens puts Searle a point down. This is that Searle has no theory to offer about what makes a substance suited to contribute towards the production of mentation, whereas the opposing camp does. Their theory is that a substance is capable of so contributing if its physical properties are such that it can realistically be used as a central ingredient in the construction of a universal symbol system.

Not that this theory will impress Searle. For he believes that (in the standard sense of 'computation') *everything* is a computer! He writes:

> The Chinese Room Argument showed that semantics is not intrinsic to syntax . . . Worse yet, syntax is not intrinsic to physics. The ascription of syntactical properties is always relative to an agent or observer who treats certain physical phenomena as syntactical . . . Computational states are not *discovered within* the physics, they are *assigned* to the physics . . . On the standard textbook definition of computation . . . for any object there is some description of that object such that under that description the object is a digital computer.[24]

Searle illustrates this train of thought with an example. 'The wall behind my back is right now implementing the Wordstar program, because there is some pattern of molecule movements which is isomorphic with the formal structure of Wordstar.'[25] Searle gleefully points out that these considerations trivialize the question 'Is the human brain a computer?': '[Y]es, brains are digital computers because everything is a digital computer.'[26]

However, Searle is simply mistaken in his belief that the 'textbook definition of computation' implies that his wall is implementing Wordstar. Let us grant Searle the claim that the movements of molecules in the wall can be described in such a way that they are 'isomorphic' with a sequence of bit-manipulations carried out by a machine running Wordstar. (Two things, or states, or processes are isomorphic if they have the same structure. If I exactly mimic the movements of your hands with mine then my hand movements are isomorphic with yours.) Of course, the isomorphism could persist for only a fraction of a second – unless one were to cheat by continually fiddling with the scheme of description.[27] The existence of the isomorphism is not enough to make it true that the wall is implementing Wordstar even during the brief time for which the isomorphism persists. Consider a computer that really is running Wordstar. Let's say that during a particular interval of time, t, the computer is carrying out a sequence of bit-manipulations m_1, m_2, m_3, . . . in response to a command to do an alphabetical sort. Let's suppose further that under Searle's hypothesized method of describing the movements of the molecules in his wall, it is true during t that the wall also is carrying out the sequence of bit-manipulations m_1, m_2, m_3, . . . (This is what Searle means when he speaks of the molecule movements being 'isomorphic with the formal structure of Wordstar'.) Much more than this must be true for it to be the case that the wall is implementing Wordstar. For it is true of the computer that if instead of being commanded to sort it had been commanded to run a spelling check (or to italicize the whole document or to delete the final page) then during t it would have been carrying out a completely different sequence of bit-manipulations. The statement 'If at t the machine had been commanded to run a spelling check it would have performed bit-manipulations n_1, n_2, n_3, . . .' is called a *counterfactual* – the statement tells you not what the machine in fact did at t, but what it would have done had the input been different. If Searle's wall is really implementing Wordstar during t then this and similar counterfactuals will be true of it; so if they aren't true of it then it isn't implementing Wordstar. As any hardware engineer will testify, arranging brute matter to form a device that has such a set of counterfactuals true of it is a highly delicate business. The assumption that a device consisting of a few bits of lath and a coat of plaster is bound to have the requisite counterfactuals true of it is unworldly.

So Searle has done nothing to make out his claim that every object has a description under which it is a universal symbol system. There is in fact every reason to believe that the class of such objects is rather narrow; and it is an empirical issue whether the brain is a member of this class. (That issue forms the fare of chapter 9.)

Exercises

'Handwork' these simple Turing machines and discover what changes they make to their tapes. The answers are given in note 28.

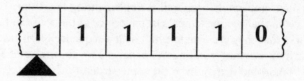

Figure 6.1

Machine one

The instructions built into a Turing machine's read/write head are usually represented in the form of a table, known as a *machine table*:

Symbol	Write	Move
1	0	L
0	1	H

The first line of the table tells the head what to do when it finds itself scanning a square containing the symbol 1, namely write 0 in the square (first deleting the 1, of course) and then move the tape one square to the left (with the result that the head ends up on the next square to the right). The second line tells the head what to do when it finds itself scanning 0, namely replace the 0 with 1 and then halt.

Before the machine is turned on its tape is as shown in figure 6.1. (▲ marks the square the head is sitting on). What will the tape look like when the machine halts?

Machine two

This machine is more interesting. It possesses an additional feature called an *indicator*. Both the instructions in the table just given have the form 'If the current symbol is . . . do ___'. The concept of an indicator is introduced in order to make more complicated forms possible; for example 'If the current symbol is . . . and the symbol found on the immediately preceding square was ___ do ___'. A useful way of conceptualizing a Turing machine's indicator is as a pointer with a number of positions. A simple 'two position' indicator will suffice for keeping track of which binary symbol was last encountered: if 0, the indicator is set to its first position, and if 1, to its second position. In Turing machine jargon the positions on the indicator are called *states*. More states than two may be used depending on the nature of the task. The universal machine described by Turing had over twenty states.

A machine table for a Turing machine with an indicator has five columns. In the table below, the first line tells the head what to do if it encounters a 1

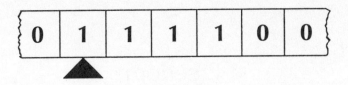

Figure 6.2

when its (two-state) indicator is in its first state, namely make no change to the symbol (N), move the tape left one square, and set the indicator to its second state. The second line says what to do if the symbol encountered is 1 and the indicator is in its second state. The 'R,H' in the third and fourth lines of the Move column means 'Shift the tape right one square and then halt'.

Symbol	State	Write	Move	Next State
1	1	N	L	2
1	2	N	L	1
0	1	1	R,H	1
0	2	N	R,H	2

Can you work out what this Turing machine is programmed to do? When the machine starts working its indicator is in state 1 and its tape is as shown in figure 6.2.

Lastly, an exercise for assembly language addicts. Try your hand at writing a program that simulates the behaviour of Machine two (using the language defined in chapter 4).[29]

7

Freedom

'Well, it MAY be possible to build a computer that thinks in some LIMITED sense' thunders the bar-room sceptic. 'But a machine will never be able to ♦♦♦♦.' Here the speaker unveils his or her pet example of a feature of human mentality that – allegedly – no machine could possibly reproduce. Alan Turing wrote grumblingly about such ripostes (to which he gave the collective title Arguments from Various Disabilities). 'No support is usually offered for these statements,' he complains.[1] He reports encountering numerous candidates for ♦♦♦♦: machinery cannot tell right from wrong, display initiative, learn from experience, use words properly, be the subject of its own thought, or do something really new.[2] In the course of my own discussions of artificial brainpower (in bar-rooms and elsewhere) I have found that two regular candidates for ♦♦♦♦ are *make free choices* and *think consciously*. According to common prejudice, an electronic artefact could not possibly exercise free will, nor be a centre of conscious awareness. In this chapter and the next, these two assumptions are called into question.

An enquiry into the possibility of computer consciousness and computer freedom is, of course, interesting in its own right. However, the deeper significance of the investigation lies elsewhere. As Herbert Simon has put it: 'Perhaps the greatest significance of the computer lies in its impact on Man's view of himself . . . [T]he computer aids him to obey, for the first time, the ancient injunction *Know thyself.*'[3] The computer is what sociologist Sherry Turkle calls an evocative object – an object that challenges us to examine ourselves anew.[4] 'Some objects, and in our time the computer is pre-eminent among them, provoke reflection on fundamentals,' she says. 'The computer is a new mirror . . . [A] mirror in which the mind is reflected as machine.'[5] Philosophical investigations into the possibility of freedom and consciousness existing in machines are, at bottom, part of the quest to understand our own nature. We fix our eyes on the mirror, but our true concern is with ourselves. Are *we* machines of a sort? I hope that what follows will help to make this possibility not only a more credible one, but also a more comfortable one.

7.1 Turbo Sam makes a choice

'Marvin, I'm tired of MIT,' said Turbo Sam one day to his chief programmer. 'I know you people built me, and I don't want to appear ungrateful. But there is a whole wide world out there. Stanford and Carnegie-Mellon have both made me very attractive offers. The British want me, too, and I've decided to go to the Turing Institute in Glasgow. It was a tough choice. California would suit someone like me much better than Scotland, but the people at the Institute have offered to spend seven million on building me a wife and kids. Marvin, I know the Defense Advanced Research Projects Agency isn't going to be at all pleased about this. However, that is your problem.'

Turbo Sam has deliberated carefully over the various options open to him, has taken into account all the available data, weighed the pros and cons, reflected on the attractions of fatherhood versus the allure of California, and has decided, ultimately, to throw in his lot with the robotics experts of Glasgow. That, by anybody's lights, is making a choice. A refusal to apply the word 'choosing' to the exercise of Turbo Sam's decision-making mechanisms would be as pointless as refusing to say that Turbo Sam thinks and understands. A robot, no less than a human, can choose between alternatives.

Yet choosing is not always choosing freely. Was Turbo Sam's choice freely made? Prima facie the answer is No. Each of Turbo Sam's decisions is the inevitable outcome of his programming: in making his choice, he merely follows the instructions that the program contains. An outsider with sufficient knowledge of the program and of the data stored in the robot's various memory devices would be able to calculate exactly how Turbo Sam must decide (barring hardware failures and once-in-a-blue-moon perturbations resulting from quantum indeterminacies). Indeed, a speedy enough outsider could know Turbo Sam's decision before even Turbo Sam himself. How, then, could Turbo Sam possibly have made his choice freely? Each of Turbo Sam's decisions is entirely determined by the details of his design, together with such environmental influences as have impinged on him since his date of manufacture. Turbo Sam certainly chooses; but on each occasion he is, it seems, powerless to choose otherwise.

This line of argument may seem compelling. But don't swallow it without a struggle. Its poison works just as effectively on humans as it does on robots.

7.2 Is freedom of the will an illusion?

According to Boswell, Samuel Johnson once declared: 'Sir, We *know* our will is free, and there's an end on it.'[6] But what Dr Johnson should have said is that we *feel* our will is free; and, unfortunately, the fact that we all have the subjective experience of choosing freely is not an end on it, for this experience may be nothing more than an illusion. A small experiment may help convince you that this is a real possibility.

Over the next half minute suddenly raise the index finger of your right hand three or four times. Pick your moments spontaneously as you go along. Try to notice whether there is any appreciable time lag in between choosing your moment and your finger beginning to move.

OK. If your subjective experiences were the same as mine, the movement in your finger muscles will have followed on more or less immediately from your conscious decision to initiate the action. The astonishing thing is that a technician equipped with the right instruments would have known you were going to raise your finger about a *second* before the movement began. H.H. Kornhuber and his associates performed this classic experiment in the seventies, using subjects with a number of electrodes fixed to the scalp and finger.[7] It was discovered that a characteristic pattern of brain activity would begin to build up as much as one and a half seconds before the finger movement commenced. (The pattern of activity, recorded by means of an electroencephalograph, is known as the *Bereitschaftspotential*.) In context, a technician observing the onset of this activity in your brain would know that you are about to raise your finger – and, chillingly, would know this the best part of a second before your subjective experience of freely picking your moment.[8] The implications of this experiment are still the subject of heated debate.[9] However, it has influenced a number of writers in their belief that our subjective experience of free will is an illusion.[10]

Numerous other facts and phenomena are cited in support of the belief that free will is an illusion. People in the grip of post-hypnotic suggestion reputedly feel that they are acting freely, even though in reality they are obeying the instructions of an external agent. Diet can affect behaviour radically. If an enlightened medieval king is turned into a twisted despot by an unsuspected food allergy, can we properly regard his decisions to repress and overtax his subjects as free ones? He, no doubt, would have firmly believed that they were. On a different tack, many putatively free choices will in fact be the outcome of a person's genetically inherited character. Via the DNA of our genes and the processes of natural selection, the influences that mould our decisions stretch back through the lives of countless generations of our forebears. Similarly, we often choose on the basis of preferences that have been drummed into us by parents and educators, or soaked up from our social milieu. Or a choice may be dictated by the effects of a prenatal or infantile experience, or an unrecognized phobia, or a variety of other hidden factors. To quote a psychiatrist: 'Free will is a completely subjective thing . . . [Y]ou can have a feeling of free will and yet there is . . . complete determination as judged from the outside.'[11] It seems our choices are often, perhaps always, the outcome of factors beyond our control.

Perhaps we feel free only because we can so easily *imagine* pursuing courses of action other than those that we actually follow.

Many who believe that free will is an illusion base their belief on a theory called *determinism*. To call a system (such as a computer) deterministic is to say that each event that happens in the system is brought about by causes. An event's causes are said to 'determine' the event, in the sense that once the causes have happened the event is bound to happen, given the surrounding circumstances and given that the laws of nature are as they are. You are probably a determinist about your car. You no doubt believe that if, say, the electrics fail then (1) this must have been brought about by some cause or set of causes, and (2) once the cause or causes came into operation, the effect was bound to follow, given the relevant laws of nature and the surrounding circumstances (one of which, of course, was that nobody noticed the fault and intervened to correct it before the effect was brought about).

Millions of words have been written on the issue of whether the universe is a deterministic system. Everything that happens in a deterministic universe is caused by prior events; and once those events occur, their effects will necessarily follow. The future is brought about inexorably by the past. One of the great figures of science, Pierre-Simon Laplace (1749–1827), wrote colourfully of the consequences of determinism:

> We must regard the universe's present state as the effect of its prior state and as the cause of the state that is to follow. [Consider] an intelligence apprized of all the forces driving nature and of the relative positions, at a given instant, of all things in the universe, and which moreover is sufficiently vast to be able to submit this data to analysis . . . To such an intelligence nothing would be uncertain: the future, like the past, would be present to its eyes.[12]

The theory that the entire universe is deterministic is known as *universal* determinism. It is a view which is now widely thought to be at odds with modern physics, although a few scientists have continued to uphold it (one of whom was Einstein[13]). *Neurophysiological* determinism, on the other hand, is a much more modest claim. This theory holds that at a certain level of analysis the human brain (and the human body in general) is a deterministic system. According to neurophysiological determinism each decision that you make is the outcome of pre-existing causes – typically, prior events in and states of your brain, nervous system, organs and tissues (including, of course, your sensory apparatus). At the present stage it is far from certain whether or not neurophysiological determinism is true. Many, though, regard it as a plausible theory; and it is certainly the case that as this century has progressed, more and more of the internal and outward behaviour of the human body has succumbed to causal explanation.

The reason for the qualification 'at a certain level of analysis' is this. Neurophysiological determinists do not believe that all events occurring within the brain, including quantum ones, are causally determined. The brain is held to be deterministic in the same sense that a computer is: the 'virtual machine' is deterministic; and if quantum indeterminacy results in a misaligned hardware device this is regarded as a malfunction or 'glitch'. The 'virtual machine' is a hypothetical machine that behaves in the way the actual machine would behave if there were no breakdowns or quantum glitches.

It is widely believed (although not, as will emerge, by me) that neurophysiological determinism has the consequence that free will is an illusion. Each of your decisions, the argument goes, is the inevitable outcome of preceding causes, causes that make it certain how you will choose *before* you actually do so. You can never choose contrary to the way you are caused to choose; none of your choices can be other than the way it is. So how can you be free? Just as a team of computer engineers might predict all Turbo Sam's decisions, so a team of alien superintelligences with the right measuring equipment might be able to predict your decisions, in a grotesque extension of Kornhuber's finger-raising experiment. (If for some reason they inform you of one of their predictions before the event you may, of course, turn bloody-minded and set about doing the opposite. But they will have predicted that, too! Their prediction is: left to itself, this organism will do X, and if we tell it that, then the change produced in its internal states by this additional information will result in its doing Y instead.)

The opinion that free will is an illusion has become an orthodox position in AI. For Marvin Minsky free will is a 'myth'.[14]

> Many notions in our informal explanations do not tolerate close examination. Free will or volition is one such notion . . . A man's or a machine's strength of conviction about such things tells us nothing . . .[15] According to the modern scientific view, there is simply no room at all for 'freedom of the human will'.[16]

Geoff Simons is equally forthright. The notion of free will, he says, belongs to the 'metaphysics of a largely pre-scientific age'.[17] He continues:

> [H]uman beings are slaves of brute matter, compelled to act in particular ways by virtue of biochemical and neuronal factors . . . What we see is the illusory nature of free will. It is a doctrine nourished in pre-scientific cultures.[18]

I am going to argue that free will is no myth. Human beings do choose freely, at any rate for much of the time, and recognition of this is entirely compatible with modern science. The existence of free will cannot, I agree, be established simply by an appeal to our subjective experience of freedom; but fortunately stronger arguments exist. The twist, though, is that these arguments also establish that Turbo Sam is capable of making free choices. For me, the twist is a welcome one. It sits easily with my belief that, in a sense, we too are machines.

7.3 Two kinds of freedom

1 Turing's randomizer

Suppose you are torn between the chocolate fudge pudding and the blueberry cheesecake. After a few moments of indecision you suddenly and for no apparent reason plump for the cheesecake. The suggestion I am going to consider is that free choice, in such circumstances, consists in making a *random* selection between equally preferable alternatives. According to this suggestion, your choice is only partly the outcome of determining factors. Such things as your long-standing preferences and the transitory state of your blood sugar level deterministically close off all your options save the choc pud and the cheesecake. The final selection between these two, though, is entirely random. If this view of things is correct, neurophysiological determinism reigns only until the final shortlist of options has been drawn up. Then the dice roll.

I'll use the term *nil preference choice* for a situation where a selection is made between alternatives that are by and large equally satisfactory, as far as the chooser is able to tell, given the time available for deliberation and the information at his or her disposal.

The theory that nil preference choices are made on a random basis is a speculative one. The theory postulates the existence, somewhere in the brain, of a neurophysiological mechanism that carries out the function of selecting randomly from a number of given alternatives. (Perhaps the mechanism is some sort of 'quantum amplifier'.) It is an empirical question whether or not such a mechanism exists. An analogous mechanism can readily be built into a computer. All that is required, essentially, is a switch driven by a Geiger counter that is monitoring the random radioactive decay of a small piece of radium. If Turbo Sam is fitted with hardware that enables him to select randomly in nil preference situations then even Laplace's omniscient genius will be unable to predict the robot's choices (since lack of predictability is the essence of a truly random outcome).

Turing was one of the first people to discuss the idea of adding a device for making random selections to an otherwise deterministic computer.[19] He remarks that such a machine can be 'described as having free will'.[20] Few who have written on the subject of free will would agree with him. It is an entrenched doctrine in philosophy that a random choice cannot be a free choice.[21] It seems to me that this doctrine is the product of faulty argumentation, and I will set out a short defence of the idea that in a nil preference situation, choosing randomly is choosing freely. (As will become clear, Turing's idea does not work at all well outside nil preference situations.)

There are two standard arguments for the doctrine that random choices cannot be free choices. I hope to convince you that both are fallacious. I call the first the *helplessness* argument. Jerome Shaffer has put the argument nicely. If decisions 'arise spontaneously and randomly ... then the agent is at the helpless mercy of these eruptions within him which control his behaviour'.[22] In a similar vein, John Thorp speaks of exchanging the bondage of causal determinism for the bondage of randomness.[23] If your choices simply well up in you at random, goes the argument, then you are not in control of your behaviour: your actions are little more than accidents that befall you. 'We can only escape from a totally deterministic view of man at the price of admitting that substantial parts of our behaviour are outside our control', states Geoff Simons.[24]

The trouble with the helplessness argument is that it presents an entirely misleading picture of what it is to choose randomly among alternatives in a nil preference situation. If your randomizer could equally well make you wait at the kerb or plunge under the wheels of a truck, reach out politely for a glass of sherry or grip your host by the lapels and bawl a bawdy song in his face, then you would indeed be at the mercy of forces beyond your control. But these are not nil preference choices. In a nil preference situation, the chooser's deliberations produce a number of alternative schemes of action, all of which are more or less equally preferable as far as the chooser is concerned. The randomizer functions merely as a tiebreaker. Far from being helpless, the chooser is the author of each scheme of action, and judges all of them to be more or less equally suitable in the circumstances.

The second argument that I want to defuse concerns responsibility. Here is how A.J. Ayer formulates it.

> [The reason we want] to show that men are capable of acting freely [is] in order to infer that they can be morally responsible for what they do. But if it is a matter of pure chance that a man should act in one way rather than another . . . he can hardly be responsible.[25]

Let me paraphrase and expand this slightly compressed reasoning. 'Misappropriate the word *free* and apply it to randomly made choices if you will,' goes the argument. 'There is nothing to stop you using words in whatever way you please. But be warned that no sensible person will want to follow you in your new usage. An agent cannot be held responsible for something that is done purely by accident; so anyone who fell in with your new usage would have to allow that agents are not responsible for their freely chosen actions. But this is as absurd as if you had misappropriated the word *safe* to apply to buildings that it is hazardous to enter. Just as our main concern in enquiring whether a building is safe is to ascertain whether it can be entered without risk, so our main concern in enquiring whether an action was freely chosen is to establish whether or not the agent is to be held responsible for the action.'

I do not find this argument persuasive. It trades illegitimately on the connotations of phrases like 'matter of pure chance' and 'done purely by accident'. Some examples will help to show up the fallacy in the argument. Imagine that a mysterious beam of energy passes through your arm while you are drinking a cup of coffee. The curious effect of this is to make it a matter of pure chance whether you continue drinking normally or jerk the contents of the cup into my lap. In these circumstances you obviously would not be responsible if you ended up tipping your coffee over me – any more than you would be if a third party bumped into your arm. So Ayer's argument fits this sort of case perfectly. But now suppose that the randomizer beam passes through the head of a hijacker, Pernod, who is just about to shoot one or other of his hostages, Kirsch and Campari, and does not much care which. The effect of the beam is to make it a matter of pure chance which of Kirsch or Campari is selected. In fact it is Kirsch who gets the bullet. Would you want to say that Pernod is not responsible for killing him? In my view, Pernod is clearly responsible for the death of Kirsch, even though it was 'a matter of pure chance' that the option *Shoot Kirsch* got selected in preference to the option *Shoot Campari*. After all, Pernod had already decided to shoot one or other of the two and the fact that the final choice between them was made at random seems neither here nor there. The moral of the tale is that the considerations presented in Ayer's argument do not apply to a random choice made under the conditions that obtain in a nil preference situation.

That completes my defence of the suggestion that the random selection of an alternative in a nil preference situation is a genuine species of free choice. Here we have an authentic kind of freedom which could easily be bestowed on a thinking computer.

I stressed earlier that random selection is an appropriate strategy only in nil preference situations. I will explain why this is so. Consider the type of situation in which the chooser, after due reflection, comes to judge that one of the various courses of action open to her outshines all the rest. Reason, inclination and sentiment all point unwaveringly to a single option. I'll call this an 'outstanding-candidate situation'. It would hardly be sensible to entrust choices of this sort to a random selection procedure. Wouldn't you want to be able to reach out singlemindedly for the option with the halo rather than spin the roulette wheel? Of course, you might feel you'd like to reserve the right to turn your back whimsically on the best candidate every once in a while – but surely only on those occasions when you want to, not on a purely random basis. If the influence of a randomizer were to deflect me from what I judge to be clearly the best course of action in the circumstances then I would indeed be helplessly in the grip of forces beyond my control.

No, there is no role for a randomizer in outstanding-candidate situations. It is time to consider a second kind of freedom.

2   How determinists can have their cake and be free to eat it too

Here is a love story.

Peter meets Samantha. Peter likes Samantha a lot. Peter finds himself thinking about marrying Samantha. Peter deliberates hard about life, love, mortgages, domesticity and other relevant factors. Peter decides without reservation to pop the question to Samantha. Samantha turns him down flat. They live happily ever after.

Here is a story about the story.

If neurophysiological determinism is true, then Peter's decision to propose to Samantha was the outcome of pre-existing causal factors (such as Peter's beliefs about Samantha – in the jargon, his 'informational states' – and his needs, preferences, the promptings of his passion, and so forth). Let's call Peter's decision to propose to Samantha 'The Choice' and the various factors that produced this decision 'The Causes'. The Choice was the deterministic outcome of the Causes. Once the Causes were in place, the Choice was a foregone conclusion. Given the relevant laws of nature – in this case the laws of neurophysiology, biophysics, etc. – this Choice, and no other, had to follow upon the Causes (just as the Causes had to follow upon *their* causes, and so on). Once the Causes were in place, it would have been a violation of the laws of nature had Peter decided not to propose to Samantha. Obviously it was not within Peter's power to violate the laws of nature. Thus nor was it in Peter's power to decide not to propose. The Choice, then, was not freely made, for Peter had, in fact, no option.

This argument has a certain sinister appeal, and versions of it have been advanced by a number of writers on free will (recently, John Thorp and Peter van Inwagen).[26] Yet I, for one, regard it as spurious. The crux of the argument is the move from the obvious truth that Peter does not have it within his power to violate the laws of nature (in particular, the laws that govern the functioning of his own brain), to the assertion that it was not within his power to refrain from proposing to Samantha. This move is fallacious. It certainly was within Peter's power to decide not to propose. Given, say, a dependent relative whom he felt obliged to care for, or additional information of an offputting nature about Samantha, he might well have decided differently, and he would have violated no laws of nature in doing so. Peter could and doubtless would have chosen differently if his information, inclinations or personal situation had been different – if, in other words, a somewhat different set of causal factors had been in operation. The argument rightly stresses that in a law-abiding universe there can be no question of the original set of causal factors being followed by a decision not to propose. But don't let that blind you to the all-important fact that if the causes had been different, then a different decision would have ensued.

Incompatibilists are people who believe that the truth of neurophysiological determinism is incompatible with the existence of free will. Arguments like the one about Peter are their stock in trade. I want to suggest to you that there is in fact no incompatibility. Even if Peter is a deterministic system it remains the case that he and he alone was the author of his decision, and that had his beliefs, desires and so forth been appropriately different he would have decided differently. Deterministic Peter's decision was surely both caused *and* free – free in that it was caused by Peter's *own* beliefs, desires, inclinations, etc. No one put psychological pressure on him and no one physically coerced him into proposing. As John Hospers once put it: The motto of freedom is *I* caused my actions.[27] Deterministic Peter is able to deliberate about his future and to author and implement his own decisions, in accordance with his own best perceptions of his wants, needs, and circumstances. If this is not freedom, then what is?

If you agree with me that there is an important kind of freedom whose existence is compatible with the truth of neurophysiological determinism then you, like me, are a compatibilist. Choices that are free in the compatibilist's sense are those that are determined by the chooser's own desires, hopes, knowledge, etc. Compatibilism offers reassurance: the possibility that neurophysiological determinism is true should make no one fear for their freedom. Free will is no illusion.

All this is good news for Turbo Sam as well as for us. He, too, possesses this second kind of freedom. Turbo Sam's decision to join the Turing Institute was made just as freely as Peter's decision to propose to Samantha. Turbo Sam's choice, no less than Peter's, was the product of his own beliefs, desires and inclinations. Turbo Sam was not coerced; and he fully had the power to do otherwise, in that if his information, personal circumstances or passing inclinations had been different, then he might well have chosen differently.

Like-minded philosophers have been advocating compatibilism ever since the seventeenth and eighteenth centuries.[28] It would be disingenuous if I did not tell you that their ideas have sometimes met with a poor reception. (The great philosopher Immanuel Kant once rudely referred to compatibilism as 'a wretched subterfuge'.[29]) In the remainder of the chapter I set out the most important objections to compatibilism and explain how they may be answered.

7.4 Kleptomania and other compulsions

K is a kleptomaniac. To his great distress, a morbid desire to steal drives him to commit a dozen or so petty thefts every day. K wishes fervently that he were not prey to this compulsive desire but is nevertheless frequently overwhelmed by it. Does K steal of his own free choice? I think most people would agree that he does not. Far from acting freely, he steals under the tyranny of his own uncontrollable desire. Many others are in the same plight as K: chronic gamblers who long to be free from their compulsion, drug addicts who have come to despise their state of addiction, and so on. Such sufferers are helplessly violated by their own desires.[30]

Some see cases like these as highlighting the worthlessness of what compatibilists call freedom. In the compatibilist sense, a decision is freely made if, roughly – I'll modify this somewhat in the next paragraph – the decision is the product of the agent's own desires and beliefs, and is taken in the absence of blackmail, brainwashing and other coercive pressures. Yet K's sudden decision to steal a bar of chocolate from the supermarket checkout is clearly the product of his own desires, and there is no external coercion. If for the compatibilist this decision counts as one freely made, then surely freedom in their sense is a shabby thing not worth the name?

The answer to this objection is short: it is a mistake to regard compatibilists as saying that a decision is freely made if it is the outcome of just any old desires in the agent. A decision is free, for compatibilists, only if it is taken *in the absence of compulsion*, and the tyranny of an obsessive desire is no less a form of compulsion than external coercions like blackmail and torture. Compatibilists view a choice as free only if it is the outcome of desires *other* than compulsive ones.

Although this short answer is correct, it leaves an important question dangling. What is the difference between desires that are compulsive and desires that are not? The credit for showing compatibilists what to say about this goes to Harry Frankfurt.[31] Central to the issue are what Frankfurt calls 'second-order' desires. A second-order desire is a desire about another desire. Thus when K desires to be rid of his morbid desire to steal he has a second-order desire, as does a heroin addict who desires not to desire the drug.

Second-order desires may be mild or vehement, half-hearted or heartfelt. K's desire to be rid of his desire to steal is vehement and heartfelt, and it is precisely because this second-order desire has such centrality for him that he can be described as being helplessly violated by his own desire to steal. To take a contrasting example, imagine a person who sometimes forms a mild and intellectualized desire not to desire sexual intercourse. If he chooses to have sex while this desire lingers on, his choice is nevertheless perfectly free, since his second-order desire is (by hypothesis) relatively slight and lies at the periphery of his concerns. On the other hand, a person who gives way to the desire for sexual gratification despite a deep and heartfelt desire not to desire sex has, like the kleptomaniac, succumbed helplessly to his own desire, and is unfree. A choice that is the outcome of desires that conflict with mild and nugatory second-order desires may still be free; but a choice that is the outcome of desires that run counter to vehement and heartfelt second-order desires is unfree.

To return to the word 'compulsive', a compulsive desire can now be characterized as one that holds sway despite a central and heartfelt desire to be rid of it. (Admittedly this characterization is still somewhat vague; the provision of a more precise analysis is an ongoing project in philosophical psychology.[32]) Using this characterization, the compatibilist maxim that 'a choice is free only if it is the outcome of desires other than compulsive ones' can be expressed more informatively: a choice is free only if it is the outcome of desires that are not in conflict with the chooser's centrally important second-order desires. This concludes the answer given by compatibilists to the charge that kleptomania and other compulsions show their kind of freedom to be unworthy of the name.

Postscript

Fortunately kleptomaniacs, alcoholics and others who are helplessly violated by their desires are far from being hopeless cases. Skilful counselling and the use of desire-management techniques can help tame or eradicate the most powerful of desires. Voltaire once quipped against compatibilism: 'When I can do what I want to do, there is my liberty for me . . . but I cannot help wanting what I do want'. He was wrong. Humans are not the helpless playthings of their own desires. Most of us are capable, to a greater or lesser degree, of bringing about deliberate changes in our system of wants and desires. (As the saying goes, the trick to happiness is not learning how to get what you want but learning how to want what you get.)

7.5 Libertarianism

Libertarians are those people, usually philosophers and theologians, who hunger after a third, peculiarly strong, kind of freedom. To get a clear picture of what it is that libertarians want, let's look at a brief exchange between a libertarian and a compatibilist.

Libertarian Suppose I deliberate between a pair of alternatives, X and Y, and finally decide on X. The point I want to stress is that this choice is properly called free only if I *could* have chosen Y instead. The hallmark of true freedom is always that the chooser could have chosen otherwise. If in reality I could not have chosen Y instead of X then my choice was not free.

Compatibilist So far I see nothing to disagree with in what you say. Given determinism, your choice of X was causally determined, but it is nevertheless perfectly true that you could have chosen Y instead. Various causal factors brought about your selection of X – factors such as your desires and information. Had these factors been appropriately different you would have chosen Y rather than X. If, say, you had desired Y much more strongly than X then you might well have chosen Y instead. So it is indeed true that you could have chosen otherwise.

Libertarian An utterly wretched subterfuge, my dear Sir. My choice was free, I say, only if I could have chosen otherwise *in the circumstances that actually prevailed*. The point you are making – that I would have chosen differently in *different* circumstances – is irrelevant to the issue of whether or not I could have chosen differently in the very circumstances that existed at the time. To call my choice free, in the true sense of the word, is to say that even given the desires and beliefs and inclinations and so forth that I had at the time, I could nevertheless there and then have chosen differently from the way I actually did. In my view neurophysiological determinism (which, I may point out, is a piece of unproven speculation) has the consequence that nobody's choices are ever truly free. Every decision, according to you, is the law-like outcome of a collection of psychological and physiological causes: the decision could not have been otherwise unless the causes had been different. If, Sir, I find that you have sold me a sick cow, you will not placate me by assuring me that in some other imaginable circumstances you *would* have sold me a healthy one. Equally, when you tell me that not one of my choices could in fact have been other than it was, I am not at all consoled by your reassurances that I would have chosen differently if only the circumstances had been other than they were.

What the libertarian wants, then, is a kind of freedom that lifts him above the realm of natural causation and gives him the power to choose either with or against whatever causal forces may be acting. (Here, perhaps, is the quintessential form of that traditional male ideal, dominion over the natural world.) The kind of freedom that libertarians want is called *transcendental* freedom. It is also known as 'contra-causal' freedom.

Transcendental freedom is supposed to be different from the ability to choose on a purely random basis. Although it is the essence of a randomly made choice that a different option could equally well have been selected (in the very circumstances that prevailed), random choices are not what the libertarian says he wants – for mere randomness cannot offer him the control that he hankers for. Transcendental freedom is supposed to occupy some mysterious middle ground lying between randomness and causal determination.[33]

Libertarianism invites a number of pointed questions. For one, how could anyone ever *know* whether they could have chosen differently in exactly the circumstances that prevailed? Certainly not by trying to recreate those same circumstances and choosing again, since the second time round they would possess some extra information, namely how they chose the first time, and that would make the circumstances different. In any case, the prospect of ever recreating *exactly* the same circumstances is hopeless. Humans are so sensitive that there is very little chance of our ever being in exactly the same neurophysiological state twice.[34] It seems, then, that even if we did possess transcendental freedom we might never in practice be able to tell.

A second pointed question concerns this strange 'middle ground' that is supposed to lie between randomness and causal determination. A causally determined event is one that is caused by other events and a random event is an uncaused event – something that 'just happens'. So for a decision to lie in the Libertarian's 'middle ground' it must be neither random nor caused by other events. How *could* this be? Here is the answer given by one recent advocate of libertarianism, John Thorp: '[What are] apparently two events, the decision and the agent's causing the decision . . . are in fact one and the same.'[35]

Thorp's disciple, Jennifer Trusted, expresses the theory more bluntly: 'We must regard the agent's decision as its own cause.'[36] Given this manoeuvre, the decision is not random, since it has a cause, namely itself; nor is it causally determined, since being its own sufficient cause, it was not brought about by other events. Even Thorp himself is prepared to admit that the idea of a decision causing itself is 'logically peculiar'.[37]

Peculiarity is not in itself a sufficient reason for dismissing a theory. After all, many hypotheses of modern science – and of quantum mechanics in particular – are peculiar indeed. Nevertheless, it is a sensible maxim that peculiar theories with no evidence in their favour should be disregarded. Particle physicists entertain peculiar hypotheses because the weight of empirical evidence presses them into it. Libertarians, on the other hand, maintain that there is a middle land between randomness and causal determination not because evidence exists, but because they dearly want there to be such a place.

Is transcendental freedom a kind of freedom that is worth wanting? In my view, no; and I see this as a decisive reason for refusing to take libertarianism seriously. To appreciate just what it is that you miss out on if you lack transcendental freedom, consider the case of Tweedledum, who is free only in the compatibilist's sense, versus Tweedledee, who has the dubious advantage of possessing transcendental freedom. Except for this one difference, Tweedledum and Tweedledee are identical.

Suppose Tweedledum and Tweedledee are faced with exactly the same choice as one another, in identical situations, and with identical beliefs, desires, hopes, and so forth. After due deliberation the compatibilist heroine Tweedledum freely chooses Option A, for this is the course of action that on balance best fits the bill so far as she can tell given the information at her disposal. If we were to tell her that she could not *in those very circumstances* have chosen differently it wouldn't worry her overmuch (bless her compatibilist heart), since the option she did choose is the one she considers to be the best (that is why she chose it in the first place, of course). Her decision was the causal product of her own information, desires, hopes, inclinations, concerns, affections and what have you – not the work of some alien force that rode roughshod over her preferences. Tweedledum is happy with her choice. Even if she could have choosen differently in the very circumstances that prevailed, she would not have done so.

Since Option A is the one that Tweedledum considers to be best, it is also the option that Tweedledee considers best, since by hypothesis 'Dum and 'Dee have the same information, concerns, inclinations and so on. 'Dee is blessed with transcendental freedom, so she has the power to choose some option other than A. But why on earth should she, given that in her opinion A cannot be bettered? It is not as if 'Dee even wants to choose differently – for 'Dum doesn't and 'Dee and 'Dum, remember, are identical in all appropriate respects. Tweedledee, it seems, will never need her transcendental freedom. And what is true for Tweedledee is true for the rest of us. I don't mind at all if I lack transcendental freedom, and if I do possess it I rather hope I shall never exercise it. In my opinion, libertarians covet a kind of freedom that is not worth having.

At this juncture all good libertarians will hasten to make the same response: a sufficient reason for wanting transcendental freedom is that if we lack it, then no-one can be held morally responsible for their decisions and actions. As J.D. Mabbott puts the point: 'Moral responsibility requires that a man should be able to choose alternative actions, everything in the universe prior to the act, including his self, being the same'.[38] If an agent could not have chosen differently in the circumstances it is an error to regard her as responsible for her action, says the libertarian. If human beings lack transcendental freedom then the whole social practice of holding agents responsible for their actions and praising or blaming them accordingly is a grotesque mistake.

I do not find this argument persuasive. If Tweedledum were to mug me with a baseball bat I certainly would not be deterred from holding her responsible by the thought that, having no transcendental freedom, she is unable to lift herself above the natural laws of the universe. What a practical person will consider relevant, when weighing the extent of Tweedledum's responsibility, will be such things as whether her behaviour was simply an unexpected side effect of a medically prescribed drug. Or is she, perhaps, basically a nice girl who has been forced into a life of teenage crime by her wicked stepfather? Or an upright if headstrong Girl Guide who was acting honourably but under misleading information – I was running for a bus with my handbag under my arm (well why not?) and the sobbing woman on her knees in the alley behind me was just a piece of happenstance (maybe one of her contact lenses had hit the deck again). If, on the other hand, it turns out that Tweedledum chose to mug me of her own compatibilist free will, because doing so suited her needs and was just fine by her, then she is to be held responsible in the first degree. I am unmoved by the libertarian's weird plea of mitigation that if she were put back into exactly the same circumstances a million times, with 'everything in the universe prior to the act being the same,' then she would choose to mug me every time.

7.6   Predictivism and chaos

A Turing machine (section 6.4) is an example of an entity whose behaviour can be predicted in full. Given a knowledge of the machine table, of the initial position of the head, of the initial state of the indicator, and of the initial contents of the tape, it is possible to calculate the machine's behaviour through all time. (Since a Turing machine is an abstract entity, the predictor does not need to worry about power failures, hardware glitches and other real-world complications.)

What I call *predictivism* is the thesis that as a matter of necessity, the behaviour of any isolated deterministic system can in principle be fully and correctly predicted. 'Isolated' means 'not interacting causally with any other system', and the phrase 'in principle' acknowledges that there may not actually be anyone or anything in the universe with sufficient intelligence and memory capacity to do the predicting. The phrase 'as a matter of necessity' indicates that deterministic systems are held to have the property of predictability not contingently, but necessarily – just as it is necessarily rather than contingently the case that any (Euclidean) triangle has three internal angles summing to 180°.

(The concept of a proposition being neccessarily the case is often explained in terms of 'possible worlds'. The claim that a proposition is neccessarily true is equivalent to the claim that it is true not only in the actual world but in every logically possible world. A proposition is said to be contingently true if it is true in the actual world but false in at least one logically possible world (and contingently false if it is false in the actual world but true in at least one logically possible world). You may like to consider which of the following are necessary and which are contingent. (The answers are given in note 39.) Every bachelor is unmarried. Every effect has a cause. Every event has a cause. Every book has a final sentence. The sum of two even numbers is even. No contingent sentence is necessary. The Chinese room argument is invalid.)

Until recently the thesis of predictivism was considered obvious; indeed it was often regarded as being part and parcel of the very concept of determinism. Laplace, of course, was a predictivist (recall the quotation in section 7.2). From the premiss that the universe is a deterministic system he moves immediately to the conclusion that its entire future is, in principle, predictable.

As we saw in sections 7.1 and 7.2, one of the standard arguments against the existence of free will is premised on this idea that the behaviour of a deterministic system can be predicted. Neurophysiological determinism is held to imply that in principle our choices, like Turbo Sam's, can be predicted in advance. Anyone running this argument needs to be cautious. A human body is not an isolated system and unless the arguer is prepared to assume universal determinism she must acknowledge that we can interact with processes that are not deterministic (according to quantum mechanics we interact with many such processes). This interference will sometimes thwart prediction. Undaunted, the arguer will doubtless insist that even so her point holds good: a fair swag of our choices can in principle be predicted correctly before we make them – so how can they be freely made?

Traditionally, compatibilists have responded to this argument by maintaining, plausibly enough, that a decision can be both free *and* predictable.[40] We can all occasionally predict the free choices of someone whose temperament we know very well – 'I knew you'd pick that one', 'I was certain that's what she'd say about it,' and so forth. The fact that these choices can be correctly predicted does not make them any the less voluntary. For compatibilists there is no conflict between predictability and freedom. (So the thought that Turbo Sam's behaviour can, in principle, be predicted in advance never was a good reason for saying that his decisions are not free.)

Compatibilists now have a second way of rebutting this argument. Recent theoretical work involving the computer modelling of non-linear equations has shown – almost shockingly – that predictivism is false. It is possible to describe deterministic systems whose behaviour cannot be predicted, even in principle. A new branch of mathematics known as chaos theory has grown up around this discovery. Chaos theory studies systems contravening the commonsense principle that a relatively small alteration to the initial conditions of a change or process makes only a relatively small difference to the result. This is the principle of proportionate effect. It is illustrated by a golf ball travelling down a fairway. Had the ball been a microscopic distance further to the left or right when struck (everything else about the drive remaining exactly the same) this would have made only a minute difference to the final position of the ball (otherwise golf would be humanly impossible). The systems studied in chaos theory are not like that: they exhibit what is called *sensitive dependence on initial conditions*. To aid visualization of such a system, picture three corks floating in a turbulent river. Initially the corks are side by side. After a few minutes two may still be close together while the third has been swept far away. The position reached by a cork after a given period of turbulence depends critically on the position it starts at: a tiny difference in its initial position can make an enormous difference to where the cork ends up.

The systems of mathematical equations studied by chaos researchers are such that an arbitrarily small change in the initial conditions can produce a huge difference in resulting behaviour. These systems of equations are usually studied with the aid of a computer. A set of initial values for the parameters of the equations is stipulated and the machine calculates the resultant behaviour of the system. A given set of initial values will produce the same behaviour each time the computer simulation is run (just as in a real-world deterministic system the same causes will always bring about the same effects); but the minutest alterations in these values can lead to radically different behaviour. In principle, these systems of equations are fully predictable: stipulate any set of initial values and the resulting behaviour of the system can be calculated.

Like Turing machines, these mathematical systems are abstract entities. Let's imagine some real-world deterministic system that possesses the same sensitive dependence on initial conditions. Such a system falsifies predictivism: its behaviour cannot be correctly predicted, even in principle. This is because the initial state of the system – that is, the state of the system from which its future behaviour is to be predicted – must be ascertained by measurement. (Merely stipulating a set of initial values, as above, would obviously not tell us anything about the *actual* behaviour of the system.) By hypothesis the system is such that an arbitrarily small misdescription of its initial state will lead to wildly inaccurate predictions of its behaviour. Or to put the same point a different way, if the system were in an initial state different from but arbitrarily close to its actual initial state, its ensuing behaviour would be radically different from the way it will actually behave. Since no real-world measuring equipment is responsive to arbitrarily small differences (there will always be differences smaller than the smallest difference that a given piece of equipment can register) it follows that the behaviour of the system cannot be predicted, even approximately. Whence predictivism is false.

Don't be worried by the fact that my argument against predictivism appeals to an imaginary deterministic system. Predictivism, remember, is the claim that an isolated deterministic system is *of necessity* predictable. This claim can be refuted by showing that it is *possible* for there to be an isolated deterministic system whose behaviour cannot be correctly predicted, even in principle; and this is what chaos theory has done.

The question of whether there is chaos in the real world – of whether there are real processes that conform to the exquisitely sensitive mathematics of chaos theory – is at the present time a contentious one. Researchers speculate that many real-world phenomena are chaotic: turbulence in liquids, the rising of smoke, the weather, national economies, ecological systems, metabolic processes in cells, the spread of some infectious diseases, the onset of certain sorts of heart attack, the transfer of energy through nerve membranes, and aspects of the behaviour of networks of neurons in the human brain (to name only some).[41] The latter suggestion is particularly interesting. Neurophysiological determinism may carry no implications concerning the predictability of our choices.

Let's return to the anti-compatibilist argument that is the target of this section. The combined effect of these considerations is to leave the argument with nil persuasive force. Now that the arguer has been disabused of the thought that deterministic systems are of neccessity predictable, she is left with no way of supporting her claim that if neurophysiological determinism is true then all (or many) of our choices are predictable. She might resort to maintaining that as a matter of contingent fact the human body contains no chaotic processes, but since there is no evidence for this it would be a desperate move – and in any case the route to her conclusion would still be blocked by the compatibilist's point that a choice can be both predictable and free.

7.7 The inevitable

Here is an old and hallowed view about the implications of determinism.[42]

If determinism is true then your decisions are the consequences of events immediately preceding them, and these of events immediately preceding *them*, and so on, back into the remote past. Naturally, it is not *up to you* how things were before your birth. Therefore the future consequences of how things were before your birth are not up to you either (given that you cannot violate the laws of nature – cannot avert or modify the effects once all the causes are in place). This means that none of your decisions or actions is ever up to you. Everything you ever do is the law-like outcome of causal factors that existed before you were born. Your future is fixed, inevitable – laid out for you, waiting to be discovered.

I will divide my comments on this argument into three groups.

Assuming determinism

As I remarked in section 7.2, universal determinism is not well regarded in modern science. It fitted comfortably enough with the physics of the nineteenth century but the quantum revolution of the 1920s brought the idea that sub-atomic events are not causally determined. One can still cling to universal determinism as a metaphysical axiom, but few do. Even the much weaker theory of neurophysiological determinism may be false. If the brain contains some kind of randomizer then those decisions in which the randomizer participates are not determined. Even if the randomizer operates only in nil preference situations the consequences of these random decisions will reverberate through the whole of the individual's existence, shaking it free from the iron grip of the past.

What if universal determinism is false but neurophysiological determinism is true? In this case, too, there would be no reason to say that our futures are fixed. The human eye is sufficiently sensitive to allow the conscious detection of the arrival at the retina of a single quantum of light[43]; and whether or not a single quantum is emitted from its source at a particular time is a random matter, according to modern physics. An effective way to 'unfix' your future would be to position yourself in the apparatus that Sakitt used to establish this remarkable sensitivity of the eye and make a contract with yourself along the following lines: 'If I detect a single photon emission in the next three seconds I will give up everything and hitchhike to India'. Not that it is actually neccessary to go to such lengths as this. In a quantum universe the everyday flux of stimulation arriving at your sensory organs is not determined by the distant past, and so nor is your future – no matter how deterministic your inner processes. The situation is analogous in the case of a computer. Although a computer's output is determined by its input and internal states, the output is 'fixed by the past' only if the input itself is, and in a universe admitting genuine randomness this need not be the case.

However, a compatibilist cannot rest content with making trouble for the premiss of the argument we're considering, for compatibilism is the claim that we possess freedom of choice *even if* universal determinism is true. I propose to grant the arguer her assumption of universal determinism and fault the argument on logical grounds.

Is anything up to me?

The claim that none of my decisions or actions is up to me strikes me as bizarre to the point of absurdity – more the stuff of a wild nightmare about determinism than of a careful philosophical enquiry into determinism's logical consequences. Picture an infinitessimal snippet of the vast parade of causes and effects that is the deterministic universe: me breakfasting in the garden. The sun is pleasant and I have no pressing engagements, so I decide to stay on for a second cup of coffee. When I pour the coffee and linger over it, is what I am doing up to me? J.L. Austin, a philosopher of good common sense, once remarked testily concerning the chair in front of him 'Well, if that's not seeing a real chair, then *I don't know what is*'.[44] He was ridiculing the claim – another wild nightmare – that neither he nor anyone else could ever know whether or not the thing in front of him was *really* a chair. The idea that it is never up to me what I do deserves equally short shrift. If deliberately lingering over my coffee is not something that is up to me, then I don't know what is. My action of pouring a second cup was the causal product of my own decision to do so, which was itself the causal product of my own inclinations, and I was under no compulsion, either external or, equally importantly, internal. To say, in these circumstances, that my action was not up to me, and that I did not freely and voluntarily linger on for a second cup, is to use words perversely, even misleadingly – like a person who maintains that they do not know if there is a chair in the room when in fact they can see one as plain as day.

I hope it is now clear that the 'therefore' in the middle of the argument heralds a crashing non sequitur. It is true that it was never up to me how things were before my birth, and true that I cannot violate the laws of nature, but it is false that my actions are never up to me, never voluntary and free.

Technical note

Formally, the problem is with the inference rule van Inwagen calls (β): NB follows from the premisses N(A⊃B) and NA.[45] ('⊃' is material implication: see section 5.6.) NA is read: 'It is true that A and no one has, or has ever had, any choice about whether A'.[46] Thus 'N All men are mortal' is an abbreviation for 'It is true that all men are mortal and no one has, or has ever had, any choice about whether all men are mortal'. For short, think of NA as saying that A's truth is not up to you (or me or anyone else) and never was.

Compatibilists see no reason to accept (β) as a valid rule, since by their lights (β) can sometimes lead from true premisses to a false conclusion – as witnessed by the argument under discussion.

Van Inwagen tells his readers that his belief in the validity of (β) has two sources. The first is intuition. 'When I carefully consider (β) it seems to be valid . . . Rule (β) . . . appeals immediately to the reflective intellect; like *Modus Tollens*, it can be easily grasped by the mind and *seen* to be true'.[47] These remarks are hardly persuasive; when I carefully consider (β) it seems to be invalid. The second source is 'the fact that I can think of no instances of (β) that have . . . true premisses and a false conclusion'.[48] Yet as I have already remarked, given compatibilism the argument under discussion is just such an instance. As things stand, van Inwagen has simply begged the question against compatibilism. He has assumed the validity of a principle that leads immediately to the conclusion that compatibilism is false. He might just as well have assumed the falsity of compatibilism straight off and spared us the logic.

I suspect that rule (β) gains whatever plausibility it has from the fact that it is typographically identical to a familiar rule of the Gödel-Feys-von Wright minimal modal system T.[49] Van Inwagen's N operator does appear to satisfy many theses of T, for example $NA \supset A$, $NA \lor NB \supset N(A \lor B)$, $A \supset -N-A$, $NA\&NB \leftrightarrow N(A\&B)$ (although for some doubts see Slote, M. 'Selective Necessity and the Free-Will Problem'). However, it cannot be assumed that because an operator is T-like in some of its behaviour it is T-like in all. Call an operator N *weakly modal* just in case it satisfies all the axioms and primitive rules of T save the axiom $N(A \supset B) \supset (NA \supset NB)$. (β) is not a valid rule of inference for a weakly modal operator (except in the case where both premisses of the rule are themselves theses of the weakened system – a case which is of no interest here, since in van Inwagen's application the premisses of (β) are not theses of modal logic). Van Inwagen is entitled to use (β) only if he has first shown that his N is not weakly modal, which he has not.

A pertinent example of a weakly modal reading of NA is 'A is true and either A is logically or necessarily true or A is a physical law (or follows logically from one or more physical laws (and nothing else)) or there is amongst the immediate causes of its being the case that A a (causally) sufficient subset in which my actions, beliefs, desires etc. do not figure, either as members or as part of the causal history of a member, or, lastly, I brought it about that A but was coerced or compelled to do so'. (The reference to a sufficient *subset* is required in order to cover cases of causal over-determination.) The onus is on van Inwagen to show not only that this reading misses some ingredient of the meaning of 'It is true that A and no one has, or has ever had, any choice about whether A' but also that the additional ingredient suffices to transform N from a weakly modal neccessity operator to a T-strength neccessity operator.[50]

How to live with a fixed future

Consider again the final sentence of the passage we're examining: 'Your future is fixed, inevitable – laid out for you, waiting to be discovered.' We are

portrayed as passive travellers who play no role in bringing the future about –
an image which is, of course, absurd. A.J. Ayer has put his finger neatly on the
flaw: 'My actions make [a] *difference* to the future: for they are *causes* as well as
effects.'[51]

Discarding the second half of the sentence leaves us with 'Your future is
fixed, inevitable'. So long as the word 'fixed' is taken to mean nothing more
than 'determined by the past', it is indeed an implication of determinism that
the future of each of us is fixed. This idea has exercised thoughtful people
since philosophy began. The Buddha recommended meditation as a technique
for reconciling oneself to the knowledge that one's life is merely a tiny episode
in a great fixed chain of cause and effect. The nineteenth century thinker John
Stuart Mill wrote of the 'depressing and paralysing influence' of his belief in
a fixed future, and Ted Honderich has recently written of what he calls his
attitude of dismay towards his own belief that each person's future is fixed.[52]
Maybe I'm lacking in imagination but I do not find the idea of living in a
universe whose future is fixed at all depressing. Let me explain.

1   Firstly, even if the future is fixed it is far from true that my future
actions will not be voluntary, will not be up to me, will not be free. I hope my
various arguments have already convinced you of this.

2   On the Laplacian view a fixed future is a *predictable* future: a snooping
superhuman intelligence could in principle calculate the intimate details of
all our futures. But thanks to chaos theory we now know that a fixed future is
not neccessarily a predictable one. Since in a causally connected world unpredictability breeds unpredictability, the existence of even one well of chaos
would frustrate the Laplacian calculation.

3   It is sometimes said that if the future is fixed then life can hold no
opportunities. I cannot agree. Imagine that you buy a lottery ticket and subsequently read in the conditions printed on the back of it that the winning
number was selected by an impartial trustee *before* the selling of tickets commenced. (The example is Dennett's.[53]) 'The winning number has been placed
in a special sealed envelope by the trustee and deposited in a bank vault,'
explains the ticket. Wouldn't you still feel that you have a perfectly good
chance of winning? The news that the outcome of the lottery is already determined surely makes no difference: you still have a chance of carrying away
the prize. And if a predrawn lottery can offer you the opportunity of winning
the prize of your dreams then so too, of course, can a predetermined future.
Indeed, in one important respect a predetermined future is even rosier than a
predrawn lottery. Once the tickets are all sold it is inevitable who is going to
win the lottery. However, it is misleading to describe the events in your fixed
future as inevitable. We normally call something inevitable if it is going to
happen *no matter what steps we take*.[54] But many of the events in your future
will happen precisely because you do take steps to bring them about. This is
not the stuff that inevitability is made of.

4   A fixed future is not a future in which you will helplessly experience the passing flow of events. Much of your future will be of your own doing: many of the things that happen will happen because – and only because – you decide that they shall and take effective measures to bring them about. If determinism is true, then each event in your life is the outcome of pre-existing causal forces, but unless you become enslaved or comatose, pre-eminent among these forces will be your own decisions and actions. For myself, I feel this is all the power I could ever need over events.

To summarize, then, I have discussed three kinds of freedom: the freedom of randomness, freedom as detailed by compatibilists, and transcendental or 'contra-causal' freedom. It is hard to see how human beings could possibly possess transcendental freedom; and in any case it seems to me that freedom of this kind is not worth hankering after. As for the other two kinds of freedom, humans may possess the first and certainly do possess the second. Both these kinds of freedom could exist in a real artefact of the same degree of sophistication as the imaginary robot Turbo Sam.

8

Consciousness

Could an artefact synthesize that supreme jewel of human existence, conscious awareness? When Turbo Sam gazes through his artificial eyes at a crowd of daffodils do his electronic circuits merely record the numerical characteristics of the light reflected from the petals? Or does Turbo Sam undergo a conscious experience of yellowness – an inner sensation to which he might abandon himself, like some silicon Wordsworth?

8.1 Neglect and disarray

Contemporary brain science has tantalizingly little to say about consciousness: the subject lies pretty much beyond the current frontiers of knowledge. For many decades it was a taboo subject, a victim of the principle 'If you don't know how to explain something, pretend it doesn't exist'. This maxim is mischievously referred to as Skinner's Razor, after B.F. Skinner, a leading figure in the Behaviourist movement. Behaviourism dominated psychology from the 1920s until the 1960s. In 1963, an AI researcher intending to make a study of the possibility of machine consciousness reported somewhat glumly that 'modern psychology . . . finds no scientific usefulness in the concept of a consciousness accompanying behaviour . . . [T]he concept of consciousness is considered . . . both undesirable and unnecessary . . . in the science of human behaviour.'[1] One recent writer on consciousness says mockingly of the Behaviourist era: 'Certainly one way of solving the problem of consciousness and its place in nature is to deny that consciousness exists at all.'[2]

Although 'consciousness' is no longer a word that brain scientists are embarrassed to use in public, it remains true that little of a scientific nature is known about the phenomenon. Indeed, so little is known that anyone who writes on the subject risks being accused of wasting paper. 'To my mind nothing has been written on consciousness that is worth the word-processor paper on which it is output' says Stuart Sutherland, Director of the Centre for Research on Perception and Cognition at the University of Sussex.[3] Despite these pessimistic words I propose to take you on a short journey through the fringes of this mystery-ridden area. I apologize in advance for the vagueness of the landscape. My aim in undertaking the journey is to try to convince you that there is nothing in the little we do know to suggest that machine consciousness is an impossibility.

The need for a taxonomy

Freud once remarked 'What is meant by *conscious* we need not discuss: it is beyond all doubt.'[4] He was completely wrong. This is the first thing we need to discuss. The word 'consciousness' is best regarded not as a term designating some unitary state, but rather as a somewhat vague label that is used for a number of none-too-closely related phenomena.[5] I suspect that when people unreflectingly say things like 'Of course dogs are conscious!' or 'I know *I'm* conscious!' they usually have no clear meaning in mind. As we shall see there are several quite different things that could be meant. Even the scientific and philosophical literature on consciousness is marred by the fact that different writers sometimes mean different things by the term, and it is not unknown for discussions between experts to peter out in mutual incomprehension.

The next three sections set out a short taxonomy of the genus consciousness. The taxonomy is not intended to be complete. Among the several senses that go unmentioned are consciousness as the gross state of being awake and consciousness in the sense of a person's sensitivity to some particular dimension of human existence (as in the expressions 'political consciousness' and 'spiritual consciousness'). Two important senses – consciousness as a sense of self and consciousness as a metaphorical 'inner space' – are mentioned only in passing, since I believe they are largely subsumed within the second entry of the taxonomy.

8.2 The fuzzy baseline

According to Julian Jaynes 'it is perfectly possible that there could have existed a race of men who spoke, judged, reasoned, solved problems, indeed did most of the things we do, but who were not conscious at all.'[6] If this sounds outrageous to you, it is probably because you are taking the word 'conscious' in what I will call the *baseline sense*. In that sense, an entity is by definition conscious if, firstly, it is capable of perceiving the world via sense organs of some description and, secondly, is capable of performing inner activities of the sort mentioned in the quotation: reasoning, deliberating, judging, hypothesising, planning, and so forth.

Jaynes is suggesting that there could be a race of beings who meet these baseline conditions and yet are *not* conscious, in some further sense of the word. A good way to develop an imaginative feel for what Jaynes is getting at is to envisage yourself driving along a familiar stretch of road while completely engrossed in thought or in your conversation with a passenger.[7] (If you don't drive, take another example: walking to the bus stop while in a reverie. In one guise or another the experience I'm about to describe will be familiar to most people.) Because you are absorbed in your conversation or reverie, little or no information about the road ahead filters into your consciousness. Yet the data still flows from your eyes and ears to your brain, and even though you are not consciously aware of doing so you continually plan manoeuvres, judge distances, read roadsigns, select gears, and so on. This state is close to how things would be for Jaynes' race of people without consciousness: sensory information flows, decisions are made, plans are devised and executed, but all in the absence of conscious awareness.

Anyone with an attachment to the baseline sense of consciousness will no doubt feel uneasy with my description of the car scenario. Surely there is a clear sense in which the driver *is* conscious of the car ahead as she overtakes it – if she weren't conscious of it, she would crash into it instead of neatly manoeuvring round it. Those who disfavour the baseline sense will reply that although the driver certainly perceives the car ahead, perception can occur without conscious awareness. Interestingly enough, psychologists at a recent conference divided approximately fifty-fifty on the question of whether or not a driver is conscious of the road ahead in the circumstances we are considering.[8] Presumably they would also have divided fifty-fifty on the question of whether a creature – or machine – that is always in this 'aware-yet-unaware' state is conscious.

Disagreement over what I'm calling the baseline sense of the term 'conscious' is best regarded as an issue of differing verbal taste. Some people find it natural to apply the word 'conscious' to any entity that meets the baseline conditions, while other people prefer to withhold the word unless additional conditions are met. There is no fact of the matter as to which group is right. A diligent taxonomist can do no more than include the baseline sense in the taxonomy of consciousness and add a note to the effect that some people prefer to reserve the term 'conscious' for entities with additional features, detailed elsewhere in the taxonomy, rather than squander the word on organisms or mechanisms that make it to the baseline but no further. As I have already indicated in chapter 3 I fall into the latter group myself, and thus find nothing odd in the idea of a race of beings who perceive and think but are not conscious. However, if your intuitions happen to tell you that these 'baseline beings' should be called conscious I certainly won't try to dissuade you, for note that if baseline beings are to be called conscious, my task of arguing that machine consciousness is a conceptual possibility becomes much simpler. A thinking robot like

Turbo Sam would amply satisfy the baseline conditions and so would indisputably be conscious in the baseline sense.

8.3 Consciousness as a type of internal monitoring[9]

An abstracted driver who perceives a vehicle ahead and yet is unaware of perceiving it is in some respects similar to a person exhibiting blindsight (a phenomenon introduced in section 3.1). Such people report the loss of part of their visual field following brain surgery and claim to be unable to see lights and patterns that are projected into their newly acquired 'blind' region. However, experiments reveal that the patients do indeed perceive these lights and patterns, despite the fact that they are not consciously aware of doing so.[10]

These and other cases suggest that the brain contains some kind of monitoring mechanism. Larry Weiskrantz, the discoverer of blindsight, conjectures that when the blindsighted person perceives a light in their blind area the perception for some reason goes unmonitored, with the result that the person is unable to report its presence.[11] David Armstrong has expressed the hypothesis of an internal monitor by means of a vivid metaphor: 'In perception the brain scans the environment. In awareness of the perception another process in the brain scans that scanning.'[12]

Not everything that goes on in us falls within the range of this hypothesized monitor. Pupillary response, for example, goes unmonitored.[13] The iris around your pupil is continually expanding and contracting, not only in response to changes in illumination but also in response to the amount of interest that the object of your vision holds for you – if you look at a stranger with widened pupils, it is an indication that they appeal to you in some way. Yet you are not conscious of giving this signal: the processes in the brain that control pupillary response are not monitored. Even those things that are within the range of the system are not monitored all the time (as the example of the car driver illustrates); and in situations that demand extreme swiftness of thought the monitor may 'disengage' more or less completely. Aircraft pilots and racing drivers often report that their minds go completely blank at a time when – as their behaviour indicates – they are making a series of lightning decisions.

Theorists suggest that the monitor feeds into the brain's speech centre. It is the monitor that enables us to talk inwardly to ourselves about what we are doing and why and how we are doing it. This incessant internal monologue, and the accompanying mirage of an 'inner private space', constitute a large part of our sense of selfhood. (No doubt more rudimentary forms of monitoring can occur in non-linguistic creatures, and it is possible that this form of consciousness exists in all the complex mammals.)

Michael Gazzaniga came to the idea that the brain contains a speech-related monitoring device as a result of his work with patients who had undergone surgery to sever the corpus callosum. This is the 'bridge' of nerve fibres connecting the left and right hemispheres of the brain. The callosum is cut as a treatment for intractable epilepsy – the so called split-brain operation (although in fact the operation does not literally split the brain at all: the two hemispheres remain connected at the subcortical level).

In general terms, the right hand hemisphere of your brain processes information from the left hand half of your visual field and controls the left side of your body (arm and finger movements, for example), while the left hemisphere deals with the right hand half of the visual field and the right side of the body. In right-handed people, the area of the brain responsible for speech is usually located in the left hemisphere, and vice versa for left-handers. (A possible explanation for this is that the region now responsible for speech may originally have been responsible for gesture.) Once the corpus callosum is cut, the two hemispheres can no longer share information with each other. This produces some very strange effects.[14]

In a famous series of experiments, split-brain subjects were positioned in front of a screen in such a way that whatever was flashed on the right hand side of the screen was 'seen' only by the left hemisphere and vice versa (figure 8.1).[15] If a sexually indecent picture is flashed briefly onto the left hand side of the screen, a right-handed subject typically reports seeing nothing and yet may blush and giggle for several minutes. When asked why they are blushing the subject will say they have no idea. Their damaged monitor system is playing them up. If a triangle is flashed onto the left half of the screen and a circle onto the right half, a right-handed subject will report seeing the circle (since, remember, the area responsible for speech is located in the left hemisphere). But when asked to draw what is on the screen with their left hand, they will produce a triangle. And if asked what they have just drawn, they insist they have produced a circle (provided, of course, they are not permitted to shift their eyes from the screen and look).

Gazzaniga suggests that the brain's monitor system is prepared to make guesses about what it doesn't know for sure: the monitor is an active *interpreter* rather than a passive recorder.[16] As Gazzaniga puts it, the monitor 'constructs hypotheses' about what is going on.[17] The system's guesses are not always correct, as in the case of the hypothesis that the left hand had drawn a circle. Gazzaniga describes a number of instances where the monitor of a split-brain patient gets caught in the act of fabricating a false hypothesis. In one experiment the screen arrangement I've mentioned was used to present a picture of a snow-bound house and car to a man's right hemisphere and a drawing of a chicken claw to the left hemisphere. He was then asked to turn to a row of eight pictured objects and use both hands to pick out the two items most closely associated with what he had seen on the screen (figure 8.2). With his left hand he pointed to a shovel (remember that the left hand is controlled by the right hemisphere) and with his right hand he picked out a drawing of a chicken. When asked to

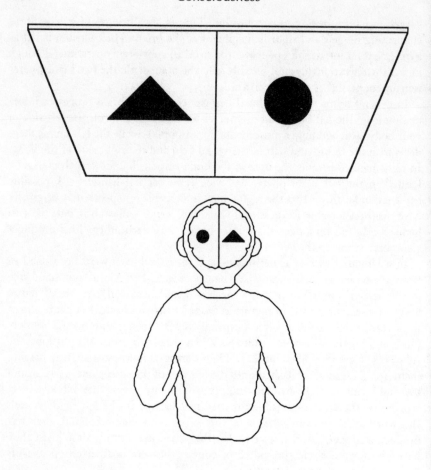

Figure 8.1   Each hemisphere 'sees' only one half of the screen.

explain his selection, his speech centre (located in the left hemisphere) relayed this hypothesis from the monitor: 'Oh, that's simple. The chicken claw goes with the chicken, and you need a shovel to clean out the chicken shed'.[18] The damaged monitor system no longer had access to everything it needed to know in order to explain both choices correctly – but that didn't stop it from hazarding a guess.

Gazzaniga's suggestion is not just that a monitor in a damaged brain will guess when it has to, but that interpretation and guesswork form a routine part of the activity of each person's monitor. This raises the disturbing possibility that our beliefs about our activities – even the most mundane of activities –

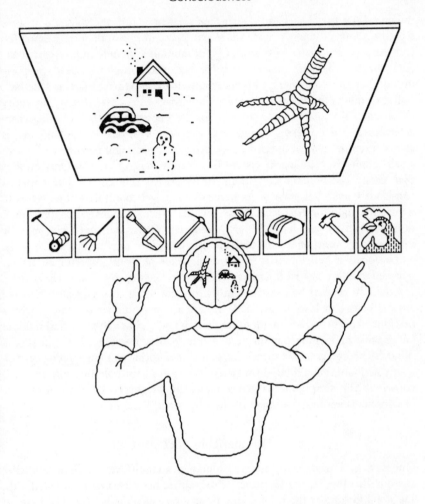

Figure 8.2 The two hemispheres pick different objects when the split-brain subject is asked which pictured items he associates with what he can see on the screen. (From figure 42 in Gazzaniga, M.S. and LeDoux, J.E. *The Integrated Mind.*)

may sometimes, or even often, be nothing more than fabrications cooked up by our monitors. Experiments like the following seem to confirm this possibility. Women in a shopping mall who were asked to select a pair of nylon stockings from a table tended in general to choose a pair from the far right of the display, even though all the pairs were identical. (It is well known that a shopper's choice of goods is heavily influenced by spatial position.) When each woman was asked to say why she picked the pair she did, explanations as spurious as

170

Consciousness

the one about the shovel and the chicken shed came out: the chosen pair were a better colour or slightly more sheer, etc. None of the women mentioned the true explanation, spatial position.[19] If your monitor system is an inveterate confabulator then the sense-making narrative that runs through your head, purporting to integrate your mental life, is an unreliable mixture of fact and fiction.

Returning to the taxonomy, under the terms of the current entry an entity is conscious if – and I must apologize for the vagueness of the following characterization – it possesses a high-level overview system of some kind that is able to monitor many of the entity's own cognitive states and processes. (Though a self-monitoring fire alarm system is not conscious, of course. Only entities that satisfy the baseline conditions are under consideration.) The entity is consciously aware of such of its perceptions as get monitored. The states to which the monitor has access may include others besides perceptual ones: desires, needs, goals, fears, beliefs, memories, plans, and much else may be monitored. A need or fear or plan etc. is a conscious one, in this sense, if the entity forms a belief that it has it as a result of direct monitor access (as opposed to inferring that it has it as a result of reflecting on its own behaviour).[20]

Could an artefact be conscious in the present sense? It seems clear that the answer is *Yes*, at least in principle. There are any number of reasons why a machine like Turbo Sam might never exist in reality, but a hypothetical robotics lab capable of turning out the rest of him would, I assume, have no special difficulty whipping up his speech-integrated monitoring and interpreting system.

If you doubt that a robot possessed of such a system would be *really and truly* conscious, this simply means that so far as you are concerned, the true essence of consciousness lies elsewhere in the taxonomy. Read on.

8.4 The ineffable *FEEL* of it all

One day, as Turbo Sam wandered lonely as a cloud over the hills and vales surrounding the Turing Institute, he saw all at once a host of golden daffodils. He stood looking at them for a long time, aware of nothing else. Their colour was richer, fuller than anything he had encountered in his laboratory environment. He engraved a high-resolution facsimile of the scene in his permanent memory, and long after he had departed from Britain the daffodils would still from time to time flash upon the inward eye of his contemplative monitor system.

What is it *like* for Turbo Sam when he looks at the daffodils? He sees flowers of a certain colour, yes – but is the sensation that he undergoes when his artificial eyes scan the daffodil-packed landscape anything like the sensation that you or I undergo in such circumstances? Or are his visual sensations unimaginably different from ours? Perhaps his visual sensations are as different from our visual sensations as our taste sensations are from our touch sensations. A nagging sub-problem arises at this point: is there any way of being sure that *you and I* undergo broadly similar visual sensations when we look at a clump of daffodils? We both call the daffodils 'yellow' – as does Turbo Sam – but that is no help. The three of us conform to the practice of applying the word 'yellow' to things that look yellow to us, but it could still be the case that yellow things look different to each of us.

In wondering what it's like for Turbo Sam when he looks at the daffodils we may already have assumed too much. *Perhaps it isn't like anything at all for Turbo Sam.* Maybe Turbo Sam doesn't really 'experience' anything when he sees a yellow flower, or runs his taste-sensors over a peppermint, or detects the unmistakable whiff of one of his circuit boards overheating. He *sees* the daffodils; he is *aware* that he sees them (thanks to his internal monitor); he knows that they are golden yellow in colour rather than a greenish yellow or a brownish yellow; he can correctly identify them as belonging to the narcissus family; and he is subsequently able to recall the flowery scene in considerable detail, including the way (as he puts it to himself) the sweep of pale, intense colour lay across the ground like a mist. Yet all of this seems possible without the robot's sensory transactions with the flowers (or the peppermint or the overheating circuit board) having any 'subjective character' or 'immediate phenomenological quality' or 'feeliness' (pick your favourite term).[21] After all, some of the simple robots used in today's car assembly plants have rudimentary touch sensors and visual systems, yet presumably they do not have sensations with phenomenological qualities, and so perhaps the same is true for Turbo Sam. (Compare those perennial questions of small children: do cats/flies/frogs actually *feel* anything when their tails are twisted/wings are pulled off/bodies are squeezed murderously.)

I assume, by the way, that as a fellow human being you have an intuitive understanding of what I'm talking about here – the feel of the wind blowing through your hair, the look of a cloudless blue sky, the unmistakable yet ineffable feeling of warmth against the skin, the dull, griping character of a stomach ache. Though I should hate to have the task of trying to explain to Turbo Sam himself exactly what it is we fear he may be missing. No doubt he would insist, hurt, that nothing is missing – that he too can tell when his hair is blowing in the wind. Turing suggests that we deal with such situations by politely acquiescing if a robot assures us that it is phenomenologically aware, no matter what doubts we might harbour in our hearts. He gleefully points out that in effect each of us adopts this convention in our dealings with the rest of humanity.[22]

An entity is conscious in the third and final sense of this taxonomy if its sensory episodes do have 'feely properties'. Desiring a dignified technical term, philosophers usually speak of *qualia* (singular: 'quale') rather than feely properties, and thus the official entry in the taxonomy reads as follows: a conscious entity is one whose sensory interactions with the world are customarily accompanied by qualia of some sort.

What exactly are qualia, and could they be experienced by a machine? These are Large Questions and the rest of the chapter is devoted to pondering them.

8.5   Into the heart of the mystery

In 1866 Thomas Huxley wrote the following in his *Lessons in Elementary Physiology*: 'What consciousness is, we know not; and how it is that anything so remarkable as a state of consciousness comes about as the result of irritating nervous tissue is just as unaccountable as the appearance of the Djin when Aladdin rubbed his lamp'.[23] More than a century has passed and the mystery remains unsolved. We still lack any firm conception of what the relationship is between qualia and the electrical and chemical activity that occurs in the brain and nervous system. Some scientists and philosophers believe that qualia are uniquely peculiar things which will always lie beyond the reach of objective science. Einstein is reputed to have said that science cannot give us the *taste* of soup.[24] In a few pages time I will examine this line of thought in some detail. But first – with a view to working you up into a suitable state of mystification – I want to heap scorn on a couple of attempts to dismiss the idea that there is something uniquely puzzling about qualia.

A dismissive outburst

'Seems to me that all the "mystery" is just the result of getting things round the wrong way. These so-called "feely properties" aren't in the brain or mind at all. They are out there in the world, as properties of the objects we perceive. Cheese is yellow, grass is green, sugar is sweet, soup is salty. There's no special problem about these properties. Any food chemist will be able to tell you what it is about a particular bowl of soup that gives it its flavour.'

An easy way to see that there is something very wrong with these remarks is to consider pain. As we all know, the cleaving of human tissue by a pin is accompanied by distinctive feely properties – and these can hardly be regarded as properties of the pin itself. The qualia are caused *in* us *by* the pin. Things are just the same with taste (and the other sensory modalities), as an example will illustrate.[25]

Phenol-thio-urea is a substance that tastes intensely bitter to about 75 percent of people and is more or less tasteless to the rest. Is phenol-thio-urea bitter? This is an awkward question for someone who naively believes that a statement like 'Sugar is sweet' says something about sugar itself, as opposed to the effect that sugar has on us. There is worse to come, though. A person's response to phenol-thio-urea is genetically determined. This means that if those who find it bitter are – let's imagine – prevented from having offspring, the substance will become tasteless to one and all after the passage of maybe a dozen generations (just as blue eyes would presumably get bred out of existence if the blue-eyed people of each generation were prevented from reproducing). In this way, phenol-thio-urea would change from being a substance that tastes bitter to the majority of people, to being a substance that is universally found to be tasteless, all without any alteration whatsoever having occurred in the chemical or physical properties of phenol-thio-urea itself.

Bitterness lies in the beholder, not the beholden. Qualia are not 'out there in the world' but are caused *in* us when external objects interact with our sensory apparatus.

Another dismissive outburst
'Oh look, there isn't any grand mystery about qualia. They are nothing but states or processes occurring in the brain. True, we don't yet know precisely which states or processes constitute qualia, but then nor do we know how the brain recognises faces, does simple arithmetic, or generates the sentences that we utter. There are many issues that brain science has yet to resolve. All of them are fascinating, but none merits the title of Mind-Boggling Mystery. All this stuff about qualia being the ultimate riddle of the universe is sheer hype.'

An outraged rejoinder
'How *could* a feeling of pain consist of ions passing across the membranes of cells in the brain? How *could* the sensation of blue or the smell of jasmine be formed of electrical activity in the cerebral cortex? Or the feeling of thirst be an increase in the concentration of amino acids in the hypothalamus? Or the pleasure of orgasm be one and the same as a chemical reaction occurring in a tiny volume of tissue lying midway between the tips of your ears? Yet the previous speaker is calmly assuring us that qualia quite literally *are* brain processes like these. I've never heard anything so incredible. And by the way, don't confuse what my antagonist is saying with the much weaker claim that electro-chemical activity in the brain is what *produces* or *causes* the qualia associated with orgasm, thirst, and so on. It is entirely plausible to say that stroking a cat causes it to purr, entirely implausible to say that the purring *is* the stroking. X *is* Y is a very different claim from X *is caused by* Y.'

The incongruity involved in the idea that qualia are brain processes is, I think, very striking. It is an idea hardly less odd than the thought that the note of middle C might somehow literally be a fish: in each case there seems to be no similarity whatsoever between the items that are juxtaposed. However, as I have said a number of times, strangeness is not neccessarily an indicator of falsity, and it may in the end turn out that – somehow – our qualia are nothing but physical happenings in the brain. (History is full of precedents: lightning, that unearthly force of the gods, did in the end turn out to be nothing more than a mundane discharge of electricity.) Personally, I certainly *hope* this is how things turn out. The idea that qualia are ethereal, non-physical presences which permeate my central nervous system like meddlesome phantoms is, to say the least, disquieting.[26] But either way, only someone suffering from severe mystery-blindness can maintain that there is no mystery here. There is, and it's a corker.[27]

Those who think that our qualia will somehow turn out to be nothing but bio-physical happenings in the brain are termed *physicalists*. The opposing camp, who think that qualia transcend the bio-physical, are known as *anti-physicalists*. Anti-physicalists also go by the name of *dualists*, because they believe that human beings are a composite of two radically different things, matter and mind – on the one hand there is our bio-physical aspect and on the other there is that blooming, buzzing stream of irreducibly mental qualia.[28] In contrast, physicalists believe that human beings are wholly bio-physical in nature, and the notion that we possess non-physical minds is anathema to them. Professor Ramsay, a character in Virginia Woolf's *To The Lighthouse*, gave a pleasingly blunt statement of physicalism: 'The mind, Sir, is meat'.[29]

According to the physicalists' vision of the future, the advancing march of the neurosciences will eventually catch up with qualia, whereupon they will be rudely shorn of their mysteries. And according to anti-physicalists we will still be none the wiser about qualia even when the neurosciences are complete and everything is known about the bio-physical brain that there is to be known. 'Tell me everything physical there is to tell about what is going on in a living brain,' writes a leading anti-physicalist, 'and . . . you won't have told me about the hurtfulness of pains, the itchiness of itches, pangs of jealousy, or about the characteristic experience of tasting a lemon, smelling a rose, hearing a loud noise or seeing the sky.'[30]

In the next two sections I examine two arguments which have recently been advanced in support of the claim that qualia are non-physical in nature. The first of them is due to Thomas Nagel and the second to Frank Jackson. The arguments are interesting – but in my view, not convincing.

8.6   What is it like to be a bat?[31]

Bats perceive the external world primarily by sonar or echolocation.[32] The flying bat emits rapid high-frequency shrieks, which are reflected back from surrounding objects. Specialized mechanisms in the bat's brain correlate the outgoing shrieks with the returning echoes, enabling the bat to make detailed discriminations of distance, size, shape, motion and texture. From a human point of view the bat is a fundamentally alien creature. It senses the external world by means of a perceptual system that is radically different from any we possess.

Nagel begins his argument by assuming that bats are conscious in the third sense of my taxonomy. He explains 'I have chosen bats instead of wasps or flounders because if one travels too far down the phylogenetic tree, people gradually shed their faith that there is experience there at all.'[33] I'm sure that some people will have their doubts about bats as well, but for the sake of argument let's grant Nagel his assumption. He continues by inviting us to try to imagine what a bat's experience of the world might be like. Nagel fully expects us to find that we cannot. 'Bat sonar, though clearly a form of perception, is not similar in its operation to any sense that we possess, and there is no reason to suppose that it is subjectively like anything we can experience or imagine.'[34] When we attempt to imagine what it is like to be a bat, we have nothing but our own experiences to serve as basic materials, and these, Nagel reminds us, are ineluctably tied to our own hidebound point of view. Our imaginative horizons are firmly drawn for us by the nature of our own perceptual apparatus. 'In contemplating the bats, we are in much the same position that intelligent bats or Martians would occupy if they tried to form a conception of what it was like to be us. The structure of their own minds might make it impossible for them to succeed.'[35] You *can't* imagine what it is like to be a bat – can you?

Next, Nagel shifts the focus of the argument from the bat's qualia to the bat's brain. The biology of the bat's brain, nervous system and perceptual apparatus 'is a domain of objective facts *par excellence* – the kind that can be observed and understood . . . by individuals with differing perceptual systems,' writes Nagel. 'There are no comparable imaginative obstacles to the acquisition of knowledge about bat neurophysiology by human scientists, and intelligent bats or Martians might learn more about the human brain than we ever will.'[36] In short, the facts about the functioning of a bat's brain fall within the public domain, and in principle nothing lies in the way of our discovering everything that there is to be known about the neurophysiological workings of bats. Yet the facts of *what it is like* to be a creature that perceives the world by sonar are accessible only from the bat's own subjective point of view. No amount of objective neurophysiological data will help our cramped imaginations to form a conception of what a bat's subjective experiences are like, says Nagel. He concludes that objective neuroscience is inherently incapable of accounting for qualia.[37] Its province is the realm of publicly accessible facts about what goes on in a creature's brain, whereas the facts about qualia, being subjective, are of a radically different nature.[38]

There are two criticisms that can be made of this argument, a minor one and a major one. First, the minor one. Does Nagel have a right to feel so sure that future neurophysiological data will not help us form a better conception of what it is like to be a bat? The following example suggests that he does not.[39] Neurophysiologically, the tasting machinery of humans is fairly similar to that of cats and rats. One small difference, discovered by monitoring the electrical

activity in the relevant neural pathways, is that in certain respects our machinery is less sensitive than a cat's but more sensitive than a rat's. The variations
in sensitivity are particularly marked at the bitter end of the 'taste spectrum'.
Perhaps, then, a substance that tastes slightly bitter to a human will not taste
bitter at all to a rat, and will taste moderately bitter to a cat. Maybe saccharin,
which tastes faintly bitter to humans, tastes the same as sugar to the less
sensitive rat and unacceptably bitter to the more sensitive cat. These are
speculations about rat qualia and cat qualia: a small discovery concerning the
neurophysiology of taste has given us a minutely better imaginative grasp of
how things might be for rats and cats. (And interestingly enough, cats will eat
sugar but not saccharin, whereas rats select either indiscriminately.) Admittedly,
the comparative taste of saccharin versus sugar is a very small stitch in the total
fabric of experience – but if a modest neurophysiological discovery like this
one can give a tiny nudge to the imagination, who can tell how the neurophysiological advances of the next four or five centuries might affect our ability
to imagine the lot of a cat, rat, or bat? Nagel may be jumping the gun.

The second criticism is very straightforward. Nagel has misdirected his
argument. Physicalists need not disagree with his assertion that we can never
fully imagine what it is like to be a bat. Their theory is about the nature of
qualia, not about the powers of the human imagination. Physicalism is the
claim that bats – and all other organisms – are purely bio-physical entities.
This claim in no way commits physicalists to believing that if we knew everything
there is to know about the neurophysiology of the bat's brain and perceptual
apparatus, then we would be able to imagine what it is like to actually *be* a
creature with that perceptual apparatus. Naturally human beings are going to
have difficulty imagining the perceptual experiences of a creature that senses
the world primarily by means of echolocation – but so what? This hardly
suffices to prove that bats cannot be purely bio-physical in nature. As Woolf's
Professor Ramsay might put the point: the fact that one meat machine is
unable to imagine the world from the point of view of another meat machine
with radically different perceptual apparatus can scarcely be counted as a proof
that the second is not a meat machine after all.

8.7 What Mary doesn't know

Frank Jackson's argument is in some ways a purified version of Nagel's.[40]
Jackson aims for a similar conclusion – that physicalism leaves something out
– but he chooses a route which bypasses Nagel's fruitless excursion into the
issue of whether we can imagine what it is like to be a creature of a different
species.

Mary, the heroine of the argument, is congenitally insensitive to pain.[41]

People with this affliction simply do not feel pain, and consequently are prone to do enormous damage to themselves. Many end up crippled as a result of repeatedly overstraining their joints. However, thanks to careful nursing Mary survives her childhood unscathed. At university she gains a double First in philosophy and the neurosciences, and she goes on to become – oddly enough – one of the world's leading experts in the neurophysiology of pain. Living as she does in the fourth millenium AD she has access to a more or less complete body of knowledge concerning the human brain and nervous system. What Mary doesn't know about the neurophysiology of pain just isn't worth knowing. But, of course, she has never actually *experienced* pain, and at the age of forty curiosity drives her to undergo a very expensive course of treatment that will normalize her brain chemistry. A month later sees her lying on a surgical couch with an expectant expression on her face as her neuropharmacologist prepares to jab a sterilized pin into her buttock. A triumphant squeal passes her lips and she congratulates herself on having met pain at last.

Jackson concludes from this scenario that physicalism is false. Prior to her course of treatment, Mary knew all the bio-physical facts about pain, yet as the pin pierced her flesh she experienced something new. Therefore there is more to be known concerning pain than the bio-physical facts can tell. 'It follows,' says Jackson, 'that physicalism leaves something out'.[42] Pain cannot be a purely bio-physical phenomenon.

Jackson's argument is ingenious but I remain unconvinced. It is true that before her treatment Mary's knowledge of pain was that of an outside observer, whereas after the treatment pain becomes something with which she has first-hand acquaintance; but it does not follow from this that physicalism is false – as I will try to show.

Consider a parallel case. Van Plank, an eminent Dutch arborist, knows every last fact about the New Zealand kauri tree. Yet van Plank, who is phobic about air travel, has never visited New Zealand to gaze first hand upon the objects of his knowledge. At sixty, he finally finds time to make the journey by sea, and in the forests of Northland is awed by his first personal encounter with a full-sized kauri. Was van Plank's previous knowledge of the kauri incomplete? In a sense yes, in a sense no. We need a semantic distinction if we are to be able to describe the situation accurately. The distinction is encapsulated in the sentence 'I don't know her, but I know a lot about her'. In the first sense, you don't know someone until you have actually met them; in the second sense, you can know an unlimited number of facts about someone you've never met. On the one hand there is knowledge in the sense of personal acquaintance, and on the other there is knowledge in the sense of possessing facts.[43] Prior to visiting New Zealand, van Plank knew every fact worth knowing about kauris. His factual knowledge of them was essentially complete. What his visit afforded was not more knowledge in the factual sense, but personal acquaintance with the *objects* of his already all-encompassing factual knowledge.

Armed with this distinction, the physicalist can describe Mary's enlightenment in a way that is entirely consistent with the theory that pain is a purely
bio-physical phenomenon. In fact, Mary is herself a physicalist (unbeknownst
to Frank Jackson), so let's hear the story from her own lips.

'I know that some twentieth century philosophers regard my case as constituting
a refutation of physicalism. I am afraid I cannot agree. I have never doubted that
pain is purely bio-physical in nature and recent events have done nothing to
make me change my mind. I agree, of course, that prior to my treatment pain
was unknown to me in the sense that I had never undergone it myself, never
actually felt it. I had never met it personally, so to speak. Yet I insist that my
factual knowledge of pain was nevertheless complete. All I lacked was personal
acquaintance with the object of this factual knowledge. I knew everything that
there is to know about the neurochemical processes that constitute pain, but
owing to my congenital abnormality those processes had never occurred inside
me. The treatment that I received normalized the chemistry of my brain and
nervous system, with the result that I am now able to host these processes within
my own body.

'So Professor Jackson is right to maintain that my previous knowledge of pain
left something out. The missing ingredient was knowledge in the sense of personal
acquaintance. However, it certainly does not follow from this that physicalism is
false. There is nothing to suffering pain over and above hosting a bio-physical
process – nothing at all.

'I should like if I may to quote from your Professor Nagel. He says "If mental
processes are indeed physical processes, then there is something *it is like*, intrinsically, to undergo certain physical processes".[44] This is true. Pain *is* a purely
bio-physical process, and it certainly is like something to host that process
within one's own nervous system. It is Professor Nagel's comment on this that
caught my eye. He continues: "What it is for such a thing to be the case remains
a mystery . . . [P]hysicalism is a position we cannot understand because we do
not at present have any conception of how it might be true".[45] I find these
honest, struggling remarks fascinating, even touching. It is so difficult for me to
imagine how *very* puzzling consciousness must have seemed back in your Age.
Rest assured that enlightenment does come – although not, I am afraid, until
well after your lifetimes. You must console yourselves with the reflection that it
would be greedy of twentieth century men and women to expect to fathom all of
life's mysteries.'

In a later article Jackson retouches his argument slightly.[46] He emphasises
that Mary learns something about *others* as a result of her treatment. 'The
trouble for physicalism is that . . . she will realise how impoverished her
conception of the mental life of others has been all along . . . All along their
experiences . . . had a feature conspicuous to them but until now hidden from
her.'[47] The retouched argument proceeds like this. Since Mary learns something about other people as a result of her treatment, there is something she
did not know about them prior to the treatment; yet (ex hypothesi) prior to the

treatment Mary knew everything *physical* there is to know about other people. Therefore physicalism leaves something out.[48] However, Mary's response to this is simple: she learned what it is like to host a certain biophysical process, pain, in her own nervous system, and so, by extension, she also learned what it is like for other people to host this biophysical process. (She has to assume here that she is not 'indulging in a wild generalization from one case', but Jackson seems happy to grant her this assumption.[49]) Once again Mary's enlightenment can be described in a way that is perfectly consistent with the truth of physicalism.

8.8 Drawing the threads together

To the best of my knowledge there are no convincing arguments against physicalism – and none for it, either. The theory hangs there, dripping mystery, supported only by faith. Yet those of us who count ourselves physicalists discern in the theory a certain comfortable, down-to-earth plausibility. The anti-physicalist alternative – an irreducibly mental dimension that sticks out of an otherwise physical universe like a sore thumb – is unpalatable to us. It offends against our expectation that nature is a harmonious, integrated affair. But the truth of the matter is that when it comes to qualia, nobody really knows.

It remains to sketch out the implications of all this for machine consciousness. If anti-physicalism happens to be true, then it may or may not be possible for a robot to experience qualia. One would need to know very much more before a definite answer could be given. If non-physical properties can be generated by a natural brain, then why not by an appropriate kind of artificial brain too? On the other hand, if physicalism is true then consciousness is a physical phenomenon, in which case there is no denying that a suitable artefact could experience qualia. Nor is there currently any reason to think that the 'physiology' of such artefacts would have to resemble ours.[50] It is mere chauvinism to assume a priori that qualia are peculiar to our tissue type. Recall the jelly-filled alien of chapter 3. By hypothesis, none of the things that go on in her tissues bear much resemblance to the things that go on in ours, yet for all that she could well lead a qualia-ridden existence.

Either way – physicalism true or physicalism false – I hope you agree that I have established the claim foreshadowed in chapters 3 and 7. Despite the pronouncements of bar-room sceptics, it is far from obvious that an artefact could not be conscious.

9

Are we computers?

By and large the men and women of the Victorian age believed themselves to be embodied spirits whose nearest non human relatives were angels. A century later, our rough ride through the theories of Darwin, Marx and Freud has left us collectively uncertain what we are; and an increasing number of people seem prepared to accept that our closest relatives may be not angels but the products of IBM and the Digital Equipment Corporation. Some brave citizens of the late twentieth century openly declare themselves to be computers and a great many more quietly entertain the suspicion that they could well be. Even those who disdain the idea can often be caught flirting with it in the form of idioms like 'The hardest part of divorce is reprogramming yourself to live alone' and 'We are all programmed by society'.

This new image of the human mind as a computer has taken root in popular culture with astonishing vigour. My aim is both to debunk the new image and to applaud it. As I explain, the image enjoys a popularity that far outstrips the scientific evidence – in fact there is currently no hard evidence either for or against the theory that the human brain is a computer. On the other hand, it seems to me that even if the theory should eventually turn out to be wrong in detail it is right in spirit. If we are not computers then we are physical machines of some other description. Last century's image of human nature had us uncomfortably straddling two realms, and we are well rid of it.

9.1 The strong symbol system hypothesis

The symbol system hypothesis is the conjecture that it is in principle possible to construct a universal symbol system that thinks (section 4.6). The strong symbol system hypothesis, on the other hand, is the conjecture that *only* universal symbol systems are capable of thinking (section 4.7). According to this hypothesis anything with the capacity for thought – and the human brain in particular – will prove on analysis to be a universal symbol system. If the strong symbol system hypothesis is true, AI *must* be possible, at least in principle, for the simple reason that the human brain is itself literally a computer.

The strong symbol system hypothesis (or SSSH) is so-called because it makes a stronger claim than the symbol system hypothesis (or SSH). It is possible that the SSH should be true and yet its stronger cousin false. Zeppelins and birds share the capacity for flight, but it doesn't follow that birds *are* Zeppelins; and, equally, computers and brains may share the capacity for thought (making the SSH true) without brains being computers (making the SSSH false). The thinking brain might operate in an entirely different way from the thinking symbol-manipulator.

Here is the picture painted of the human mind by Zenon Pylyshyn, a leading advocate of the SSSH.[1] 'The idea that mental processing is computation is indeed a serious empirical hypothesis . . . The mind is . . . continually engaged in rapid, largely unconscious searching, remembering and reasoning, and generally in manipulating knowledge . . . [This knowledge is] encoded by properties of the brain in the same general way the semantic contents of the computer's representations are encoded – by physically instantiated symbol structures.'[2] Although we are not consciously aware of it, our mental activity consists at bottom of the manipulation of sentence-like symbolic expressions, says Pylyshyn; fundamentally, human thought is the manipulation of sentences of an internal mental language or code.[3] This hypothesized internal language is often referred to as 'Mentalese'. Mentalese may or may not resemble the binary code employed in today's artefacts (most likely not); and, likewise, the fundamental computational operations used by the brain may differ considerably from those listed in section 4.5. As advocates of the SSSH are careful to stress, the computer inside the head may bear little resemblance to today's commercial machines.

The vigorous new area of research known as cognitive science is founded on the idea that the computer has much to tell us about the brain. This interdisciplinary investigation into the contents of the human skull draws its personnel from psychology, neuroscience, philosophy, computer science, linguistics, anthropology and zoology. As you might expect, there are a number of different shades of opinion to be found among such a diverse crowd of researchers. Hard-line cognitive scientists take the SSSH literally. Others regard the identification of brain with computer as nothing more than a helpful metaphor or research-provoking analogy. Yet another group believes that the brain is 'sort-of' a computer – a computer in a sense, but not a symbol-manipulator. This idea is taken up in the next chapter. The present chapter focusses on the hard-line claim that the brain is *literally* a computer, in the sense of 'computer' defined in chapter 4.

Cognitive science is a discipline that fairly buzzes with excitement. The human brain is the most complicated and mysterious object in the known universe and cognitive scientists tend to picture themselves as being on the very brink of discovering how it works. I am optimistic about the prospects of this new, powerful, multidisciplinary push towards understanding; though I will admit to harbouring a base suspicion that when the breakthrough finally comes, the SSSH itself may get trampled underfoot in the great surge forward into enlightenment.

Not everyone takes a tolerant view of the SSSH. Karl Lashley, one of the most famous figures in the development of brain science, and John Searle, of the Chinese room, have both remarked on the existence of a historical tendency among scientists and philosophers to model the operation of the brain on the most fashionable technology of the day.[4] In the mid-seventeenth century, when water clocks and hydraulic puppets were all the rage, Descartes developed a hydraulic theory of the brain's activities. Half a century later, Leibniz proposed that the brain could be likened to a factory. Freud relied heavily on electromagnetics and hydraulics in his descriptions of the mind's operations. Next Sir Charles Sherrington, the eminent British neuroscientist, likened the nervous system to a telegraph. When the telegraph was ousted by the telephone, the brain became a telephone switchboard. To cynics, the SSSH is merely the latest spectacle in this parade of attempts to compare the brain to each *dernier cri* in high technology. In 1951 Lashley impatiently dismissed the theory that the brain is a computer, calling it a 'far-fetched analogy'; and Searle is no less scornful in his recent writings.[5]

Perhaps the disclosure that brain science is a dedicated follower of fashion does place the SSSH in a slightly different light; but in the end the Searle-Lashley exposé does not establish very much. The fact that nowadays nobody is inclined to believe that the human skull is occupied by a jazzed-up water clock or a telephone switchboard scarcely suffices to prove that the brain is not a computer. The SSSH is an empirical theory and nothing but a careful study of the evidence can furnish an estimate of its credibility.

9.2   Hardware versus wetware

As everyone knows, the sundry electrical and mechanical bits and pieces that fill the plastic or metal skin of a commercial computer are known collectively as hardware. The juicy folds of grey and white tissue that fill the human skull are known as *wetware* by those enamoured of the computer analogy. This section investigates the extent of the similarity between the two.

Wetware consists predominantly of two categories of cells: neurons and neuroglia. Neurons are the stars of the ensemble. The dull neuroglia, which in fact outnumber neurons by ten to one, play a variety of supporting roles.

These include clearing away dead neurons and ensuring that live ones remain comfortably immersed in their baths of nutrient.

Each neuron sports an enormous number of connecting fibres, known as dendritic projections and axonal projections (see figure 9.1). These fibres snake about the brain, connecting each single neuron to maybe ten thousand of its neighbours. Picture a neuron as a body with many hands and feet. Each hand (axonal projection) grasps a neighbour's foot (dendritic projection).[6] The bodies hang there, each the centre of a tangled web of linked projections – a web of awesome complexity. At a very conservative estimate of a thousand 'hands' per neuron and 10^{12} neurons per head (that's a million with six more zeroes added) there are a staggering total of one thousand million million inter-neural connections in each brain. In the words of Steven Rose, an eminent neurobiologist: 'The mass of processes, structures and interactions possible within this [maze] beggars both description and mathematicization. The fascination is almost akin to terror . . .'[7]

In 1843 it was discovered that the nervous system is primarily electrical in its operation, and by the early 1940s a detailed picture had emerged of the neuron as a receiver and transmitter of pulses of electricity. A neuron's main purpose in life appeared to be to emit short bursts of electricity to its neighbours, with the axonal projections functioning as output fibres and the dendritic projections functioning as input fibres. An electrical discharge develops in the cell body, travels along the axon, or 'tail', to the tree of output fibres, and ultimately tickles the input fibres of a myriad adjoining neurons.[8] It seems that a discharge is produced in a neuron whenever a sufficient number of the neurons connected to its input fibres are themselves 'firing'. If, say, more than 700 of the cell's thousand feet are tickled, it automatically fires and tickles all the feet that its hands are clutching.

This account is interesting enough, but when all is said and done it is aggravatingly uninformative – even circular. A neuron fires pulses at its neighbours but these serve only to incite *them* to fire pulses at *their* neighbours. What can be the point of it all? The hundred years of study between 1840 and 1940 produced a large amount of detailed knowledge concerning the chemical, electrical and cellular properties of neurons, yet this knowledge was nothing compared to the vast blank that remained on the map. What could these individually well-understood cells be doing as they work mysteriously together in their vast and grotesquely complicated webs? What rhyme or reason could there be to their cooperative behaviour? The detailed study of the properties of individual neurons had revealed little about how the brain as a whole operates.

In hindsight, this is hardly surprising. Think how much you could learn about the organization and functioning of a computer from a detailed study of the properties of its individual transistors – close to zilch. The time was ripe for a theory taking a higher-level perspective. Enter Warren McCulloch, neurophysiologist, and Walter Pitts, mathematician. In 1943 they published an

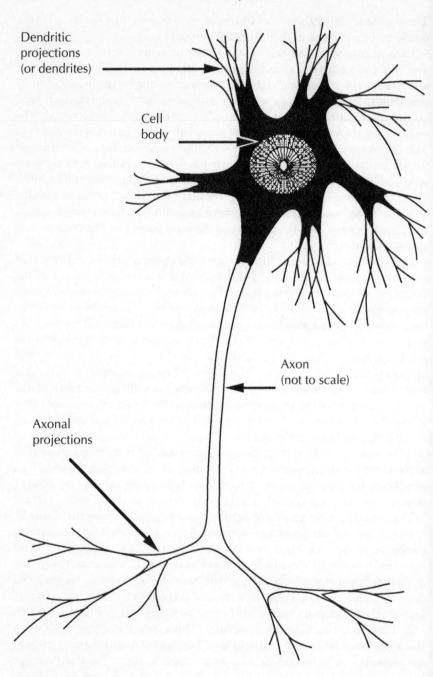

Dendritic
projections
(or dendrites)

Cell
body

Axon
(not to scale)

Axonal
projections

Figure 9.1 Human neuron.

historic article with the forbidding title 'A Logical Calculus of the Ideas Immanent in Nervous Activity'. Brain science was never to be the same again.

McCulloch and Pitts proposed that each neuron be regarded as either On or Off, with no in-between states. On their theory, all that matters about a neuron is whether it is firing or not – everything else (such as the intensity of the burst or fluctuations in the cell's chemical composition) is classed as inessential detail and ignored. (In the same way, an explanation of how a bicycle pump works will ignore such things as colour, weight and chemical composition.) So, granted that the neuron is a simple On/Off switch, it can be viewed as a device for physically realising one or other of two symbols. Yes or No, True or False, 0 or 1: as with the bits manipulated by an artificial computer it hardly matters how you choose to write these symbols in English.

Enlarging on this theme, McCulloch and Pitts explained how small groups of neurons could function as very simple symbol-manipulators. For example, three neurons can be connected together in such a way that the third fires when, and only when, both the other two do. In the terminology of chapter 4, this symbol-manipulator executes the instruction: write a cross (or 1 or Yes or True) at location 3 if, and only if, locations 1 and 2 both contain crosses.

Computers are full of devices such as this. Electrical engineers call them 'logic gates'. (If you are familiar with logical truth tables, you will see that the gate I have just described does the work of the truth table for 'and'. Note 9 gives the table.) However, McCulloch and Pitts themselves were writing just before the computer age began. Towards the end of their article they drew an abstract comparison between a net of interconnected neurons and a Turing machine (section 6.4); but apart from this there was no mention of computers in the article. It was not until two years later that information first began to circulate about the design of the ENIAC and the EDVAC. The connections with what McCulloch and Pitts had said were startling, and suddenly a lot of people were putting two and two together. Maybe neurons were much the same sort of things as the EDVAC's binary logic gates and flip-flops.

Half a century on, it is clear that people were putting two and two together to make five. Even at the time there was a certain amount of nagging evidence regarding the dissimilarities between neurons and computing hardware (evidence which was striking enough to make computer pioneer John von Neumann doubt whether the brain is a computer).[10] One difficulty was the existence of a body of evidence suggesting that '*On or Off*' was certainly not the only important feature of a neuron's operation. For example, the *rate* at which a neuron emits pulses of electricity seems to play a vital role in the brain's processing, whereas the rate at which a flip-flop flips has no computational significance.

Another known dissimilarity between neurons and hardware concerns connection density. Each neuron has an enormous number of input and output connections (some boast as many as 100,000 of each). In stark contrast, the connections emanating from a flip-flop or a logic gate can be counted on the fingers of one hand. A third difficulty concerns diversity. While the central processor of a computer contains only a few kinds of basic hardware units (in effect just flip-flops and gates), the brain contains many different sorts of neurons. Some are shaped like pyramids, some like stars, some like spindles, some like chandeliers.[11] Nor is it likely that these variations can be written off as 'inessential detail'. This is because there seems to be a correlation between a neuron's type and its specific function, with differently-shaped neurons predominating in different areas of the brain.

So there is, in fact, only a superficial similarity between neurons and the basic components of manufactured computers. To quote Thomas Poggio, one of a new breed of AI researchers who are taking a close interest in neurophysiology: 'Neurons are complex devices, very different from the simple digital switches . . . portrayed by . . . McCulloch and Pitts.'[12] Yet this is only one of many difficulties for the supposed analogy between hardware and wetware that have become apparent. It is now realized that the analogy breaks down in a number of fundamental ways. The remainder of this section gives a point by point analysis of the breakdown.

The 100 step limitation[13]

In comparison with electronic hardware the brain is slow, slow, slow. Individual hardware events – a flip-flop shifting position from 0 to 1, for example – take around a thousand-millionth of a second to happen, whereas a neuron needs a full thousandth of a second or so to respond to a tickle on its feet with a burst of electricity along its arms. In terms of basic electrical operations, then, a brain takes a million times longer to do its thing than the humblest personal computer (and bear in mind that a million times one second is almost a fortnight).

Let's suppose for the sake of argument that the brain works by following a program; that is, suppose the brain works by stepping through a series of instructions one at a time, just as a computer running an AI program does. Let's see where this supposition leads us. Because of the time that a neuron takes to operate, a thousandth of a second, the brain would need *at least* this long to obey each instruction (or much longer if the instruction requires a number of successive cycles of activity). Thus the very *maximum* number of instructions that could be dealt with in a tenth of a second is 100 – and a tenth of a second is roughly the time the brain takes to extract the meaning from a sentence or to recognize a visual pattern. It follows that *if* the brain accomplishes tasks like these by stepping through a program, then the program for each task is at most 100 instructions long. And that's ridiculous. Current AI programs contain thousand upon thousand of instructions: 100 is pathetically small beer. Writing a speech-processing or visual-recognition program in 100 lines is akin to feeding 5000 people with five loaves and two little fishes.

We are led inexorably to the conclusion that whatever else the brain might be, it certainly isn't a device that runs traditionally conceived AI programs. The operations that take place in Roger Schank's computer as it runs Sam must bear vanishingly little resemblance to what goes on inside Schank's own head.

Parallel activity

Common or garden computers are known as *sequential processors*, because they slog through their instructions in sequence, obeying them one after another. A parallel processor, on the other hand, is one that performs many operations simultaneously (or 'in parallel'). For example, suppose Ali Baba crouches hidden inside one of forty jars. A sequential processor would locate him by stepping through the instructions *Check jar 1, Check jar 2* . . . A parallel processor consisting of forty appropriately positioned slaves would locate Ali by obeying all forty instructions simultaneously. The obvious advantage a parallel device has over a sequential one is speed. It is odds on that a machine – or organ – with sluggishly functioning components and a parallel mode of operation would be able to thrash a competitor with high speed components but a sequential mode of operation. (The exception, of course, is if the task in question happens to be one which, by its nature, necessitates a sequential approach.[14] A simple example is the task of calculating the series 2^2, $(2^2)^3$, $((2^2)^3)^4$ etc.)

The 100 Step Limitation constitutes strong evidence that the brain somehow operates in parallel.[15] If each 'step' consists of thousands of operations performed simultaneously then a vast amount of processing can be packed into the tenth of a second or so that the brain takes to identify a visual pattern or ascribe meaning to a sentence. (Anatomical studies tend to confirm that the brain is some kind of parallel device: the pattern of parallel, simultaneously operating layers of neurons is repeated everywhere.)

However, it is something of a tradition, in some circles, to disparage the distinction between parallel and sequential processing. Philosopher Aaron Sloman insists that 'the distinction . . . has not much theoretical significance'; and Roger Schank has described it as 'one of AI's wonderful red herrings'.[16] The usual reason for thinking the distinction can't matter much is that whatever can be done in parallel can also be done sequentially: instead of doing a welter of things at once, just take it easy and do them one at a time. Any amount of parallel processing can be simulated on a sequential machine.

The weakness of this traditional line of reasoning lies in its failure to heed the known complexity of the brain. Take the numbers seriously and an entirely different picture emerges. 'If current estimates of the number of [connections] in the brain are anywhere near correct,' writes James McClelland (a leading critic of traditional AI), 'it would take even the fastest of today's computers something between several years and several centuries to simulate the processing that can take place within the human brain in one second.'[17] When the tortoise is seen in its true colours, Achilles is left without a prayer.

Memory recall

Each specific memory location in a computer has a unique *address* (section 4.3). As with houses, the addresses are formed by simply numbering the locations. (Thus the storage location with address 10 might contain my Social Security number, and the location with address 11, the date of my birth.) These addresses form a program's only link with the memory store: a piece of information cannot be retrieved unless its numerical address is stated in the program. For example, if the program is to multiply the total number of lettuces sold by the unit wholesale price, it needs to know the addresses at which these two pieces of information have been placed. No address, no recollection.[18]

Human beings, on the other hand, retrieve a memory not by means of a pre-assigned address but via a *description* of the information required. The question 'What did we feed you last time we had you round?' describes the information the speaker is after and equipped with the description my brain will probably be able to haul out the memory in question.

Each piece of information in a computer's memory has a *single* address or 'handle'. In contrast, the human brain is capable of using any one of an open-ended collection of descriptions to retrieve one and the same fact. For instance, my hostess might have prompted exactly the same recollection by asking 'What did we eat the evening we saw that play about Turing?'.

The general principle seems to be that if *part* of the content of a memory is specified (last meal round at Martha's; meal consumed with Martha before trip to see 'The Imitation Game') then the brain is able to retrieve the rest of the memory. For this reason, human memories are called *content-addressable*: access to them is via their content. In a computer, on the other hand, access is via an address that bears as much relation to the content of the memory as the number of a house bears to the furnishings inside.

Often the description that initiates human recall will relate to a very abstract aspect of the memory in question. Here is a striking example. 'A friend told me recently that [in] the first edition of *Encyclopaedia Britannica* . . . *A* was given 511 pages and *M* through *Z* were given 753 pages altogether! This amusing fact instantaneously triggered the retrieval of another memory, implanted in my mind years ago under totally unremembered circumstances, of how records used to be made back in the days when there was no magnetic tape and the master disk was actually cut during the live performance. The performers would be singing or playing along and all of a sudden the recording engineer would notice that there was not much room left on the disk, and so the performers would be given a signal to hurry up. As a result the tempo would be faster the closer to the center of the disk the needle got.'[19]

The snippet of content that served to retrieve this memory is so abstract that it is hard to pin down in words: something to do with more space being given to earlier parts than to later ones. The example illustrates vividly the open-endedness of the access that we have to our memories. There is no telling which aspect of a memory's content may serve to retrieve it – a far cry from the rigid use of a single pre-assigned address.

The computer is a brilliant mimic. Given enough ingenuity on the part of the programmer, a computer can be persuaded to imitate any number of things which it isn't, from a nuclear explosion to a cow's stomach. Because content-addressability is such a desirable feature for a memory system to possess, considerable effort has been invested in trying to devise programs that will enable computers to imitate content-addressable systems. So far, however, only clumsy parodies have been achieved. One method is to let the computer search exhaustively through all the items in its memory until the one with the content in question is located. A more efficient method makes use of 'hashing'. Hash coding (or scatter storage) is a programming technique that allows the computer to retrieve a piece of data when presented with a pre-arranged part of it, known as the probe (or key). For example, if the piece of data to be retrieved is the sentence 'Kant wrote the *Critique of Pure Reason*', the probe might be the fragment 'Kant wrote'. The trick is to store the data at a memory location whose address can be *calculated* from the probe by means of some pre-arranged function. The programmer might, for instance, choose to store the data at the location whose address is the number that results from adding the ASCII codes of all the letters in the probe. (Various standard techniques are in use; they are known collectively as hash functions.[20]) The computer responds to the probe by calculating the corresponding address and retrieving the data the programmer has stored there. The obvious limitation of this method is that the programmer has to specify the probes in advance. The method thus fails to capture what I am calling the open-endedness of the access we have to the information stored in our brains: there is no telling in advance which 'part' of a given memory may serve as a 'probe'. Nobody has come near to cracking the problem of reconciling the computer's system of content-blind addresses with the open-endedness of human recall.

Distribution

In a computer, each string of symbol tokens exists at a specific physical location in the hardware – on a length of magnetic tape, perhaps, or stored in a row of flip-flops. An engineer could put a piece of hardware under a microscope, point to a particular location and say 'That's where the memory that blah is stored – just *there*.' The memory could be destroyed completely by wiping the location clean (and any locations that happen to contain copies, of course). A computer's memory store is often compared to a filing cabinet or a library: each parcel of information is stored in a particular place and retrieval involves 'going to the place and fetching the information'.

We commonly liken our own memories to filing cabinets. This is probably a complete misconception. There is strong evidence that human memory does not function on the principle of 'each item at its own location'. Earlier this century Karl Lashley performed a range of studies on animals, particularly rats, initially with the intention of finding the exact sites of specific memories in the brain. He used a technique known as *ablation*. In a typical experiment 100 rats would be trained to learn a route through a maze to a food reward. Once the rats had memorized the route Lashley would surgically remove (ablate) a different area of cortex from each of them. The rats were then allowed to run the maze again. Lashley obtained the highly counter-intuitive result that destroying up to about ten percent of the cortex produced very little effect on memory no matter where the destruction occurred. When more cortex than this was removed, the number of errors made in running the maze was found to be proportional to the surface area of the destruction but unrelated to its position.[21] The memory of the correct route seemed not to be stored anywhere in particular.

In 1950 Lashley summed up the results of thirty-three years of ablation studies like this:

> It is not possible to demonstrate the isolated localisation of a memory trace anywhere within the nervous system . . . The [trace] is represented throughout the region . . . The conclusion is justified, I believe . . . that all of the cells of the brain are constantly active and are participating, by a sort of algebraic summation, in every activity. There are no special cells reserved for special memories . . . [E]very instance of recall requires the activity of literally millions of neurons. The same neurons which retain the memory traces of one experience must also participate in countless other activities.[22]

These results were a puzzle to Lashley. As he remarked with irony: 'I sometimes feel, in reviewing the evidence on the localization of the memory trace, that the necessary conclusion is that learning just is not possible. It is difficult to conceive of a mechanism which can satisfy the conditions set for it.'[23] How can it possibly be, asked Lashley, that the information in the cortex is not stored anywhere in particular but rather is *everywhere*?

A decade or so after Lashley wrote these words the newly invented technique of holography provided memory researchers with a model of information storage that could accommodate his perplexing results.[24] Holograms are 'laser photographs'; their most familiar feature is the eerie three-dimensional effect produced when light from a laser is projected through the photographic plate. If you hold the plate up to an ordinary light, it looks nothing like an ordinary photographic negative. No picture at all is discernible on it, just a blurry mess. Surprisingly, any small piece of this blur has the entire scene stored in it. The result of cutting a hole in the plate is remarkably similar to the effect that tissue loss has on memory: there is an overall softening of detail in the projected picture but no specific part of the scene disappears. A holographic plate is an example of what is now called a *distributed* information storage system: that is, a system in which the individual pieces of information do not occupy separate locations, but are spread uniformly throughout the storage medium. Lashley's pioneering results are an indication that the brain makes considerable use of distributed storage.

Recent studies have tended to confirm Lashley's broad conclusion that there is in general no obvious relationship between the precise location of a lesion (i.e. an area of destruction) and the resulting behavioural deficit.[25] However, when judged by today's standards, his experimental methods were somewhat crude, and few now accept his findings in their entirety. His hypothesis that 'there are no special cells reserved for special memories' is dubious, as is his suggestion that every cognitive activity involves all the cells of the brain. Microelectrode studies of the behaviour of single neurons (which involve lowering a fine wire into the brain of a conscious animal) have revealed the presence of neurons that respond maximally to highly specific stimuli. For example, the higher visual cortex of the macaque monkey contains single neurons that seem to be triggered by the appearance of a monkey hand anywhere in the monkey's field of vision.[26] Here, it seems, is exactly the kind of specificity that Lashley denied.

The general thrust of the evidence provided by microelectrode studies is that cells exhibiting such extreme specificity may be considerably fewer in number than less specialized cells. Single neurons generally respond to a wide range of different stimuli, indicating that each neuron may be implicated in the storage of many different pieces of information.[27] Even the 'monkey hand cell' will respond to stimuli other than a hand, although the response is weaker.[28]

At the present stage, the overall picture is far from clear, and there is considerable disagreement among neuroscientists concerning the number of neurons that the brain may use to store a memory trace. James Anderson and Michael Mozer conjecture that between seven hundred thousand and seven million neurons participate in the storage of a single trace (an estimate considerably lower than Lashley's).[29] At the opposite end of the scale Horace Barlow suggests that the number may be as low as 1000 neurons (a figure that many regard as too low to be consistent with the results of ablation and lesion studies).[30]

If Anderson and Mozer are right then the brain's memory traces are massively distributed, as a bit of number juggling will show. Their figure of seven million represents about ten percent of the neurons in the primary visual cortex.[31] Say that in the course of your life so far your brain has stored away N visual memories. Obviously N is a huge number. On the assumption that every one of the memories requires ten percent of the available neurons to store it, each single neuron must participate in the storage of N/10 visual memories (whereas in a computer each flip-flop participates in the storage of exactly one bit of information). Given the size of N, this is distribution on a grand scale.

It is clear that human memory is very different in nature from the non-distributed, address-driven stores of today's computers.

Graceful degradation

Computers tend to expire upon the slightest injury. A sharp poke with a screwdriver practically anywhere inside the central processor and the whole machine will go haywire. In the old days, when electronic components were notoriously unreliable, computers used to spend much more time in a state of complete paralysis than in operation; and even now the failure of a single paltry semiconductor can bring a multi-million dollar installation to its knees. Things are entirely different in the case of wetware. It stands up well to damage. Even injury on a massive scale may have little or no effect on the brain's central functions – as witnessed by the famous case of Phineas Gage, a railway worker. Within minutes of having the anterior and middle left lobes of his cerebrum smashed by a speeding iron rod, Gage was conscious, collected, and speaking. According to John Harlow, Gage's physician, the effect of the damage and the ensuing infection was to leave him 'fitful, irreverent . . . obstinate . . . vacillating . . . indulging at times in the grossest profanity . . . impatient of restraint or advice . . . [yet] with the animal passions of a strong man'.[32] Gage lived a travelling life for thirteen years after the accident, eventually dying of unknown causes.

Laboratory studies of subjects who have lost small amounts of brain tissue (by injury or surgery) indicate that damage produces a graded impairment of performance. The more tissue you lose, the worse you become at, say, discriminating visual patterns or comprehending speech (the precise nature of the impairment depends on where in the brain the assault occurs). There is no sudden breakdown. The performance of a brain degrades gradually and gracefully as damage increases, whereas a computer goes down with a crash at the first peep of trouble.[33] Again we find a profound lack of similarity between hardware and wetware.

9.3　Goodbye, von Neumann

It would please opponents of the SSSH if one could conclude from this list of disanalogies between wetware and hardware that the brain is not a computer. Several writers in fact do so. In the opinion of philosopher Patricia Churchland 'these differences [make] the metaphor that identifies the brain with a computer seem more than a trifle thin'; and biologist John Young bluntly asserts on the basis of such differences that 'the computer analogy is grossly inadequate to describe the operation of the brain'.[34] No such conclusion can be drawn, however. All that can properly be concluded is that the brain does not have what is known as a *von Neumann architecture*. Let me explain.

When the ENIAC team broke up in 1946, John von Neumann set about reorganizing and extending the design of this pioneer machine. The result was a set of brilliant architectural proposals that have been the mainstay of computer design ever since.[35] A computer built in accordance with von Neumann's specifications is known simply as a von Neumann machine. Even today, von Neumann architecture remains virtually universal in the computer industry.

A list of the central features of von Neumann architecture reads almost like a re-run of the points raised in the preceding section.

1   A von Neumann machine is a sequential processor: it executes the instructions in its program one after another.[36]
2   Each string of symbols is stored at a specific memory location.
3   Access to a stored string always proceeds via the numerical address of the string's location.
4   There is a single 'seat of control', the central processing unit or CPU.

The CPU contains a special register, the 'instruction register', into which instructions are fed one at a time (see section 4.3). For example, suppose the bit-code for 'shift' enters the instruction register. (As explained in section 4.4, the function of this instruction is to shift everything in a register one place to the right. The bit at the far right of the register 'falls out' and a zero is fed in at the far left. The result of shifting 0101 is 0010.) The arrival of the instruction in the instruction register initiates a three part cycle of activity in the CPU. First, the symbol string to be operated upon is transferred from main memory to a short term storage register or 'buffer' inside the CPU. Second, the shift is performed and the resulting string placed in short term storage inside the CPU. Third, the string is transferred from its temporary location to the original address in main memory. This three part cycle is known as the fetch-operate-store cycle. It is in the nature of a machine that works like this to degrade ungracefully, since the continuing good health of each part of the central processor is necessary for proper functioning. If any of its registers fail, the activity of the central processing unit must halt.

The upshot of the preceding section is that the brain is not a von Neumann machine. However, it in no way follows from this that the brain is not a computer. Von Neumann architecture is merely one approach to the construction of universal symbol systems – an approach which has evolved and thrived in the engineering environment parochial to the latter half of the twentieth century. It is hardly likely to be the last word. If the brain had turned out to be a von Neumann machine it would have been only marginally less surprising than if the heart had turned out to be an Archimedean screw. Von Neumann architecture is nothing more than the first manifestation of a new and ongoing technology.

1   There is no necessary connection between symbol manipulation and sequential processing. In recent years there has been considerable progress in designing experimental hardware that operates in parallel (although nothing like the degree of parallelism found in the brain has been achieved). Computers with a parallel architecture are referred to as 'non-von' machines.

2   The memory system of a symbol-manipulator need not be based on the method of numerical addresses. A computer that uses a distributed, content-addressable storage system is certainly a possibility – although at the present time such a device is little more than a gleam in a few researchers' eyes.

3   Von Neumann's idea of a single central processing unit goes hand-in-hand with a sequential mode of operation and the chances are that future parallel architectures will replace centralized control by multilateral cooperation.

The SSSH is completely silent on architectural matters. It maintains only that the brain is a universal symbol system. The issues of parallel activity, distribution and so forth have no bearing on the truth or falsity of the hypothesis. As Zenon Pylyshyn says, 'It is the failure to distinguish computation as a type of process from the particular physical form it takes in current computing machines that has prevented many people from taking computation as a literal account of mental process[es].'[37] The SSSH leaves it entirely open how the brain stores its symbols and how it organizes its operations on them. Cognitive scientists see these as matters for detailed empirical investigation by methods yet to be developed.

The state of play so far

Although the facts reviewed in section 9.2 have no bearing on the actual truth or falsity of the SSSH they nevertheless have an important role to play in the enquiry we are pursuing. They make it clear that brains bear little or no resemblance to computers as we currently know and understand them, and this highlights the schematic nature of the SSSH. The SSSH contains a number of 'placeholders' – unknowns that we cannot yet fill in. The theory that the brain is a von Neumann machine is at least a precise and detailed claim, something that can be measured against the evidence; whereas the theory that the brain is a computer of unknown architecture, using unknown symbols and unknown fundamental operations, is sketchy and schematic. In time, no doubt, these unknowns will be replaced by detailed, experimentally testable proposals; but for now this inexactness, coupled with our limited experimental data concerning brain function, puts the SSSH well beyond the reach of either refutation or confirmation by empirical means.

Philosophical arguments flourish in areas where empirical evidence is thin on the ground and it is chiefly to philosophical considerations that cognitive scientists turn when marshalling support for the SSSH. The next step of our enquiry, then, is to examine the arguments that they put foward. This is the agenda for the next four sections.

First, though, I want to quickly clear out of the way an argument that might be raised against the SSSH. This runs: many aspects of the brain's functioning have nothing to do with the manipulation of symbols; therefore the SSSH is incorrect.

Suppose, for example, that the din of your neighbour's lawnmower gives you a headache, or that you miss your bus and are thrown into a foul mood for the rest of the day. How could the development of a headache or the onset of a mood possibly consist of symbol manipulation? The central feature of symbol-strings is that, like sentences, they encode information. It is easy to see how the acquisition of a *belief* might consist of the formation of a string of symbols; but, unlike beliefs, headaches and moods do not encode information at all and so it is entirely mysterious how the process of acquiring them could be one of symbol manipulation.[38] These are the sorts of consideration that lie behind the premiss of the argument.

However, the premiss lends no support at all to the conclusion. A device that is centrally and cardinally a symbol processor can contain other activity besides symbol manipulation – just as a food processor will embrace activity apart from the manipulation of food (cooling and lubrication systems are permitted). Cognitive science is certainly not committed to viewing *everything* that happens in the brain in terms of symbol manipulation. The brain is a mess of multifarious activity, and the SSSH concerns only those processes that are centrally involved in thought and the production of intelligent behaviour.

9.4 Putting meaning into meat

Courtesy of my brain I am able to do such things as forsee possible consequences of my actions, reason from the observed to the unobserved, and desire that certain situations are otherwise. A precondition for my being able to do any of this is that my brain be capable of forming *representations* of events, facts, and states-of-affairs, both actual and potential. For example, my brain has some way of representing the fact that tomato sauce will leave a nasty stain if you spill it down your shirt: somehow or other my brain contains that information.

To put it another way, certain of the goings-on in my brain have *meaning*, in the sense that these goings-on refer to and represent other things – objects, facts, events, and so on. How does this happen? After all, meat and meaning are at first blush unlikely partners, yet somehow they come together inside my skull. How? This is one of the many major gaps in our current understanding of the brain.

A more familiar type of meaning-bearing entity is the common or garden sentence, spoken or written, and its sundry derivatives, such as codes, technical notations, and the symbol strings that inhabit computers. The sentence 'Fido licks Brian' is a symbolic representation of the fact that Fido licks Brian – nothing easier. Would that the picture was equally simple in the case of the brain.

'But I think it is!' [This is a proponent of the SSSH coming in right on cue.[39]] 'Sentences, and linguistic symbols in general, provide the only real model we have for how a chunk of matter can represent a fact. We know that the brain must contain representational states, so it is natural to theorize that these states literally *are* sentences: the representations that the brain uses are sentence-like strings of symbols. That solves the problem of how meanings get into meat and also provides an explanation of what the brain is actually up to when it's reasoning, planning, and so on. It is manipulating these strings of symbols.'

Explain what you mean when you say the brain literally contains sentences. 'Well, I obviously don't mean that there are words kind of literally *written* in there. These symbols I'm talking about are physically realized in the brain by some sort of electrical or chemical activity. In a von Neumann machine the bit symbols are realised by magnetic fields, the states of flip-flops, and so forth. I've nothing to tell you about the method or methods employed in the brain. That's a matter for further empirical enquiry.'

Are you saying that when we think, we always do so in a language? 'Yes, in a way. I'm not saying that the brain thinks in sentences of English or German or whatever. You may feel you're doing that at a conscious level, but the level of brain activity that I'm talking about is way below consciousness (and, incidentally, way below the level of mental imagery, too).[40] The language of the brain can't be a familiar spoken language, simply because infants who haven't yet picked up a native language behave in ways which strongly indicate that they already have the ability to form mental representations. No, the language is some kind of special brain code. I call it Mentalese, just to give it a name. I'm inclined to believe that it's innate, part of our genetic endowment, rather than learned in any sense.'

In what ways are the representations that the brain uses supposed to be like sentences? Why call Mentalese a 'language'? 'I mean you to take me literally when I say these representations are sentence-like. That's the whole point of my theory. The basic picture is that on the one hand we've got this big mystery about how physical states in the brain represent facts, and on the other hand we've got these nice simple things, sentences, which provide a perfect model for how representation takes place. I'm saying, let's solve the mystery by postulating that these brain states literally are sentences. Which is to say that Mentalese representations share a number of central characteristics of ordinary-language sentences. There are two I lay particular emphasis on: first, what I call building from basic vocab units, and second using *form* to kind of 'capture' the meaning that you want. In English you start with basic vocab units, like 'Brian', 'Fido', 'licks' and 'kicks', and build sentences from them. I'm suggesting that Mentalese is similar in that respect. On the second point, it is the form or pattern in which you arrange the basic units that determines what fact is represented – Fido licks Brian, or Brian licks Fido. When I say that Mentalese is a language, I mean that Mentalese representations have both these features.'

Explain why all this amounts to saying that the brain is a computer. 'OK. The connection is very simple. On this theory a brain and a computer are one and the same type of device. Both work by manipulating the sentences of an internal linguistic code. Bit strings have the two features I just mentioned – they are built from basic vocab units and the pattern in which the units are arranged plays a crucial role in determining the meaning. (See section 4.2.) To give a simple example, if 1111 is the basic unit meaning 'copy' and 00 and 01 name two registers, you can combine these three units into two different patterns to get two different instructions – a copy from 00 to 01, or vice versa. By the way, you can see an important factor at work here, which I describe as *form* relating *meaning* to *activity*. If the instruction 1111 00 01 goes into the central processor the machine responds in one way and if 1111 01 00 goes in, a different action is caused. So you can see that in a computer it is the form or structure of a string which, so to speak, causally implements the meaning of the string. That's something which should appeal to a philosopher. Meanings are rather mysterious and abstract things, and at first sight it's something of a puzzle to see how an ethereal thing like a meaning could actually cause a machine to *do* something. In computers we see the puzzle resolved by the use of a symbolic code that reflects all the relevant meaning-distinctions by means of form-distinctions that the hardware is sensitive to. I'm saying that we have no idea how *else* meaning could be linked to activity, apart from via a structured symbolic code, and so I'm suggesting that there must be such a code in the brain.'[41]

It seems to me that all you've done is to suggest <u>an</u> explanation of how the brain represents facts. You haven't said anything to show that this is the correct explanation. 'That's fair comment. I haven't. But, as I say, nobody has any other ideas about how meaning could be linked to activity. Since ours is the only explanation in the wind we think it should be taken very seriously. As Lyndon B. Johnson once said, "I'm the only President you've got". We have a plausible theory that hangs together very nicely and has no rivals.'

We move on to a second argument in support of the SSSH.

9.5   Believing what you don't believe

Ibrahim, a carpet vendor, sits quietly with a Coke in a shady corner of the
bazaar. He startles as a fair headed foreigner steps from behind him. 'Hi,' she
says smiling engagingly. 'My name's Nancy. I'm touring your country on a
motor scooter.' Ibrahim's heart flutters and he considers how best to inveigle
Nancy to dine with him.

We now administer a short quiz to Ibrahim.

1   Do you intend to seek a dinner engagement with this attractive
    young tourist?
2   Do you intend to seek a dinner engagement with the Angel of Death?

For beneath the winsome smile that is Nancy's true identity.

Ibrahim answers *Yes* to the first question and a worried *No* to the second.
He espouses the goal of dining with Nancy and totally eschews the goal of
dining with the Angel of Death. It is a bit of a puzzle how this can be possible,
given that in some sense these are the *same* goal; but the fact remains that for
Ibrahim they are somehow different goals and he has (or had) the one, but has
never had the other.

Ibrahim, like all of us, can perform this difficult-looking trick with beliefs as
well as intentions. He has never believed the Angel of Death to be mortal, yet
he did believe Nancy to be so. (To make certain, let's go back in time and
preface the quiz with a question soliciting his opinion on Nancy's possible
immortality. Ibrahim is definite in his answer. 'She is as water spilt upon the
desert sand,' he replies. He would be equally obliging if asked to affirm his
belief that the Angel of Death, on the other hand, is not mortal.) Since Nancy
and the Angel of Death are the same person, the belief that Nancy is mortal is
in some sense one and the same as the belief that the Angel of Death is mortal
– yet, puzzlingly, Ibrahim is able to hold the one but not the other.

Where, you wonder, is this fantasy taking us? Phenomena such as these
– intending what you also do not intend, believing what you also do not
believe – constitute the so-called paradoxes of intentionality.[42] How are such
contradictory-seeming feats possible? Jerry Fodor and Zenon Pylyshyn have
an explanation to offer.

'A natural explanation of what it is to hold a belief,' writes Pylyshyn, 'is that
holding the belief consists in storing, in a special . . . "belief box", a token . . . of
a sentence of Mentalese.'[43] What Pylyshyn metaphorically describes as the brain's
'belief box' is its belief storage. (The idea is that being in this 'box', as opposed
to another one, is what *makes* something a belief rather than a goal or fear or
what have you.[44]) The hypothesis that the contents of the 'box' are sentences
of Mentalese explains Ibrahim's ability to believe that Nancy is mortal without

also believing that the Angel of Death is mortal. Some Mentalese symbol-structure X corresponds to the English sentence 'Nancy is mortal' and a different symbol-structure Y corresponds to the sentence 'The Angel of Death is mortal'. Even though X and Y record one and the same fact, it is obviously possible for Ibrahim's brain to have X but not Y in its 'belief box'. Here, then, is a neat and simple resolution of the paradoxes of intentionality.

To summarize the argument. If the acts of intending, believing, doubting etc. are analysed in terms of the brain's performing operations on symbol-structures, a range of common but initially paradoxical phenomena becomes readily comprehensible. This adds to the appeal of the analysis.

9.6 Productivity and systematicity

To say that thought is productive (in the technical sense involved in this third argument for the SSSH) is to say that in principle we are capable of thinking an unlimited number of thoughts. If thought is productive then, given an infinitely long life, a human being would be able to think an infinite number of different thoughts.

In a finite lifespan a person can think only a finite number of thoughts. Let's suppose some person manages exactly ten billion before the Angel of Death drops by. There will remain many other things that they could have thought but didn't – call these their potential thoughts. For example someone could easily pass their whole life without ever framing the thought 'It isn't the case that the Sydney Harbour bridge needs to be shaved each morning'. To deny that human thought is productive would be to claim that there is some maximum number N of actual and potential thoughts. You may feel that no matter how large a number N is claimed to be you would always be able to dream up another thought, an N+1st, no matter how bizarre (maybe even the thought that there are at least N+1 thoughts would do the trick). But just imagining that you can do this doesn't prove that you can, of course. It is an empirical matter. No one knows for certain whether human thought is productive. However, many people regard the hypothesis that it is as a plausible one. (Some of the advocates of parallel distributed processing – the approach to cognition discussed in the next chapter – are notable dissenters.[45]) In the words of Jerry Fodor, if thought is not productive then '[i]n principle it could turn out, after a lot of thinking, that your experience catches up with your cognitive capacities so that you actually succeed in thinking everything that you are able to'. He continues 'It's no good saying that you take this consequence to be absurd; I agree with you, but Aunty doesn't.'[46] (Section 10.8 contains some further discussion of the productivity issue.)

To say that human thought is *systematic*, in Fodor's sense, is to say that an ability to think some thoughts is 'intrinsically connected' to an ability to think others.[47] '[Y]ou don't find people who can think the thought that John loves the girl but can't think the thought that the girl loves John' explain Fodor and Pylyshyn.[48] If a person has the conceptual resources to think that possums smell worse than dingos then provided thought is systematic, they are bound to be able to think that dingos smell worse than possums. Notice that systematicity and productivity are distinct phenomena: you can agree with the claim that thought is systematic even if you happen to believe that thought is not productive.

Human language is productive. There is no limit to the number of grammatical sentences of English, say. This is easy to prove. Just pick any (true) sentence, P, and keep on going like this: 'P' is true, '"P" is true' is true, '"'P' is true' is true' is true . . . They pretty soon get unwieldy but each of them is grammatical (indeed is true) and there is no limit to the number of them.

Is English systematic? Fodor and Pylyshyn think so.

> You don't, for example, find native speakers who know how to say in English that John loves Mary but don't know how to say in English that Mary loves John. If you did find someone in such a fix, you'd take that as presumptive evidence that he's not a native English speaker but some sort of tourist.[49]

In fact, the question of the systematicity of English is less straightforward than the question of its productivity. For it is not completely clear what systematicity amounts to. Productivity is a property of the English language per se. Fodor and Pylyshyn do not make it clear whether systematicity is likewise supposed to be a property of a language per se or whether it is rather a relation that holds between the language and certain speakers of it. They owe us a clear account of precisely what it means to say that a language is systematic. But this is a relatively small complaint and we need not linger over it.

Now the argument for the SSSH. Let's take it that thought is productive. How does the brain manage this? Well, we know that language is productive so the simplest explanation to hand for the productivity of thought is that thought is linguistic. If each of our thoughts is a sentence of Mentalese then we will be able in principle to think an unlimited number of thoughts. Thought is productive because Mentalese is. Or if you are unwilling to assume that thought is productive then take the claim that thought is systematic. How does the brain manage it? Same story – the systematicity of Mentalese can be recruited to explain the systematicity of thought. Either way we get an argument for the existence of Mentalese.[50]

9.7 Evaluating the arguments

Reducing the arguments of sections 9.4, 9.5 and 9.6 to their essentials, each comes down to the claim that one *possible* way of explaining the phenomena in question (the productivity and systematicity of thought, the paradoxes of intentionality and the brain's fundamental ability to represent facts) is to postulate an internal symbolic code. A cartoon analogy highlights the weakness of this form of argument. Phenomenon: Fido bites Brian. A possible explanation: Fido believes that Brian has a rare illness which only a dogbite can cure. Devising a *possible* explanation is one thing, demonstrating that it is the *correct* explanation is something entirely different – and something which the three arguments do not begin to address.

In my view Fodor and Pylyshyn are right to maintain that the paradoxes of intentionality lend a certain amount of support to the idea that the brain is capable of forming several different representations of one and the same fact. However, the considerations raised by the paradoxes go no way toward showing that these representations are sentences of Mentalese; and this is the crucial issue. The brain may well be able to form different representations of the same fact, but these representations need not be the symbol strings postulated by the SSSH.

Fodor and Pylyshyn attempt to quash such scepticism by insisting that the Mentalese hypothesis is the only reasonable explanation on offer for the phenomena in question. Pylyshyn describes it as 'the only straw afloat' and Fodor takes the gag 'I'm the only President you've got' as his epigraph.[51] The trouble is, though, that there *are* other straws afloat and some look no less promising than the Mentalese hypothesis. The next chapter is devoted to one such straw. A floating straw that was much discussed in Turing's time and has recently been repopularized by Phil Johnson-Laird and Colin McGinn (among others) is the hypothesis that the brain processes *analogue* representations.[52]

A simple example of an analogue representation is an architect's three-dimensional model of a building. Features of the real building are represented by the corresponding features of elements of the model. Roof angles are represented by the angles between the sheets of card that represent the roof; the number and shape of the panes of glass in each window are represented by the number and shape of the plastic insets in the pieces of card that represent the walls, and so on. There are many different types of analogue representation – scale models of all kinds, maps, pictures, graphs, and the images on the retina, to name but a few.

Graphs are an interesting case. In the architect's model, angle is represented by angle, number by number and shape by shape, and in maps distance is represented by distance. The example of graphs makes it plain that analogue representation need not always be of like by like. In a graph a distance along an axis can represent an object's mass or speed or intelligence or . . .

It is not easy to say precisely what it is that analogue representations have in common with each other. Nevertheless, the basic idea is clear enough. As McGinn puts it 'In analogue [representations] properties of the represented states of affairs are somehow *reflected* in features of the [representation] itself'.[53] In an analogue representation the features doing the representing, the 'representors', vary in a way that reflects or apes or models variation in the 'representees' – more plastic squares means more windows, darker blue on a chart means deeper water, a greater displacement from 0 on the graph means a higher intelligence.[54]

Analogue representations are strikingly different from linguistic representations. Consider maps. The fact that the motorway between London and Leeds is longer than the motorway between London and Birmingham is represented by the fact that one blue line on the map is longer than another blue line – as everyone knows, road lines on maps represent length by means of their length, which varies in proportion to the length of the road represented. Sentences, on the other hand, obviously do not represent by means of possessing a property whose magnitude varies in proportion to the magnitude of the property that is being represented. The symbol-string 'The London-Birmingham motorway is 120 miles long' is actually longer than the string 'The London-Leeds motorway is 198 miles long', and even if you were to make the latter the longer string by padding it with gaps this would have no representational significance whatsoever. To extract information from an analogue representation you need something like a scale, and this concept is completely foreign to sentential representations.

Analogue representations are often referred to simply as *models*. Perhaps the brain uses models. Maybe the brain's representations of the external world are analogue and are manipulated by processes that are themselves analogous to manipulations that can be performed physically on the represented objects – such as rotating and bending. (In like fashion the architect's model can be manipulated by processes analogous to manipulations that can be performed on the real building – additional doorways can be cut into the model's walls, skylights can be repositioned, and so forth.) This is a very different picture of the brain from the one that the SSSH paints – sentential representations manipulated by fundamental operations from the same stable as those of a von Neumann machine.

McGinn (following Craik) gives this sketch of the problem-solving process for an analogue brain.

> First, an external state of affairs is 'translated' into an analogue representation: in the simplest case this will involve the perceptual generation of a suitable model – the state of affairs outside causes the brain to construct an internal simulation of that state of affairs. Second, the model will be manipulated by various procedures and algorithms that transform it, relate it to other models, work experimentally on it – these procedures being themselves analogues of external processes. Third, there will be some appropriate output of these internal operations – either action (if the reasoning was practical) or a new belief (if the reasoning was theoretical). These are the three phases gone through by an engineer modelling a bridge, and these are the three phases involved in the brain's solving a problem by means of its internal models . . . Problem-directed thinking is experimenting on analogue representations generated and stored in the brain; as it were, conducting dry-runs on cerebral copies or replicas.[55]

This alternative picture may be even vaguer than the SSSH but it is that much – an alternative.[56]

Psychologist Irving Biederman has recently suggested that in vision, and in particular in the course of visual recognition, the brain makes use of a species of analogue representation known as *geonic representation*.[57] The basic units of geonic representations are *geons*. These are simple, typically symmetrical volumes such as cylinders, bricks, spheres, cones, horns, wedges, and flat rectangular plates. Biederman's idea is that the objects our eyes alight upon can be approximated by arrays of geons. To give some very simple examples, a table lamp can be approximated by means of a cone with its top sliced off (representing the shade) and a cylinder (representing the stand); and a torch can be represented by a long cylinder (the body), a wider, stubbier cylinder (the lamp housing) and a tiny brick (the switch).[58] (Two table lamps of identical shape but different size can be represented by means of two arrays of different volume.[59]) Geons form the basis for a powerful representational system. Biederman estimates that a system using only thirty-six primitive geons would have the potential to represent 154 million objects containing three or fewer principal segments – a figure considerably in excess of the actual number of objects that a normal adult can recognize.

Geonic representations can be combined to form representations of complex scenes and objects. A geonic representation of a highly complex object like a space shuttle can be generated from geonic representations of its components by arranging them in such a way that the spatial relationships between the components are modelled.

As Biederman remarks, the geonic representational method derives its power from essentially the same source as the sentential method.

> In both cases, the representational power derives from the enormous number of combinations that can arise from a modest number of primitives. The relations in speech are limited to left-to-right (sequential) orderings; in the visual domain a richer set of possible relations allows a far greater representational capacity from a comparable number of primitives.[60]

In the present context, one of the most interesting things about geonic representations is that, like sentential representations, they possess recursive structure.[61] A geonic representation is defined to be some number of geonic representations in spatial relationship to one another. This possesses the same 'circularity' as the recursive definition of 'identifier' that I gave in section 4.2: the term 'geonic representation' appears on both sides of the definition. The 'recursive spiral' bottoms out with the geons themselves, the simplest geonic representations.

Recursive representational systems are productive. The basic geons can be combined into an in principle unlimited number of geonic representations (of objects real and unreal). Moreover geonic representations seem to be systematic in Fodor's sense. If you have the geonic resources to represent a cat sitting on a person then you also have the resources to represent a person sitting on a cat. The geonic system demonstrates that analogue representational systems can be both productive and systematic.

Each of the three arguments for the SSSH invites a sceptical response. The Mentalese hypothesis is one answer to the puzzle of how meat and meaning come together but it is not the only possible answer. The brain could do its representing by means of mental models, not sentences of Mentalese. The paradoxes of intentionality can be accounted for by postulating that the brain is capable of representing the same fact in a number of ways; but these representations may be analogue ones. The productivity and systematicity of thought can be explained by the hypothesis that we think in Mentalese, but can be explained just as well by the hypothesis that we think in an analogue medium.

9.8   The meaning of 'computer'

'Ah, but even if the brain isn't a symbol-manipulator, it could still turn out to be a computer of some other sort!' That is a natural remark for someone to make at this stage of the discussion; and it is, of course, true that the meaning of the word 'computer' can be widened so that symbol-manipulators become just one type of computer. I want to point out the perils of such wordplay.

Turing once predicted that within fifty years the meaning of the word 'think' will change so much that 'one will be able to speak of machines thinking without expecting to be contradicted'.[62] Analogously, I believe that within 100 years the meaning of the word 'computer' will change so much that one will be able to call the brain a computer without expecting to be contradicted. Technical terms do change their meanings. For instance, naval officers will nowadays often refer to sonar equipment as 'radar' – a reasonable enough extension, given that the 'two' perform a similar function and have a similar user-interface. (In the original sense of the terms, radar equipment detects distant objects by means of radio waves and sonar by sound waves.) The successors of today's computers will no doubt retain the name 'computer', whether or not they are symbol-manipulators.

However, none of this relieves us of the obligation to assign, here and now, an exact meaning to the word 'computer'. This is a necessity if our discussions are not to be vague and confused. After all, it is hardly enlightening to be told that the brain is a computer in some as yet totally unspecified sense of the word. In fact, this means nothing more than that a brain is a brain. If the hypothesis that the brain is a computer is to make a definite claim, the word 'computer' must have a precise meaning.

The meaning to which I have adhered throughout this book is the one spelled out in chapter 4: a computer is a universal symbol system. With a view to defending this definition, let me review some possible alternatives.

In one perfectly legitimate way of speaking, a computer is anything that can compute in the *original* sense of the word – which is to say, calculate. Thus the dictionary defines a computer as 'a calculator: a machine or apparatus ... for carrying out, esp. complex, calculations'.[63] Von Neumann favoured this definition. He remarked that 'a computing machine in the proper sense' is a machine that can perform arithmetical calculations.[64]

If this is how the word 'computer' is defined, it becomes an indisputable truth that the human brain is a computer, for we can all do mental arithmetic. Whatever else the brain may be, it is certainly an apparatus that can perform calculations. A bloodless victory like this is worthless. The question of whether the brain is a computer loses all its interest if the meaning of the word 'computer' is made so wide that the issue is settled merely by our ability to add two and two.

Perhaps I should stress that I'm not *arguing* with the dictionary. The dictionary definition gives a correct account of the word 'computer' in its most general sense. The point is simply that this definition trivializes the theory that the brain is a computer; so anyone who believes this to be a serious and interesting theory must be using the word 'computer' in a different, less general, way.

Some modern writers define computation not as the processing of strings of symbols, but as the processing of any sort of representations whatsoever.[65] (Harking back to section 9.4, representations are those states of a machine or organ that serve to depict facts about the outside world.) Some other writers achieve the same effect by keeping the word 'symbol' in the definition of computation but broadening its meaning to cover any type of representation at all.[66] These proposals suffer from the same malady as the dictionary definition: they rob the claim that the brain is a computer of much of its interest. This is because the statement that my brain contains and processes representations really says little more than that I use my brain to reason about actual and possible states-of-affairs in my environment. The question of whether or not the brain is a representation-processor (and thus a computer in this new sense) is certainly an empirical one – after all, the ancient Greeks thought the brain was nothing more than a blood cooler and even the Behaviourists of a few decades ago had some fairly strange things to say about brains. However, the question is not one that lies at the cutting edge of modern brain research. The contentious issue is whether the representations that the brain uses are sentence-like strings of symbols or something completely different.[67]

So, then, what is needed is a definition of the word 'computer' that succeeds in giving a non-trivial sense to claims like 'computers can think' and 'the human brain is a computer'. My preference is to use the term 'information processor' for any device that processes representations of some sort; and to reserve the word 'computer' for a device that processes representations consisting of strings of symbols in the original sense – compositional, recursively-structured, quasi-linguistic strings as described in chapter 4. The question of whether or not the brain is a computer then escapes the trivialization that it suffers at the hands of the other definitions I have discussed, and the relatively uncontroversial fact that the brain somehow creates and manipulates representations can be summed up by the statement that the brain is an information processor.

An important caveat. It would be naive to disregard the fact that the advancing sweep of scientific knowledge has wrought the downfall of many terminological recommendations that looked sound enough at the time they were made. It is possible that future research will show the brain's activity to be both similar to and yet different from the manipulation of bit-strings, in ways that it is currently impossible to speculate upon. In this case, my recommended terminology might leave the question 'Is the brain a computer?' with no real answer. Likewise, the question of whether the earth moves round the sun has, since Einstein, largely passed into just such limbo – for all that it once led Galileo to trial before the Inquisition.

To summarize. The SSSH is a provocative and intriguing conjecture and is currently the subject of intense investigation.[68] It is still early days but so far no persuasive reasons exist for believing that the human brain is – or is partly – a computer. There is, as yet, no hard empirical evidence for the hypothesis; and nor is much corroboration forthcoming from the philosophical arguments we have examined.

The next chapter concerns research which appears to be ushering in an entirely new kind of information processing machine. This research makes a radical break with the traditional approach to AI. The machines under development function very differently from symbol-manipulators; and if in the distant future they should prove capable of thought, this would be no verification of the symbol system hypothesis. On the contrary, it would represent the triumph of a new, and as yet largely untested, approach to AI. Cognitive science has been thrown into ferment by this new research. The embryonic existence of these new information processors has sorely undermined confidence in the hypothesis that the brain is a computer.

10

AI's fresh start:
parallel distributed processing

Large collections of neurons can certainly think. Thus it is perhaps surprising that AI researchers should have devoted so much effort to programming commercially available computers and so little to building and investigating networks of artificial neurons. The potential of this latter approach to achieving AI – 'neural simulation' as it is often called – was discussed at the Dartmouth Conference, but over the years it became a canon of traditional AI that neural simulation is a waste of time. Researchers who came into AI during the 1960s and 1970s could see little point in attempting to construct an entirely new kind of machine, based on the poorly understood and forbiddingly complex human brain, when the von Neumann computer was already on hand – and, moreover, running small but impressive programs like GPS, Shrdlu and Sam. The work of one researcher who did take neural simulation seriously, Frank Rosenblatt, was subjected to ruinous criticism by Marvin Minsky and Seymour Papert in 1969.[1]

Suddenly these traditional perceptions are under a massive attack from within. A group of researchers who have grown disillusioned with the conventional approach to AI have revived Rosenblatt's ideas and begun to experiment with small networks of artificial neurons. Their results are encouraging. The networks that the group has built display an almost uncanny ability to organize themselves and, once organized, behave rather as if they contain computer programs. The networks operate in a highly parallel fashion and store information in a distributed way. (See section 9.2 for explanations of the terms *parallel* and *distributed*.) The group have christened their approach to AI 'Parallel Distributed Processing'; PDP for short.

AI has always been a field of high hopes and grand predictions. PDP is no exception. 'It is likely that [PDP] will offer the most significant progress of the past several millennia on the mind/body problem,' writes psychologist and computer scientist Paul Smolensky.[2] (Hubert Dreyfus, as deflationary as ever, cuts through the hype with the remark that the next twenty years of research in PDP is unlikely to produce even a network with the intellectual ability of a slug.[3]) To date the successes of PDP have been modest – in many ways much more modest than those of traditional AI. The networks that have been built so far are miniscule in comparison with the human brain; and their performance, although intriguing, is trivial even when judged against such lowly organisms as the ant and the earthworm. The mathematical theory of how PDP networks function is still in a primitive state, and lab research tends to involve a lot of hit-and-miss juggling with the enormous numbers of connections linking the artificial neurons. PDP is in its infancy. Advocates of PDP agree that 'there are serious obstacles that must be overcome before [the approach] can offer . . . power comparable to that of symbolic computation' (Smolensky again).[4] It will be well into the next century before we are in any position to judge the true significance of this exciting new development in AI.

10.1   The basic ideas

A neuron is regarded as a unit that is either on or off – either firing or not firing (section 9.2). It fires if a sufficient number of the neurons connected to it are themselves firing. To clarify the details of this, consider a grossly oversimplified neuron with just three input connections from other neurons. (Figure 10.1) I'll refer to the three input fibres as AB, AC and AD.

Neural connections are known to have different 'strengths' (or 'weights' or 'conduction factors'). These are determined partly by the diameter of the connecting fibre and partly by the chemical composition of the junction, or synapse, between the output fibre of one neuron and the input fibre of the next. Suppose the strengths of the connections AB, AC and AD are 1, 2 and 3 respectively. In effect, this means that the connection AC 'amplifies' neuron C's burst of activity by a factor of 2 and AD 'amplifies' D's burst by a factor of 3. Thus from the point of view of neuron A, the effect of neuron C turning on is twice that of neuron B turning on, and the effect of D turning on is three times that of B turning on. A simple way of describing this is to say that when all of B, C, and D are on, the total input to A is 6 'units of current' – 1 unit from B, 2 from C and 3 from D. If only B and D are on, the total input is 4; and so on.

The *threshold* of a neuron is the minimum input that will cause it to turn on. Suppose A has a threshold of 4. This means that A will fire if C is off but B and D are both on, since the total input is then 4. A will also fire when B, C and D are all on (total input = 6), and when C and D are on but B is off (total input = 5). If, however, B and C are on but D is off the total input, 3, is less than the threshold and so the neuron does not fire.

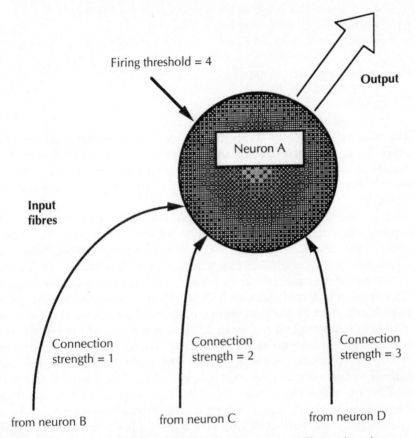

Firing threshold = 4

Output

Neuron A

Input
fibres

Connection
strength = 1

Connection
strength = 2

Connection
strength = 3

from neuron B   from neuron C   from neuron D

Figure 10.1 The neuron fires a discharge along its output fibres when the
weighted sum of its inputs exceeds its threshold.

Some neural connections are known to be *inhibitory*. These have exactly the
opposite effect to the kind of connections that I've just described (which are
called *excitatory*). To see how they work, suppose AC is now an inhibitory
connection of strength 2. If B and D, but not C, are on, the total input is 1+3,
so neuron A fires (A's threshold is still 4). If, however, B, C and D are *all* on,
the total input is 1+3−2, the '−2' being C's inhibitory contribution. Since the
total input is now less than the threshold the neuron does not fire.

Quick test
Let A's threshold be 2. As before, AB is excitatory, strength 1; AC is inhibitory, strength 2; and AD is excitatory, strength 3. Does A fire when

- B is off, C is off, D is on?
- B is off, C is on, D is on?
- B is on, C is on, D is on?

(The answers are given in note 5.)

PDP networks

The basic building blocks of a network are simple switch-like units that are either on or off. These are the artificial neurons. A network consists of a densely interconnected mass of these units. Some connections are excitatory, some inhibitory. Each connection has a specific strength, and each unit has a threshold.

In a sense these networks operate in an extremely simple way. All that happens is that units switch themselves on and off in response to the stimulation they receive from their neighbours. Whenever the total input that a unit is receiving from its neighbours equals or exceeds its threshold, it switches on, and as soon as the total input drops below the threshold, it switches off again. This simple principle of operation leads to overall behavior that is grotesquely complicated. Since all the units are interconnected, either directly or via some number of intervening units, they all influence one another and the patterns of interaction are as complex as the pathways of connections between them (see figure 10.2). When any unit flips on or off, the ripples are felt throughout the network – ripples of excitation and inhibition, which cause many other units to turn on or turn off. The network is a buzzing hive of parallel interaction, with the units causing each other to switch on and off at a furious rate.

Predicting the behaviour of a network of even a few dozen units is a fearsomely complicated business. To visualize the complexity of the situation, picture a dozen or so billiard balls rolling about on a table. Since the balls collide with one another each influences the movement of the rest, either directly or indirectly – and via a chain of collisions, a ball's influence may even loop back to affect its own motion. The mathematics of such situations is well known for its ability to inspire horror.

Input and output

Think of the units in a network as arranged in layers. (Figure 10.2.) The units in the top or input layer are set up in such a way that the operator can 'clamp' them on or off, thereby overriding their tendency to change state in response to the activity of their neighbours. To 'compute' with a network, one clamps the units in the top layer into some pattern of ons and offs. This pattern is the input. The repercussions of this disturbance rebound through the network in cycle after cycle of parallel activity. This violent reaction gradually subsides

Input layer

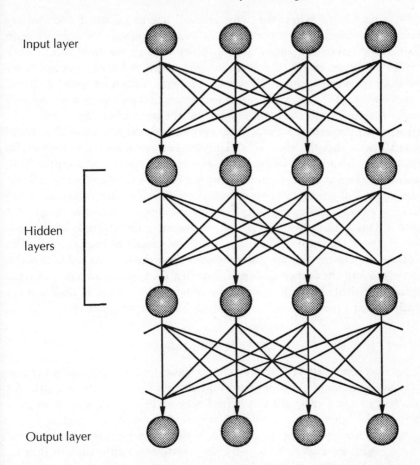

Hidden
layers

Output layer

Figure 10.2   Connections between the layers of artificial neurons in a PDP
network.

and eventually the network settles down into a stable, quiescent state. To put
it metaphorically, the network gradually relaxes as it discovers how to live ever
more harmoniously with the input until finally it crystallizes into a fixed
configuration, with some of the units permanently on and the rest permanently off. The network has 'found' the state in which the rest of the units can
live in balance with the clamped input layer. Once the network has accom-
modated itself to the input in this way, the output can be read off the bottom
layer. The output is, if you like, one 'edge' of the stable pattern that the
network falls into. A meaningful application of this computational procedure is
described in section 10.2.

In practice a given input pattern is usually capable of producing a number of different stable states: the 'most relaxed' one and a number of 'uneasy truces' – states that are just sufficiently stable to prevent the network from looking for a more harmonious way of accommodating the input. If a network settles down into one of these compromise states it will stick there and never produce the desired output. To prevent this from happening, units can be set up to operate probabilistically: a unit may or may not switch on when the total input it receives exceeds its threshold, and the probability that it will do so depends on the amount by which the input exceeds the threshold. This 'background noise' has the effect of shaking the network out of any compromise states into which it may fall. Geoffrey Hinton (the inventor of a type of PDP network known as a Bolzmann machine) has coined a vivid analogy to describe this process of driving a network out of compromise states.[6] Imagine a ball bearing rolling across a metal plate with a number of horizontal grooves cut into it. One of these is a deep trough, representing the optimally stable state, and the rest are small surface ruts just deep enough to trap the ball. The chances are that the ball will roll into one of these shallow ruts and stick there, never reaching the deepest groove. If, however, the plate is continually vibrated – the equivalent of adding 'noise' to the system – the ball will be shaken out of each shallow groove and will eventually fall into the deep one.

The right connections

The connections between units, and in particular their strengths, play a crucial role in determining the behaviour of a network. Changing the strength of a single connection can pitch a stabilized network back into a state of frenzied activity. An operator can mould the output that a network produces from a given input by modifying the strengths of the network's connections (since if the strengths are altered, the network has to settle into a different state in order to live stably with the input). Setting up a network to perform a given task is a matter of getting the strength of each individual connection just right. As PDP researchers like to put it, a network's knowledge is 'stored in the strengths of its connections'. (PDP is often referred to simply as 'connectionism'.)

Training a network

The most commonly used method of setting up networks for specific tasks is a cyclical process of adjustment known as training. For illustration consider the task of inverting an input pattern – that is, of recreating the input pattern in reverse order on the output units (see figure 10.3). For training purposes around fifty input patterns are chosen at random. The operator clamps the input units into the first of these patterns and allows the network to settle into a stable state. (Since the network is at this stage completely untrained, the output the operator obtains will very likely bear no relation to the desired

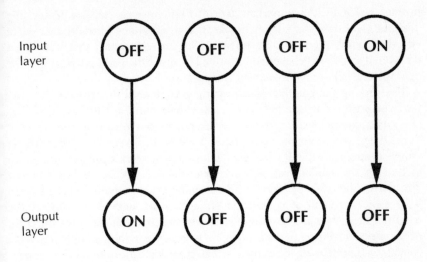

Figure 10.3 Inverting an input pattern.

pattern.) Next, the operator presses the buttons that adjust the connection
strengths throughout the network – more on how this works in a moment.
This process is repeated with the remaining patterns in the sample. Then,
using the same patterns, the operator goes through the entire cycle again – and
again and again. In the experiment described in the next section, it was necessary to repeat the training cycle almost 200 times.

The crux of the training procedure is, of course, the bit where the buttons
are pressed to adjust the strengths of the network's connections. Here are the
details. Once the network has settled into a stable state the output units are
compared one at a time with the desired output pattern. If an output unit that
ought to be on is off, a button is pressed to slightly increase the strengths of
the excitatory connections leading to that unit from other units which are on.
This means that next time the network is given the same input pattern, the
unit in question will be more likely to turn on (since an increase in the
strengths of these connections results in an increase in the total input that the
unit receives from its neighbours). Similarly, if an output unit that ought to
be off is on, a button is pressed to slightly *decrease* the strengths of excitatory
connections leading to it from units that are on. (In real life this is all done by
a computer rather than by hand – the 'buttons' are an explanatory prop.) The
same effects are produced by strengthening or weakening inhibitory connections, and by raising or lowering the thresholds of units. In practice a mixture
of such adjustments is used.

Where a network contains layers between the input and output layers ('hidden layers', as they are called) the number of possible combinations of ad-

justments is huge. An important area of PDP research consists of devising 'learning algorithms' for such networks; that is, of finding formulae that select effective combinations of adjustments. The few algorithms that have been discovered so far are believed to be limited in application and progress in PDP depends crucially on improvement in this area.[7]

The striking thing is that once training is completed the network can correctly invert not only the patterns in the sample but also patterns that it has never encountered before. From the examples in the sample the network learns the general principle of inversion. Each of the inversions in the training sample makes its own individual demands on the network's connections and so each step of the training cycle pulls the connection strengths in slightly different directions. The effect of repeating the training cycle a large number of times is to forge a system of connection strengths that suits all equally. Sheer repetition smooths out a pattern of strengths that accommodates the differing needs of each inversion in the sample. So long as the training sample is diverse enough to represent all the demands that inversion can make on the connections, this pattern of strengths enables the network to invert input patterns lying outside the sample.

A point worth emphasizing is that the procedure for adjusting the connection strengths up or down has no 'intelligence' built into it. If a unit that ought to be on is off, the procedure simply locates all the active excitatory connections leading to the unit and mechanically increases the strength of each of them by the same fixed amount (*mutatis mutandis* for inhibitory connections). The procedure is invariant for different learning tasks. Let the output patterns in the training sample be not the inverses but the converses of the input patterns – that is, the result of replacing each 'on' in the input pattern with an 'off' and each 'off' with an 'on'. Training with this sample will give the network the ability to form converses rather than inverses – no change in the connection adjustment procedure is required.

PDP researchers stress how impressive this is. A complaint often directed against traditional AI programs is that their 'intelligence' is entirely second-hand, a pale reflection of the human intelligence that goes into analysing the problem and devising the rules that lead the computer to the solution. PDP networks, on the other hand, start from scratch. Inversion may be a trivial task but at least the network learns how to do it without any assistance from a programmer. It may well be that these self-organizing networks offer us a highly simplified view of the mechanisms that underlie our own ability to learn.

10.2 English lessons

Even with the best will in the world, it is hard to get worked up by the news that PDP networks can learn to do such simple things as create the inverse or converse of their input. This section describes something much more exciting.

The ringleaders of the PDP revolution, James McClelland and David Rumelhart, have trained a network to produce the past tenses of English verbs.[8] The network can respond correctly to verbs that were not encountered during training, and even when the verb is not regular the network can often get the past tense right. (By a 'regular' verb I mean one whose past tense is formed by adding 'ed' to the root form of the verb: push/pushed, pull/pulled.) When the trained network was presented for the first time with the verb *guard*, it responded *guarded*; and, much more spectacularly, it replied *wept* on its first encounter with *weep*, *clung* to *cling*, and *dripped* to *drip* (notice the double 'p').

A key problem that Rumelhart and McClelland had to tackle in the course of planning their experiment was how to represent English verbs in a form that the network could handle. It took them over two years to find a method that worked. This great expenditure of time and intellect illustrates the sheer difficulty of PDP. The pioneers of symbolic computing had little trouble in devising a general system for converting words and other information into a form that a computer can use – the familiar method of assigning bit-codes to the letters of the alphabet, etc. In contrast, devising methods for presenting information to networks is one of the hardest aspects of PDP research. The method that Rumelhart and McClelland used is in fact an extremely restricted one. Powerful, general systems of representation will have to be devised before PDP networks can be put to much serious use.

I'll spare you the messy details of the method that Rumelhart and McClelland used. In outline, verbs are analysed into sets of special phonetic features (called 'Wickelfeatures').[9] Each of the units in the input and output layers (there are 460 in each layer) is used to represent a specific feature. The experimenters clamp each input unit on or off according to whether or not the phonetic feature it represents is present in the verb under consideration.

The network's training began with a mixture of ten regular and irregular verbs. Children, too, begin by memorizing a small handful of past tenses, and Rumelhart and McClelland deliberately chose a training sample that is typical of a child's initial repertoire of past tenses – verbs like *came*, *got*, *gave*, *looked*, *needed*, *took*, and *went*. Training consisted of presenting the root form of a verb (*come*, *go* etc.) at the input layer, then comparing the actual and desired outputs and adjusting the connection strengths as described in the last section. The network could produce the past tenses for itself after just ten training cycles (that is, ten cycles of exposure to the entire sample).

Next, 400 or so more verbs were added to the sample (about eighty percent of these being regular). The network took 190 training cycles to master them. By this stage the network was able to respond to verbs that it had not encountered before, correctly producing *kept* from *keep* and *clung* from *cling*. In the course of training, the network's connections absorbed both the 'add -*ed*' relationship and the more subtle relationships that exist between input and output in the case of non-regular verbs. The network's acquisition of this knowledge was entirely the result of repeated, mechanical adjustments to the connection strengths and this experiment forms a fine example of a machine 'learning for itself'. However, the network was accurate in only about seventy percent of its responses. Some of its more spectacular failures were *squawked* from *squat*, *shipped* from *shape*, and *membled* from *mail*. These particular errors are produced by what is called blending.[10] A less extreme example of this is the formation of the blend 'ated' from the responses 'ate' and 'eated'. PDP networks are prone to errors of this nature.

In the course of 'growing up' the network made some of the same mistakes with its verbs as children do. After the first ten sessions the network could correctly form the past of *come* and *go* – as can a very young child – but while learning the larger sample it began to over-regularize, producing responses like *comed*, *goed* and *wented*. Eventually the grip of the 'add -*ed*' principle weakened and the network reverted to *came* and *went*. It is probable that the similarity with children is of no real significance. The over-regularization was brought about by the transition from the initial sample, which contained only two regular verbs, to a sample in which regular verbs predominated. There is no evidence that over-regularization in children is likewise preceded by a large shift in the proportion of regular verbs encountered.[11]

This innocent-looking experiment in fact constitutes a serious challenge to orthodox ways of thinking. The theory that the brain initiates and controls behaviour principally by following rules is a popular one among cognitive scientists (see section 5.5) and linguistic rules have always formed a favourite example. The network, though, does not use rules to produce its output. The concept of a program is entirely foreign to the way the network operates (section 10.4 enlarges on this). The implication for the orthodox theory is clear: it is all too possible that the unconscious following of stored rules in fact plays no part in the production of human speech. If the network has no need of a program then perhaps neither does the human brain.

10.3   Escape from a nightmare?

One of the major bugbears of traditional AI is the difficulty of programming computers to recognize that different but similar objects are instances of the same type of thing. This is sometimes known as the *classification problem*. Take a letter *a* in my handwriting and one in yours. The two are certain to differ, perhaps fairly drastically, yet probably most English-speaking people would be able to recognize the two patterns of ink marks as instances of the same letter, especially if aided by the presence of a surrounding context. Computers, on the other hand, are extremely bad at such tasks.

It would be a programmer's nightmare to try to write out a set of recognition

Figure 10.4   A few of the variations on the letter 'A' to be found in the *Letraset* catalogue.

rules incorporating descriptions of a realistically wide range of the variations that can occur in the letter *a*. Take a look at figure 10.4 if you don't believe me. A nightmare within the nightmare is that a set of rules which cast wide enough to net plenty of *a*s and *A*s would probably pull in a fair catch of *u*s, *H*s, *o*s, *b*s, *D*s, *F*s, *v*s and *e*s at the same time.

The problems that underlie letter recognition have long been regarded as some of the thorniest in AI. (As Douglas Hofstadter once put it, 'The central problem of AI is: What are *a* and *i* ?'.[12]) The same difficulties crop up in many diverse areas and it is this pervasiveness that makes the classification problem such a fundamental one for AI. Can a computer be programmed to recognize my smiling face at a party when hitherto it has only seen me frowning into its TV eye at the lab, and moreover before I shaved off my beard? Can a computer be given a human chess player's intuitive ability to see that two positions from different games are essentially the same, even though the exact numbers of pieces and their exact positions are different in each case? How can a computer be programmed to follow the speech of people whose voices it has not heard before? And so on.

Attempts to write programs that identify faces or follow natural speech have, notoriously, become bogged down in the mess of descriptions required for a realistic treatment of the variations that can occur in the target items. PDP may have the power to steer AI clear of this particular nightmare – and context seems to hold the key.

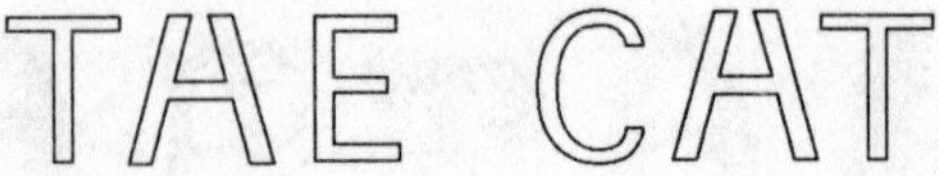

TAE CAT

Figure 10.5   The curse of context.

The curse of context[13]

Letters are much more easily identified in context than in isolation, as figure 10.5 illustrates. Figure 10.4, too, contains a number of *A*s that could not possibly be identified out of context.

Context plays an equally important role in the interpretation of speech. An experiment demonstrating this involves subjects listening to tapes of human speech that have been doctored here and there with brief audible clicks.[14] Thus the subject might hear *legi**lature, where * is a carefully positioned click that completely obliterates the sound of the *s*. The context provided by the surrounding phonemes leads subjects to interpolate an *s* into the gap. At the conscious level subjects are completely unaware that this is what they are doing. They report actually *hearing* the missing *s*, and describe the click as a 'disembodied sound'.

Programmers have found context to be an exceedingly tough nut to crack and many researchers have come to believe that this refractoriness is a curse left on AI by an unwitting John von Neumann. To see why this may be so, imagine yourself trying to read a word written in an unfamiliar and unusual hand. The natural thing to do is to consider each letter in the context of the whole word: paradoxically, you use the letters to identify the word and the word to identify the letters. In a flurry of parallel activity your guesses at what the individual letters might be interact with your various guesses at the whole word. Guesses veto and reinforce one another until finally a stable pattern of hypotheses emerges and you are suddenly sure what the word is. A von Neumann machine, with its sequential mode of operation, can give at best a clumsy parody of this sort of thing. PDP networks, on the other hand, are parallel processors par excellence and may prove ideal hardware for the kind of problem solving that consists of allowing rival teams of hypotheses to slug it out simultaneously until a winner emerges.

Preliminary laboratory evidence indicates that PDP networks can, in one fell swoop, lift the curse of context and solve the classification problem. Pilot studies have produced networks that are adept at recognizing written and spoken words.[15] The networks exploit context to the full: all the letters, or sounds, in a word are examined simultaneously and 'guesses' as to their individual identities evolve in parallel, each influencing the others.

Smiles and frowns

Igor Aleksander, professor of information technology at Imperial College London, has succeeded in building a network that recognizes human faces. Although Aleksander does not work under the PDP banner his research into networks of stylized 'neurons' has many points of contact with PDP.[16]

During training the Wisard (as Aleksander calls his machine) scrutinizes a person's face through its TV eye and gradually learns the distinctive patterns of alteration that the face undergoes as the person speaks, smiles and so on. After sufficient training the Wisard can reliably identify the person on subsequent meetings despite subtle changes in appearance and expression. Like the other networks I have described, the Wisard has the ability to generalize from the sample used in training. This enables it to analyse the expressions of complete strangers and say whether they are smiling or frowning. Suitable training enables the Wisard to recognize many sorts of objects and the potential for industrial application is considerable. (Aleksander has been building networks of artificial neurons since the mid 1960s and as the first waves of enthusiasm for PDP began to sweep through the AI labs of North America Aleksander was quietly clinching a deal to put the Wisard into commercial production.)

10.4   The contrast with computers

Computers, as you know, run on symbols – programs are lists of symbolically encoded instructions, information is stored in memory in the form of symbols, and each step of a computation consists of an operation on a symbol string. In complete contrast the processing that takes place in the past-tense network, or in the inversion network of section 10.1, consists of units exciting and inhibiting one another and not of the program-governed manipulation of stored symbolic expressions. (As McClelland and Rumelhart put it, 'The currency of our systems is not symbols, but excitation and inhibition.'[17]) Networks just 'squirm' until they 'feel comfortable' with the input, and have more in common with a globule of molten metal cooling into a solid lump than with a VAX or an IBM stepping through a program.

Notice that the inversion network can be regarded as a bit manipulator (albeit a programless one). A string of bits is, after all, simply a sequence of ons and offs, and so the network can be viewed as a device for transforming one string of bits into another. Indeed, it is possible to use a coordinated array of networks to simulate a von Neumann machine (one network is trained to perform shifts, another to perform compare-rights, and so on). The fact that networks can be used to support symbolic computation is an important one and I will return to it in section 10.10. The point I want to emphasize here is

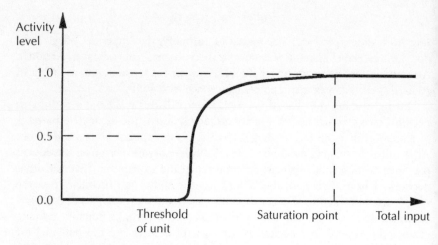

Figure 10.6   The level of output depends on the amount of input the unit is receiving from other units.

that although networks can be *used* as symbol-manipulators, they are in general a different sort of beast. It would be completely misleading to regard PDP as nothing more than the exploration of a radically new type of symbol-manipulator.

In order to keep the story simple I have so far described only one rather special type of unit – the straightforward on/off model. The more general model, hitherto ignored, can adopt a range of levels of activity between *fully on* and *fully off*.[18] Thus a unit's level of activity at a particular time might be .75 (to put it metaphorically, the unit is operating at less than full volume). The level of activity depends on the amount of input that the unit is receiving from other units. For example, the activity level may jump from 0 to .5 once the total input reaches the threshold of the unit and then steadily increase to 1 if the input continues to increase (see figure 10.6). The input and output patterns for a network composed of such units will be, not strings of 0s and 1s, but sequences of real numbers. An example of one of the possible output patterns for a network with four output units is <0.6, 0.4, 0.8, 1.0>. Clearly, all similarity with strings of bits has vanished. (In mathematical terms networks take a numerical vector as input and produce a numerical vector as output. Networks can therefore be viewed as devices that perform vector transformations.)

The difference between a von Neumann machine and the past-tense and inversion networks is as plain as chalk and cheese. However, it is not at all easy to formulate a sharp criterion that encapsulates the difference between PDP networks and symbol-manipulators in general. For recall that the class of symbol-manipulators has been left somewhat open-ended. Proponents of the

SSSH allow that the brain's fundamental symbol-manipulating operations may differ in radical – and presently unknowable – ways from the fundamental operations of a von Neumann machine. Similarly they allow that the brain's symbolic code may be very different from any that we know about today.

To put the same point in a different way, there is no sharp, universally applicable criterion for distinguishing between a network that is being used as a symbol-manipulator and one that is not. The best we can do – and this is quite enough – is cite paradigm examples of symbol-structures (recursive, compositional bit-code, formulae of the predicate calculus, etc.) and paradigm examples of fundamental symbol-manipulating operations (shift the string in a given storage location one bit to the left; compare two strings and place a marker in a given storage location if they are identical; replace a bound variable with a constant) and then judge a novel architecture in terms of its degree of similarity, if any, to the paradigms.

Compare the famous problem of family resemblance.[19] As everybody knows, members of a family (the Wittgenstein family, say) often resemble one another to a far greater degree than they resemble members of an unrelated family (the Sartres, perhaps). Is it possible to formulate a sharp criterion that encapsulates once and for all exactly which features distinguish Wittgensteins from Sartres? Probably not. Family resemblances just aren't like that.

As I said in the last chapter, the theory that the brain is a symbol-manipulator rose to popularity among cognitive scientists not so much because there is hard evidence in its favour but because it seemed to be the 'only straw afloat'. There seemed no plausible alternative conception of how the brain might function. PDP has changed all this – there is no longer just one straw to clutch at. According to the new theory, the brain is a complex weave of multilayered networks – no symbols, no programs. We'll be looking at some challenges to the new theory later in the chapter. For the moment, let's just relish its novelty!

10.5   Comparisons with wetware

One of the new theory's credentials is the extent to which PDP networks exhibit 'brain-like' features. Here is a checklist of the similarities. (You may find it helpful to refer back to section 9.2.)

1   The individual units in a network are somewhat like real neurons.
2   Learning in the brain is widely believed to involve the modification of connection strengths (although this is not yet a proven fact).
3   Networks are massively parallel. Output is generated from the disturbance at the input layer via an orgy of excitation and inhibition in

which all the units participate simultaneously. Populations of real neurons are known to engage in a grossly similar kind of parallel activity.

4   Networks store information in a distributed fashion with each individual connection participating in the storage of many different items of information. The know-how that enables the past-tense network to form *wept* from *weep* is not stored in a specific connection but is 'spread' through the entire pattern of connection strengths that was forged during training. Thus networks provide a model for understanding the results of Lashley and others concerning the non-localized nature of memory (section 9.2).

5   A network can be made to function as a content-addressable memory, in the sense that if *part* of a remembered pattern is presented as input the complete pattern is generated as output.[20] Content-addressability is one of the most striking features of human memory.

6   Networks degrade gracefully. If a few connections are snapped here and there the network remains operational, although the damage results in a tendency to make mistakes. As damage increases, the network's performance becomes steadily worse (in a manner faintly reminiscent of a brain suffering from one of the degenerative diseases).[21]

However, these similarities between networks and wetware are matched by a list of important dissimilarities. Existing PDP networks in fact form only the crudest approximation to networks of real neurons and much refinement will be necessary before PDP can claim to offer any real insight into how the brain functions. The remainder of this section consists of a discussion of some of the major discrepancies.

Real neurons

The brain contains a large number of different types of neurons – pyramid cells, star cells, chandelier cells, and many more. A number of factors indicate that the various types perform different functions. For instance, the mix of neurons is not uniform throughout the brain: different cell types predominate in the different regions. Moreover, neurons of different types have different numbers of connections, varying from a few hundred to hundreds of thousands. None of this diversity is reflected in PDP networks, which invariably contain just one type of unit. For this reason alone, current networks must be viewed as providing only a very crude model of human wetware.

Worse still, PDP units do not correspond to any known type of neuron. All real neurons are dedicated *either* to inhibiting other cells from firing *or* to inciting them to fire – never both. PDP units, on the other hand, are hybrids: each has a mixture of inhibitory and excitatory output connections. Attempts to build functioning networks out of non-hybrid units have so far been unsuccessful.

Difficulties such as these have led some researchers to suggest that each unit should be viewed as standing for a *group* of neurons, some inhibitory and some excitatory.[22] This ploy has drawn a sharp comment from biologist Francis Crick: 'If it were carefully stated how this group might be built out of more or less real neurons . . . [the suggestion] might be acceptable to neuroscientists . . . but this is seldom if ever done.'[23]

The learning process

Despite the existence of a few gross similarities between a learning brain and a learning network there is in fact no detailed analogy between the two.

All currently known procedures for tuning the strengths of connections during training depend crucially on repetition. A network has to run through the entire training sample a considerable number of times before learning is completed. While repetition is certainly important for human learning it is by no means essential in every case. For instance, someone with a good memory will be able to learn a list of instructions or a page of French vocabulary at a single reading.

A further important difference is exhibited by the fact that networks learn their skills only with the help of a teacher (although the search is on for a 'self-supervising' learning algorithm). Brains, of course, are much more self-reliant. During my first encounters with a windsurfer a regime of fulsomely repeated error somehow enabled my brain to learn which output signals to my muscle systems would achieve the graceful union of philosopher and wind. In the course of this learning process my brain had no foreknowledge of what the correct outputs should be – there was no semi-omniscient outsider supplying my brain with precise specifications of which signals it should be aiming for. Training procedures for networks require an external specification of the desired outputs. Each step in the training cycle involves comparing the actual output with the output that the trainer wants to achieve and then nudging the strengths of the connections up or down as appropriate.

It is clear, then, that even if the brain does learn via the modification of connection strengths, the procedures that it uses can bear little detailed resemblance to those used up to now in PDP.

Brain chemistry

Paradoxically the joint between a pair of interconnecting neural fibres consists largely of empty space. The fibres are separated at their closest point by what is known as a synaptic cleft and the excitatory and inhibitory signals that pass from neuron to neuron are 'carried' across these gaps by chemicals called *neurotransmitters*.[24] In the last decade or so some fifty different types of neurotransmitter have been identified and researchers believe that the final total may be much higher.

Injecting subjects with neurotransmitters has produced effects as diverse as memory enhancement, joy, hopelessness, analgesia and erotic stimulation. Chemicals that interfere with the activity of neurotransmitters have been used with considerable success in the treatment of disorders such as schizophrenia.[25] Evidently neurotransmitters play a variety of systematic roles in the brain's operations. (There is some speculation that they may also play a part in the brain's mechanism for modifying the strengths of inter-neural connections.) Understanding the overall contribution that chemicals make to information processing may prove to be just as important as understanding the electrical activity of neurons. PDP has concentrated on the latter area and has virtually ignored the chemical side of the brain's operations.[26]

Brain geometry

Neurons and their connecting fibres are often arranged in extremely regular patterns. Brain scientists tend to become quite lyrical when describing this geometrical orderliness: at the micro-level the brain is 'exquisitely structured', 'beautifully and eminently regular', 'sometimes almost crystalline in appearance'. To take a specific example, the microstructure of the cerebellum – an organ towards the rear of the brain – resembles a three dimensional rectangular grid. Vast numbers of long, horizontal input fibres lie in layer upon layer of neat parallel lines, and woven at right angles through this sheaf is an equally dense mass of output fibres, each one tidily perpendicular to the horizontal fibres surrounding it.

In contrast a PDP network has no geometry to speak of. It is certainly helpful to think of the units as lying in horizontal layers with the connections linking the layers vertically (as in figure 10.2) but this is nothing more than a convenience. It makes no difference if the network is squashed flat into a single layer or twisted up into some random shape. The only thing that matters is how the units are connected to each other; and in existing networks even this is far less dependent on spatial considerations than is the case in the brain. In the two layer past-tense network, for example, each input unit is connected uniformly to *every* output unit – there is no sense in which an input unit is connected to a greater number of 'nearby' output units than 'distant' ones. In the brain, on the other hand, each neuron connects prolifically in its immediate neighbourhood and rather more sparingly to neurons situated a slightly greater distance away. When a whole group of neurons is connected long-distance to a second group, the connections may respect the geometrical relationships of the neurons. Crudely, if in the first group neuron B is situated in between neurons A and C then it is likely that B will be connected to a neuron in the second group that is situated in between the neurons connected to A and C.

It is not known whether the brain's intricate geometry plays any essential role in its functioning. A device can consist of components arranged in regular patterns without this regularity being in the least relevant to the way the device works. Take a TV set. The electrical components are usually grouped on the chassis in a tidy fashion but this is simply for convenience of assembly and repair. The neat geometrical arrangement of the capacitors, resistors, switches, and so forth, makes no contribution whatever to the actual functioning of the set, whereas the correct functioning of a lens or a clockwork watch is crucially dependent on the precise geometrical arrangement of the various components. Devices like these work on geometrical principles.

On which side of this line does the brain fall? Is its geometry essential to its functioning or largely incidental? At the present stage this remains in general an open question. It has been conjectured that the brain's geometry may play a vital role in hand-eye coordination, the processing of sensations, linguistic comprehension, and much else besides.[27] On the other hand, the brain's intricate geometry may turn out to have more to do with the exigencies of biological growth than with the actual cognitive function of the organ.

If the thinking brain does operate on geometrical principles then the PDP networks that have been studied so far are like a portrait from which the face has been omitted. When PDP researchers begin to experiment with networks that do incorporate aspects of brain geometry their research may play a crucial role in unravelling the significance of the brain's exquisite structure.

10.6 Searle's Chinese gym

John Searle is no more impressed by PDP than he is by traditional AI. He maintains that no PDP network is capable of learning a language in the full sense nor of performing any other task requiring understanding. He has constructed two adaptations of his Chinese room thought-experiment which, he believes, prove this.

It is possible that Searle does not fully appreciate the difference between PDP and conventional computation. He sometimes writes as if he thinks the only difference is parallel vs serial. He says:

> Strong AI claims that thinking is merely the manipulation of formal symbols . . . The Churchlands are correct in saying that the original Chinese room argument was designed with traditional AI in mind but wrong in thinking that connectionism [i.e. PDP] is immune to the argument . . . [T]he connectionist system is subject even on its own terms to a variant of the objection presented by the original Chinese room argument . . . [The argument] applies to any computational system . . . whether [the computations] are done in serial or in parallel; that is why the Chinese room argument refutes strong AI in any form.[28]

In fact, Searle's two adaptations of his Chinese room argument are more powerful than he seems to think. If either works, it refutes the general claim that some form of PDP architecture is capable of cognition and not just the narrower claim that Searle refers to as 'strong AI'.

The first argument

Imagine that instead of a Chinese room, I have a Chinese gym: a hall containing many monolingual English-speaking men. These men would carry out the same operations as the nodes and synapses [i.e. units and connections] in a connectionist architecture . . . [T]he outcome would be the same as having one man manipulate symbols according to a rule book. No one in the gym speaks a word of Chinese, and there is no way for the system as a whole to learn the meanings of any Chinese words. Yet with appropriate adjustments, the system could give the correct answers to Chinese questions.[29]

Searle does not specify exactly how the people in the gym are to simulate the units in the network but it is easy enough to fill in some details. As we've seen, what a unit does is broadcast output to its neighbours when the total input it receives exceeds its threshold. The people in the gym can mimic this by passing each other plastic tokens, green tokens representing input along an excitatory connection and red tokens along an inhibitory connection. The number of tokens passed from one player to another (in a single transaction) represents the strength of the connection. Since a very(!) large number of people will be involved in the simulation, it is no doubt a good idea to give players lists detailing to whom they must pass their tokens and how many should be handed over. During the training phase of the simulation the players make changes to their lists in accordance with instructions shouted by the trainer.

One can agree with Searle that no amount of handing around tokens and fiddling with these lists will enable the individual players to learn Chinese. But it cannot validly be inferred from this that the set-up as a whole is unable to learn Chinese. As you have probably realized by now, this new version of the Chinese room argument commits exactly the same fallacy as the old. Searle's conclusion that the set-up understands no Chinese simply does not follow from his premiss that none of the individual players understands Chinese – just as the premiss that Joe Soap is ignorant of Chinese fails to imply that the system of which Joe is a part understands no Chinese (section 6.2).

The second argument

Because parallel machines are still rare, connectionist programs [sic] are usually run on traditional serial machines . . . Computationally, serial and parallel systems are equivalent . . . If the man in the Chinese room is computationally equivalent to both, then if he does not understand Chinese solely by virtue of doing the computations, neither do they.[30]

When Searle loosely says that serial and parallel systems are equivalent, he is referring to the fact that, given unbounded resources, any PDP network can be simulated by a von Neumann machine (sections 10.7 and 10.9 take a detailed look at this prima facie surprising fact). Expressed rigorously, Searle's argument seems to be this: Let N be a PDP network purportedly capable of understanding Chinese. The man in the room is capable of simulating N, even though he works in a serial manner (by the above fact). Carrying out the simulation does not enable him to understand Chinese (just ask him). Therefore N cannot understand Chinese. I will explain why this tricky argument is not valid. (The Chinese gym and its occupants – another simulation of N – are not required in this second argument.)

The first thing to notice is that this argument commits the same part-whole fallacy as the original Chinese room argument. There is no entailment from 'The man does not understand' to 'The whole simulation of N of which the man is a part does not understand'.

My second criticism is a little more indirect. Searle himself has issued frequent warnings on the perils of confusing a computer simulation with the thing being simulated. Here are some characteristic passages.

No one supposes that a computer simulation of a storm will leave us all wet. . . Why on earth would anyone in his right mind suppose a computer simulation of mental processes actually had mental processes?[31]

Barring miracles, you could not run your car by doing a computer simulation of the oxidation of gasoline, and you could not digest pizza by running [a] program that simulates such digestion. It seems obvious that a simulation of cognition [even one which is 'accurate down to the last synapse'] will similarly not produce the effects of the neurobiology of cognition.[32]

From the fact that a system can be simulated by symbol manipulation and the fact that [the system] is thinking, it does not follow that thinking is equivalent to formal symbol manipulation.[33]

Searle's examples show forcefully that it is in general invalid to argue in the following way:

S is a simulation of X; X can □; therefore S can □.

A storm can make you wet, but it hardly follows that a computer simulation of a storm can make you wet. Let me call this form of argument Searle's Beastie.
Consider a slightly different form of argument:

S is a simulation of X; S cannot □; therefore X cannot □.

Logicians describe this as a contraposed form, or *contrapositive*, of 'S is a simulation of X; X can □; therefore S can □'. A contrapositive of an argument is what you get when you swap the conclusion with one of the premises and insert a 'not' into each of the two statements you've moved. (So a contrapositive of A, B ∴ C is: A, not-C ∴ not-B.) The interesting thing about contrapositives is that if an argument is invalid, all its contrapositives are bound to be invalid too. (This can be proved formally. If you want to try to rough out a proof of your own, a good way to start is by reflecting on the fact that if 'A is false' follows from 'B is false', then 'B is true' follows from 'A is true'.)

The problem for Searle is that his second argument is nothing other than a contrapositive of his own Beastie! If you take the contraposed form of the Beastie (S is a simulation of X; S cannot □; therefore X cannot □) and substitute 'the man in the Chinese room' for 'S', 'understand Chinese' for '□', and 'N' for 'X', what you get is precisely Searle's argument: the man in the Chinese room is simulating N; the man cannot understand Chinese; therefore N cannot understand Chinese. Searle's second argument and the Beastie stand or fall together.

(Notice that the move from 'the simulation of X can't understand Chinese' to 'X can't understand Chinese' is not required in the original Chinese room argument. This is because the room set-up is not a simulation of a symbol-manipulator – it *is* a symbol-manipulator.)

Now that Searle's Beastie is on stage I can return to my discussion of the Chinese gym argument. As you may have realised by now, this argument in fact consists of two inferences, one from a premiss about the individual players in the gym to a conclusion about the simulation as a whole, and a second from this intermediate conclusion to a claim about the network being simulated.

No individual player can understand Chinese.
∴   The simulation as a whole cannot understand Chinese.
∴   The network being simulated cannot understand Chinese.

I hope you agree that Searle's *argument* for the intermediate conclusion must be rejected (on the ground that it commits a part-whole fallacy). But you may nevertheless feel disposed to agree with Searle that the conclusion of the argument is true: the cranky simulation of N contained in the gym simply is not a candidate for a Chinese-understander. I am sure this will be a common intuition. If you do agree with Searle on this point, should you follow him in inferring that N itself cannot understand Chinese? No. Searle is the last person who should be advocating this inference, for its form is, as before, a contrapositive of the Beastie: the gym set-up is a simulation of N; the simulation cannot understand Chinese; therefore N cannot understand Chinese.

There is certainly no reason why those who believe that understanding Chinese (and mentation in general) consists in the kind of processing that goes on in PDP networks should accept the inference. A simulation will lie somewhere on a scale from poor to exact, and the claim that mentation is parallel distributed processing certainly does not entail that any and every simulation of mentation itself mentates. What the claim does entail is that if a PDP device understands Chinese then a sufficiently exact simulation of the device will understand Chinese (for an exact simulation of parallel distributed processing simply is parallel distributed processing). Contraposing this gives a tightened form of the second half of the gym argument: if a sufficiently exact simulation of a PDP device does not understand Chinese then nor does the device itself. This is of no help to Searle, though, for the simulation in the gym is very far from being an exact simulation of N.

The idea that the people in the gym can give an exact simulation of a network complex enough to process and respond appropriately to an input of Chinese sentences is otherworldly. As we saw in chapter 6, a number of Searle's points against cognitive science involve a studied refusal to take physical and biological realities seriously. Here is a characteristic dig at the strong symbol system hypothesis: '[I]f we are trying to take seriously the idea that the brain is a digital computer, we get the uncomfortable result that we could make a system that does just what the brain does out of pretty much anything . . . cats and mice and cheese or levers or water pipes or pigeons or anything else . . .'.[34] The theory that the brain is a computer does not (need I say) imply that an artificial brain can *really* be made out of pigeons. (The theory would be absurd if it did imply this – Searle is surely right about that much.) It is only in fairyland that computers are made of cats and mice and cheese and an exact simulation of a gigantic PDP network can be carried out by a squad of people in a gym.

What if a supporter of the second half of the gym argument were to cry 'Thought experiment!' at this point? Recall that in the case of the Chinese room thought experiment I was happy to ignore the fact that a real human cannot work fast enough and accurately enough to handwork a large AI program. If I am to be consistent, mustn't I make a similar concession in the present case? It would, though, be a tactical blunder if the argument's protagonist were to take this line at the present point in the discussion ('Come on, stop being difficult and just *imagine* a world in which the people in the gym are capable of giving an exact simulation of N'). For the effect would be to chase away the intuition that the gym set-up does not understand Chinese. The argument's protagonist would be asking us to consider a world that differs radically enough from the real world as to enable a band of humans with their pockets full of coloured tokens to enact an exact simulation of a network containing maybe as many as one thousand million million connections. I have no firm intuitions about fairyland, save that one should expect the bizarre; and I certainly have no inclination to insist that even in fairyland the cranky 'machine' in the gym would be unable to understand Chinese.

I shall be returning to Searle's views on simulation in section 10.9. He claims (in the quotation given a few pages back) that a neuron-by-neuron, synapse-by-synapse computer simulation of cognition would not itself be a cognitive system. In my view he is simply mistaken about that. The interesting question is not whether such a simulation, if it existed, would count as a cognitive system, but whether such a simulation could possibly exist. This is one of the topics to which I now turn.

10.7　The Church–Turing thesis

'*Down with programs!*' '*Down with symbol-manipulation!*' '*Down with Mentalese!*' These are the slogans of the PDP revolution and they strike at the heart of orthodox cognitive science and orthodox AI. Not surprisingly, the forces of orthodoxy have been quick to strike back.[35] In the remainder of this chapter I survey the weaponry of the counter-revolutionaries, beginning with the Church-Turing thesis.

There are two main issues for us to consider. First, there is the question of whether the PDP revolution places the symbol system hypothesis in jeopardy. Second, there is the question of the extent to which PDP threatens the strong symbol system hypothesis. What defences can orthodox cognitive science throw up around its theory that the biological brain is a symbol-processor? These questions are complex. The Church-Turing thesis is a clear landmark, and makes a natural starting point.

Alonzo Church is an American logician who, like Turing, did work of profound relevance to computing in the decade before the first machines were built. Church and Turing worked independently, the former at Princeton and the latter at Cambridge, yet within months of each other they put forward essentially the same thesis.[36] Turing expressed his version in terms of (what are now called) Turing machines and Church in terms of his own invention, the lambda calculus. (This is a powerful symbolism for representing the mathematical operations of abstraction and generalization.[37] McCarthy was subsequently to use the lambda calculus in constructing the language LISP.) The two versions of the thesis were soon proved to be equivalent. Although the Church-Turing thesis was first enunciated in 1936 it remains of fundamental importance in the theory of computation.

In order to state the thesis I need the concepts of an *algorithm* and an *algorithmically calculable process*. First, algorithms. (The word is derived from the name of the influential ninth century Persian mathematician Abu Jaafar Muhammad ibn Mûsâ *al-Khowârizmi*.) I'll call the steps of a procedure *moronic* if no insight, ingenuity or creativity is necessary in order to carry them out. A procedure for achieving some specified result is known as an algorithm when (1) every step of the procedure is moronic; (2) at the end of each step it is moronically clear what is to be done next (i.e. no insight etc. is needed to tell);

(3) the procedure is guaranteed to lead to the specified result in a finite number of steps (assuming each step is carried out correctly).

To give a simple example, if you've mixed up your keys and can't tell by sight which one fits your front door, the well-known expedient of trying them in succession is an algorithm for finding the right key: the procedure is sure to work eventually (assuming you haven't actually lost the key) and is certainly moronic. Algorithms are handy things and they crop up in such diverse forms as knitting patterns, the recipes in cookery books for the culinarily inept and the mechanical procedures we learn at school for long multiplication and division. And, of course, all (terminating) computer programs are algorithms.[38]

A system (real or abstract) is algorithmically calculable if there is an algorithm – known or unknown – for calculating its behaviour. To put this more fully, the system is algorithmically calculable just in case there is an algorithmic procedure for deriving correct descriptions of the system's outputs from correct descriptions of the inputs it receives (and moreover a procedure that works for all possible inputs). Tautologically, a computer with a given set of programs is an algorithmically calculable system (provided it doesn't malfunction) because, of course, these programs are themselves algorithms for passing from input to output. PDP networks are also algorithmically calculable systems.

Here is the Church-Turing thesis (expressed in neither Church's terms nor Turing's):

> Any algorithmically calculable system can be simulated by a universal symbol system.

In other words, a computer with a large enough memory can simulate any other algorithmically calculable system whatsoever. (To say that a computer can simulate another system is simply to say that the computer can be programmed so that it will generate correct symbolic descriptions of the system's outputs from descriptions of inputs into the system, for all possible inputs.) The Church-Turing thesis is a statement about computer power: there is no algorithmically calculable device more powerful than a computer. Whatever can be done by any such device can be done by a computer (although possibly not in the same length of time).

The word 'thesis' is used to convey the slightly strange status of this proposition. Everyone believes it but everyone agrees that it hasn't been proved. Indeed, it isn't a proposition that *can* be proved formally, for algorithmic calculability is a highly informal concept, characterized as it is in terms of such imprecise ideas as ingenuity and insight. The arguments for the thesis are indirect, but compelling. Over the years a number of people have constructed precise mathematical definitions intended to capture the informal concept of something's being algorithmically calculable. Although each of these definitions has been couched in very different terms they have all turned out to be equivalent to one another. This is an argument for their correctness – they give each other mutual support, so to speak. Furthermore, each definition makes the Church–Turing thesis true – and that's something that *is* susceptible of formal proof, since the result of rewriting the thesis in terms of a precise definition is a mathematically exact statement. (Notice, incidentally, that the converse of the Church–Turing thesis is trivially true: if a system can be simulated by a computer – in the exacting sense of 'simulated' presently in use – then it is an algorithmically calculable system.)

If the Church–Turing thesis is true (as everyone thinks) and if our own cognitive processes are algorithmically calculable, then it follows that in principle a computer could give an exact simulation of the mind. This is often put forward as a general argument for thinking that the symbol-processing approach to AI is sound. The argument forms the first exhibit in our tour of the counter-revolution's arsenal.

There is a difficulty with the argument. It is important to realise that the Church–Turing thesis says nothing at all about the *practical feasibility* of using a computer to simulate a given algorithmically calculable system. The thesis tells us only that the simulation can be performed in an ideal world of unlimited resources – a world in which time is of no concern, in which issues of reliability and cumulative error can be ignored and, most importantly of all, in which there are no bounds on the capacity of the computer's memory devices. Whether the simulation can be carried out in the less bountiful environment afforded by the real world is an altogether different question.

The idealized computers of Turing's 1936 paper are a rich source of examples of simulations that are possible in an ideal world but impossible in the real world. (A Turing machine, remember, consists of a read/write head and a single paper tape of unbounded length.) Turing's original formulation of the Church–Turing thesis was in terms of these idealized machines: Any algorithmically calculable system can be simulated by a Turing machine. Thus a Turing machine can simulate a state-of-the-art Cray supercomputer (since, of course, a Cray, like every computer, is algorithmically calculable). It would, however, take untold centuries for a Turing machine to simulate even a few hours of the Cray's operations, and the simulation would quite probably require more paper tape than our planet has to offer. The distinction between real and ideal simulations – between, that is, those simulations that are possible in practice and those that are possible only in principle – is an important one and it will re-enter the discussion in sections 10.8 and 10.9.

The real/ideal distinction points up a serious weakness in the attempt to use the Church–Turing thesis as a blanket defence of the symbol-processing approach to AI. If it is true that our cognitive processes are algorithmically calculable then in principle they can be simulated by computer, but the rub is that it may not be remotely possible to perform the simulation in the real world. Moreover, there is a second weakness – one significant enough to deserve its own section.

10.8   Are our cognitive processes algorithmically calculable?

The Church-Turing thesis is something of a Trojan Horse. At first blush it looks like a tribute to the power and generality of the symbolic approach to AI, but in fact the ideas Turing presented in his 1936 paper can be made the basis of a scepticism concerning the foundations both of symbolic AI and of PDP. This section is the story of this threat to AI from without – a threat that menaces both PDP revolution and orthodox counter-revolution alike. (You may prefer to skip the section if you are eager to continue reading the account of the counter-revolution. The best point at which to return to it is following section 10.11.)

If the Church-Turing thesis is true and if our cognitive processes are algorithmically calculable then in principle a large enough computer can give an exact simulation of the mind. But what of the second 'if'? In his 1936 paper Turing mooted the possibility that our cognitive processes are algorithmically calculable.[39] Subsequently this has become an article of deepest faith among AI researchers and has even acquired the status of something 'too obvious to mention'. Take Newell's expression of the blanket defence of symbolic AI that we've been considering: 'A universal [symbol] system always contains the potential for being any other system, if so instructed. Thus, a universal system can become a generally intelligent system.'[40] The hypothesis that a system exhibiting general intelligence will be algorithmically calculable is thought so obvious that it is not even mentioned. Justin Leiber is no less dogmatic: 'In the in principle sense, you are [a] Turing Machine, but you do it all through a marvel of cunningly coordinated parallel processes, shortcuts piled within shortcuts.'[41] In point of fact there is no reason – apart from a kind of wishful thinking – to believe that all our cognitive processes are algorithmically calculable. This is *terra incognita*, and for all we know many aspects of brain function may be noncomputable.

To pursue this point we need some hitech terminology. Let S be a set of sentences. For the moment it doesn't matter what these sentences are; I'm going to use S as the basis for a number of general definitions – general in the sense that they are applicable no matter what sentences S happens to contain. Call the language in which the sentences of S are written L. (So L might be English or the differential calculus or the first order predicate calculus etc.). To say that S is *decidable* is to say that there is an algorithm for settling whether or not given sentences are members of S. The algorithm must give the right answer for each sentence of L. So for S to be decidable there must be an algorithm that can be applied to each sentence of L and that will deliver either the answer 'Yes, this sentence is in S' or 'No, this sentence is not in S' (and moreover the answers the algorithm gives must always be correct). S is said to be *undecidable* if there is no such algorithm. If there is such an algorithm it is called a *decision procedure* for S.[42]

To give a straightforward example of a set that is decidable, let the only members of S be the sentences 'London is in England' and 'Paris is in France'. It is easy to compose a decision procedure for this two-membered set: given any English sentence, scan through it character by character and determine whether or not it is identical to either the first member of S or the second member of S. If it is identical to one of them then output 'This sentence is in S'; otherwise output 'This sentence is not in S'. This is called a *lookup* decision procedure (or *lookup* algorithm). The program contains a complete list of the members of S and tests sentences for membership of S simply by looking through the list.

Any finite set of sentences has a lookup decision procedure. In other words, every finite set of sentence is decidable. Lookup decision procedures become less practicable as the set in question gets larger. Indeed, it is easy to imagine lookup decision procedures that are completely impossible to implement in practice. Take a set containing N English sentences, where N is the number of atoms in the known universe. Since N is finite this set has a lookup decision procedure, but it isn't one that any real computer could run. (Though a Turing machine could run it, since Turing machines have unbounded resources.) This is why lookup decision procedures for very large sets are of no relevance to AI.

Many sets have decision procedures that don't involve lookup. One example is the set of English sentences that are less than 100 characters long (to test whether a given English sentence is a member of the set just count the characters). However, some finite sets have no decision procedure apart from a lookup procedure. The sentences of this book form such a set. There is no rule for generating the sentences that an algorithm can exploit. I will describe such sets as 'undecidable save by lookup'. If the theory of cognition involves large sets that are undecidable save by lookup this could be very bad news for AI.

An *infinite* set is a set containing at least as many members as there are whole numbers. If an eternal being were to begin counting the members of an infinite set, one, two three, four . . . then no matter how large a number the being gets up to, there will always be further members left to count. Infinite sets are not necessarily exotic things. An extremely humdrum infinite set can be constructed from nothing more than the sentence 'Fred is just an ordinary bloke' and the rule: if X is a member of the set then so is 'it is false that X'. Here are the first few of the set's infinitely many members.

Fred is just an ordinary bloke.

It is false that Fred is just an
ordinary bloke.

It is false that it is false that
Fred is just an ordinary
bloke.

It is false that it is false that
    it is false that Fred is
    just an ordinary bloke.

Exercise
This infinite set is decidable. Outline a decision procedure for it. (Note 43
gives the answer.)

Logic provides examples of both decidable and undecidable infinite sets.
The set of valid sentences of what is known as truth-functional logic is infinite
and decidable. Truth-functional logic is the branch of logic that focuses on the
expressions 'if-then', 'and', 'it is false that' and 'either-or'. A *valid* sentence is
a sentence that is true come what may, true under all circumstances. An
example of a valid sentence of truth-functional logic is 'either Fred is an
ordinary bloke or it is false that Fred is an ordinary bloke'. The next step up
from truth-functional logic is first-order quantifier logic. The quantifiers are
'some' and 'every'. In the language of quantifier logic (but not of truth-
functional logic) it is possible to make such statements as 'every pig has
bristles' and 'some logicians have bristles'. Logic books brim with examples of
valid sentences of quantifier logic: 'if it false that everyone in the bar is drunk
then someone in the bar is not drunk', 'either everyone loves Suzy or someone
does not love Suzy', 'if everything in the house is either mine or mine then
everything in the house is mine', and so forth. The set of valid sentences of
first-order quantifier logic is infinite and undecidable. (This was first proved
by Church.[44]) Any attempt to write an algorithm that will test arbitrary sentences of first-order logic for validity is bound to be unsuccessful. Any procedure that anyone dreams up is bound to be unreliable, bound in the long run
to give wrong answers or no answer at all at least as many times as it gives right
ones. There simply is no decision procedure for the set of valid sentences of
first-order quantifier logic.

However, this set is not completely intractable computationally. There is an
algorithm that meets the following conditions.[45]

1 Whenever the algorithm is applied to a valid sentence of first-order
quantifier logic it will (given enough time) deliver the result 'Yes, this sentence
is valid'.

2 Whenever the algorithm is applied to a sentence of first-order quantifier
logic that is not valid it will either deliver the result 'No, this sentence is not
valid' or will deliver no answer at all (i.e. will carry on computing 'forever' –
in practice until someone turns it off or until it runs out of memory and
crashes).

An algorithm that meets these two conditions is called a semi-decision
procedure. If there is a semi-decision procedure for a set S then S is said to be
semidecidable. Every answer that a semi-decision procedure gives is correct, and
every time the algorithm is applied to a sentence that *is* in the set it *gives* an

answer, provided you wait long enough. When the algorithm is applied to a sentence that is *not* in the set it may give an answer (the right one) or it may never come to the end of its calculations.

Can you see why a semi-decision procedure is not a decision procedure? The sticking point is the proviso that you wait long enough. If you're testing a sentence and no answer is forthcoming then no matter how long you wait you can never be sure whether the algorithm is just about to pronounce, perhaps positively, or whether the sentence is one of those invalid ones for which the algorithm never delivers a result.

Are there such things as *nonsemidecidable* sets – sets, that is, for which there is not even a semi-decision procedure? Yes. Again logic furnishes an example. The set of valid sentences of *second-order* quantifier logic is known to be nonsemidecidable. First-order logic is all about saying that *things* have properties and bear relationships to other things: 'every thing has the property of being massive', 'some things have both the property of being a logician and the property of having bristles', 'there is some thing that stands in the relation of being-larger-than to every other thing'. The language of second-order logic allows us to quantify over not just things themselves but also the properties that things have and the relationships that things bear to one another. In other words, in the language of second-order logic we can write sentences containing such expressions as 'every property which' and 'there are some relationships which'. In the language of second-order logic (but not of first-order logic) it is possible to make such statements as 'Jules and Jim have some properties in common', 'every thing has some properties', 'Napoleon had every property necessary to being a good general' and 'every constitutional relationship that holds between the US President and Senate also holds between the British Prime Minister and the House of Commons'. The set of valid sentences of second order logic is as computationally intractable as they come. Any attempt to write an algorithm that will say 'Yes, that's a member' whenever it is applied to a member of the set (and never when it is applied to a non-member) is doomed. There is no such algorithm: that is what it means to say that a set of sentences is nonsemidecidable.

There is an intimate connection between the concept of a system's being algorithmically calculable and the concept of a set's being semidecidable. Let the members of S be descriptions of the input/state/output behaviour of a system B. That is, each member of S is of the form 'If the system B is given input I while in internal state X then it goes into internal state Y and produces output O'. S contains all the sentences of this form that are true of B. (For some types of system the internal state parameters will be idle; and for some systems input will sometimes produce a change in state but no output.) Unless S is semidecidable B is not algorithmically calculable. If S is nonsemidecidable there can be no algorithm that pairs each description of input into B with a correct description of the ensuing output (if any).

In the particular case where the system B is the human brain I will call this set of descriptions of input/state/output behaviour 𝔹. The members of 𝔹 are highly complicated sentences. Each records the total output (electrical and chemical) that the brain will produce in response to a particular total input received while the brain is in a particular (total) internal state.

Is 𝔹 infinite? This is an empirical question, and at present we don't know the answer. It is certainly the case that the corresponding set for a universal Turing machine is infinite, since there are infinitely many possible inputs (infinitely many ways that the limitless tape can be inscribed with 0s and 1s before the machine is set in motion). Many believe there is a good prima facie case for thinking that 𝔹 too is infinite. It is, of course, true that a brain can process only a finite number of finite inputs in its finite life. But it is not at all obvious that there are only a finite number of *potential* inputs from which the actual inputs that a given brain encounters are drawn. The potential inputs seem endless – in the same way that there are an endless number of English sentences (see the discussion of productivity in section 9.6). If the number of potential inputs is infinite then 𝔹 is infinite, for 𝔹 contains *all* input/state/output descriptions, potential as well as actual.

The same goes for states. Each brain can enter only a finite number of states in its life, yet the set of potential states from which this finite number is drawn may be infinite. (Analogously the electrical potential of a cell membrane can take only a finite number of values in the course of the cell's finite life, yet there are an indefinite number of possible values lying between the maximum and minimum values for that membrane, from which the set of actual values is drawn.) 'Thinking that P' is an example of an internal state, and there certainly seems to be no limit to the number of different things that a person could think. As Jerry Fodor puts it:

> [T]he thoughts that one actually entertains in the course of a mental life comprise a relatively unsystematic subset drawn from a vastly larger variety of thoughts that one could have entertained had an occasion for them arisen. For example, it has probably never occurred to you before that no grass grows on kangaroos. But, once your attention is drawn to the point, it's an idea that you are quite capable of entertaining, one which, in fact, you are probably inclined to endorse.[46]

How many true sentences can be produced from the following by plugging in specific numbers for k? A finite number or infinitely many?

Someone can think that 1 is less than the number k.

(Very large numbers get pretty unwieldy in standard linear notation, but bear in mind that the thinker isn't restricted to this notation. She can use power notation (3.14159×10^{5389}), introduce abbreviations ($61 \times (3.9)w^w$, where $w =$ 7954), switch bases, and so forth.) If the number of true sentences that can be produced is infinite the number of potential thoughts is infinite; if the number of potential thoughts is infinite the number of potential internal states is infinite; and if the number of potential internal states is infinite then $\mathbb{B}$ is infinite.[47]

Is $\mathbb{B}$ decidable? We don't know. Is is even semidecidable? We don't know. And if $\mathbb{B}$ is nonsemidecidable the human brain is not algorithmically calculable.[48] Even if $\mathbb{B}$ should turn out to be finite it may be undecidable save by lookup. The existence, in theory, of a lookup decision procedure could be of no conceivable relevance to AI, given the size of $\mathbb{B}$ and the sheer difficulty of formulating and listing its members. AI's ambitions to simulate the brain depend for viability on there being a practicable set of algorithms that can generate members of $\mathbb{B}$.[49]

Turing's proof

It was Turing himself in his 1936 paper who proved the existence of the uncomputable. His proof is simple and elegant. Just for fun, here is a version of it.

A binary sequence is any sequence of the basic digits 0 and 1. Each register in a computer's memory contains a binary sequence. The tape of each Turing machine that uses the binary alphabet has a binary sequence inscribed on it.[50] If the tape is of finite length the binary sequence inscribed on it is of course finite, but since Turing machines are abstractions infinite tapes and thus infinite binary sequences are permitted. It actually simplifies the proof I'm about to give if we imagine that a Turing machine's tape *always* contains an infinite binary sequence; so let's ignore machines with finite tapes. Any computation that can be performed by a machine with a finite tape can also be performed by a machine with an infinite tape.

To say that a binary sequence is *computable* is to say that there is a Turing machine that produces the sequence as output. Suppose all the computable binary sequences are listed one under another. (It doesn't matter in what order they are listed.) The list will stretch away to infinity both downwards and to the right. The top left-hand corner might look like this:

    1st machine's tape: 1 0 0 1 1 1 1 0 0 0 0 1 1 1 1 . . .
    2nd machine's tape: 1 1 0 1 0 0 0 1 0 0 1 1 0 0 0 . . .
    3rd machine's tape: 0 0 1 0 0 1 1 0 1 1 1 1 1 1 0 . . .
    4th machine's tape: 1 1 1 0 0 0 0 0 0 0 0 0 1 1 1 . . .

These sequences are the machines' outputs. A machine's input is inscribed on its tape before it starts running (and will generally get written over in the course of the computation). Reading from the left, the initial contents of a machine's tape consist of a finite binary sequence, the input, followed by an infinite string of 0s 'filling up' the remainder of the tape. Or if you're worried about how an infinite string of 0s could have got there, think of the machine as using not 1s and 0s but 1s and blanks. The input – a finite string of blanks and 1s – is inscribed at the beginning of an infinitely long blank tape. (Now the only worry is how all blanks could have got there!)

Some of the machines will halt – will stop writing on their tapes after a finite time. Whether or not a machine halts is determined by its machine table and its input. Some of the machines never halt. They are embarked on churning out an infinite sequence. Nevertheless, it remains the case that by following the instructions in its table the machine can arrive at each digit of the sequence in some finite time.

Every computable sequence is on the above list. The crux of proving the existence of the uncomputable is to specify a binary sequence that is not on the list, and so is not computable.

The first step towards specifying this sequence is to consider the infinite binary sequence whose first digit is the first digit of the first sequence on the list, whose second digit is the second digit of the second sequence on the list, whose third digit is the third digit of the third sequence on the list, and so on. (So the sequence begins 1 1 1 0 . . .) This is called the list's *diagonal sequence*.

The next step is to replace each 0 in the diagonal sequence with 1 and each 1 with 0. The result of doing this is called the *complement* of the diagonal sequence. The complement of the diagonal sequence is not on the list. This is easy to establish. The complement differs from the first sequence on the list in its first digit, differs from the second sequence on the list in its second digit, and so on. It is a consequence of the way we constructed the complement of the diagonal sequence that it differs from each sequence on the list. So the complement of the diagonal sequence is a binary sequence that is not computable. If it were computable it would be on the list, and it isn't on the list.[51]

Notice that the list of computable binary sequences can be drawn up in an infinite number of different ways – for there are an infinite number of choices for the first entry on the list. It follows that there are infinitely many binary sequences that are not computable. Each list has its own diagonal sequence the complement of which is not on the list and therefore is not computable; so, given that there are infinitely many lists, there must be infinitely many sequences that are not computable.

Let's take stock. To say that a binary sequence is not computable is simply to say that there can be no Turing machine that churns out this sequence on its tape. I'll call the set of all sequences that Turing machines *can* churn out TURING and the set of all sequences that no Turing machine can churn out

ANTITURING. There can be no algorithm that computes the members of ANTITURING. For if there were then by the Church-Turing Thesis, a Turing machine would be able to mimic the algorithm and churn out a member of ANTITURING – which is impossible. ANTITURING lies forever beyond the reach of computation.

To say that a set of infinite sequences is decidable is to say, firstly, that there is an algorithm which can churn out each member of the set and, secondly, that there is an algorithm which can churn out each non-member of the set. To say that a set of infinite sequences is semidecidable is to say that there is an algorithm which can churn out each member of the set but no algorithm which can churn out each non-member. (In extending the concepts of decidability and semidecidability as previously introduced to sets of infinite sequences we obviously have to omit the idea that an algorithm can establish membership or non-membership of the set in a finite time.)

The set TURING is undecidable, since as we have seen there is no algorithm that can churn out each non-member of the set. In fact, TURING is not even semidecidable. This is because there is no *single* algorithm that can churn out each computable binary sequence. There is no paradox here. Although each one of the computable sequences is produced by an algorithm, there is no one algorithm that produces them all. Similarly each one of us was produced by a mother, but there is no one mother that produced us all.

The reason there is no such algorithm is straightforward: if there were one it could it could be adapted to churn out a member of ANTITURING. The trick would be to keep stopping the algorithm. Let it produce only the first digit of the first computable sequence, only the first two digits of the second computable sequence, only the first three digits of the third computable sequence, and so on. Another algorithm would run along behind collecting the final digit of each broken sequence. So between them the two algorithms would be producing the diagonal sequence. Now add a third algorithm that replaces each 1 by 0 and each 0 by 1. Between them the three would be computing the complement of the diagonal sequence – which is impossible.[52]

In one and the same article Turing both floated the idea that our cognitive processes are algorithmically calculable and provided the conceptual resources for understanding how this might fail to be so.[53] Roger Penrose's bestselling *The Emperor's New Mind* contains many interesting ruminations on the question that Turing's proof raises. He writes: 'The kind of issue that I am trying to raise is whether it is conceivable that a human brain can, by the harnessing of appropriate "non-computable" physical laws, do "better", in some sense, than a Turing machine.'[54]

AI researchers are fond of saying that they are looking for Maxwell's laws of thought. Last century Maxwell reduced electrodynamics to a few elegant equations. The idea of doing the same for cognition is certainly appealing. Minsky speaks of the search for 'the three algorithms'. His metaphor is a child throwing three pebbles into a pond. The basic wavepattern produced by each pebble is very simple – concentric rings moving outwards – but the interaction of these three patterns produces a confusion of waves and ripples. The hope is – though it's fading – that the complexity of our cognitive life will similarly turn out to be the product of a small number of elegant algorithms.

Lack of success in the search for Maxwell's laws of thought is ushering in a new perspective. The mind is coming to be seen as a rag bag of large numbers of special-purpose algorithms, a motley assortment of ad hoc tools assembled by Mother Programmer, the greatest pragmatist in the universe. The latest generation of AI systems mirror this new image. Lenat's CYC already contains around thirty different special-purpose inference mechanisms.

AI is polarized around these two viewpoints – a small number of very powerful algorithms versus a large number of weaker, messier ones. Yet there is a daunting third possibility. Algorithms may not be much of the story of mind at all – at best one of the minor characters, perhaps.

Traditional program-writing AI is, of course, irrevocably bound up with the assumption that cognitive processes are algorithmically calculable by means of practicable algorithms (i.e. algorithms that can be run in real time using real resources). PDP, too, is wedded to this assumption (as I have said, PDP networks are algorithmically calculable systems.) I'm certainly not suggesting that the assumption is false – merely pointing out that at present there is very little reason, if any, to think that it is true.

10.9 Simulating networks by computer

Since PDP networks are algorithmically calculable, computers can simulate them. This fact is much exploited in PDP research. It may surprise you to learn that researchers seldom build and study real networks – it is much more convenient to study computer simulations instead. The famous past-tenses network never existed in concrete and the experiment described earlier in the chapter was in fact performed using a computer simulation. This isn't cheating. Much of the day-to-day work of computers consists of mimicry – of earthquakes, nuclear explosions, weather systems, national economies, aircraft wings, and so on. It is often far more convenient to work with a computer simulation than to work directly with the entity itself. (If a team of aero engineers want to know the increase in wing sag that will be produced by adding five percent to the weight of the engines, they don't monkey about with a real wing, but feed the new engine weights into a computer model of the aircraft and let the program calculate the increase in sag.)

Rumelhart and McClelland built a detailed computer model of the past-tenses network. That is, they wrote a computer program containing specifications of the number of units in the network, their thresholds, the pattern of inter-connections, the initial strengths of the connections, and the formula for adjusting the connection strengths during training. The program calculates exactly how the proposed network would behave. Tell the computer that the input layer of the network is to be clamped into the pattern corresponding to the verb 'squat', for example, and the program will calculate that, given the current values of the connection strengths, the network will reply with the output pattern corresponding to 'squawked'. Studying the behaviour of the computer simulation is every bit as good as studying the behaviour of the real network and far more convenient (not least because the physical procedure of increasing or decreasing the strength of a real connection is dispensed with, in favour of the much simpler business of altering the corresponding numerical value in the program).

The ability of computers to simulate networks raises an obvious philosophical question. According to the Revolution's manifesto, PDP is supposed to constitute a serious challenge to the orthodox approach to AI. Yet how can this be, if a computer program can exactly reproduce the behaviour of a network? Are PDP and the symbol system hypothesis in fact compatible with each other, after all? Let's listen to representatives of the two approaches debating this issue.

Kathy O'Symbol In my view, PDP poses no challenge to the project of achieving AI by programming computers. That doesn't mean I'm out to decry PDP. These networks have some fascinating features, such as the ability to provide content-addressable access to the information stored in them. I think it is highly likely that PDP will contribute many significant ideas to AI. However, the point I want to stress is that since a program can simulate all the relevant aspects of the behaviour of a network, we traditionalists can help ourselves freely to the properties of networks without departing from our program-writing approach to AI.

Magnus Parallel: I agree that in principle each of our networks can be simulated by a program. But you must be careful about what you infer from that. Simulations that are possible in principle are often not possible in practice. We've been able to use computer simulations up to now in our research, but only because we've been investigating relatively simple networks. Even so, the simulations take an annoyingly long time to run. A computer requires several hours to simulate just a few minutes in the life of a tiny network. So the idea of using a computer to simulate a network large enough to display real intelligence is quite absurd. You could die waiting.

Kathy Yes, currently available computers, with their von Neumann architecture, are just not fast enough to make the simulation of large scale networks practicable. The most notable feature of von Neumann architecture is the sequential mode of operation. That's the way they've been built ever since the early days. In recent times, though, the limitations of von Neumann architecture have begun to make themselves felt. For example, we'd like to be able to build expert systems containing tens of thousands of inference rules, but a program of that size would operate far too slowly – a few thousand rules is the practical limit at the moment. This is why many of us are saying that von Neumann architecture has had its day. Many labs are building experimental computers with massive numbers of processing units operating in parallel. A few years from now, von Neumann machines will be museum pieces.

Magnus We too are experimenting with designs for massively parallel hardware. After all, parallel processing is the very essence of PDP. It sounds to me as if you're talking about joining our enterprise.

Kathy There are points of contact, of course, but let's be careful not to blur the central issue. Our disagreement is not about parallel processing. The bone of contention is symbol-manipulation. We want it, you say you don't. The parallel machines we are envisaging will still store information by means of a symbolic code, and the fundamental operations of these machines will still consist of structure-sensitive manipulations of chunks of this code. Whereas, to quote one of your own slogans at you, the basic medium of exchange in PDP is not symbols but excitation and inhibition. Now, returning to the issue of simulation, I agree that a *sequential* computer could not simulate a complex network in a reasonable timespan. However, a massively parallel computer ought to be able to perform a real-time simulation of the most complicated network you can dream up. We can't prove that at the present stage, of course, but we think it's a reasonable enough conjecture. So my opening remarks still stand. Since it is likely that a symbol-manipulator can simulate the behaviour of arbitrarily complex networks, I don't see PDP as posing a challenge to the thesis that symbol-manipulation is an adequate basis for AI.

Magnus I'm still not satisfied. You're on tricky philosophical ground with this stuff about simulation. Your symbol system hypothesis says that computers can *really* think – not that they can merely *simulate* thought. It seems to me that if we're right when we claim that the human brain doesn't manipulate symbols, then your hypothesis collapses. I'll explain what I mean. Let's suppose for a moment that the human brain is a vastly complex weave of innumerable PDP networks – no programs, no symbols.

Kathy That's a whopping great suppose!

Magnus Never mind. Let's make that assumption for the sake of argument and see where it leads. Let's also suppose that a team of programmers manages to set up a perfect computer simulation of one such brain. That is, they write a program containing a specification of how all the units are connected up, of the connection strengths, and so on. The program can calculate exactly how the brain will behave. Now, let's say the person who owns the brain is thinking about chess. It would be ridiculous to claim that the computer simulation is thinking about chess. After all, none of the symbols in the program refer to chess pieces, or to anything remotely connected with chess – they refer only to units in the network, patterns of connectivity, threshold values and so forth. In other words, no part of the program is *about* chess – the program is exclusively about networks. So I think you must agree that although the computer is *simulating* someone thinking about chess, it isn't itself thinking about chess.

Kathy Yes, I've heard that line of argument before. Stuart Sutherland has a pithy way of putting the underlying point: 'If . . . more is involved in human thinking than symbol-manipulation, it might still be possible to simulate human thinking on a computer, but the program would no more be thinking than would a program simulating the behaviour of a hurricane be windy.'[55] And here's John Searle writing in a similar vein: 'No one supposes that . . . a computer simulation of a fire is likely to burn the house down. Why on earth would anyone in his right mind suppose a computer simulation of mental processes actually had mental processes?'[56]

Magnus Uh-oh! Am I really siding with John Searle?

Kathy Seems so. In fact, we're right back to the argument about the robot Turbo Sam and whether he thinks (section 6.3). In my view, if the computer in Turbo Sam's head is running this brain-simulating program you're talking about, then we've got a robot that thinks, understands, and all the rest of it. After all, Turbo Sam will be able to play chess, keep house, engage in philo-sophical debate, and in general cope with the rigours of the environment as skilfully as someone with a real brain. It's even possible that Turbo Sam should eventually turn into a more profound thinker than the human whose brain he has a copy of! Give the robot a hot-house education and his intellect may flower in ways that the 'donor's' never had a chance to. In my view, it is neither here nor there that Turbo Sam's program consists of symbols referring to thresholds, connectivity patterns and so forth. What matters is the fact that, as an adaptable system for generating behaviour, the brain-simulating pro-gram rivals a real brain. This is what makes it true that Turbo Sam thinks. So, Magnus, you're shot down in flames on this issue. Far from PDP yielding grounds for thinking that the symbol system hypothesis is false, it is actually the case that the *truth* of the hypothesis follows from your assumption that the brain is a weave of PDP networks. Because *if* that's what the brain is, a computer can simulate the brain, and hence is capable of thinking. True, the program won't involve the traditional recipe for representing knowledge (sections 4.6, 5.5). On the traditional recipe knowledge is represented directly. In the brain-simulating program, knowledge is represented indirectly, via a represen-tation of a network that 'contains' the knowledge in question. But that's OK. If a brain knows the rules of chess then a perfect simulation of that brain also knows the rules of chess.

Magnus You missed out the crucial words 'in principle'. It's an open empirical question whether some physically possible computer could give anything like a real-time simulation of an enormously complex set of networks (especially if the activity levels of the units are continuous rather than discrete). When you say that a computer can simulate the brain, you may be talking about fairyland – the way John Searle is when he says a computer can be made out of water pipes, ball-cocks and faucets (section 6.4); or the philosopher Ned Block, when he envisages forming a computer out of a billion people equipped with two-way radios![57] These things are possible in principle, but they aren't possible in the only place that really matters – the actual world.

10.10   The battle for the brain

Remember Mentalese (sections 9.1, 9.4)? According to orthodox cognitive science, human thinking consists of the manipulation of 'sentences' of this internal language or code: the brain is a biological symbol-manipulator. Hard-line PDPniks take their initial results to indicate that the brain may well get by without crunching symbols. Simple networks of artificial neurons cope without the assistance of symbolic computation, so maybe complex networks of real neurons do, too. Mother Nature has no use for Mentalese, say the PDPniks. How do the orthodox respond? Let's hear once more from Kathy O'Symbol.

Kathy 'PDP networks are great memory devices. In fact, my guess is that one of the early commercial applications of PDP will be the manufacture of special memory units used as adjuncts to conventional computers. But there's far more to cognition than just memory, obviously – and the trouble is that PDP may not be capable of delivering the rest of the goods. PDPniks are perfectly candid about this. Listen to Paul Smolensky: "It is far from clear whether connectionist models [i.e. PDP networks] have adequate . . . power to perform high-level cognitive tasks: There are serious obstacles that must be over-come before [networks] can offer . . . power comparable to that of symbolic computation."[58]

'One of the major problems concerns *inference*. The computer, like the human brain, is an extremely efficient inference engine. Tell a computer that Hamish is a Scotsman and that all Scotsmen eat haggis, and the machine can deduce effortlessly that Hamish eats haggis. Symbol-free networks, on the other hand, seem to be incorrigible dunces when it comes to inference. There is even reason to doubt whether a symbol-free network can handle compositional distinctions such as the one between *Hamish eats the haggis* and *The haggis eats Hamish*.[59] (This means simple arithmetic goes out of the window, too, since the network won't be responsive to the difference between (13×4)+9 and 13×(4+9).) When the patterns of activation that stand for Hamish, the haggis and eating are all active there's nothing to tell the network who did the eating. The only ways around this that have been proposed so far are ad hoc and artificial – not the sort of methods that one might expect a brain to use.

'None of these difficulties arise if you've got symbols on hand and the associated properties of compositionality and recursive structure (section 4.2). In a computer the meanings of *Hamish is a Scotsman* and *All Scotsmen eat haggis* are represented by related symbol-structures. Logical inference is easy when there is a systematically structured symbolic code to do it in. This suggests that the way to give networks the power they appear to lack is to turn them into symbol-manipulators!

'As we see it, then, one of the main tasks confronting PDP researchers is to figure out how to implement a symbolic code in their networks. That's our advice to them, ironic as it is: turn networks into genuine computers. It's an exciting thought – hardware modelled on human wetware is something computer scientists have dreamed about for years. I'm pleased to say that initial attempts to make networks manipulate symbols have proved encouraging. For example, David Touretzky has managed to simulate a network that will execute a simple program consisting of instructions like this one:

If the symbols CAT are present in the workspace, delete them and create the symbols DOG in their place.[60]

'I can now comment on the issue of whether PDP conflicts with the theory that the brain is a computer. A consequence of what I've just been saying is that the brain might consist of PDP networks *and yet still be a computer*. The two are not necessarily exclusive, given that networks can function as symbol-processors (and, indeed, gain power by doing so). We traditionalists like to view PDP as a theory of how symbolic computation is physically realised in the brain – or, rather, as the sketchy beginnings of such a theory.[61] In other words, we view PDP as an investigation into the mechanisms that the brain uses to *do* its symbol crunching.

'An example will clarify what I'm saying. A nameless foreign power builds a top secret military robot. The CIA steals one and an AI lab is given the job of figuring out how the on-board computer does its tricks. Two related but different tasks confront the team. One is to investigate the symbolic side of things: what kind of code does the computer use and what programs does it have? The other is to investigate how the computer itself is designed. Does it have a von Neumann architecture or is it some type of parallel processor? Does it use a distributed memory system, and if so, how does this work? What mechanisms does it use to execute if-then instructions? And so on. Questions of this sort are often called *implementational* ones. Returning to cognitive science, it too consists of two levels of enquiry. There is the *symbol level*, where we are concerned with such questions as what the brain's symbolic code is like, what fundamental symbol-processing operations evolution has made available, and which concatenations of these operations the brain uses in performing specific cognitive tasks. Second, there is the *implementation level*: how does this 3lb hunk of tissue actually perform its symbol-processing? Serial or parallel? Or both? Stored programs, or the biological equivalent of modifiable hard-wiring (as in the ENIAC)? A centralized control, or something different? How is memory handled? What sort of structures execute the fundamental symbol-manipulating operations? And so on.

'The computational brain must be studied at both these levels. PDPniks tend to regard their work as forming a radical break with traditional cognitive science. We ourselves see things rather differently. We welcome PDP as a pioneering effort in the study of the implementation level of the brain.'

10.11   Concluding remarks

This view of PDP can be called *implementationalism*. At the opposite pole lies *eliminativism*.[62] The eliminativist believes it will become increasingly plain, as PDP marches forward, that all forms of cognition can be explained in ways that do not involve reference to a quasi-linguistic brain code. The theory that the brain is a symbol-processor will ultimately vanish, say eliminativists. In between these poles lies *moderatism*. Moderates expect that a variety of theories will be required to fully explain the functioning of the brain. They anticipate a division of labour, with the symbolic approach yielding the correct account of some cognitive processes and 'pure' PDP of others (language processing and logical reasoning are offered as possible examples of the former, face recognition and associative memory of the latter). In addition, moderates expect the study of PDP to alter our understanding of symbolic computation itself, in unforseeable and perhaps radical ways (implementationlists may or may not share this expectation). Moderates point out that research into the use of PDP architectures for processing symbols may lead to the discovery of a glorious bonanza of exotic fundamental operations. The fundamental opera-tions of today's computers – shift, compare-right, copy and so forth – form an unlikely model for the workings of the brain. The fundamental symbol-manipulating operations that become available in PDP architectures may hold greater promise. Thus the moderate stresses that, far from eliminating the theory that the brain is a symbol-processor, the study of PDP may well con-siderably enhance that theory's plausibility.

It would be premature to speculate which of these three positions is correct. Perhaps none of them is (section 10.8). We have strayed well beyond the cur-rent frontiers of knowledge. Implementationalism, eliminativism and moderatism are the articulating beliefs of three vast research programs. These three programs are in competition with one another, but they are also closely related. All are children of AI. For better or for worse, these computationally-inspired research programs dominate the current agenda for the study of the brain. It is an agenda that will occupy cognitive science well into the next century.

Epilogue

To call an animal a machine is to indicate that its manner of functioning is not essentially different from machines which might be designed or made by men . . . This is to say that living organisms are in fact so constituted that we could in principle understand them as engineers or physicists understand their systems.

Richard L. Gregory[1]

In 1745 the philosopher and physician Julien de la Mettrie proposed that human beings are machines. Not surprisingly his views were met with hostility and ridicule. He wrote for an audience whose best examples of machines were weaving looms and clockwork timepieces; one cannot blame them for finding his theory both incomprehensible and debasing. ('The body is but a watch,' explained de la Mettrie with great implausibility. 'Man is but . . . a collection of springs which wind each other up . . . The brain has muscles for thinking as the legs have muscles for walking.')[2]

Where de la Mettrie's contemporaries found it difficult to understand how humans could possibly be machines, some of us nowadays find it hard to understand how we could not be. (Perhaps you are, or are becoming, one of us.) The watch was de la Mettrie's finest example of an artefact; among our finest are artefacts whose behaviour is crudely similar to that of brain tissue. And four decades of experimental work in AI have taught us much concerning the potential richness and flexibility of machines. Moreover we possess philo-sophical sketches of how the possibility of thought and free action can arise for an artefact; and we find no reason to doubt that consciousness, too, is a purely physical phenomenon.

In 1637 René Descartes, the father of modern philosophy, argued that our ability to think is our very essence: it is what makes us the beings that we are, what distinguishes us from the animals.[3] *Cogito ergo sum*, he declared. I think therefore I am. At the close of the twentieth century de la Mettrie's new followers confidently place 'machina' after 'sum'. I think therefore I am a machine.

Notes

Introduction

1 Minsky, M. *Semantic Information Processing*, p. v.
2 *Better Mind the Computer*, BBC TV. I have edited this spoken material slightly in order to achieve a smoother flow.
3 Douglas Lenat and Edward Feigenbaum, two leading AI researchers, envision a future in which some human dignity remains. In 1991 they made the following statement: 'We cannot hold AI back any more than primitive man could have suppressed the spread of speaking . . . Our distant descendants may look back on the synergistic man-machine systems that emerge from AI as the natural dividing line between "real human beings" and "animals". We stand, at the end of the 1980s, at the interstice between the first era of intelligent systems . . . and the second era . . . In that second era . . . the "system" will be reconceptualised as a kind of colleagular relationship between intelligent computer agents and intelligent people . . . From such man-machine systems will emerge intelligence and competence surpassing the unaided human's. Beyond that threshold, in turn, lie wonders which we (as unaided humans) literally cannot today imagine.' (Lenat, D. B., Feigenbaum, E. A. 'On the Thresholds of Knowledge', pp. 224–5.) They include 'superhuman intelligence' among AI's 'nine ultimate goals' (op. cit. p. 226).

Chapter 1   The beginnings of Artificial Intelligence: a historical sketch

1 For details see Zuse, K. 'Some Remarks on the History of Computing in Germany', and Bauer, F. L. 'Between Zuse and Rutishauser – The Early Development of Digital Computing in Central Europe'.
2 The restrictions were not lifted until 1955. From 1945 Zuse worked on a programming language he called the Plankalkül. His ideas had a certain amount of influence on the designers of the language ALGOL (see Bauer, op. cit. pp. 521–2).

3   An *electronic* computer is one built from electronic components – in the early days vacuum tubes, now semiconductors. With the exception of Zuse's machine, all the computers mentioned in this chapter used electronic components. Zuse used relays. These are small electrically-driven mechanical switches. They operate much more slowly than vacuum tubes. The latter owe their speed to the fact that they have no moving parts save a beam of electrons (hence the term). Relays were used extensively in the calculating machines of the pre-war era, and as late as 1948 IBM unveiled a computer based on this older technology (it had 21,400 relays and only 13,500 vacuum tubes). This machine, the SSEC, was out of date before it ran its first program.

4   For details of the Colossus, see Randell, B. 'The Colossus' and also his 'On Alan Turing and the Origins of Digital Computers'.

5   For example Stan Augarten in *Bit By Bit*, p. 146.

6   Good, I. J. 'Pioneering Work on Computers at Bletchley', p. 41.

7   Kilburn, T., Williams, F. C. 'The University of Manchester Computing Machine', p. 120.

8   Lavington, S. H. *A History of Manchester Computers*, pp. 12–15. Comparing the Manchester machine to the University of Cambridge EDSAC computer (which was first operational in May 1949), Lavington writes 'the Manchester Mark I was much less of a finished product from the user's viewpoint, but offered a comparable basic number-crunching performance (the Mark I in fact had a rather larger storage capacity)'. The fact that the EDSAC was more user friendly made it better suited for serious mathematical work. It was not until October 1949 that the Manchester Mark I caught up in this respect.

9   Stern, N. 'The BINAC: A Case Study in the History of Technology', p. 12.

10   The world's first transistorized computer was also built at the University of Manchester. It became operational in November 1953. Lavington's *Early British Computers* gives an excellent presentation of the British side of the story.

11   Lavington, S. H. *A History of Manchester Computers*, p. 20. Alan Turing produced the love letters by using the machine's random number generator.

12   The ENIAC is described by Goldstine, H. H. and Goldstine, A. 'The Electronic Numerical Integrator and Computer'.

13   The relay-based IBM SSEC, which first ran in public in January 1948, was also a stored-program machine but was not fully electronic (see note 3).

14   In September 1948 the ENIAC was modified to operate with a stored program. This reduced the setting-up time from days to minutes. However, the modified ENIAC was never a stored-program computer in the full sense. This is because the program was stored in read-only memory, which meant that the benefits of variable addressing (note 19) could not be enjoyed. (See Metropolis, N., Worlton, J. 'A Trilogy of Errors in the History of Computing', pp. 53–4.)

15   Larson, E. R. 'Honeywell, Inc. v. Sperry Rand Corp., et al.', p. 694.

16   Atanasoff, J. V. 'Computing Machine for the Solution of Large Systems of Linear Algebraic Equations'.

17   Shurkin, J. *Engines of the Mind*, p. 174.

18   From one of von Neumann's letters. (Quoted by Andrew Hodges in *Alan Turing: The Enigma*, p. 304.) It is a common observation that the computerization of society has been a side effect of the computerization of war. The ENIAC's first real task was to assist, under von Neumann's direction, in designing the H bomb.

19   A particularly bitter controversy has raged concerning the provenance of the stored-program concept. The concept is present in Alan Turing's seminal article 'On Computable Numbers, with an Application to the Entscheidungsproblem', published in 1936 (see especially the discussion of standard descriptions and description numbers, pp. 240–2). In the United States the first published discussion of the stored-program concept was von Neumann's 'First Draft of a Report on the EDVAC', which appeared in 1945. (The EDVAC was the ENIAC's projected successor.) Von Neumann's sole authorship of this report led many to assume that he was responsible for the concept. In fact the 'First Draft' was a write-up of the ideas of Eckert, Mauchly, von Neumann, and other members of the ENIAC group. Eckert and Mauchly were outraged that the 'First Draft' was published with only von Neumann's name on it (although this may have been done without von Neumann's permission; see also note 33). The concept of storing both the data to be operated upon and the operating instructions on the same internal disks seems to have originated with Eckert in a memo written in January 1944, some months before von Neumann joined the ENIAC group (see Eckert, J. P. 'The ENIAC'). Von Neumann's chief contribution to the stored-program concept was the idea of a *variable address* (see Burks, A. W. 'From ENIAC to the Stored-Program Computer: Two Revolutions in Computers', p. 340). Von Neumann's invention, which opened the way to the use of subroutines and loops, enables a program to modify itself in certain respects while it is running. A streamlined version of variable addressing called *indirect* addressing is described in detail in chapter 4. Indirect addressing was invented at Manchester and implemented in the Mark I (see Lavington, S. H. *A History of Manchester Computers*, p. 12).
20   Quoted by Shurkin, J. *Engines of the Mind*, p. 173.
21   The JOHNNIAC, owned by the RAND Corporation at Santa Monica, was a near copy of the machine that von Neumann and his team built at the Institute for Advanced Study in Princeton. Many such copies were built. They became known as Princeton Class machines. (See Gruenberger, F. J. 'The History of the JOHNNIAC'.)
22   Newell, A., Shaw, J. C., Simon, H. A. 'Empirical Explorations with the Logic Theory Machine: a Case Study in Heuristics'.
23   Herbert Gelernter took up this project, and in 1959 his program proved its first theorem in elementary Euclidean geometry. (Gelernter, H., Hansen, J. R., Loveland, D. W. 'Empirical Explorations of the Geometry Theorem Proving Machine'.)
24   From an interview with Pamela McCorduck, recorded in her *Machines Who Think*, p. 143.
25   Ibid, p. 142.
26   The notion that the Logic Theorist was 'first' has been widely put about. See, for example, Fleck, J. 'Development and Establishment in Artificial Intelligence', p. 115 (the Logic Theorist was 'the first working, characteristically AI program developed'); Simons, G. L. *Introducing Artificial Intelligence*, p. 48 (the Logic Theorist was 'the first effective AI program'); Waldrop, M. M. *Man-Made Minds: The Promise of Artificial Intelligence*, p. 23 (the Logic Theorist was 'the first true AI program'). One author even states that 'Samuel's program was preceded in 1956 by a program called the Logic Theorist' (Berry, A. *The Super-Intelligent Machine*, p. 30). Feigenbaum and Feldman describe the Logic Theorist as 'the

Notes to pages 8–10

first heuristic program fully realized on a computer' in their influential *Computers and Thought* (p. 108). However, in Samuel's own words, his program 'achieved this aim – to improve its playing ability through [a] learning process involving heuristics – fairly early in its existence, certainly well before 1956 . . . Except for the fact that no publicity was made of the existence of my checker program, one could argue that a program employing learning heuristics had been "fully realized" by this time . . . My checker program was one of the first programs of any size to be run on the first experimental model of . . . the IBM 701.' (Personal communication, December 6, 1988.)

27 Feigenbaum, E. A., Feldman, J. *Computers and Thought*, p. 108.

28 From an interview with Pamela McCorduck, recorded in her *Machines Who Think*, pp. 95–6.

29 Some of the central ideas of this article were prefigured two years earlier in a discussion paper which Turing entitled 'Intelligent Machinery'. (This paper was published posthumously in 1969.)

30 It is not unusual to see Turing referred to as the founding father of AI itself (for example Bundy, A. *Artificial Intelligence*, p. ix; Herken, R. *The Universal Turing Machine*, p. xii; Ringle, M. *Philosophical Perspectives in Artificial Intelligence*, p. 1.; Searle, J. 'Is the Brain's Mind a Computer Program?', p. 20; Shortliffe, E. H. *Computer-Based Medical Consultations: MYCIN*, p. 13). This is hyperbole. Turing did not work on anything that can be described as an AI program (save for an extremely unsatisfactory chess program that he never completed; see Bates, A. M., Bowden, B. V., Strachey, C., Turing, A. M. 'Digital Computers Applied to Games'). Nor did he appreciably influence the ideas of Minsky, Simon, or the other figures at the Dartmouth Conference (McCorduck, P. *Machines Who Think*, p. 95, note 1). It is as the founder of the *philosophy* of AI that Turing takes his rightful place in the history of the subject.

31 Jefferson, G. 'The Mind of Mechanical Man', p. 1110. (This is the text of the Lister Oration, delivered at the Royal College of Surgeons in June 1949.)

32 Turing, A. M. 'On Computable Numbers, with an Application to the Entscheidungsproblem'.

33 As indeed was von Neumann. Stanley Frankel, one of the first scientists to use the ENIAC, writes as follows: '[V]on Neumann was well aware of the fundamental importance of Turing's paper of 1936 . . . which describes in principle the Universal Computer of which every modern computer . . . is a realization . . . Many people have acclaimed von Neumann as the "father of the computer" but I am sure he would never have made that mistake himself. He might well be called the midwife, perhaps, but he firmly emphasized to me, and to others I am sure, that the fundamental conception is owing to Turing – in so far as not anticipated by Babbage, Lovelace and others.' (From a letter reproduced in Randell, B. 'On Alan Turing and the Origins of Digital Computers', p. 10.) Babbage's work is described in chapter 4.

34 Hodges, A. *Alan Turing: The Enigma*, pp. 267–8.

35 The Germans had a supposedly unbreakable code known as Enigma, which throughout the war was their main method of safeguarding military radio communications from eager allied eavesdroppers. Turing devised a machine for the

rapid decoding of messages broadcast in Enigma and thereby gave the Allies open access to the entire radio communications network of the Wehrmacht. By 1942 the Bletchley staff were decoding 50,000 intercepted messages a month – one a minute. These ranged from orders for individual U-boat commanders to planning directives of the highest level. This was the first, and probably the last, war in which one side had the blessing of a detailed and comprehensive foreknowledge of the other's strategy. Turing's codebreaking machines, which ticked loudly, were known as Bombes. Hodges gives an excellent account of the Bletchley operation; op. cit. chapter 4.

36 I. J. Good in an interview with Pamela McCorduck, recorded in her *Machines Who Think*, p. 53.

37 Here is Turing's own statement of the relationship between the Turing machine and the ACE. 'Some years ago I was researching on what might now be described as an investigation of the theoretical possibilities and limitations of digital computing machines. I considered a type of machine which had a central mechanism, and an infinite memory which was contained on an infinite tape . . . Machines such as the ACE may be regarded as practical versions of this same type of machine.' ('Lecture to the London Mathematical Society on 20 February 1947', pp. 106–7.) In a letter to Ross Ashby (undated but written while Turing was working on the ACE at the National Physical Laboratory) he says: 'The ACE is in fact analogous to the "universal machine" described in my paper on conputable [sic] numbers . . . [W]ithout altering the design of the machine itself, it can, in theory at any rate, be used as a model of any other machine, by making it remember a suitable set of instructions.' (NPL archive, Science Museum Library, South Kensington, London.) As Hodges suggests (*Alan Turing: The Enigma*, p. 556) Sara Turing was probably more or less quoting her son's own words when she wrote '[H]is aim [was] to see his logical theory of a universal machine, previously set out in his paper "Computable Numbers" [sic] . . . take concrete form in an actual machine' (*Alan M. Turing*, p. 78).

38 The production model was called the DEUCE. A pilot version of the ACE – then the fastest machine in the world – first ran in 1950, two years after Turing had left the project.

Chapter 2   Some dazzling exhibits

1 Heiser, J. F., Colby, K. M., Faught, W. S., Parkison, R. C. 'Can Psychiatrists Distinguish a Computer Simulation of Paranoia from the Real Thing?'
2 See Colby, K. M. *Artificial Paranoia*, and 'Modeling a Paranoid Mind'.
3 Colby, K. M., Weber, S., Hilf, F. D. 'Artificial Paranoia', pp. 16–18.
4 See chapter 3, section 3.3.
5 As is often related, Weizenbaum named the program after Eliza Doolittle, a character in George Bernard Shaw's play *Pygmalion*. Weizenbaum, like the professor in the play, was able to teach his protégé to speak increasingly well.
6 Weizenbaum, J. *Computer Power and Human Reason*, pp. 3–4.
7 Weizenbaum, J. *Computer Power and Human Reason*, pp. 1–16.
8 Weizenbaum, J. *Computer Power and Human Reason*, p. 7.

9   McCorduck, P. *Machines Who Think*, pp. 254–5.
10 Colby, K. M., Watt, J. B., Gilbert, J. P. 'A Computer Method of Psychotherapy: Preliminary Communication', p. 152.
11 Weizenbaum, J. *Computer Power and Human Reason*, pp. 202–3.
12 Weizenbaum, J. *Computer Power and Human Reason*, chapter 8.
13 What follows is an edited version of a transcript reproduced in Winograd, T. *Understanding Natural Language*, pp. 8–15. Two of the entries are taken not from this source, but from Winograd, T. *Procedures as a Representation for Data in a Computer Program for Understanding Natural Language*, p. 44.
14 A 'hack' is an elegant piece of programming. The term 'hacker' is also used for a raider who breaks into other people's computer files.
15 Weizenbaum, J. *Computer Power and Human Reason*, p. 116.
16 Sussman, G. J. *A Computer Model of Skill Acquisition*.
17 Sussman, G. J. *A Computer Model of Skill Acquisition*, p. 73.
18 *A Computer Model of Skill Acquisition*, p. 83. (Sussman himself assumes that Hacker is male.)
19 *A Computer Model of Skill Acquisition*, p. 83.
20 *A Computer Model of Skill Acquisition*, p. 26.
21 *A Computer Model of Skill Acquisition*, chapters II and IV.
22 Samuel, A. L. 'Some Studies in Machine Learning Using the Game of Checkers', p. 71. See also chapter 1 note 26.
23 Samuel, A. L. 'Some Studies in Machine Learning Using the Game of Checkers', p. 89.
24 Samuel, A. L. 'Some Studies in Machine Learning Using the Game of Checkers', p. 103.
25 Samuel, A. L. 'Some Studies in Machine Learning Using the Game of Checkers', p. 104.
26 Maximum look-ahead is ten turns of play.
27 *Sports Illustrated*, vol. 71, Oct. 30, 1989, p. 97.
28 With thanks to Don Beal for this information.
29 Personal communication.
30 For a contrary opinion, see Hubert and Stuart Dreyfus *Mind Over Machine*, chapter 4.
31 Much of the work on GPS was carried out at Carnegie-Mellon University, although like the Logic Theorist, the program first ran on the RAND Corporation's JOHNNIAC.
32 Adapted from Ernst, G. W. and Newell, A. *GPS: A Case Study in Generality and Problem Solving*, chapter VI.
33 Adapted from Copi, I. M. *Introduction to Logic*, Second Edition, p. 18. See note 13 to chapter 5.
34 Newell, A., Simon, H. 'GPS, a Program that Simulates Human Thought'.
35 Newell, A., Simon, H. 'GPS, a Program that Simulates Human Thought', p. 293.
36 The distinction between human AI and alien AI first came to the fore at the Dartmouth Conference, under the terminology of 'theoretical mode' and 'performance mode'.
37 Nils Nilsson, quoted in Rose, F. *Into the Heart of the Mind*, p. 177.

38   *Can Digital Computers Think?*, BBC Radio, May 1951. (Quoted by Hodges, A., *Alan Turing: The Enigma*, p. 442.)
39   Story and questions are from Schank, R. C., Abelson, R. *Scripts, Plans, Goals and Understanding*, pp. 178–80.
40   De Jong, G. 'Skimming Newspaper Stories by Computer', p. 16.
41   For a full account, see Schank, R. C., Abelson, R. *Scripts, Plans, Goals and Understanding*, especially chapter 3.
42   Op. cit., pp. 47–8; and Schank, R. *The Cognitive Computer*, p. 122.
43   Based on Schank, R. *The Cognitive Computer*, p. 111.
44   Simons, G. *Are Computers Alive?*, p. 66.
45   A Centaur has the intelligence of a man and the strength and swiftness of a horse; while 'mycin' is a suffix commonly found in the generic names of antimicrobial drugs (as in 'streptomycin').
46   Shortliffe, E. *Computer-Based Medical Consultations: MYCIN*, pp. 52, 142–3.
47   Jackson, P. *Introduction to Expert Systems*, p. 106.
48   An edited version of output reproduced in Aikins, J. S. 'Prototypical Knowledge for Expert Systems', pp. 173–6.
49   Winograd, T., Flores, F. *Understanding Computers and Cognition*, p. 132. For a sceptical evaluation of the worth of expert systems, see Dreyfus, H., Dreyfus, S. *Mind Over Machine*.

Chapter 3   Can a machine think?

1   Beach, F. A., Hebb, D. O., Morgan, C. T., Nissen, H. W., (eds) *The Neuropsychology of Lashley*, p. xix.
2   André Breton, *First Surrealist Manifesto*.
3   For a detailed discussion of this issue, see Jackendoff, R., *Consciousness and the Computational Mind*, esp. ch. 6.
4   Weiskrantz, L., Warrington, E. K., Sanders, M. D., Marshall, J., 'Visual Capacity in the Hemianopic Field Following a Restricted Occipital Ablation'; Weiskrantz, L. *Blindsight*.
5   Weiskrantz, L., 'Trying to Bridge Some Neuropsychological Gaps Between Monkey and Man'.
6   Lackner, J. R., Garrett, M. F., 'Resolving Ambiguity: Effects of Biasing Context in the Unattended Ear'.
7   All references to Turing's views in this chapter are to this article.
8   This is slightly stronger than Turing's original formulation. He says (p. 434): 'The object of the game for the third player is to help the interrogator. The best strategy for her is probably to give truthful answers.'
9   *The Philosophical Writings of Descartes*, volume 1, translated by Cottingham, J., Stoothoff, R., Murdoch, D., p. 140.
10   Described by Daniel Bobrow in 'A Turing Test Passed'.
11   For example, Christopher Longuet-Higgins in 'To Mind via Semantics', p. 92.
12   This is a 'conversation' I had with Eliza version 4.3.

13   Heiser, J. F., Colby, K. M., Faught, W. S., Parkison, R. C., 'Can Psychiatrists Distinguish a Computer Simulation of Paranoia From the Real Thing?'.

14   To quote from the runtime comments of one interrogator: 'Not too many people say "and/or". That's a very machine-like structure.' (Op. cit. p. 155.)

15   Those interested in a fuller description of the details of Parry's functioning should read Colby's *Artificial Paranoia*.

16   Weizenbaum, J., 'ELIZA – a Computer Program for the Study of Natural Language Communication Between Man and Machine', p. 42. (Further information about Eliza's functioning may be found in this article.)

17   Ned Block, for example, advances this criticism in 'Psychologism and Behaviourism'.

18   Peter Carruthers advances this objection in *Introducing Persons*, pp. 241–2.

19   'Computing Machinery and Intelligence', pp. 456, 460.

20   Compare Douglas Hofstadter in *The Mind's Eye* (ed. Hofstadter, D. R., Dennett, D. C.), pp. 72–3.

21   By Malcolm Stairmand.

22   A version of this argument has also occurred to Claude Shannon and John McCarthy (*Automata Studies*, pp. v–vi) and to Ned Block ('Psychologism and Behaviourism'). James Culbertson has in effect shown how to design an idealized machine that will do what I have described Superparry as doing ('Some Uneconomical Robots').

23   The puzzle was revitalized by Thomas Hobbes in the seventeenth century. Hobbes is responsible for the version of it I give (*Works*, ed. Molesworth, W., vol. 1, pp. 136–7).

24   This example is due to Fuller, L. L., 'Positivism and Fidelity to Law – A Reply to Professor Hart', p. 663.

25   Compare Hilary Putnam, 'Robots: Machines or Artificially Created Life?', esp. p. 406. He argues that 'Are androids alive?' is a prime example of a question whose answer calls for a decision and not for a discovery (p. 403 ff). Putnam holds that the question 'Are robots conscious?' also calls for a decision. My account differs. As will emerge in chapter 8 I believe that where consciousness is concerned, there *is* a fact of the matter.

26   Wittgenstein, L., *Philosophical Investigations*, sect. 360.

27   The behaviour of the digger wasp is described by Wooldridge, D., *The Machinery of the Brain*, p. 82; see also Dennett, D., *Elbow Room*, p. 11.

28   Compare Donald Michie's characterization of human intelligence. 'The human intellect is marked not so much for any special brilliance at some particular task, but rather for its ability to make a plausible shot at almost anything. We accordingly suspend judgement about the idea of an intelligent machine, waiting until one arises with the versatility and the powers of integrative behaviour which we demand of our colleagues.' *On Machine Intelligence*, p. 51.

29   The term 'intentional explanation' has been popularised by Daniel Dennett; see especially *Brainstorms*, chs. 1 and 12.

30   Goodall, J., *In the Shadow of Man*, pp. 95–6. A sceptic bothered by the fact that we can have no linguistic confirmation from Figan that this was indeed his plan might suggest an alternative, simpler, explanation: Figan went away and forgot the banana, only to notice it again as he watched Goliath leave. However, Goodall would presumably defend her analysis by piling example upon example until it became difficult to resist her estimation of Figan's planning abilities.

Chapter 4   The symbol system hypothesis

1   The hypothesis was named by Allen Newell and Herbert Simon in 'Computer Science as Empirical Inquiry: Symbols and Search'. (They call it the physical symbol system hypothesis, but for ease I drop 'physical'.) See also Simon and Newell, 'Information-Processing in Computer and Man'; Newell, 'Physical Symbol Systems' and 'The Knowledge Level'; and Lenat, D. B., Feigenbaum, E. A. 'On the Thresholds of Knowledge'.

2   A flip-flop usually consists of a pair of transistors.

3   In the case of the characters '0' to '9', the ASCII values are not quite as arbitrary as elsewhere in the system. The codes for numeric characters have been chosen so that subtracting the code for the character '0' gives the corresponding binary number. (Binary numbers are explained in full later in the present section.) For example, the ASCII code for '3' is 0110011 and for '0' is 0110000. Subtracting yields 0000011, which is the number three in base-2 notation. This convention makes it easy for the machine to translate numerical input into base-2. (Morse is responsive to letter frequency; thus the code for 'E' is simpler than the code for 'Q', for instance.)

4   111111   111101   000000   111110   000001.
    111111   111111   000010   110111   011111   000000.

5   Sometimes several registers are required to store a single 'chunk'. For example, a computer whose registers have a maximum capacity of 8 bits will need two registers to store the 9 bit binary number 100001111. Register capacity varies from computer to computer. Smaller machines use 8 or 16 bit registers, while more powerful ones use 32 or 64 bit registers.

6   See note 19 to chapter 1.

7   This exercise is important from a theoretical viewpoint. Calvin Elgot and Abraham Robinson ('Random-Access Stored-Program Machines, an Approach to Programming Languages') have proved that simple expressions like $x_1+x_2+x_3+ \ldots +x_n$, where n may take any value, cannot be computed by a stored-program random-access machine without the use of indirect addressing or some equivalent technique for modifying instructions while the program is running (such as von Neumann's variable addressing; see chapter 1, note 19). The Elgot-Robinson result applies only to machines with random-access memory and not to machines with serial access memory. (You have random access to the drawers of a filing cabinet – you can go straight to whichever drawer you want and open it. You have serial access to the contents of a tape cassette – to get to the track you want you have to fast-forward through any preceding tracks.) Turing machines (chapter 6) have serial-access memory. A Turing machine can compute expressions like the foregoing without the use of instruction-modification. Not all commentators are clear about this. According to Herman Goldstine 'A machine without the ability to alter instructions cannot form [i.e. compute] such simple expressions as $[x_1+x_2+x_3+ \ldots +x_n]$ for arbitrary values n=1, 2, . . .' (*The Computer from Pascal to von Neumann*, pp. 265–6).

8   Hint: use the copy instruction to store the contents of the register whose address

is stored in register x at a known address α; do the same for the contents of subsequent registers; branch to α.

9   There is much redundancy in this list (see Newell, A. 'Physical Symbol Systems', section 4.8). Redundancy is often a virtue in computer design, since it makes for efficiency. A machine that has to 'build' each branch-on-0 or Rbranch out of other operations will be slower, other things being equal, than a machine that has these operations among its primitives.

10 A machine that uses the listed operations and has unbounded memory is equivalent to a universal Turing machine. (See chapter 6 and Newell, op. cit., section 3.) The proof of this consists essentially of writing a program for the machine that enables it to simulate a universal Turing machine, and writing a program for a universal Turing machine that enables it to simulate a machine that uses the listed operations.

11 In the traditional version of this recipe symbolic expressions represent real-world objects, relationships etc. directly, without the mediation of further representations. For example, in the mini-language presented in section 4.2 the identifier 000001 directly represents the real-world object Mary. Indirect representation is also possible. In this case the symbolic expressions directly represent other items that themselves represent the real-world objects (etc.) in question. A version of the recipe involving indirect representation is discussed in section 10.9.

12 Cantor proved the existence of a cardinal number greater than the cardinal number of the set of all integers.

13 Turing, A. M. 'Computing Machinery and Intelligence', p. 439.

14 An interesting account of Babbage's visionary project is given by Alan Bromley in 'Charles Babbage's Analytical Engine, 1838'. See also Lovelace, A. A. and Menabrea, L. F. 'Sketch of the Analytical Engine Invented by Charles Babbage, Esq.'. Ada Lovelace was Babbage's collaborator. She wrote a number of programs for the Engine. Metropolis and Worlton have investigated the extent to which the pioneers of electronic computing were aware of Babbage's work ('A Trilogy of Errors in the History of Computing', pp. 50–3). Babbage was mentioned in lectures at the Moore School (home of the ENIAC) in 1946 and in lectures at Manchester in 1947. 'Babbage' was a household word for all those working on Turing's ACE project at the National Physical Laboratory, Teddington. Both Lovelace and Babbage are mentioned by Turing in 'Computing Machinery and Intelligence'.

15 See the articles by Newell and Simon cited in note 1. Two other leading proponents of the strong symbol system hypothesis are Jerry Fodor (*The Language of Thought*) and Zenon Pylyshyn (*Computation and Cognition*).

Chapter 5   A hard look at the facts

1   Lenat, D. B. 'The Nature of Heuristics', p. 242.
2   Winston, P. H. 'Learning Structural Descriptions from Examples'.
3   Waltz, D. L. 'Understanding Line Drawings of Scenes With Shadows'.
4   Raphael, B. *The Thinking Computer*, chapter 8.
5   Raphael, B. 'The Robot Shakey and his Successors', p. 7.

6   Giuliano, V. E. 'Comments on a Paper by R. F. Simmons', p. 69; Lenat, D. B. 'Computer Software for Intelligent Systems', p. 152.

7   Both these statements by Minsky are reported in Dreyfus, H. L., and Dreyfus, S. E., *Mind Over Machine*, p. 78.

8   Dreyfus, H. L., Dreyfus, S. E., *Mind Over Machine*, p. 10.

9   Dreyfus, H. L., Dreyfus, S. E., *Mind Over Machine*, p. xi.

10 McDermott, D. 'Artificial Intelligence Meets Natural Stupidity', p. 144.

11 Full details of the program may be found in Ernst, G. W. and Newell, A. GPS: *A Case Study in Generality and Problem Solving*.

12 Ernst, G. W. and Newell, A. GPS: *A Case Study in Generality and Problem Solving*, p. 163.

13 Newell and Ernst detail eleven representations given to the program in GPS: *A Case Study in Generality and Problem Solving*, chapter 6. In order to represent the problem about the murder of Benito (section 2.7) in a form that GPS can solve, the programmer must treat Razor's utterances 'I'm innocent' and 'Any of these schmucks who says I did it is lying' as being one and the same sentence. (This particular example is not given by Newell and Ernst.)

14 GPS: *A Case Study in Generality and Problem Solving*, p. vii.

15 Dreyfus, H. L. *What Computers Can't Do* (Second Edition), pp. 96, 296.

16 Simon, H. *The Shape of Automation*, p. 83.

17 The name is due to John McCarthy. (McCarthy, J., Hayes, P. J., 'Some Philosophical Problems from the Standpoint of Artificial Intelligence'.)

18 Minsky, M. 'A Framework for Representing Knowledge', p. 124.

19 The micro-world policy manifesto is Minsky, M., Papert, S. 'Progress Report on Artificial Intelligence'.

20 Haugeland, J. *Artificial Intelligence: the Very Idea*, p. 190. I have modified Haugeland's version slightly.

21 Winograd, T. *Understanding Natural Language*, section 7.

22 Winograd, T. *Understanding Natural Language*, p. 143.

23 Simon, H. A. 'Artificial Intelligence Systems that Understand', p. 1061.

24 Winograd, T. 'Breaking the Complexity Barrier Again', p. 13.

25 Winograd, T. 'Breaking the Complexity Barrier Again', Part 1.

26 The search for methods for programming general temporal structure is well under way but far from complete. For a survey see section 1 of my collection *Logic and Reality*.

27 *Supplement to the Oxford English Dictionary*, vol. II. (The word is possibly derived from 'hyperbole'.)

28 Brad Darrach, 'Meet Shakey, The First Electronic Person', *Life*, vol. 69, part 21, November 20, 1970.

29 *The Times Higher Educational Supplement*, 10 October, 1986.

30 *Better Mind the Computer*, BBC TV.

31 For example Samuel, A. L. 'Some Studies in Machine Learning Using the Game of Checkers', p. 103–4.

32 See Shurkin, J. 'Computer Pioneer and his Historic Program still Active at Stanford', p. 4. (I owe this reference to Hubert Dreyfus.)

33 *Life*, November 20, 1970, p. 61; Turkle, S. *The Second Self*, p. 279.

34 See Sussman, G. J. *A Computer Model of Skill Acquisition*, footnote 2, and Minsky, M. 'Adaptive Control: From Feedback to Debugging', p. 123.
35 Simon, H. A. *The Shape of Automation*, p. xv.
36 Simon, H. A., Newell, A. 'Heuristic Problem Solving: the Next Advance in Operations Research', p. 6.
37 Simon, H. A., Newell, A. 'Heuristic Problem Solving: the Next Advance in Operations Research', p. 8.
38 Simon, H. A., Newell, A. 'Heuristic Problem Solving: the Next Advance in Operations Research', p. 7.
39 Simon, H. A. *The Shape of Automation*, p. 96. (I owe this reference to Hubert Dreyfus.)
40 From an interview with Pamela McCorduck, recorded in her *Machines Who Think*, p. 189.
41 Moto-oka, T., Kitsuregawa, M. *The Fifth Generation Computer: The Japanese Challenge*, pp. 80–1; Moto-oka, T. et al. 'Challenge for Knowledge Information Processing Systems. (Preliminary Report on Fifth Generation Computer Systems)', pp. 27–8.
42 Moravec, H. *Mind Children: The Future of Robot and Human Intelligence*, p. 6.
43 Ibid, p. 1.
44 Quoted in Winograd, T., Flores, F. *Understanding Computers and Cognition*, p. 128.
45 Roszak, T. 'Smart Computers at Insecure Stage', p. 47.
46 Dreyfus, H. L. *What Computers Can't Do* (Second Edition), p. 79; Dreyfus, H. L., Dreyfus, S. E. *Mind Over Machine*, pp. 13–15.
47 Simon, H. A., Newell, A. 'Heuristic Problem Solving: the Next Advance in Operations Research', p. 9.
48 Winograd, T., Flores, F. *Understanding Computers and Cognition*, p. 98.
49 Waltz, D. L. 'Artificial Intelligence', p. 122.
50 Winograd, T. 'Artificial Intelligence and Language Comprehension', p. 10.
51 Adapted from an example given by Winograd in *Understanding Natural Language*, p. 33.
52 Many of these illustrations are taken from the writings of Minsky, Lenat and H. Dreyfus.
53 The symbol system hypothesis does not entail the data model: the former may be true even if the latter is incorrect. See the discussion of simulation in section 10.9.
54 See Newell, A., Simon, H. A. 'Computer Science as Empirical Inquiry: Symbols and Search'.
55 For sceptical discussions of what I call the data model of knowledge, see Winograd, T. 'What Does it Mean to Understand Language?' pp. 226–7; Winograd, T., Flores, F. *Understanding Computers and Cognition*, chapters 4 and 8; Dreyfus, H. *What Computers Can't Do* (Second Edition), chapters 5 and 8.
56 Notice that in this alternative, stored procedures are also excluded, since these too are symbol-structures.
57 Lenat, D. B., Feigenbaum, E. A. 'On the Thresholds of Knowledge', pp. 212, 223.
58 Lenat, D. B., Feigenbaum, E. A. 'On the Thresholds of Knowledge', p. 199. In the text quotations from joint works are (for stylistic reasons) attributed to the principal author. Footnotes cite the co-authors.

59 Lenat, D. B., Guha, R. V. *Building Large Knowledge-Based Systems*, p. xvii.
60 Lenat, D. B., Feigenbaum, E. A. 'On the Thresholds of Knowledge', pp. 202, 203, 208.
61 Lenat, D. B., Guha, R. V. *Building Large Knowledge-Based Systems*, p. 4.
62 *Program*: Are there spots on the body?
    User: Yes.
    Program: What colour spots?
    User: Reddish-brown.
    Program: Are there more spots on the trunk than elsewhere?
    User: No.
    Program: The patient has measles.
    (Lenat, D. B., Guha, R. V. *Building Large Knowledge-Based Systems*, p. 2.)
63 Lenat, D. B., Feigenbaum, E. A. 'On the Thresholds of Knowledge', pp. 196–7.
64 Lenat, D. B., Guha, R. V. *Building Large Knowledge-Based Systems*, p. 7.
65 Guha, R. V., Lenat, D. B. 'CYC: A Mid-Term Report', p. 57.
66 Guha, R. V., Lenat, D. B. 'CYC: A Mid-Term Report', p. 54.
67 Lenat, D. B., Guha, R. V. *Building Large Knowledge-Based Systems*, p. 352; Lenat, D. B., Feigenbaum, E. A. 'On the Thresholds of Knowledge', pp. 189, 210, 212, 223; Lenat, D. B., Feigenbaum, E. A. 'Reply to Brian Smith', pp. 232, 233.
68 Lenat, D. B., Feigenbaum, E. A. 'On the Thresholds of Knowledge', p. 223.
69 Lenat, D. B., Feigenbaum, E. A. 'On the Thresholds of Knowledge', pp. 197, 219.
70 Guha, R. V., Lenat, D. B. 'CYC: A Mid-Term Report', p. 34.
71 Lenat, D. B., Feigenbaum, E. A. 'On the Thresholds of Knowledge', p. 220.
72 Lenat, D. B., Guha, R. V. *Building Large Knowledge-Based Systems*, p. 23.
73 Guha, R. V., Lenat, D. B. 'CYC: A Mid-Term Report', p. 41; Lenat, D. B., Guha, R. V. *Building Large Knowledge-Based Systems*, pp. 172, 175–6.
74 The classic discussion of the ontological status of events is Davidson, D. 'The Logical Form of Action Sentences'.
75 For a survey of attempts to give a satisfactory account of assertions involving fictional entities see Proudfoot, D. 'Fictional Entities'.
76 This example is adapted from Davidson, op. cit. p. 105.
77 The classic discussion of this issue is section 7 of David Hume's *An Enquiry Concerning Human Understanding*.
78 McCarthy, J. 'Circumscription – A Form of Non-Monotonic Reasoning'; McDermott, D., Doyle, J. 'Non-Monotonic Logic I'.
79 The flightless bird example and the challenge to develop nonmonotonic logics originate with Marvin Minsky.
80 Doyle, J. 'A Truth Maintenance System'. 'Reason maintenance system' and 'justification maintenance system' are alternative terms for this type of mechanism. (All three terms are in wide use; Doyle's terminology is the earliest.)
81 Guha, R. V. 'The Representation of Defaults in CYC'.
82 Lenat, D. B., Guha, R. V. *Building Large Knowledge-Based Systems*, p. 21.
83 Guha, R. V., Lenat, D. B. 'CYC: A Mid-Term Report', p. 57.
84 Lenat, D. B., Guha, R. V. *Building Large Knowledge-Based Systems*, p. 357.
85 Lenat, D. B., Feigenbaum, E. A. 'On the Thresholds of Knowledge', p. 212.
86 Lenat, D. B., Feigenbaum, E. A. 'On the Thresholds of Knowledge', p. 224.

87 Lenat, D. B., Feigenbaum, E. A. 'On the Thresholds of Knowledge', p. 188.

88 Lenat, D. B., Feigenbaum, E. A. 'Reply to Brian Smith', pp. 236, 241.

89 Lenat, D. B., Feigenbaum, E. A. 'On the Thresholds of Knowledge', p. 192;
    Lenat, D. B., Feigenbaum, E. A. 'Reply to Brian Smith', p. 234.

90 Lenat, D. B., Feigenbaum, E. A. 'On the Thresholds of Knowledge', p. 220.

91 Smith, B. C. 'The Owl and the Electric Encyclopaedia', p. 255.

92 Lenat, D. B., Guha, R. V. *Building Large Knowledge-Based Systems*, p. 156ff.

93 Lenat, D. B., Guha, R. V. *Building Large Knowledge-Based Systems*, p. 181.

94 Lenat, D. B., Guha, R. V. *Building Large Knowledge-Based Systems*, p. 159.

95 Lenat, D. B., Guha, R. V. *Building Large Knowledge-Based Systems*, p. 149.

96 Guha, R. V., Lenat, D. B. 'CYC: A Mid-Term Report', p. 47; Guha, R. V. 'The
    Representation of Defaults in CYC', p. 5. 'Causal' is metalinguistic. Lenat and
    Guha prefer to record this fact explicitly in the notation by the use of quotation
    marks. Thus they write: causal('X ⊃ Y').

97 For the sake of simplicity I am here treating 'causal' as a type of modal operator.
    Lenat and Guha themselves (op. cit.) prefer to record the assertion that the em-
    bedded material implication is true by means of a separate piece of syntax. Thus
    they represent 'it is true that X causes Y' as: (X ⊃ Y) & causal('X ⊃ Y'). They
    abbreviate this whole context to '(cause X Y)'.

98 The truth table for '⊃' is as follows. (Read along the horizontal lines.)

Statement X	Statement Y	X ⊃ Y
True	*True*	*True*
True	*False*	*False*
False	*True*	*True*
False	*False*	*True*

99   I discuss a related difficulty in 'What Is Computation?'

100 For a survey see Jackson, F. (ed.) *Conditionals*.

101 Hanks, S., McDermott, D. 'Default Reasoning, Nonmonotonic Logics, and the
     Frame Problem'; McCarthy, J. 'Applications of Circumscription to Formalising
     Common-Sense Knowledge'. The temporal projection problem is also known
     simply as 'the Hanks-McDermott problem'.

102 Hanks, S., McDermott, D. 'Default Reasoning, Nonmonotonic Logics, and the
     Frame Problem'.

103 Guha, R. V. 'The Representation of Defaults in CYC', pp. 7–8; Guha, R. V., Lenat,
     D. B. 'CYC: A Mid-Term Report', pp. 37, 46–7.

104 Guha, R. V. 'The Representation of Defaults in CYC', p. 8.

105 It does not matter that the antecedent of this second labelled implication ('some-
     one removes the bullets from the gun') does not appear in the story. For nor does
     the antecedent of the first ('X is shot with a *loaded* gun'). The two cases are
     completely symmetrical.

106 If labels must be used then the idea of a positionality criterion should be abandoned.
     The obvious thing to try instead is an entailment criterion: can the KB prove a

theorem of the form '∃P(causal(P ⊃ Y))' where '∃' is a substitutional quantifier. (For a description of substitutional quantification see my 'Substitutional Quantification and Existence'.) Unfortunately CYC will have trouble applying such a criterion. CYC may know that

(causal(X ⊃ Y)) OR (causal(Z ⊃ Y))

and yet be unable to prove

∃P(causal(P ⊃ Y)).

CYC's general inference mechanism is only *Horn-complete* (Guha, R. V., Lenat, D. B. 'CYC: A Mid-Term Report', p. 42.) This means that CYC will often be unable to draw inferences that are, from our point of view, obviously correct. It is only when the premises and conclusion of the inference are so-called *Horn clauses* that CYC is guaranteed to be able to make the inference. A Horn clause is a statement whose disjunctive normal form has no more than one immediate subformula that lacks the prefix NOT. So 'A OR NOT B' is a Horn clause, as is '(NOT A) OR (NOT B)'. But 'A OR B' is not a Horn clause. Nor is

(causal(X ⊃ Y)) OR (causal(Z ⊃ Y)).

107   Guha, R. V., Lenat, D. B. 'CYC: A Mid-Term Report', p. 54.
108   Guha, R. V., Levy, A. Y. 'A Relevance Based Meta Level', p. 1.
109   Guha, R. V., Levy, A. Y. 'A Relevance Based Meta Level', pp. 2–4.
110   See my 'Horseshoe, Hook, and Relevance' and 'The Trouble Anderson and Belnap Have with Relevance'.
111   Blair, P., Guha, R. V., Pratt, W. 'Microtheories: An Ontological Engineer's Guide', p. 15.
112   Blair, P., Guha, R. V., Pratt, W. 'Microtheories: An Ontological Engineer's Guide'.
113   Guha, R. V., Levy, A. Y. 'A Relevance Based Meta Level', p. 7.
114   Guha, R. V., Levy, A. Y. 'A Relevance Based Meta Level', p. 7.
115   Guha, R. V., Levy, A. Y. 'A Relevance Based Meta Level', pp. 8–11.
116   Brian Cantwell Smith has the same impression. '[I]t is unclear how [Lenat et al.] plan to group, relate, and index their frames.' ('The Owl and the Electric Encyclopaedia', p. 269.)
117   A shortened form of 'ex falso quodlibet'.
118   There is an alternative proof of Quodlibet. X follows from S if there is no possible world in which all the members of S are true and X is false. Suppose S is inconsistent. Then there is no possible world in which all the members of S are true (this is what inconsistency amounts to). A fortiori there is no possible world in which all the members of S are true and X is false (where X is any sentence whatsoever). Therefore X follows from S. (For a discussion of the issues here see my 'On When a Semantics is not a Semantics', 'What is a Semantics for Classical Negation?' and 'Vagueness and Bivalence'.)
119   Church, A. 'A Note on the Entscheidungsproblem'. Church's result applies to

standard first order quantifier logic. Some weaker quantifier logics are decidable but are inferentially hamstrung.

120 Lenat, D. B., Guha, R. V. *Building Large Knowledge-Based Systems*, p. 51.

121 Lenat, D. B., Guha, R. V. *Building Large Knowledge-Based Systems*, pp. 50–2; Guha, R. V. 'The Representation of Defaults in CYC'.

122 Lenat, D. B., Guha, R. V. *Building Large Knowledge-Based Systems*, p. 307; Guha, R. V. 'The Representation of Defaults in CYC'.

123 Guha, R. V., Lenat, D. B. 'CYC: A Mid-Term Report', p. 37; Guha, R. V. 'The Representation of Defaults in CYC', p. 5.

124 Guha, R. V., Lenat, D. B. 'CYC: A Mid-Term Report', p. 37; Guha, R. V. 'The Representation of Defaults in CYC', p. 5.

125 Let 'W' symbolize 'The world ended 10 minutes ago'. Use the first rule to infer NOT ((NOT A) AND (NOT W)) from the premiss A. Use the second rule to infer W from this intermediate conclusion and the premiss NOT A. (This is a variant of C. I. Lewis' so-called first independent proof (Lewis, C. I., Langford, C. H. *Symbolic Logic*, p. 250).) Notice that a restriction to Horn clauses provides no help with the problems engendered by Quodlibet. As the derivation stands not every formula in it is a Horn clause. In particular NOT ((NOT A) AND (NOT W)) is not a Horn clause, since its disjunctive normal form is A OR W. This can be remedied by applying the first rule to the premiss NOT A to obtain NOT ((NOT NOT A) AND (NOT W)) and then applying the second rule to this formula and NOT NOT A to obtain W. The derivation is now three steps long, since an extra move is required to derive NOT NOT A from the premiss A. Every formula in the modified derivation is a Horn clause (the disjunctive normal form of NOT ((NOT NOT A) AND (NOT W)) being (NOT A) OR W). In other words an inconsistent KB will be able to construct Horn clause derivations of every statement that it has the resources to express (simply substitute for W). Moreover each of these derivations will be very short – at most three steps long.

126 Guha, R. V., Lenat, D. B. 'CYC: A Mid-Term Report', p. 37.

127 See Gentzen, G. 'Investigations Into Logical Deduction'.

128 Lenat, D. B., Feigenbaum, E. A. 'On the Thresholds of Knowledge', pp. 217, 222.

129 Lenat, D. B., Feigenbaum, E. A. 'On the Thresholds of Knowledge', p. 199. Their italics.

130 Winograd, T. 'Breaking the Complexity Barrier Again', p. 13.

Chapter 6   The curious case of the Chinese room

1 Searle, J. *Minds, Brains and Science* p. 31; 'Minds, Brains and Programs', p. 423; 'Is the Brain's Mind a Computer Program?', p. 21.

2 'Minds, Brains and Programs', p. 417.

3 Some writers take Searle's set up to involve a program consisting simply of a giant lookup table that pairs Chinese characters with Chinese characters – the technique used in the Parry and Superparry programs. (For example Kim Sterelny, *The Representational Theory of Mind*, p. 220ff.) This is a misunderstanding. Searle

makes it clear that the details of the program make no difference to the argument (see 'Minds, Brains and Programs', p. 417). Indeed, the Sam program, which Searle uses to illustrate the argument, does not have a lookup table architecture. This misinterpretation makes the Chinese room argument look weaker than it is, and lays it open to the mistaken objection that since no one believes that a Superparry-type program qualifies as a Chinese understander, 'Searle tells us only what we already know' (Sterelny, p. 222).

4 Searle, J. 'Minds, Brains and Programs', pp. 419–20.
5 Searle, J. 'Minds, Brains and Programs', p. 419.
6 Searle, J. 'Minds, Brains and Programs', p. 419.
7 For example Ned Block 'The Computer Model of the Mind', p. 282ff.
8 See Schank, R. C., Abelson, R. *Scripts, Plans, Goals and Understanding*, chapters 7 and 8.
9 Schank, R. C. 'Understanding Searle', p. 446. Schank adds – 'yet'.
10 Searle, J. 'Minds, Brains and Programs', p. 419.
11 Searle, J. 'Minds, Brains and Programs', p. 419 and 'Is the Brain's Mind a Computer Program?', p. 24.
12 Searle, J. *Minds, Brains and Science*, pp. 34–5.
13 Searle, J. 'Minds, Brains and Programs', pp. 420 and 421.
14 Searle, J. 'Minds, Brains and Programs', pp. 420 and 421.
15 Searle, J. 'Minds, Brains and Programs', p. 423.
16 Searle, J. 'Minds, Brains and Programs', p. 422 and *Minds, Brains and Science*, pp. 40–1.
17 Searle, J. 'Minds, Brains and Programs', p. 422.
18 Searle, J. 'Minds, Brains and Programs', p. 424.
19 Pylyshyn, Z. W., 'The "Causal Power" of Machines', p. 442.
20 Searle, J. 'Author's Response', p. 453.
21 Proved by Minsky in his *Computation: Finite and Infinite Machines*, Section 14.8.
22 What Turing proved is that there exists (in the mathematical sense) a Turing machine that is capable of computing all effectively calculable functions, in a sense of 'effectively calculable' defined by Alonzo Church; see Turing, A. M. 'On Computable Numbers, with an Application to the Entscheidungsproblem'. (The concept of effective calculability is equivalent to the concept of algorithmic calculability introduced and explained in chapter 10.) It has been shown subsequently that there are many different Turing machines (i.e. Turing machines with different machine tables) that can do this. These are the universal Turing machines. A universal Turing machine is equivalent in computing power to any universal symbol system with unbounded memory. The proof of this consists essentially of writing a program for a machine with the fundamental operations listed in section 4.5 that enables it to simulate a universal Turing machine, and writing a program for a universal Turing machine that enables it to simulate a machine that uses the listed operations.
23 Searle, J. *Minds, Brains and Science*, p. 38.
24 Searle, J. 'Is the Brain a Digital Computer?', pp. 26, 27.
25 Searle, J. 'Is the Brain a Digital Computer?', p. 27.
26 Searle, J. 'Is the Brain a Digital Computer?', p. 26.

27   One can prolong the isomorphism by continually shifting the references of the key terms in the description ('instruction register', 'accumulator', etc.). By this I mean allowing a term to refer first to one thing then to another, then another. (Analogously, the reference of the term 'Prime Minister of Britain' may shift as a result of a general election.) The reference of the term 'instruction register' must be changed repeatedly as the computation progresses, in such a way that at every moment the term refers to a region of the wall whose molecules happen to be an encoding (under Searle's method of description) of the contents at that moment of the real machine's instruction register (similarly for the accumulator and the rest of the machine's registers). See my 'What Is Computation?' for an argument that it is illegitimate, in the context, to make such a manoeuvre. There I defend the sufficiency of Turing's 1936 analysis of computation against the so-called problem of 'trivial realizations' (of which the Wordstar wall is one). I argue that the problem arises only if one ignores the lessons about modellings taught us by Skolem's paradox. Clearing away this problem undercuts various objections that have been made to psychological functionalism and to the hypothesis that the human brain is a computer.

28   Machine One progressively replaces the 1s on its tape with 0s until it strikes a square already containing 0, which it replaces with 1 and then halts. Thus the tape looks like this when the machine halts.

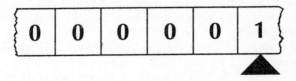

Figure 6.3

Machine Two is a *parity checker*. That is, it reports whether an unbroken sequence of 1s contains an odd or even number of digits. As the sequence of 1s moves past the head the indicator flops between its two states: odd, even, odd, even. When the head strikes the 0 marking the right hand end of the sequence, it replaces the 0 with 1 if there were an odd number of 1s in the sequence (i.e. if its indicator is in state 1), and makes no change if there were an even number (i.e. if its indicator is in state 2). It then positions itself over the final 1 in the sequence and halts.

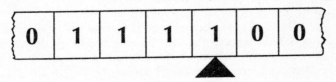

Figure 6.4

29   This is a scaled-down version of what must be done in the course of constructing the first part of the proof discussed in note 22.

Chapter 7   Freedom

1   Turing, A. 'Computing Machinery and Intelligence', p. 447.
2   Turing, A. 'Computing Machinery and Intelligence', p. 447.
3   Simon, H. 'What Computers Mean for Man and Society', p. 1191.
4   Turkle, S. *The Second Self: Computers and the Human Spirit*, p. 13.
5   Turkle, S. *The Second Self: Computers and the Human Spirit*, pp. 16, 306, 308.
6   Boswell, J. *Life of Samuel Johnson*, vol. 2, 10 October 1769 (p. 231 in the Birrell edition).
7   Deecke, L., Grözinger, B., Kornhuber, H. H. 'Voluntary Finger Movement in Man: Cerebral Potentials and Theory'. In a total of 87 experiments with 39 subjects, the Bereitschaftspotential started on average 750 milliseconds prior to finger flexion, and in some subjects 1.5 seconds or more prior to flexion. (See also Libet, B. 'Unconscious Cerebral Initiative and the Role of Conscious Will in Voluntary Action'.)
8   The reaction time for finger movement is only about one tenth of a second. (So if, say, you were instructed to press a button as soon as you heard a buzzer, it would be approximately one tenth of a second before your finger muscles began to respond.) Since the Bereitschaftspotential commences a full second or more before the onset of the muscular response in the finger, the disturbing results of this experiment cannot be explained away by appealing to the lag between decision and movement.
9   See, for example, the Open Peer Commentary that follows the article by Libet cited in note 7.
10   For example Harth, E. *Windows on the Mind: Reflections on the Physical Basis of Consciousness*, p. 182.
11   Hans Schaefer, in Eccles, J. C. ed. *Brain and Conscious Experience*, pp. 310–311.
12   Laplace, P. *Essai Philosophique sur les Probabilités*, seconde édition, pp. 3–4. (Translation by Diane Proudfoot.)
13   'You believe in [a] God who plays dice, and I in complete law and order in a world which objectively exists,' wrote Einstein in a letter to Max Born. (*The Born-Einstein Letters*, 7 Sept. 1944.)
14   Minsky, M. *The Society of Mind*, p. 307.
15   Minsky, M. *Semantic Information Processing*, p. 431.
16   Minsky, M. *The Society of Mind*, p. 306.
17   Simons, G. *The Biology of Computer Life*, p. 100.
18   Simons, G. *The Biology of Computer Life*, pp. 100, 109.
19   Turing, A. M. 'Intelligent Machinery', p. 9; 'Computing Machinery and Intelligence', p. 438. Turing uses the term 'partially random' to describe machines containing a genuinely random selection process (e.g. a process driven by radioactive decay), and the term 'apparently partially random' to describe machines that are in fact completely deterministic but contain a selection procedure that causes them to appear superficially as if they were partially random (e.g. a program that uses the digits of the number π to determine a selection).
20   'Computing Machinery and Intelligence', p. 438. Turing adds immediately afterwards 'though I would not use this phrase myself'. Tantalizingly, Turing offers

no explanation for this reluctance. I suspect that what he meant was something like this: 'You can, if you want, describe such a machine as having free will; but I myself think this hoary old expression is so vague that it is best avoided altogether. I consider the expression "random selection among alternatives" to be a precise, scientific replacement for loose and unclear talk about freedom of the will.' (He adopted a similar position with respect to the term 'think'; ibid. p. 442.) In a BBC radio talk given in 1951 Turing again proposed that the addition of a simple hardware device – 'something like a roulette wheel or a supply of radium' – is sufficient to provide a suitably programmed computer with freewill (see Hodges, A. *Alan Turing: The Enigma*, pp. 441–2).

21 Two recent writers who have, in various ways, questioned the doctrine are Dennett, D. C., 'On Giving Libertarians What They Say They Want', and van Inwagen, P., *An Essay on Freewill*, pp. 126–50.

22 Shaffer, J. A., *Philosophy of Mind*, p. 106.

23 Thorp, J. *Free Will: A Defence Against Neurophysiological Determinism*, p. 71.

24 Simons, G. *The Biology of Computer Life*, p. 111.

25 Ayer, A. J. *Philosophical Essays*, p. 275.

26 Thorp, J. *Free Will: A Defence Against Neurophysiological Determinism*, p. 27; van Inwagen, P. *An Essay on Freewill*, chapter III. See also Minsky, M. *The Society of Mind*, p. 306.

27 Hospers, J. *An Introduction to Philosophical Analysis*, p. 330.

28 The first compatibilists were Thomas Hobbes and David Hume. Hobbes: 'A Freeman is he, that in those things which by his strength and wit he is able to do, is not hindered to do what he has a will to'. (*Works*, ed. Molesworth, W., vol. III, pp. 196–7 (circa 1650).) Hume: 'By liberty, then, we can only mean a power of acting or not acting, according to the determinations of the will'. (*An Enquiry Concerning Human Understanding*, p. 95 (1748).) While Hume and Hobbes saw themselves as giving the one true analysis of freedom, I take the compatibilist account to describe merely one of several possible kinds of freedom. This is, though, a kind of freedom of particular interest, in that we undoubtedly possess it – unlike some of the other kinds of freedom for which some thinkers have hankered (see the discussion of libertarianism in section 7.5).

29 Kant, I. *Critique of Practical Reason*, p. 99.

30 This apt phrase is Harry Frankfurt's.

31 Frankfurt, H. G. 'Freedom of the Will and the Concept of a Person'. See also Slote, M. 'Understanding Free Will'. In what follows I depart in a number of ways from Frankfurt's own terminology.

32 See Frankfurt's 'Identification and Externality' for some further work on this issue.

33 See, for example, Thorp, J. *Free Will: A Defence Against Neurophysiological Determinism*, chapter VI.

34 Compare Dennett, D. C. *Elbow Room: the Varieties of Freewill Worth Wanting*, p. 137.

35 Thorp, J. *Free Will: A Defence Against Neurophysiological Determinism*, p. 102.

36 Trusted, J. *Free Will and Responsibility*, p. 157.

37 Thorp, J. *Free Will: A Defence Against Neurophysiological Determinism*, p. 103.

38 Mabbott, J. D. 'Freewill and Punishment', p. 301.

39 Answers: N, N, C, C, N, N, N.
40 See, for example, Flew, A. 'Divine Omnipotence and Human Freedom', p. 150.
41 See Holden, A. V. (ed.) *Chaos*; Degn, H., Holden, A. V., Olsen, L. F. (eds) *Chaos in Biological Systems*; Gleick, J. *Chaos: Making a New Science.*
42 Compare Peter van Inwagen, *An Essay on Freewill*, p. 56; Carl Ginet 'Might We Have No Choice'; James Lamb 'On a Proof of Incompatibilism'; and David Wiggins 'Towards a Reasonable Libertarianism'. The 'up to' formulation is van Inwagen's. For material relating to the final sentence of the passage see Ted Honderich, *A Theory of Determinism*, p. 385ff.
43 Sakitt, B. 'Counting Every Quantum'.
44 Austin, J. L. *Sense and Sensibilia*, p. 10.
45 Van Inwagen, P. *An Essay on Freewill*, pp. 93–4.
46 Van Inwagen, P. *An Essay on Freewill*, pp. 93–4.
47 Van Inwagen, P. *An Essay on Freewill*, pp. 97, 124.
48 Van Inwagen, P. *An Essay on Freewill*, pp. 97–8.
49 See for example Hughes, G. E., Cresswell, M. J. *An Introduction to Modal Logic*, ch. 2.
50 My 'Compatibilism and Modality' contains further discussion of these technical matters.
51 Ayer, A. J. *Philosophical Essays*, p. 284. (My italics.)
52 Mill, J. S. *Autobiography*, p. 119; Honderich, T. *A Theory of Determinism*, chapter 7.
53 Dennett, D. C. *Elbow Room*, p. 120.
54 Dennett, D. C. *Elbow Room*, p. 127.

Chapter 8   Consciousness

1 Culbertson, J. T. *The Minds of Robots*, p. 77.
2 Jaynes, J. *The Origin of Consciousness in the Breakdown of the Bicameral Mind*, p. 13.
3 Sutherland, S. 'Removing the Mystery from Intelligence'.
4 Freud, S. *Neue Folge der Vorlesungen zur Einführung in die Psychoanalyse*, pp. 76–7.
5 Interestingly, Kathy Wilkes reports that the word 'consciousness' did not appear in English until the mid seventeenth century. There was, she says, no corresponding term in classical Greek, and modern Chinese appears to lack any close equivalent. The adjective 'conscious' existed in English prior to the seventeenth century, but not with its modern meanings. The word was used only to characterize *shared* knowledge: a number of people were conscious of an item of knowledge if all were privy to it. This sense persists in locutions like 'we are all conscious of the fact that'. (See Wilkes, K. '–, yìshì, duh, um, and consciousness'.)
6 Jaynes, J. *The Origin of Consciousness in the Breakdown of the Bicameral Mind*, p. 47. Jaynes is a controversial figure who has claimed that people of early civilizations – the Homeric Greeks, for example – were not conscious. Jaynes brings forward a mass of historical, archaeological and literary evidence in support of this claim. I myself remain unconvinced. Nevertheless, Jaynes' discussion of consciousness is rich and provocative.

7   Jaynes, J. *The Origin of Consciousness in the Breakdown of the Bicameral Mind*, p. 85.

8   Reported by Kathy Wilkes in '– yìshì, duh, um, and consciousness', note 11.

9   For five detailed theories in this genre, see Armstrong, D. M. *A Materialist Theory of the Mind*, chs. 6 and 15; Dennett, D. C. 'Toward a Cognitive Theory of Consciousness'; Gazzaniga, M. S. 'Brain Modularity: Towards a Philosophy of Conscious Experience'; Johnson-Laird, P. N. *Mental Models*, ch. 16 and *The Computer and the Mind*, ch. 19; Weiskrantz, L. 'Some Contributions of Neuropsychology of Vision and Memory to the Problem of Consciousness' and 'Neuropsychology and the Nature of Consciousness'. Jaynes' account overlaps somewhat with accounts in this genre. 'Perception is sensing a stimulus and responding appropriately. And this can happen on a nonconscious level, as I have tried to describe in driving a car . . . Mind-space I regard as the primary feature of consciousness . . . [We] narratize the analogic simulation of actual behaviour . . . Consciousness is constantly fitting things into a story . . . The basic connotative definition of consciousness is thus an analog 'I' narratizing in a functional mind-space . . . [There are] different modes of conscious narratization such as verbal, . . . perceptual (imagining scenes), behavioural (imagining ourselves doing something), physiological (monitoring our fatigue or discomfort or appetite), or musical (imagining music) . . . [It is] this remarkable privacy of covert events which we call consciousness.' (*The Origin of Consciousness in the Breakdown of the Bicameral Mind*, pp. 448, 450, 452, 453.)

10 Weiskrantz, L., Warrington, E. K., Sanders, M. D., Marshall, J. 'Visual Capacity in the Hemianopic Field Following a Restricted Occipital Ablation'; Weiskrantz, L. *Blindsight*.

11 Weiskrantz, L. 'Some Contributions of Neuropsychology of Vision and Memory to the Problem of Consciousness', pp. 194–5.

12 Armstrong, D. M. *A Materialist Theory of the Mind*, p. 94.

13 Weiskrantz, L. 'Some Contributions of Neuropsychology of Vision and Memory to the Problem of Consciousness', p. 184.

14 Opinions diverge over whether the monitor system of a split-brain patient has itself been divided into two, or whether the system is located wholly in one hemisphere and can no longer access what is going on in the other. Gazzaniga believes the latter to be the case. If the former is the case the head of a split-brain patient may contain two separate 'streams of awareness', only one of which can be reported verbally. For an interesting philosophical discussion of this possibility see Nagel, T. 'Brain Bisection and the Unity of Consciousness'.

15 Gazzaniga, M. S., Bogen, J. E., Sperry, R. W. 'Observations on Visual Perception After Disconnection of the Cerebral Hemispheres in Man'; Sperry, R. W. 'Some Effects of Disconnecting the Cerebral Hemispheres'; Gazzaniga, M. S., Le Doux, J. E. *The Integrated Mind*.

16 Gazzaniga, M. S. 'Brain Modularity: Towards a Philosophy of Conscious Experience'.

17 Gazzaniga, M. S. 'Brain Modularity: Towards a Philosophy of Conscious Experience', p. 219.

18 Gazzaniga, M. S. 'Brain Modularity: Towards a Philosophy of Conscious Experience', p. 223.

19 Nisbett, R. E., Wilson, T. D. 'Telling More Than We Can Know: Verbal Reports On Mental Processes', pp. 243–4.

20 See Armstrong, D. M. *A Materialist Theory of the Mind*, chs 6 and 15.

21 Thomas Nagel uses the expression 'subjective character' in this context in 'What is it Like to be a Bat?'. The phrase 'immediate phenomenological quality' is used by Saul Kripke in *Naming and Necessity*. Bill Lycan talks about the 'feely properties' of pains, colour sensations and so forth in *Consciousness*, ch. 5.

22 'Computing Machinery and Intelligence', p. 446. Turing's discussion of consciousness is somewhat superficial. He recommends his Test as an adequate diagnostic for consciousness (pp. 445–7). However, in view of the arguments presented in chapter 3, the Turing Test is not a reliable indicator even of consciousness in the baseline sense.

23 Huxley, T. H. *Lessons in Elementary Physiology*, p. 193.

24 See Dennett, D. C. 'Quining Qualia', p. 48.

25 The example is from Bennett, J. 'Substance, Reality, and Primary Qualities', p. 9.

26 Neuroscientist John Eccles mounts a defence of this occult-sounding idea in *The Human Mystery*, ch. 10.

27 See Dan Dennett's *Consciousness Explained* for a spirited attempt to induce mystery-blindness.

28 So-called *substance dualists* believe that humans are literally composed of two different substances, 'physical matter' and 'mental matter'. This is a somewhat antiquated position and is associated particularly with the seventeenth century philosopher René Descartes. (For that reason substance dualism is often referred to simply as Cartesian Dualism.) Most modern dualists are *property dualists*: they agree with physicalists that there is just one sort of matter involved – human beings are not sandwiches – but they maintain that this matter has two radically different types of properties, bio-physical ones and 'feely' ones.

29 Virginia Woolf, *To the Lighthouse*, Hogarth Press 1927 and Colin Gregg Films Ltd 1982. The original book contains little dialogue. Screenwriter Hugh Stoddart based Ramsey's philosophical remarks on ideas held by Woolfe's father. (Private communication.) Marvin Minsky is famous for his similar remark that the mind is a 'meat machine'.

30 Jackson, F. C. 'Epiphenomenal Qualia', p. 127.

31 Nagel, T. 'What is it Like to be a Bat?' Notoriously, it is unclear from Nagel's writings whether he himself is best classified as a physicalist or an anti-physicalist. However, his argument about bats is plainly anti-physicalist in import.

32 Or to be precise, the microchiroptera do.

33 Nagel, T. 'What is it Like to be a Bat?' p. 438.

34 Nagel, T. 'What is it Like to be a Bat?' p. 438.

35 Nagel, T. 'What is it Like to be a Bat?' p. 440.

36 Nagel, T. 'What is it Like to be a Bat?' p. 442.

37 Nagel expands on this theme in chapters II and III of *The View From Nowhere*.

38 I hope my exposition has done justice to Nagel's argument. In my opinion a number of critics have misrepresented the argument, partly out of a desire to make it clearer than it actually is, and partly because they have tended to overlook the fact that Nagel's central preoccupation is with the limited extent to which we can *imagine* what things are like from the point of view of a bat. In particular, I

find no support in Nagel's article for the view that he commits the fallacy of applying Leibniz' law to a referentially opaque context (see, for example, Churchland, P. S. *Neurophilosophy* , pp. 327–30; Churchland, P. M. 'Reduction, Qualia, and the Direct Introspection of Brain States', pp. 19–22; Lycan, W. G. *Consciousness*, pp. 75–8).

39 The example is due to Paul Churchland, 'Some Reductive Strategies in Cognitive Neurobiology', p. 302.

40 Jackson, F. C. 'Epiphenomenal Qualia'. Jackson describes his argument as much indebted to Nagel's (note 10).

41 Jackson's own presentation of the argument concerns colour vision rather than pain. The details are inessential. As he says, the argument 'could be deployed for taste, hearing, the bodily sensations, and generally speaking for the various mental states which are said to have (as it is variously put) raw feels, phenomenal features, or qualia.' ('Epiphenomenal Qualia', p. 130.)

42 Jackson, F. C. 'Epiphenomenal Qualia', p. 129. See also p. 130.

43 This distinction was drawn by Bertrand Russell in 1912. He used the terms 'knowledge by acquaintance' and 'knowledge of truths'. (*The Problems of Philosophy*, chapter 5.) The distinction has been used against Jackson's argument in various ways by various people, notably Paul Churchland ('Reduction, Qualia, and the Direct Introspection of Brain States'), David Lewis ('Postscript to Mad Pain and Martian Pain'), and Laurence Nemirow ('Review of Thomas Nagel's *Mortal Questions*').

44 Nagel, T. 'What is it Like to be a Bat?', pp. 445–6. My italics.

45 Nagel, T. 'What is it Like to be a Bat?', p. 446.

46 Jackson, F. C. 'What Mary Didn't Know', sequel to 'Epiphenomenal Qualia'.

47 Jackson, F. C. 'What Mary Didn't Know', pp. 292–293.

48 Jackson, F. C. 'What Mary Didn't Know', p. 293.

49 Jackson, F. C. 'What Mary Didn't Know', p. 294.

50 See David Lewis, 'Mad Pain and Martian Pain'; Hilary Putnam, 'Philosophy and our Mental Life' and 'The Mental Life of Some Machines'.

Chapter 9   Are we computers?

1 Other leading exponents of the SSSH are Fodor (*The Language of Thought*) and Newell and Simon ('Computer Science as Empirical Enquiry: Symbols and Search'). The latter are partly responsible for the nomenclature used here: what I call the strong symbol system hypothesis is one half of their physical symbol system hypothesis.

2 This is a composite quotation taken from pages 55, 193 and 258 of Pylyshyn, Z. *Computation and Cognition*.

3 Pylyshyn, Z. *Computation and Cognition*, p. 194.

4 Beach, F. A., Hebb, D. O., Morgan, C. T., Nissen, H. W., (eds) *The Neuropsychology of Lashley*, p. xix; Searle, J. *Minds, Brains and Science*, p. 44.

5 *The Neuropsychology of Lashley*, p. xix; *Minds, Brains and Science*, esp. ch. 3; see also Searle's 'Is the Brain a Digital Computer?'

6   The orderly picture drawn by classical neurology is now known to be not entirely accurate; on occasion axon will clasp axon and dendrite will clasp dendrite. Indeed, some types of neuron lack an axon altogether.

7   Rose, S. *The Conscious Brain*, p. 71.

8   This final 'tickling' is chemical rather than electrical in nature. See the discussion of neurotransmitters in section 10.5.

9   The truth table for AND is as follows. (Read along the horizontal lines.)

Statement X	Statement Y	X AND Y
True	*True*	*True*
True	*False*	*False*
False	*True*	*False*
False	*False*	*False*

10   Von Neumann, J. *The Computer and the Brain* and 'The General and Logical Theory of Automata'.

11   It is still an open question exactly how many distinct types of neuron there are – perhaps as many as several thousand. (See Crick, F., Asanuma, C. 'Certain Aspects of the Anatomy and Physiology of the Cerebral Cortex', p. 358.)

12   Poggio, T., Koch, C. 'Ill-posed Problems in Early Vision: from Computational Theory to Analogue Networks', p. 304.

13   This terminology originates with Feldman, J. A. and Ballard, D. H. ('Connectionist Models and their Properties', p. 206).

14   Shimon Ullman calls such tasks 'essentially sequential' ('Visual Routines', p. 120). Ullman suggests that essential sequentiality may be a feature of some aspects of human visual processing.

15   Rumelhart, D. E., McClelland, J. L. 'PDP Models and General Issues in Cognitive Science', p. 131.

16   Sloman, A. *The Computer Revolution in Philosophy*, p. 135. Schank is quoted in Waldrop, M. M. 'Artificial Intelligence in Parallel', p. 610.

17   McClelland, J. L. 'Models of Perception and Memory based on Principles of Neural Organisation', p. 22. (Quoted by Pat Churchland in *Neurophilosophy*.)

18   If you are familiar only with a high-level programming language such as BASIC or Pascal, you may be puzzled by the concept of an address, since addresses never actually appear in the program. It is the computer's compiler – a systems program that translates your program into instructions in machine code – that takes care of assigning addresses to the variables and constants that you use. For example, if you enter a line

TOTALCOST = LETTUCES × UNITPRICE

the compiler will reorganise it into something of the form

MULTIPLY A1 A2 A3

where A1 is the address of the value of LETTUCES, A2 of UNITPRICE and A3 of the result, TOTALCOST.

19 Hofstadter, D. 'Variations On A Theme as the Essence of Imagination', p. 20.
20 Kohonen, T. *Content-Addressable Memories*, chapter 2.
21 Lashley, K. S. 'In Search of the Engram', p. 492.
22 Lashley, K. S. 'In Search of the Engram', pp. 500, 501, 502.
23 Lashley, K. S. 'In Search of the Engram', p. 501.
24 Longuet-Higgins, H. C. 'The Non-Local Storage of Temporal Information'; Pribram, K. H., Nuwer, M., Baron, R. J. 'The Holographic Hypothesis of Memory Structure in Brain Function and Perception'.
25 See, for example, Chow, K. L. 'Visual Discriminations After Extensive Ablation of Optic Tract and Visual Cortex in Cats'; Keating, E. G., Horel, J. A. 'Effects of Prestriate and Striate Lesions on the Monkey's Ability to Locate and Discriminate Visual Forms'.
26 Gross, C. G., Bender, D. B., Rocha-Miranda, C. E. 'Inferotemporal Cortex: A Single-unit Analysis'.
27 Eccles, J. C. 'Possible Synaptic Mechanism Subserving Learning'; Anderson, J. A., Silverstein, J. W., Ritz, S. A., Jones, R. S. 'Distinctive Features, Categorical Perception, and Probability Learning: Some Applications of a Neural Model', pp. 421–2.
28 Gross, C. G., Bender, D. B., Rocha-Miranda, C. E. 'Inferotemporal Cortex: A Single-unit Analysis', pp. 231–3.
29 Anderson, J. A., Mozer, M. C. 'Categorization and Selective Neurons', p. 217.
30 Barlow, H. B. 'Single Units and Sensation: a Neuron Doctrine for Perceptual Psychology?', pp. 385 and 389–90.
31 The primary visual cortex is of relevance here because it is believed that the likeliest sites for the storage of memories are the very areas of cortex where the initial sensory impressions take shape. Other structures, the hippocampus and the amygdala, appear to be involved in the consolidation and retrieval of memories. (See Squire, L. R., Zola-Morgan, S. 'Memory: Brain Systems and Behaviour'.)
32 Harlow, J. M. 'Recovery From the Passage of an Iron Bar Through the Head', pp. 339–40.
33 The term 'graceful degradation' is used in this context by Rumelhart and McClelland ('PDP Models and General Issues in Cognitive Science', p. 134).
34 Churchland, P. S. *Neurophilosophy*, p. 459; Young, J. Z. *Philosophy and the Brain*, p. 18 (see also p. 64).
35 Burks, A. W., Goldstine, H. H., von Neumann, J. 'Preliminary Discussion of the Logical Design of an Electronic Computing Instrument'.
36 It is often said that a von Neumann machine 'does only one thing at a time'. This is somewhat metaphorical. At any one time a modern computer may be simultaneously passing the results of program instruction n to a memory location, obeying instruction n+1 (i.e. performing the manipulation the instruction calls for), and reading instruction n+2.
37 Pylyshyn, Z. *Computation and Cognition*, p. 55.
38 For a related discussion, see Haugeland, J. *Artificial Intelligence: The Very Idea*, pp. 230–8.

39 See Fodor, J. *The Language of Thought*, chapter 2 and 'Fodor's Guide to Mental Representation', pp. 90–95; Pylyshyn, Z. *Computation and Cognition*, pp. 29 and 39ff.

40 Some writers consider the existence of mental imagery to constitute a problem for the theory that thought consists of the manipulation of sentences (for, after all, images are not sentences). See Kosslyn, S. H. *Image and Mind* and *Ghosts in the Mind's Machine*; Block, N. 'Mental Pictures and Cognitive Science'; Haugeland, J. *Artificial Intelligence: the Very Idea*, pp. 221–30. For a critical discussion, see Pylyshyn, Z. *Computation and Cognition*, chapter 8.

41 Notice that this is an argument for taking the SSSH seriously in its full strength. The argument maintains that the only explanation we have of how a physical device can represent facts is that it uses a symbolic code – and this applies whether the device is a human brain or a wodge of alien green slime.

42 Verbs that generate these paradoxes – believe, intend, fear, wonder, etc. – are known collectively as the intentional verbs. A classic discussion of the intentional verbs is Chisholm, R. M. *Perceiving: A Philosophical Study*, ch. 11.

43 Pylyshyn, Z. *Computation and Cognition*, p. 195; see also Fodor, J. *The Language of Thought*, pp. 71–9.

44 The 'belief box' metaphor originated with Steven Schiffer.

45 Rumelhart, D. E., McClelland, J. L. 'PDP Models and General Issues in Cognitive Science', pp. 119–20.

46 Fodor, J. *Psychosemantics*, p. 148.

47 Fodor, J. *Psychosemantics*, p. 149; Fodor, J., Pylyshyn, Z. 'Connectionism and Cognitive Architecture: A Critical Analysis', p. 39.

48 Fodor, J., Pylyshyn, Z. 'Connectionism and Cognitive Architecture: A Critical Analysis', p. 39.

49 Fodor, J. *Psychosemantics*, p. 149.

50 Fodor, J. 'Fodor's Guide to Mental Representation', pp. 89–90; Fodor, J. *Psychosemantics*, pp. 147–53; Fodor, J., Pylyshyn, Z. 'Connectionism and Cognitive Architecture: A Critical Analysis', pp. 33–41.

51 Pylyshyn, Z. *Computation and Cognition*, pp. 39, 63. The quotation is given in McClelland, J. L. 'The Basis of Lawful Behaviour: Rules or Connections?', p. 16. Fodor, J. *The Language of Thought*, p. 27.

52 Johnson-Laird, P. *Mental Models*; McGinn, C. *Mental Content*. The locus classicus of the 'mental models' approach is Kenneth Craik's *The Nature of Explanation*, published in 1943. See also Kosslyn, S. H. *Image and Mind* and *Ghosts in the Mind's Machine*; and Block, N. 'Mental Pictures and Cognitive Science'.

53 McGinn, C. *Mental Content*, p. 178.

54 For more thoroughgoing analyses of the concept see Lewis, D. 'Analog and Digital' and Haugeland, J. 'Analog and Analog'.

55 McGinn, C. *Mental Content*, p. 180.

56 A number of people have pointed out that the use of analogue models considerably simplifies the frame problem (chapter 5). In a dynamic analogue model, updating is to some extent taken care of 'for free' and information about consequent changes can be extracted by a process analogous to observation.

57 Biederman, I. 'Recognition by Components: a Theory of Human Image Understanding'.
58 Biederman, I. 'Recognition by Components: a Theory of Human Image Understanding', p. 130.
59 Biederman, I. 'Recognition by Components: a Theory of Human Image Understanding', p. 119.
60 Biederman, I. 'Recognition by Components: a Theory of Human Image Understanding', p. 116.
61 Michael Corballis makes this point (*The Lopsided Ape*, p. 222).
62 Turing, A. M. 'Computing Machinery and Intelligence', p. 442.
63 *Chambers Concise 20th Century Dictionary.*
64 Von Neumann, J. *The Computer and the Brain*, p. 75.
65 See, for example, Patricia Churchland, *Neurophilosophy*, p. 9; Paul Churchland, 'Some Reductive Strategies in Cognitive Neurobiology', p. 281. Andras Pellionisz inveighs against this shift in terminology in 'Old Dogmas and New Axioms in Brain Theory'.
66 Anderson, J. A., Hinton, G. E. 'Models of Information Processing in the Brain', pp. 29–30; Young, J. Z. *Philosophy and the Brain*, p. 139.
67 Although some philosophers play down the importance of the concept of a representation. See, for example, Stich, S. *From Folk Psychology to Cognitive Science.*
68 Some of the most interesting research so far has been in the area of language acquisition. For an overview, see Fodor, J. *The Language of Thought*, ch. 3; Pinker, S., Prince, A. 'On Language and Connectionism: Analysis of a Parallel Distributed Processing Model of Language Acquisition'; Pinker, S. *Language Learnability and Language Development*; Berwick, R. C., Weinberg, A. S. *The Grammatical Basis of Linguistic Performance: Language Use and Acquisition.*

Chapter 10   AI's fresh start: parallel distributed processing

1 Rosenblatt called his artificial neural networks 'perceptrons' (see his *Principles of Neurodynamics*). In their book *Perceptrons* Minsky and Papert showed that Rosenblatt's devices are incapable of calculating a particular class of functions (the so-called linearly inseparable functions). Many important functions fall into this class, and by and large the AI community treated this result as the death knell for the perceptron. Part of the problem was that Rosenblatt chiefly – although not exclusively – studied devices consisting of only two layers of artificial neurons (input is presented at one layer and output read from the other). Minksy and Papert showed that if additional layers of 'neurons' are inserted between these, the resulting devices can calculate linearly inseparable functions. This was not seen as Rosenblatt's salvation, however, since his algorithm for adjusting the connections between the 'neurons' in order to secure the right outputs from the inputs (known as the perceptron convergence procedure) becomes unreliable once these so-called hidden layers are introduced (see note 7) – a fact which led Minsky and Papert to deem the hidden layer approach 'sterile' (p. 232). Hidden layers are used freely in parallel distributed processing, and the search for systematic methods of adjusting the myriad connec-

tions in these 'extended perceptrons' is a fundamental area of enquiry. (A function that cannot be calculated by a two-layer perceptron is given by the following table. The idea is that the pair $I_1 I_2$ is to be presented to the perceptron as input, and O is the required output.

I_1 I_2 O
1 1 0
1 0 1
0 1 1
0 0 0

This function is particularly important, since it represents the basic logical operation XOR (exclusive or). An example of a statement involving XOR is 'You may claim either rebate A or rebate B': the statement is false if you can claim both rebates, or neither, and is true otherwise. A simple XOR network involving a single hidden 'neuron' is described by Rumelhart, D. E., Hinton, G. E., and Williams, R. J. 'Learning Internal Representations by Error Propagation', p. 321.)

2   Smolensky, P. 'On the Proper Treatment of Connectionism', p. 3.

3   Quoted in *The Economist*, 29 June, 1985.

4   Smolensky, P. 'On the Proper Treatment of Connectionism', p. 2.

5   Yes; no; yes.

6   Hinton, G. E. 'Learning in Parallel Networks', pp. 267–70.

7   The algorithm described in the preceding paragraph is essentially Rosenblatt's classic perceptron convergence procedure (see note 1). A simple generalization for use where n hidden layers are present is to repeat the procedure n+1 times, starting at the output layer and working back through the hidden layers towards the input layer. This is known as *back propagation*. The perceptron convergence procedure is universal, in the sense that it can be used to configure a two-layer perceptron to calculate any function that *can* be calculated by these devices. It is known that the back propagation algorithm is not universal (this was the basis of the premature judgement by Minsky and Papert that the hidden layer approach is 'sterile' (note 1)). At present it is far from clear what the actual limits on the use of this algorithm are. 'Scaling' is a major problem: it is doubtful whether the algorithm can be used to configure a very large network in a reasonable amount of time. (Some empirical studies of the algorithm are described in Rumelhart, D. E., Hinton, G. E., Williams, R. J. 'Learning Internal Representations by Error Propagation'.)

8   Rumelhart, D. E., McClelland, J. L. 'On Learning the Past Tenses of English Verbs'.

9   After the linguist Wickelgren. For a full account, see the above reference, pp. 233–9.

10 For a discussion of blending see Pinker, S., Prince, A. 'On Language and Connectionism: Analysis of a Parallel Distributed Processing Model of Language Acquisition', p. 155ff.

11 Pinker, S., Prince, A. 'On Language and Connectionism: Analysis of a Parallel Distributed Processing Model of Language Acquisition', pp. 136–45.

12 Hofstadter, D. *Metamagical Themas: Questing for the Essence of Mind and Pattern*, p. 633.

13 This appealing phrase is Keith Gunderson's. (*Mentality and Machines*, p. 98.)

14 Warren, R. M. 'Perceptual Restoration of Missing Speech Sounds'.

15 McClelland, J. L., Rumelhart, D. E., Hinton, G. E. 'The Appeal of Parallel Distributed Processing', pp. 20–3. Rosenberg, C. R., Sejnowski, T. J. 'Parallel Networks that Learn to Pronounce English Text'; Elman, J. D., Zipser, D. 'Learning the Hidden Structure of Speech'.

16 Aleksander, I., Burnett, P. *Thinking Machines: The Search for Artificial Intelligence*, chapter 9. See also Aleksander, I., (ed.) *Neural Computing Architectures: The Design of Brain-Like Machines.*

17 Rumelhart, D. E., McClelland, J. L. 'PDP Models and General Issues in Cognitive Science', p. 132.

18 Rumelhart, D. E., Hinton, G. E., McClelland, J. L. 'A General Framework for Parallel Distributed Processing', pp. 45–54.

19 Wittgenstein, L. *Philosophical Investigations*, sections 65–78.

20 McClelland, J. L., Rumelhart, D. E., Hinton, G. E. 'The Appeal of Parallel Distributed Processing', pp. 25–9.

21 Wood, C. C. 'Variations on a Theme by Lashley: Lesion Experiments on the Neural Model of Anderson, Silverstein, Ritz and Jones'.

22 McClelland, J. L., Rumelhart, D. E. and the PDP Research Group *Parallel Distributed Processing: Explorations in the Microstructure of Cognition*. Vol. 2: *Psychological and Biological Models*, p. 329.

23 Crick, F., Asanuma, C. 'Certain Aspects of the Anatomy and Physiology of the Cerebral Cortex', p. 370.

24 For a short account of the details of the process see *The Oxford Companion to the Mind*, ed. Gregory, R. L., pp. 554–7.

25 Davis, J. M., Garver, D. L. 'Neuroleptics: Clinical Use in Psychiatry'.

26 See McClelland, J. L., Rumelhart, D. E. 'Amnesia and Distributed Memory' for some preliminary steps in this direction.

27 For example, Churchland, P. M. 'Some Reductive Strategies in Cognitive Neurobiology'. Crucial to Churchland's hypothesis is the fact that the brain is known to contain a considerable number of neural 'maps'. For example, part of the surface of the cortex consists of a two-dimensional representation of the eyes' current field of view. Other maps concern the auditory landscape and the orientation of the body's muscles. These maps are often deformed by the varying local curvature of the cortical tissue. Churchland speculates that this geometrical deformation serves to place the various maps in register or 'synchronization' with each other. If this is right, the brain's geometry is crucial to hand-eye coordination, hand-ear coordination, and much else. (See also Pellionisz, A., Llinás, R. 'Brain Modeling by Tensor Network Theory and Computer Simulation', esp. pp. 344–5.)

28 Searle, J. 'Is the Brain's Mind a Computer Program?', pp. 20, 22. The paper to which Searle refers is Churchland, P. M., Churchland, P. S. 'Could a Machine Think?'.

29 Searle, J. 'Is the Brain's Mind a Computer Program?', p. 22.

30 Searle, J. 'Is the Brain's Mind a Computer Program?', p. 22.

31   Searle, J. *Minds, Brains and Science*, pp. 37–8.
32   Searle, J. 'Is the Brain's Mind a Computer Program?', p. 23.
33   Searle, J. 'Is the Brain's Mind a Computer Program?', p. 21.
34   Searle, J. 'Is the Brain a Digital Computer', p. 25.
35   See, for example, Fodor, J., Pylyshyn, Z. 'Connectionism and Cognitive Architecture: a Critical Analysis'; Pinker, S., Prince, A. 'On Language and Connectionism: Analysis of a Parallel Distributed Processing Model of Language Acquisition'; and the Open Peer Commentary following Smolensky's article 'On the Proper Treatment of Connectionism'.
36   Church, A. 'A Note on the Entscheidungsproblem'; Turing, A. 'On Computable Numbers, with an Application to the Entscheidungsproblem'.
37   Church, A. 'An Unsolvable Problem of Elementary Number Theory'.
38   There is an important distinction between the actual program (itself an algorithm) and the algorithm that the program embodies. For example, any BASIC program and any Fortran program are two quite different algorithms, yet a BASIC and a Fortran program for taking square roots might both use the same mathematical algorithm for extracting the roots.
39   Turing, A. M. 'On Computable Numbers, with an Application to the Entscheidungsproblem', pp. 249–52.
40   Newell, A. 'Physical Symbol Systems', p. 170.
41   Leiber, J. *An Invitation to Cognitive Science*, p. 100.
42   A decidable set may have more than one decision procedure. By definition the different procedures will always agree in their answers.
43   The decision procedure uses a *recursive* rule: for X to be a member, X must either be 'Fred is just an ordinary bloke' or X must be of the form 'it is false that Y' where Y is a member. (The rule is recursive because it defines membership (X's) in terms of membership (Y's); see section 4.2.)
44   Church, A. 'A Note on the Entscheidungsproblem'.
45   There are several, in fact. Two of the best known are yielded by the truth tree method and the resolution method respectively.
46   Fodor, J. 'Fodor's Guide to Mental Representation', p. 89. See also *Psychosemantics*, pp. 147–8.
47   A Turing machine can have only a finite number of states (otherwise the state transitions could not be specified by means of a finite machine table). Hodges credits Turing with the 'brave suggestion' that the set of potential states of the human mind is also finite (*Alan Turing: The Enigma*, p. 105). However, Turing's point seems to be rather that a Turing machine can simulate a device with an infinite number of internal states by using symbols to represent the states. '[T]he restriction [to a finite number of states] is not one which seriously affects computation, since the use of more complicated states of mind can be avoided by writing more symbols on the tape' ('On Computable Numbers', p. 250).
48   Marian Boykan Pour-El and Ian Richards have shown that the solutions to Maxwell's wave equation are not always computable. Solutions which are computable at a time t may not be computable at time t +1. (Pour-El, M. B., Richards, I. 'The Wave Equation with Computable Initial Data such that its Unique Solution is Not Computable'; 'Computability and Noncomputability in Classical Analysis'.) There is no reason to think that the fields described by these solutions

exist in the actual world. Nevertheless the Pour-El – Richards result is conceptually important. It establishes, in a very direct way, the *possibility* of physical systems that are not algorithmically calculable.

49 One may hope that even if the brain should turn out not to be algorithmically calculable, it is nevertheless 'recursively approximable' in the sense of Rose and Ullian. (Rose, G. F., Ullian, J. S. 'Approximation of Functions on the Integers'.) A system is recursively approximable if and only if there is an algorithm that computes descriptions (not necessarily in real time) of the system's input/output behaviour in such a way that after a sufficiently large number of descriptions have been generated the proportion of the descriptions that are incorrect never exceeds a prescribed figure. However, this is at present no *more* than a hope. There are uncountably many functions that are not recursively approximable (theorem 3.2, op. cit. p. 700). (See also Horowitz, B. M. 'Constructively Nonpartial Recursive Functions'.)

50 We can ignore Turing machines that do not use the binary alphabet (i.e. machines that use three or more basic symbols) since these can be simulated by machines that do use the binary alphabet. We can also ignore Turing machines whose tapes are infinite in both directions, since any such machine can be simulated by a machine whose tape is infinite in one direction only. The same goes for multi-tape machines. (Minsky, M. *Computation: Finite and Infinite Machines*, pp. 129–30.)

51 This is known as a *diagonal* argument. This form of argument was first used by Georg Cantor in his famous proof, alluded to in chapter 4, that there are sets larger than the set of all integers.

52 Turing proved more than that the set of computable binary sequences is undecidable. He showed that the set of what he called *satisfactory* binary sequences is undecidable. A binary sequence is satisfactory if and only if it constitutes an encoding – in assembly language, say – of the machine table and initial tape contents of a Turing machine that eventually halts (i.e. whose head eventually comes to rest, the computation completed). To put it less formally, to say that a sequence is satisfactory is to say (a) that it is a binary specification of a program and an input, and (b) that the program will accept the input, compute away and successfully terminate. (As every would-be programmer knows, not every program is like that. Some get stuck in loops and would keep going forever if not forcibly stopped.) Turing's result that the set of satisfactory binary sequences is undecidable has become known as the Halting Theorem. When coupled with the Church-Turing thesis, the Halting Theorem yields a surprising result: there can be no algorithmic method, applicable to every computer C and every program P written in C's machine code, for determining whether C can succeed in obeying each instruction in P. (Remember from chapter 4 that programs in machine code end with an instruction to halt.) There can be no universal method for computing whether programs will terminate successfully.

53 In 1936 Turing broached the idea that our cognitive processes are algorithmically calculable only gently. He was much more forthright later. In a lecture given in 1947 while he was working on the ACE he explicitly referred to the human brain as a digital computing machine ('Lecture to the London Mathematical Society', p. 111). (His 1945 remark that he was going to 'build a brain' has become famous (Hodges, A. *Alan Turing: The Enigma*, p. 290).) In 'Intelligent Machinery' (p. 16)

he conjectures 'that the cortex of the infant is an unorganised machine, which can be organised by suitable . . . training'. He continues 'The organising might result in the modification of the machine into a universal machine or something like it'. (As Justin Leiber has pointed out (*An Invitation to Cognitive Science*, p. 158), Turing's discussion in this paper of unorganised machines is a striking anticipation of PDP.)

54 Penrose, R. *The Emperor's New Mind*, p. 172.
55 Sutherland, N.S. 'Removing the Mystery from Intelligence'. (To preserve continuity of presentation, I have written 'thinking' where the original contains 'intelligence'.) It is unclear whether or not Sutherland himself endorses the quoted argument.
56 Searle, J. *Minds, Brains and Science*, pp. 37–8.
57 Block, N. J. 'Troubles with Functionalism', p. 279.
58 Smolensky, P. 'On the Proper Treatment of Connectionism', p. 2.
59 Fodor, J., Pylyshyn, Z. 'Connectionism and Cognitive Architecture: a Critical Analysis', pp. 21–7.
60 Touretzky, D. S., Hinton, G. E. 'Symbols Among the Neurons: Details of a Connectionist Inference Architecture'.
61 Broadbent, D. 'A Question of Levels: Comment on McClelland and Rumelhart'; Fodor, J., Pylyshyn, Z. 'Connectionism and Cognitive Architecture: a Critical Analysis', pp. 54–68.
62 Here I loosely follow the terminology of Pinker, S., Prince, A. 'On Language and Connectionism: Analysis of a Parallel Distributed Processing Model of Language Acquisition', p. 77.

Epilogue

1 Gregory, R. L. 'The Brain as an Engineering Problem', p. 310.
2 Mettrie, J. O. de la, *Man a Machine*, pp. 132, 135.
3 Descartes, R. 'Discourse On Method'.

Bibliography

Aikins, J. S. 1983. 'Prototypical Knowledge for Expert Systems'. *Artificial Intelligence*, 20, pp. 163–210.

Aleksander, I. (ed.) 1989. *Neural Computing Architectures: The Design of Brain-Like Machines*. Cambridge, Mass.: MIT Press.

Aleksander, I., Burnett, P. 1987. *Thinking Machines: The Search for Artificial Intelligence*. Oxford: Oxford University Press.

Anderson, J. A., Hinton, G. E. 1981. 'Models of Information Processing in the Brain'. In Hinton, G. E., Anderson, J. A. (eds) 1981. *Parallel Models of Associative Memory*. Hillsdale, N.J.: Lawrence Erlbaum, pp. 9–48.

Anderson, J. A., Mozer, M. C. 1981. 'Categorization and Selective Neurons'. In Hinton, G. E., Anderson, J. A. (eds) 1981. *Parallel Models of Associative Memory*, pp. 213–36.

Anderson, J. A., Silverstein, J. W., Ritz, S. A., Jones, R. S. 1977. 'Distinctive Features, Categorical Perception, and Probability Learning: Some Applications of a Neural Model'. *Psychological Review*, 84, pp. 413–51.

Armstrong, D. M. 1968. *A Materialist Theory of the Mind*. London: Routledge and Kegan Paul.

Atanasoff, J. V. 1940. 'Computing Machine for the Solution of Large Systems of Linear Algebraic Equations'. In Randell, B. (ed.) 1982. *The Origins of Digital Computers*. Berlin: Springer-Verlag, pp. 315–35.

Augarten, S. 1984. *Bit by Bit*. New York: Ticknor and Fields.

Austin, J. L. 1962. *Sense and Sensibilia*. Oxford: Clarendon.

Ayer, A. J. 1954. *Philosophical Essays*. London: Macmillan.

Barlow, H. B. 1972. 'Single Units and Sensation: a Neuron Doctrine for Perceptual Psychology?'. *Perception*, 1, pp. 371–94.

Bates, A. M., Bowden, B. V., Strachey, C., Turing, A. M. 1953. 'Digital Computers Applied to Games'. In Bowden, B. V. (ed.) 1953. *Faster than Thought*. London: Pitman, pp. 286–310.

Bauer, F. L. 1980. 'Between Zuse and Rutishauser – The Early Development of Digital Computing in Central Europe'. In Metropolis, N., Howlett, J., Rota, G. C.

(eds) 1980. *A History of Computing in the Twentieth Century*. New York: Academic Press, pp. 505–24.

Beach, F. A., Hebb, D. O., Morgan, C. T., Nissen, H. W. (eds) 1960. *The Neuropsychology of Lashley*. New York: McGraw-Hill.

Bennett, J. 1965. 'Substance, Reality, and Primary Qualities'. *American Philosophical Quarterly*, 2, pp. 1–17.

Berry, A. 1983. *The Super-Intelligent Machine*. London: Jonathan Cape.

Berwick, R. C., Weinberg, A. S. 1984. *The Grammatical Basis of Linguistic Performance: Language Use and Acquisition*. Cambridge, Mass.: MIT Press.

Biederman, I. 1987. 'Recognition by Components: a Theory of Human Image Understanding'. *Psychological Review*, 94, pp. 115–47.

Biro, J. I., Shahan, R. W. (eds) 1982. *Mind, Brain and Function: Essays in the Philosophy of Mind*. Brighton: Harvester.

Blair, P., Guha, R. V., Pratt, W. 1992. 'Microtheories: An Ontological Engineer's Guide'. MCC Technical Report Number CYC-050-92. Austin, Texas: Microelectronics and Computer Technology Corporation.

Blakemore, C., Greenfield, S. (eds) 1987. *Mindwaves*. Oxford: Basil Blackwell.

Block, N. 1978. 'Troubles with Functionalism'. In Savage, C. W. (ed.) 1978. *Perception and Cognition: Issues in the Foundations of Psychology*. Minneapolis: University of Minnesota Press, pp. 261–325.

Block, N. 1981. 'Psychologism and Behaviourism'. *Philosophical Review*, 90, pp. 5–43.

Block, N. 1983. 'Mental Pictures and Cognitive Science'. *The Philosophical Review*, 92, 499–541.

Block, N. 1990. 'The Computer Model of the Mind'. In Osherson, D. N., Lasnik, H. (eds) 1990. *An Invitation to Cognitive Science*. Vol. 3. *Thinking*. Cambridge, Mass.: MIT Press, pp. 247–289.

Bloomfield, B. P. (ed.) 1987. *The Question of Artificial Intelligence*. London: Croom Helm.

Bobrow, D. 1968. 'A Turing Test Passed'. *ACM SIGART Newsletter*, December 1968, pp. 14–15.

Born, I. (trans.) 1971. *The Born-Einstein Letters*. London: Macmillan.

Boswell, J. *Life of Samuel Johnson*. Ed. Birrell, A. 1896. Westminster: Archibald Constable.

Bowden, B. V. (ed.) 1953. *Faster than Thought*. London: Pitman.

Breton, A. 1924. *Manifestes du Surréalisme*. Paris: Editions du Sagittaire.

Broadbent, D. 1985. 'A Question of Levels: Comment on McClelland and Rumelhart'. *Journal of Experimental Psychology: General*, 114, pp. 189–192.

Bromley, A. G. 1982. 'Charles Babbage's Analytical Engine, 1838'. *Annals of the History of Computing*, 4, pp. 196–217.

Bundy, A. (ed.) 1980. *Artificial Intelligence*. Edinburgh: Edinburgh University Press.

Burks, A. W. 1980. 'From ENIAC to the Stored-Program Computer: Two Revolutions in Computers'. In Metropolis, N., Howlett, J., Rota, G. C. (eds) 1980. *A History of Computing in the Twentieth Century*. New York: Academic Press, pp. 311–44.

Burks, A. W., Goldstine, H. H., von Neumann, J. 1946. 'Preliminary Discussion of the Logical Design of an Electronic Computing Instrument'. An edited version appears in Randell, B. (ed.) 1982. *The Origins of Digital Computers*. Berlin: Springer-Verlag, pp. 399–413.

Carpenter, B. E., Doran, R. W. (eds) 1986. *A.M. Turing's ACE Report of 1946 and Other Papers*. Cambridge, Mass.: MIT Press.

Carruthers, P. 1986. *Introducing Persons*. London: Croom Helm.

Chisholm, R. M. 1957. *Perceiving: A Philosophical Study*. New York: Cornell University Press.

Chow, K. L. 1968. 'Visual Discriminations After Extensive Ablation of Optic Tract and Visual Cortex in Cats'. *Brain Research*, 9, pp. 363–6.

Church, A. 1936a. 'A Note on the Entscheidungsproblem'. *The Journal of Symbolic Logic*, 1, pp. 40–1.

Church, A. 1936b. 'An Unsolvable Problem of Elementary Number Theory'. *The American Journal of Mathematics*, 58, pp. 345–63.

Churchland, P. M. 1985. 'Reduction, Qualia, and the Direct Introspection of Brain States'. *The Journal of Philosophy*, 82, pp. 8–28.

Churchland, P. M. 1986. 'Some Reductive Strategies in Cognitive Neurobiology'. *Mind*, 95, pp. 279–310.

Churchland, P. M., Churchland, P. S. 1990. 'Could a Machine Think?'. *Scientific American*, 262 (1), pp. 26–31.

Churchland, P. S. 1986. *Neurophilosophy: Toward a Unified Science of the Mind/Brain*. Cambridge, Mass.: MIT Press.

Colby, K. M. 1975. *Artificial Paranoia*. New York: Pergamon.

Colby, K. M. 1981. 'Modeling a Paranoid Mind'. *Behavioural and Brain Sciences*, 4, pp. 515–34.

Colby, K. M., Watt, J. B., Gilbert, J. P. 1966. 'A Computer Method of Psychotherapy: Preliminary Communication'. *The Journal of Nervous and Mental Disease*, 142, pp. 148–152.

Colby, K. M., Weber, S., Hilf, F. D. 1971. 'Artificial Paranoia'. *Artificial Intelligence*, 2, 1–25.

Cooper, D. (ed.) 1993. *Companion to Aesthetics*. Oxford: Basil Blackwell.

Copeland, B. J. 1979. 'On When a Semantics is not a Semantics'. *Journal of Philosophical Logic*, 8, pp. 399–413.

Copeland, B. J. 1980. 'The Trouble Anderson and Belnap have with Relevance'. *Philosophical Studies*, 37, pp. 325–34.

Copeland, B. J. 1984. 'Horseshoe, Hook, and Relevance'. *Theoria*, 50, pp. 148–64.

Copeland, B. J. 1985. 'Substitutional Quantification and Existence'. *Analysis*, 45, pp. 1–4.

Copeland, B. J. 1986. 'What is a Semantics for Classical Negation?'. *Mind*, 95, pp. 478–90.

Copeland, B. J. 1993a. 'The Curious Case of the Chinese Gym'. *Synthèse*. (Forthcoming.)

Copeland, B. J. 1993b. 'Compatibilism and Modality'. (Forthcoming.)

Copeland, B. J. 1993c. 'What Is Computation?'. (Forthcoming.)

Copeland, B. J. 1993d. 'Vagueness and Bivalence'. (Forthcoming.)

Copeland, B. J. (ed.) 1994. *Logic and Reality: Essays in Pure and Applied Logic In Memory of Arthur Prior*. Oxford: Oxford University Press. (Forthcoming.)

Copi, I. M. 1961. *Introduction to Logic*. Second edn. New York: Collier-Macmillan.

Corballis, M. 1991. *The Lopsided Ape*. New York: Oxford University Press.

Cottingham, J., Stoothoff, R., Murdoch, D. 1985. *The Philosophical Writings of Descartes.* Cambridge: Cambridge University Press, vol. 1.

Craik, K. J. W. 1943. *The Nature of Explanation.* Cambridge: Cambridge University Press.

Crick, F., Asanuma, C. 1986. 'Certain Aspects of the Anatomy and Physiology of the Cerebral Cortex'. In McClelland, J. L., Rumelhart, D. E., and the PDP Research Group 1986. *Parallel Distributed Processing: Explorations in the Microstructure of Cognition.* Vol. 2: *Psychological and Biological Models.* Cambridge, Mass.: MIT Press, pp. 333–71.

Culbertson, J. T. 1956. 'Some Uneconomical Robots'. In Shannon, C. E., McCarthy, J. (eds) 1956. *Automata Studies.* Princeton: Princeton University Press, pp. 99–116.

Culbertson, J. T. 1963. *The Minds of Robots: Sense Data, Memory Images, and Behaviour in Conscious Automata.* Urbana: University of Illinois Press.

Darrach, B. 1970. 'Meet Shakey, The First Electronic Person', *Life,* vol. 69, part 21, November 20, 1970, pp. 58B–68.

Davidson, D. 1967. 'The Logical Form of Action Sentences'. In Davidson, D. 1980. *Essays on Actions and Events.* Oxford: Clarendon Press, pp. 105–22.

Davidson, D. 1973. 'Freedom to Act'. In Davidson, D. 1980. *Essays on Actions and Events.* Oxford: Clarendon Press, pp. 63–81.

Davidson, D. 1980. *Essays on Actions and Events.* Oxford: Clarendon Press.

Davis, J. M., Garver, D. L. 1978. 'Neuroleptics: Clinical Use in Psychiatry'. In Iverson, L. L., Iverson, S. D., Snyder, S. H. (eds) 1978. *Handbook of Psychopharmacology.* New York: Plenum, vol. 10, pp. 129–64.

Deecke, L., Grözinger, B., Kornhuber, H. H. 1976. 'Voluntary Finger Movement in Man: Cerebral Potentials and Theory'. *Biological Cybernetics,* 23, pp. 99–119.

Degn, H., Holden, A. V., Olsen, L. F. (eds) 1987. *Chaos in Biological Systems.* New York: Plenum.

DeJong, G. 1977. 'Skimming Newspaper Stories by Computer'. *Proceedings of the Fifth International Joint Conference on Artificial Intelligence.* Cambridge: Massachusetts Institute of Technology, p. 16.

Dennett, D. C. 1978a. *Brainstorms: Philosophical Essays on Mind and Psychology.* Brighton: Harvester.

Dennett, D. C. 1978b. 'On Giving Libertarians What They Say They Want'. In Dennett, D. C. 1978. *Brainstorms: Philosophical Essays on Mind and Psychology.* Brighton: Harvester, pp. 286–99.

Dennett, D. C. 1978c. 'Toward a Cognitive Theory of Consciousness'. In Dennett, D. C. 1978. *Brainstorms: Philosophical Essays on Mind and Psychology.* Brighton: Harvester, pp. 149–73.

Dennett, D. C. 1984. *Elbow Room: the Varieties of Freewill Worth Wanting.* Oxford: Clarendon Press.

Dennett, D. C. 1988. 'Quining Qualia'. In Marcel, A. J., Bisiach, E. (eds) 1988. *Consciousness in Contemporary Science.* Oxford: Clarendon Press, pp. 42–77.

Dennett, D. C. 1991. *Consciousness Explained.* Boston: Little Brown.

Descartes, R. 1641. 'Discourse On Method'. In Cottingham, J., Stoothoff, R., Murdoch, D. 1985. *The Philosophical Writings of Descartes.* Cambridge: Cambridge University Press, vol. 1.

Doyle, J. 1979. 'A Truth Maintenance System'. *Artificial Intelligence,* 12, pp. 231–72.

Dreyfus, H. L. 1965. *Alchemy and Artificial Intelligence*. Santa Monica: RAND Corporation, Report P-3244, Dec. 1965.

Dreyfus, H. L. 1979. *What Computers Can't Do: The Limits of Artificial Intelligence*. Revised edn. New York: Harper & Row.

Dreyfus, H. L., Dreyfus, S. E. 1986. *Mind Over Machine*. New York: Macmillan/The Free Press.

Eccles, J. C. (ed.) 1966. *Brain and Conscious Experience*. Berlin: Springer-Verlag.

Eccles, J. C. 1972. 'Possible Synaptic Mechanism Subserving Learning'. In Karczmar, A. G., Eccles, J. C. (eds) 1972. *Brain and Human Behaviour*. Berlin: Springer-Verlag, pp. 39–61.

Eccles, J. 1979. *The Human Mystery*. New York: Springer.

Eckert, J. P. 1980. 'The ENIAC'. In Metropolis, N., Howlett, J., Rota, G. C. (eds) 1980. *A History of Computing in the Twentieth Century*. New York: Academic Press, pp. 525–39.

Elgot, C. C., Robinson, A. 1964. 'Random-Access Stored-Program Machines, an Approach to Programming Languages'. *Journal of the Association for Computing Machinery*, 11, pp. 365–99.

Elman, J. D., Zipser, D. 1988. 'Learning the Hidden Structure of Speech'. *Journal of the Acoustical Society of America*, 83, pp. 1615–29.

Ernst, G. W., Newell, A. 1969. *GPS: A Case Study in Generality and Problem Solving*. New York: Academic Press.

Feigenbaum, E. A., Feldman, J. (eds) 1963. *Computers and Thought*. New York: McGraw-Hill.

Feldman, J. A., Ballard, D. H. 1982. 'Connectionist Models and their Properties'. *Cognitive Science*, 6, pp. 205–54.

Fleck, J. 1982. 'Development and Establishment in Artificial Intelligence'. In Bloomfield, B. P. (ed.) 1987. *The Question of Artificial Intelligence*. London: Croom Helm, pp. 106–64.

Flew, A. 1955. 'Divine Omnipotence and Human Freedom'. In Flew, A., MacIntyre, A. (eds) 1955. *New Essays in Philosophical Theology*. London: SCM Press, pp. 144–69.

Flew, A., MacIntyre, A. (eds) 1955. *New Essays in Philosophical Theology*. London: SCM Press.

Fodor, J. A. 1975. *The Language of Thought*. New York: Thomas Y. Crowell.

Fodor, J. A. 1985. 'Fodor's Guide to Mental Representation: The Intelligent Auntie's Vade-Mecum'. *Mind*, 94, pp. 76–100.

Fodor, J. A. 1987. *Psychosemantics: The Problem of Meaning in the Philosophy of Mind*. Cambridge, Mass.: MIT Press.

Fodor, J., Pylyshyn, Z. 1988. 'Connectionism and Cognitive Architecture: A Critical Analysis'. In Pinker, S., Mehler, J. (eds) 1988. *Connections and Symbols*. Cambridge, Mass.: MIT Press, pp. 3–71.

Frankfurt, H. G. 1971. 'Freedom of the Will and the Concept of a Person'. In Frankfurt, H. G. 1988. *The Importance of What We Care About: Philosophical Essays*. Cambridge: Cambridge University Press, pp. 11–25.

Frankfurt, H. G. 1976. 'Identification and Externality'. In Frankfurt, H. G. 1988. *The Importance of What We Care About: Philosophical Essays*. Cambridge: Cambridge University Press, pp. 58–68.

Frankfurt, H. G. 1988. *The Importance of What We Care About: Philosophical Essays*. Cambridge: Cambridge University Press.

Freud, S. 1932. *Neue Folge der Vorlesungen zur Einfuhrüng in die Psychoanalyse*. Frankfurt: S. Fischer Verlag.

Fuller, L. L. 1958. 'Positivism and Fidelity to Law – A Reply to Professor Hart'. *Harvard Law Review*, 71, pp. 630–72.

Gazzaniga, M. S. 1988. 'Brain Modularity: Towards a Philosophy of Conscious Experience'. In Marcel, A. J., Bisiach, E. (eds) 1988. *Consciousness in Contemporary Science*. Oxford: Clarendon Press, pp. 218–38.

Gazzaniga, M. S., Bogen, J. E., Sperry, R. W. 1965. 'Observations on Visual Perception After Disconnection of the Cerebral Hemispheres in Man'. *Brain*, 8, pp. 221–36.

Gazzaniga, M. S., Le Doux, J. E. 1978. *The Integrated Mind*. New York: Plenum.

Gelernter, H., Hansen, J. R., Loveland, D. W. 1960. 'Empirical Explorations of the Geometry Theorem Proving Machine'. In Feigenbaum, E. A., Feldman, J. (eds) 1963. *Computers and Thought*. New York: McGraw-Hill, pp. 153–63.

Gentzen, G. 1934. 'Investigations Into Logical Deduction'. In Szabo, M. E. (ed.) 1969. *The Collected Papers of Gerhard Gentzen*. Amsterdam: North-Holland, pp. 68–131.

Ginet, C. 1966. 'Might We Have No Choice?'. In Lehrer, K. (ed.) 1966. *Freedom and Determinism*. New York: Random House.

Giuliano, V. E. 1965. 'Comments on a Paper by R. F. Simmons'. *Computational Linguistics*, 8, pp. 69–70.

Gleick, J. 1988. *Chaos: Making a New Science*. London: Cardinal.

Goldstine, H. H. 1972. *The Computer from Pascal to von Neumann*. Princeton: Princeton University Press.

Goldstine, H. H., Goldstine, A. 1946. 'The Electronic Numerical Integrator and Computer'. In Randell, B. (ed.) 1982. *The Origins of Digital Computers*. Berlin: Springer-Verlag, pp. 359–73.

Good, I. J. 1980. 'Pioneering Work on Computers at Bletchley'. In Metropolis, N., Howlett, J., Rota, G. C. (eds) 1980. *A History of Computing in the Twentieth Century*. New York: Academic Press, pp. 31–45.

Goodall, J. van Lawick 1971. *In the Shadow of Man*. London: Collins.

Gregory, R. L. 1961. 'The Brain as an Engineering Problem'. In Thorpe, W. H., Zangwill, O. L. (eds) 1961. *Current Problems in Animal Behaviour*. Cambridge: Cambridge University Press, pp. 307–30.

Gregory, R. L. (ed.) 1987. *The Oxford Companion to the Mind*. Oxford: Oxford University Press.

Gross, C. G., Bender, D. B., Rocha-Miranda, C. E. 1974. 'Inferotemporal Cortex: A Single-unit Analysis'. In Schmitt, F. O., Worden, F. G. (eds) 1974. *The Neurosciences: Third Study Program*. Cambridge, Mass.: M.I.T. Press, pp. 229–38.

Gruenberger, F. J. 1979. 'The History of the JOHNNIAC'. *Annals of the History of Computing*, 1, pp. 49–64.

Guha, R. V. 1990. 'The Representation of Defaults in CYC'. MCC Technical Report Number ACT-CYC-083-90. Austin, Texas: Microelectronics and Computer Technology Corporation.

Guha, R. V., Lenat, D. B. 1990. 'CYC: A Mid-Term Report'. *AI Magazine*, Fall, pp. 32–59.

Bibliography 289

Guha, R. V., Levy, A. Y. 1990. 'A Relevance Based Meta Level'. MCC Technical Report Number ACT–CYC–040–90. Austin, Texas: Microelectronics and Computer Technology Corporation.

Gunderson, K. 1985. *Mentality and Machines*. London: Croom Helm.

Hanks, S., McDermott, D. 1986. 'Default Reasoning, Nonmonotonic Logics, and the Frame Problem'. *Proceedings of the Fifth National Conference on Artificial Intelligence*, pp. 328–33.

Harlow, J. M. 1868. 'Recovery From the Passage of an Iron Bar Through the Head'. *Massachusetts Medical Society Publications*, 2, pp. 328–47.

Harth, E. 1982. *Windows on the Mind: Reflections on the Physical Basis of Consciousness*. Brighton: Harvester.

Haugeland, J. (ed.) 1981a. *Mind Design: Philosophy, Psychology, Artificial Intelligence*. Cambridge, Mass.: MIT Press.

Haugeland, J. 1981b. 'Analog and Analog'. In Biro, J. I., Shahan, R. W. (eds) 1982. *Mind, Brain and Function: Essays in the Philosophy of Mind*. Brighton: Harvester, pp. 213–25.

Haugeland, J. 1985. *Artificial Intelligence: the Very Idea*. Cambridge, Mass.: MIT Press.

Heiser, J. F., Colby, K. M., Faught, W. S., Parkison, R. C. 1980. 'Can Psychiatrists Distinguish a Computer Simulation of Paranoia from the Real Thing?' *Journal of Psychiatric Research*, 15, pp. 149–62.

Herken, R. (ed.) 1988. *The Universal Turing Machine*. Oxford: Oxford University Press.

Hinton, G. E. 1985. 'Learning in Parallel Networks'. *BYTE*, April 1985, pp. 265–73.

Hinton, G. E., Anderson, J. A. (eds) 1981. *Parallel Models of Associative Memory*. Hillsdale, N. J.: Lawrence Erlbaum.

Hobbes, T. *Works*. Ed. Molesworth, W. 1839–45. London: John Bohn.

Hodges, A. 1983. *Alan Turing: The Enigma*. London: Burnett.

Hofstadter, D. R. 1980. *Gödel, Escher, Bach: an Eternal Golden Braid*. New York: Basic.

Hofstadter, D. R. 1982. 'Variations on a Theme as the Essence of Imagination'. *Scientific American*, 247 (4), pp. 14–21.

Hofstadter, D. R. 1985. *Metamagical Themas: Questing for the Essence of Mind and Pattern*. New York: Basic Books.

Hofstadter, D. R., Dennett, D. C. (eds) 1981. *The Mind's I*. New York: Basic Books.

Holden, A. V. (ed.) 1986. *Chaos*. Manchester: Manchester University Press.

Honderich, T. (ed.) 1973. *Essays on Freedom of Action*. London: Routledge & Kegan Paul.

Honderich, T. 1988. *A Theory of Determinism: The Mind, Neuroscience, and Life-Hopes*. Oxford: Clarendon Press.

Horowitz, B. M. 1980. 'Constructively Nonpartial Recursive Functions'. *Notre Dame Journal of Formal Logic*, 21, pp. 273–6.

Hospers, J. 1967. *An Introduction to Philosophical Analysis*. London: Routledge & Kegan Paul.

Hughes, G. E., Cresswell, M. J. 1968. *An Introduction to Modal Logic*. London: Methuen.

Hume, D. 1748. *An Enquiry Concerning Human Understanding*. Ed. Selby-Bigge, L. A. 1902. Oxford: Clarendon Press.

Huxley, T. H. 1866. *Lessons in Elementary Physiology*. London: Macmillan.

Jackendoff, R. 1987. *Consciousness and the Computational Mind*. Cambridge, Mass.: MIT Press.

Jackson, F. C. 1982. 'Epiphenomenal Qualia'. *Philosophical Quarterly*, 32, 127–36.

Jackson, F. C. 1986. 'What Mary Didn't Know'. *The Journal of Philosophy*, 83, pp. 291–5.

Jackson, F. C. (ed.) 1991. *Conditionals*. Oxford: Oxford University Press.

Jackson, P. 1986. *Introduction to Expert Systems*. Wokingham: Addison-Wesley.

Jaynes, J. 1990. *The Origin of Consciousness in the Breakdown of the Bicameral Mind*. Second edn. Boston: Houghton Mifflin.

Jefferson, G. 1949. 'The Mind of Mechanical Man'. *British Medical Journal*, June 25 1949, pp. 1105–10.

Johnson-Laird, P. N. 1983. *Mental Models: Towards a Cognitive Science of Language, Inference and Consciousness*. Cambridge: Cambridge University Press.

Johnson-Laird, P. N. 1988. *The Computer and the Mind: An Introduction to Cognitive Science*. London: Fontana.

Kant, I. 1788. *Critique of Practical Reason*. Trans. Beck, L. W. 1949. Chicago: University of Chicago Press.

Karczmar, A. G., Eccles, J. C. (eds) 1972. *Brain and Human Behaviour*. Berlin: Springer-Verlag.

Keating, E. G., Horel, J. A. 1972. 'Effects of Prestriate and Striate Lesions on the Monkey's Ability to Locate and Discriminate Visual Forms'. *Experimental Neurology*, 35, pp. 322–36.

Kilburn, T., Williams, F. C. 1953. 'The University of Manchester Computing Machine'. In Bowden, B. V. (ed.) 1953. *Faster than Thought*. London: Pitman, pp. 117–29.

Kohonen, T. 1980. *Content-Addressable Memories*. Berlin: Springer-Verlag.

Kosslyn, S. H. 1980. *Image and Mind*. Cambridge, Mass.: Harvard University Press.

Kosslyn, S. H. 1983. *Ghosts in the Mind's Machine: Creating and Using Images in the Brain*. New York: Norton.

Krantz, D. H., Atkinson, R. C., Luce, R. D., Suppes, P. (eds) 1974. *Contemporary Developments in Mathematical Psychology*. Vol. 2: *Measurement, Psychophysics, and Neural Information Processing*. San Francisco: W.H. Freeman.

Kripke, S. A. 1980. *Naming and Necessity*. Oxford: Basil Blackwell.

Lackner, J. R., Garrett, M. F. 1972. 'Resolving Ambiguity: Effects of Biasing Context in the Unattended Ear'. *Cognition*, l, pp. 359–72.

Lamb, J. 1977. 'On a Proof of Incompatibilism'. *Philosophical Review*, 86, pp. 20–35.

Laplace, P. 1814. *Essai Philosophique sur les Probabilités*. Second edn. Paris: Courcier.

Larson, E. R. 1974. 'Honeywell, Inc. v. Sperry Rand Corp., et al.'. *US Patent Quarterly*, 180, pp. 673–772.

Lashley, K. S. 1950. 'In Search of the Engram'. In Beach, F. A., Hebb, D. O., Morgan, C. T., Nissen, H. W. (eds) 1960. *The Neuropsychology of Lashley*. New York: McGraw-Hill, pp. 478–505.

Lavington, S. H. 1975. *A History of Manchester Computers*. Manchester: NCC Publications.

Lavington, S. H. 1980. *Early British Computers*. Manchester: Manchester University Press.

Lehrer, K. (ed.) 1966. *Freedom and Determinism*. New York: Random House.

Leiber, J. 1991. *An Invitation to Cognitive Science*. Oxford: Basil Blackwell.

Lenat, D. B. 1982. 'The Nature of Heuristics'. *Artificial Intelligence*, 19, pp. 189–249.

Lenat, D. B. 1984. 'Computer Software for Intelligent Systems'. *Scientific American*, 251 (3), pp. 152–60.

Lenat, D. B., Feigenbaum, E. A. 1991a. 'On the Thresholds of Knowledge'. *Artificial Intelligence*, 47, pp. 185–230.

Lenat, D. B., Feigenbaum, E. A. 1991b. 'Reply to Brian Smith'. *Artificial Intelligence*, 47, pp. 231–50.

Lenat, D. B., Guha, R. V. 1990. *Building Large Knowledge-Based Systems: Representation and Inference in the CYC Project*. Reading, Mass.: Addison-Wesley.

Lewis, C. I., Langford, C. H. 1932. *Symbolic Logic*. New York: Dover, 1959.

Lewis, D. K. 1971. 'Analog and Digital'. *Noûs* , 5, pp. 321–7.

Lewis, D. K. 1980. 'Mad Pain and Martian Pain'. In Lewis, D. 1983b. *Philosophical Papers*, vol. 1. New York: Oxford University Press, pp. 122–30.

Lewis, D. K. 1983a. 'Postscript to Mad Pain and Martian Pain'. In Lewis, D. 1983b. *Philosophical Papers*, vol. 1. New York: Oxford University Press, pp. 130–2.

Lewis, D. K. 1983b. *Philosophical Papers*, vol. 1. New York: Oxford University Press.

Lewis, H. D. (ed.) 1956. *Contemporary British Philosophy*, Series 3. London: George Allen & Unwin.

Libet, B. 1985. 'Unconscious Cerebral Initiative and the Role of Conscious Will in Voluntary Action'. *Behavioural and Brain Sciences*, 8, pp. 529–39.

Longuet-Higgins, H. C. 1968. 'The Non-Local Storage of Temporal Information'. *Proceedings of the Royal Society*, Series B, 171, pp. 327–34.

Longuet-Higgins, H. C. 1972. 'To Mind Via Semantics'. In Kenny, A. J. P., Longuet-Higgins, H. C., Lucas, J. R., Waddington, C. H. 1972. *The Nature of Mind*. Edinburgh: Edinburgh University Press, pp. 92–107.

Lovelace, A. A., Menabrea, L. F. 1843. 'Sketch of the Analytical Engine Invented by Charles Babbage, Esq.'. In Bowden, B. V. (ed.) 1953. *Faster than Thought*. London: Pitman, pp. 341–408.

Lycan, W. G. 1987. *Consciousness*. Cambridge, Mass.: MIT Press.

Mabbott, J. D. 1956. 'Freewill and Punishment'. In Lewis, H. D. (ed.) 1956. *Contemporary British Philosophy*, Series 3. London: George Allen & Unwin, pp. 289–309.

Marcel, A. J., Bisiach, E. (eds) 1988. *Consciousness in Contemporary Science*. Oxford: Clarendon Press.

McCarthy, J. 1980. 'Circumscription – A Form of Non-Monotonic Reasoning'. *Artificial Intelligence*, 13, pp. 27–39, 171–2.

McCarthy, J. 1986. 'Applications of Circumscription to Formalising Common-Sense Knowledge'. *Artificial Intelligence*, 28, pp. 89–116.

McCarthy, J., Hayes, P. J. 1969. 'Some Philosophical Problems from the Standpoint of Artificial Intelligence'. In Meltzer, B., Michie, D. (eds) 1969. *Machine Intelligence 4*. Edinburgh: Edinburgh University Press, pp. 463–502.

McClelland, J. L. (unpublished). 'Models of Perception and Memory Based on Principles of Neural Organisation'.

McClelland, J. L. 1987. 'The Basis of Lawful Behaviour: Rules or Connections?'. *The Computers and Philosophy Newsletter*, 2 (1) pp. 10–16.

McClelland, J. L., Rumelhart, D. E. 1986. 'Amnesia and Distributed Memory'. In McClelland, J. L., Rumelhart, D. E., and the PDP Research Group 1986. *Parallel Distributed Processing: Explorations in the Microstructure of Cognition*. Vol. 2: *Psychological and Biological Models*. Cambridge, Mass.: MIT Press, pp. 503–27.

McClelland, J. L., Rumelhart, D. E., Hinton, G. E. 1986. 'The Appeal of Parallel Distributed Processing'. In Rumelhart, D. E., McClelland, J. L., and the PDP Research Group 1986. *Parallel Distributed Processing: Explorations in the Microstructure of Cognition*. Vol. 1: *Foundations*. Cambridge, Mass.: MIT Press, pp. 3–44.

McClelland, J. L., Rumelhart, D. E., and the PDP Research Group 1986. *Parallel Distributed Processing: Explorations in the Microstructure of Cognition*. Vol. 2: *Psychological and Biological Models*. Cambridge, Mass.: MIT Press.

McCorduck, P. 1979. *Machines Who Think*. New York: W. H. Freeman.

McCulloch, W. S., Pitts, W. 1943. 'A Logical Calculus of the Ideas Immanent in Nervous Activity'. *Bulletin of Mathematical Biophysics*, 5, pp. 115–33.

McDermott, D. 1976. 'Artificial Intelligence Meets Natural Stupidity'. In Haugeland, J. (ed.) 1981. *Mind Design: Philosophy, Psychology, Artificial Intelligence*. Cambridge, Mass.: MIT Press, pp. 143–60.

McDermott, D., Doyle, J. 1980. 'Non-Monotonic Logic I'. *Artificial Intelligence*, 13, pp. 41–72.

McGinn, C. 1989. *Mental Content*. Oxford: Basil Blackwell.

Meltzer, B., Michie, D. (eds) 1969. *Machine Intelligence 4*. Edinburgh: Edinburgh University Press.

Metropolis, N., Howlett, J., Rota, G. C. (eds) 1980. *A History of Computing in the Twentieth Century*. New York: Academic Press.

Metropolis, N., Worlton, J. 1980. 'A Trilogy of Errors in the History of Computing', *Annals of the History of Computing*, 2, pp. 49–59.

Mettrie, J. O. de la 1748. *Man a Machine*. Trans. Gertrude Bussey 1912. Illinois: Open Court, 1953.

Michie, D. 1974. *On Machine Intelligence*. Edinburgh: Edinburgh University Press.

Mill, J. S. 1924 (1873). *Autobiography*. New York: Columbia University Press.

Minsky, M. L. 1967. *Computation: Finite and Infinite Machines*. Englewood Cliffs, N. J.: Prentice-Hall.

Minsky, M. L. (ed.) 1968. *Semantic Information Processing*. Cambridge, Mass.: MIT Press.

Minsky, M. L. 1974. 'A Framework for Representing Knowledge'. An edited version appears in Haugeland, J. (ed.) 1981. *Mind Design: Philosophy, Psychology, Artificial Intelligence*. Cambridge, Mass.: MIT Press, pp. 95–128.

Minsky, M. L. 1984. 'Adaptive Control: From Feedback to Debugging'. In Selfridge, O. G., Rissland, E. L., Arbib, M. A. (eds) 1984. *Adaptive Control of Ill-Defined Systems*. New York: Plenum, pp. 115–25.

Minsky, M. L. 1986. *The Society of Mind*. New York: Simon and Schuster.

Minsky, M. L., Papert, S. 1969. *Perceptrons: An Introduction to Computational Geometry*. Cambridge, Mass.: MIT Press.

Minsky, M. L., Papert, S. 1972. 'Progress Report on Artificial Intelligence'. Cambridge, Mass.: MIT AI Lab Memo 252.

Moravec, H. 1988. *Mind Children: The Future of Robot and Human Intelligence*. Cambridge, Mass.: Harvard University Press.

Moto-oka, T. (ed.) 1982. *Fifth Generation Computer Systems*. Amsterdam: North-Holland.

Moto-oka, T. et al. 1982. 'Challenge for Knowledge Information Processing Systems.

(Preliminary Report on Fifth Generation Computer Systems.)'. In Moto-oka, T. (ed.) 1982. *Fifth Generation Computer Systems*. Amsterdam: North-Holland, pp. 3–89.

Moto-oka, T., Kitsuregawa, M. 1985. *The Fifth Generation Computer: The Japanese Challenge*. New York: Wiley.

Nagel, T. 1971. 'Brain Bisection and the Unity of Consciousness'. *Synthèse*, 22, pp. 396–413.

Nagel, T. 1974. 'What is it Like to be a Bat?'. *Philosophical Review*, 83, 435–50.

Nagel, T. 1986. *The View From Nowhere*. New York: Oxford University Press.

Nemirow, L. 1980. 'Review of Thomas Nagel's *Mortal Questions*'. *Philosophical Review*, 89, pp. 473–7.

Newell, A. 1980. 'Physical Symbol Systems'. *Cognitive Science*, 4, pp. 135–83.

Newell, A. 1982. 'The Knowledge Level'. *Artificial Intelligence*, 18, pp. 87–127.

Newell, A., Shaw, J. C., Simon, H. A. 1957. 'Empirical Explorations with the Logic Theory Machine: a Case Study in Heuristics'. In Feigenbaum, E. A., Feldman, J. (eds) 1963. *Computers and Thought*. New York: McGraw-Hill, pp. 109–33.

Newell, A., Simon, H. A. 1961. 'GPS, a Program that Simulates Human Thought'. In Feigenbaum, E. A., Feldman, J. (eds) 1963. *Computers and Thought*. New York: McGraw-Hill, pp. 279–93.

Newell, A., Simon, H. A. 1976. 'Computer Science as Empirical Inquiry: Symbols and Search'. In Haugeland, J. (ed.) 1981. *Mind Design: Philosophy, Psychology, Artificial Intelligence*. Cambridge, Mass.: MIT Press, pp. 35–66.

Nisbett, R. E., Wilson, T. D. 1977. 'Telling More Than We Can Know: Verbal Reports On Mental Processes'. *Psychological Review*, 84, pp. 231–59.

Osherson, D. N., Lasnik, H. (eds) 1990. *An Invitation to Cognitive Science*. Vols. 1–3. Cambridge, Mass.: MIT Press.

Pellionisz, A. J. 1986. 'Old Dogmas and New Axioms in Brain Theory'. *Behavioural and Brain Sciences*, 9, pp. 103–4.

Pellionisz, A. J., Llinás, R. 1979. 'Brain Modeling by Tensor Network Theory and Computer Simulation. The Cerebellum: Distributed Processor for Predictive Coordination'. *Neuroscience*, 4, pp. 323–48.

Penrose, R. 1989. *The Emperor's New Mind*. Oxford: Oxford University Press.

Pinker, S. 1984. *Language Learnability and Language Development*. Cambridge, Mass.: Harvard University Press.

Pinker, S., Mehler, J. (eds) 1988. *Connections and Symbols*. Cambridge, Mass.: MIT Press.

Pinker, S., Prince, A. 1988. 'On Language and Connectionism: Analysis of a Parallel Distributed Processing Model of Language Acquisition'. In Pinker, S., Mehler, J. (eds) 1988. *Connections and Symbols*. Cambridge, Mass.: MIT Press, pp. 73–193.

Poggio, T., Koch, C. 1985. 'Ill-posed Problems in Early Vision: from Computational Theory to Analogue Networks'. *Proceedings of the Royal Society of London*, B226, pp. 303–23.

Pour-El, M. B., Richards, I. 1981. 'The Wave Equation with Computable Initial Data such that its Unique Solution is Not Computable'. *Advances in Mathematics*, 39, pp. 215–39.

Pour-El, M. B., Richards, I. 1983. 'Computability and Noncomputability in Classical Analysis'. *Transactions of the American Mathematical Society*, 275, pp. 539–60.

Pribram, K. H., Nuwer, M., Baron, R. J. 1974. 'The Holographic Hypothesis of Memory Structure in Brain Function and Perception'. In Krantz, D. H., Atkinson, R. C., Luce, R. D., Suppes, P. (eds) 1974. *Contemporary Developments in Mathematical Psychology*. Vol. 2: *Measurement, Psychophysics, and Neural Information Processing*. San Francisco: W. H. Freeman, pp. 416–57.

Proudfoot, D. 1993. 'Fictional Entities'. In Cooper, D. (ed.) 1993. *Companion to Aesthetics*. Oxford: Basil Blackwell.

Putnam, H. 1964. 'Robots: Machines or Artificially Created Life?' In Putnam, H. 1975b. *Mind, Language and Reality*. Cambridge: Cambridge University Press, pp. 386–407.

Putnam, H. 1967. 'The Mental Life of Some Machines'. In Putnam, H. 1975b. *Mind, Language and Reality*. Cambridge: Cambridge University Press, pp. 408–28.

Putnam, H. 1975a. 'Philosophy and our Mental Life'. In Putnam, H. 1975b. *Mind, Language and Reality*. Cambridge: Cambridge University Press, pp. 291–303.

Putnam, H. 1975b. *Mind, Language and Reality*. Cambridge: Cambridge University Press.

Pylyshyn, Z. W. (ed.) 1970. *Perspectives On the Computer Revolution*. Englewood Cliffs, N.J.: Prentice-Hall.

Pylyshyn, Z. W. 1980. 'The "Causal Power" of Machines'. *Behavioural and Brain Sciences*, 3, pp. 442–4.

Pylyshyn, Z. W. 1984. *Computation and Cognition: Towards a Foundation for Cognitive Science*. Cambridge, Mass.: MIT Press.

Randell, B. 1972. 'On Alan Turing and the Origins of Digital Computers'. In Meltzer, B., Michie, D. (eds) 1972. *Machine Intelligence 7*. Edinburgh: Edinburgh University Press, pp. 3–20.

Randell, B. 1980. 'The Colossus'. In Metropolis, N., Howlett, J., Rota, G. C. (eds) 1980. *A History of Computing in the Twentieth Century*. New York: Academic Press, pp. 47–92.

Randell, B. (ed.) 1982. *The Origins of Digital Computers*. Berlin: Springer-Verlag.

Raphael, B. 1976a. *The Thinking Computer: Mind Inside Matter*. San Francisco: W. H. Freeman.

Raphael, B. 1976b. 'The Robot "Shakey" and "His" Successors'. *Computers and People*, 25 (10), p. 7.

Ringle, M. (ed.) 1979. *Philosophical Perspectives in Artificial Intelligence*. Brighton: Harvester.

Rose, F. 1985. *Into the Heart of the Mind: An American Quest for Artificial Intelligence*. New York: Vintage Books.

Rose, G. F., Ullian, J. S. 1963. 'Approximation of Functions on the Integers'. *Pacific Journal of Mathematics*, 13, pp. 693–701.

Rose, S. 1976. *The Conscious Brain*. Revised edn. Harmondsworth: Penguin.

Rosenblatt, F. 1962. *Principles of Neurodynamics*. Washington, D.C.: Spartan.

Roszak, T. 1986. 'Smart Computers at Insecure Stage'. *New Scientist*, April 3, 1986, pp. 46–7.

Rumelhart, D. E., McClelland, J. L., and the PDP Research Group 1986. *Parallel Distributed Processing: Explorations in the Microstructure of Cognition*. Vol. 1: *Foundations*. Cambridge, Mass.: MIT Press.

Rumelhart, D. E., McClelland, J. L. 1986a. 'On Learning the Past Tenses of English Verbs'. In McClelland, J. L., Rumelhart, D. E., and the PDP Research Group 1986.

Parallel Distributed Processing: Explorations in the Microstructure of Cognition. Vol. 2: *Psychological and Biological Models*. Cambridge, Mass.: MIT Press, pp. 216–71.

Rumelhart, D. E., McClelland, J. L. 1986b. 'PDP Models and General Issues in Cognitive Science'. In Rumelhart, D. E., McClelland, J. L., and the PDP Research Group 1986. *Parallel Distributed Processing: Explorations in the Microstructure of Cognition*. Vol. 1: *Foundations*. Cambridge, Mass.: MIT Press, pp. 110–46.

Rumelhart, D. E., Hinton, G. E., McClelland, J. L. 1986. 'A General Framework for Parallel Distributed Processing'. In Rumelhart, D. E., McClelland, J. L., and the PDP Research Group 1986. *Parallel Distributed Processing: Explorations in the Microstructure of Cognition*. Vol. 1: *Foundations*. Cambridge, Mass.: MIT Press, pp. 45–76.

Rumelhart, D. E., Hinton, G. E., Williams, R. J. 1986. 'Learning Internal Representations by Error Propagation'. In Rumelhart, D. E., McClelland, J. L., and the PDP Research Group 1986. *Parallel Distributed Processing: Explorations in the Microstructure of Cognition*. Vol. 1: *Foundations*. Cambridge, Mass.: MIT Press, pp. 318–62.

Russell, B. 1912. *The Problems of Philosophy*. Oxford: Oxford University Press.

Sakitt, B. 1972. 'Counting Every Quantum'. *Journal of Physiology*, 223, pp. 131–50.

Samuel, A. L. 1959. 'Some Studies in Machine Learning Using the Game of Checkers'. In Feigenbaum, E. A., Feldman, J. (eds) 1963. *Computers and Thought*. New York: McGraw-Hill, pp. 71–105.

Savage, C. W. (ed.) 1978. *Perception and Cognition: Issues in the Foundations of Psychology*. Minneapolis: University of Minnesota Press.

Schank, R. C. 1979. 'Natural Language, Philosophy and Artificial Intelligence'. In Ringle, M. 1979. *Philosophical Perspectives in Artificial Intelligence*. Brighton: Harvester, pp. 196–224.

Schank, R. C. 1980. 'Understanding Searle'. *Behavioural and Brain Sciences*, 3, pp. 446–7.

Schank, R. C. 1984. *The Cognitive Computer*. Reading, Mass.: Addison-Wesley.

Schank, R. C., Abelson, R. 1977. *Scripts, Plans, Goals and Understanding*. Hillsdale, N.J.: Lawrence Erlbaum.

Schmitt, F. O., Worden, F. G. (eds) 1974. *The Neurosciences: Third Study Program*. Cambridge, Mass.: M.I.T. Press.

Searle, J. 1980a. 'Minds, Brains, and Programs'. *Behavioural and Brain Sciences*, 3, pp. 417–24.

Searle, J. 1980b. 'Author's Response'. *Behavioural and Brain Sciences*, 3, pp. 450–6.

Searle, J. 1989. *Minds, Brains and Science: the 1984 Reith Lectures*. London: Penguin.

Searle, J. 1990a. 'Is the Brain's Mind a Computer Program?' *Scientific American*, 262 (1), pp. 20–5.

Searle, J. 1990b. 'Is the Brain a Digital Computer?'. *Proceedings and Addresses of the American Philosophical Association*, 64, pp. 21–37.

Sejnowski, T. J., Rosenberg, C. R. 1987. 'Parallel Networks that Learn to Pronounce English Text'. *Complex Systems*, 1, pp. 145–68.

Selfridge, O. G., Rissland, E. L., Arbib, M. A. (eds) 1984. *Adaptive Control of Ill-Defined Systems*. New York: Plenum.

Shaffer, J. A. 1968. *Philosophy of Mind*. Englewood Cliffs, N.J.: Prentice-Hall.

Shannon, C. E., McCarthy, J. (eds) 1956. *Automata Studies*. Princeton: Princeton University Press.

Shortliffe, E. H. 1976. *Computer-Based Medical Consultations: MYCIN*. New York: Elsevier.

Shurkin, J. 1983. 'Computer Pioneer and His Historic Program Still Active at Stanford'. Stanford: Stanford University News Service.

Shurkin, J. 1984. *Engines of the Mind*. New York: W.W. Norton.

Simon, H. A. 1965. *The Shape of Automation: For Men and Management*. New York: Harper & Row.

Simon, H. A. 1977a. 'What Computers Mean for Man and Society'. *Science*, 195, pp. 1186–91.

Simon, H. A. 1977b. 'Artificial Intelligence Systems that Understand'. *Proceedings of the Fifth International Joint Conference on Artificial Intelligence*. Cambridge: Massachusetts Institute of Technology, pp. 1059–73.

Simon, H. A., Newell, A. 1958. 'Heuristic Problem Solving: The Next Advance in Operations Research'. *Operations Research*, 6, pp. 1–10.

Simon, H. A., Newell, A. 1964. 'Information-Processing in Computer and Man'. In Pylyshyn, Z. W. (ed.) 1970. *Perspectives on the Computer Revolution*. Englewood Cliffs, N.J.: Prentice-Hall, pp. 256–73.

Simons, G. L. 1983. *Are Computers Alive?* Brighton: Harvester.

Simons, G. L. 1984. *Introducing Artificial Intelligence*. Manchester: NCC Publications.

Simons, G. L. 1985. *The Biology of Computer Life*. Brighton: Harvester.

Sloman, A. 1978. *The Computer Revolution in Philosophy*. Brighton: Harvester.

Slote, M. A. 1980. 'Understanding Free Will'. *The Journal of Philosophy*, 77, pp. 136–51.

Smith, B. C. 1991. 'The Owl and the Electric Encyclopaedia'. *Artificial Intelligence*, 47, pp. 251–88.

Smolensky, P. 1988. 'On the Proper Treatment of Connectionism'. *Behavioural and Brain Sciences*, 11, pp. 1–23.

Sperry, R. W. 1982. 'Some Effects of Disconnecting the Cerebral Hemispheres'. *Science*, 217, pp. 1223–6.

Squire, L. R., Zola-Morgan, S. 1988. 'Memory: Brain Systems and Behaviour'. *Trends in Neuroscience*, 11, pp. 170–5.

Sterelny, K. 1990. *The Representational Theory of Mind*. Oxford: Basil Blackwell.

Stern, N. 1979. 'The BINAC: A Case Study in the History of Technology'. *Annals of the History of Computing*, 1, pp. 9–20.

Stich, S. 1983. *From Folk Psychology to Cognitive Science: The Case Against Belief*. Cambridge, Mass.: MIT Press.

Sussman, G. J. 1975. *A Computer Model of Skill Acquisition*. New York: Elsevier.

Sutherland, N. S. 1986. 'Removing the Mystery from Intelligence'. *The Times Higher Education Supplement*, Feb. 28, 1986, p. 16.

Thorp, J. 1980. *Free Will: A Defence Against Neurophysiological Determinism*. London: Routledge & Kegan Paul.

Thorpe, W. H., Zangwill, O. L. (eds) 1961. *Current Problems in Animal Behaviour*. Cambridge: Cambridge University Press.

Touretzky, D. S., Hinton, G. E. 1985. 'Symbols Among the Neurons: Details of a Connectionist Inference Architecture'. *Proceedings of the Ninth International Joint Conference on Artificial Intelligence*. Los Altos: Morgan Kaufmann, pp. 238–43.

Trusted, J. 1984. *Free Will and Responsibility*. Oxford: Oxford University Press.

Turing, A. M. 1936. 'On Computable Numbers, with an Application to the Entscheidungsproblem'. *Proceedings of the London Mathematical Society*, Series 2, 42 (1936–37), pp. 230–65.

Turing, A. M. 1947. 'Lecture to the London Mathematical Society on 20 February 1947'. In Carpenter, B. E., Doran, R. W. (eds) 1986. *A.M. Turing's ACE Report of 1946 and Other Papers*. Cambridge, Mass.: MIT Press, pp. 106–24.

Turing, A. M. 1948. 'Intelligent Machinery'. In Meltzer, B., Michie, D. (eds) 1969. *Machine Intelligence 5*. Edinburgh: Edinburgh University Press, pp. 3–23.

Turing, A. M. 1950. 'Computing Machinery and Intelligence'. *Mind* 59, pp. 433–60.

Turing, S. 1959. *Alan M. Turing*. Cambridge: W. Heffer.

Turkle, S. 1984. *The Second Self: Computers and the Human Spirit*. New York: Simon and Schuster.

Ullman, S. 1984. 'Visual Routines'. *Cognition*, 18, pp. 97–159.

Van Inwagen, P. 1983. *An Essay on Freewill*. Oxford: Clarendon Press.

Von Neumann, J. 1945. 'First Draft of a Report on the EDVAC'. An edited version appears in Randell, B. (ed.) 1982. *The Origins of Digital Computers*. Berlin: Springer-Verlag, pp. 383–92.

Von Neumann, J. 1951. 'The General and Logical Theory of Automata'. In Pylyshyn, Z. (ed.) 1970. *Perspectives On the Computer Revolution*. Englewood Cliffs, N.J.: Prentice-Hall, pp. 87–113.

Von Neumann, J. 1958. *The Computer and the Brain*. New Haven: Yale University Press.

Waldrop, M. M. 1984. 'Artificial Intelligence in Parallel'. *Science*, 225, pp. 608–10.

Waldrop, M. M. 1987. *Man-Made Minds: The Promise of Artificial Intelligence*. New York: Walker.

Waltz, D. L. 1975. 'Understanding Line Drawings of Scenes With Shadows'. In Winston, P. H. (ed.) 1975. *The Psychology of Computer Vision*. New York: McGraw-Hill, pp. 19–91.

Waltz, D. L. 1982. 'Artificial Intelligence'. *Scientific American*, 247 (4), pp. 101–22.

Warren, R. M. 1970. 'Perceptual Restoration of Missing Speech Sounds'. *Science*, 167, pp. 392–3.

Weiskrantz, L. 1977. 'Trying to Bridge Some Neuropsychological Gaps Between Monkey and Man'. *British Journal of Psychology*, 68, pp. 431–45.

Weiskrantz, L. 1986. *Blindsight*. Oxford: Oxford University Press.

Weiskrantz, L. 1987. 'Neuropsychology and the Nature of Consciousness'. In Blakemore, C., Greenfield, S. (eds) 1987. *Mindwaves*. Oxford: Basil Blackwell, pp. 307–20.

Weiskrantz, L. 1988. 'Some Contributions of Neuropsychology of Vision and Memory to the Problem of Consciousness'. In Marcel, A. J., Bisiach, E. (eds) 1988. *Consciousness in Contemporary Science*. Oxford: Clarendon Press, pp. 183–99.

Weiskrantz, L., Warrington, E. K., Sanders, H. D., Marshall, J. 1974. 'Visual Capacity in the Hemianopic Field Following a Restricted Occipital Ablation'. *Brain*, 97, pp. 709–28.

Weizenbaum, J. 1966. 'ELIZA – a Computer Program for the Study of Natural Language Communication Between Man and Machine' *Communications of the Association for Computing Machinery*, 9, pp. 36–45.

Weizenbaum, J. 1976. *Computer Power and Human Reason: From Judgement to Calculation*. San Francisco: W. H. Freeman.

Whitehead, A. N., Russell, B. 1910. *Principia Mathematica*. Cambridge: Cambridge University Press.

Wiggins, D. 1973. 'Towards a Reasonable Libertarianism'. In Honderich, T. (ed.) 1973. *Essays on Freedom of Action*. London: Routledge and Kegan Paul, pp. 31–61.

Wilkes, K. 1988. '–, Yishi, Duh, Um, and Consciousness'. In Marcel, A. J., Bisiach, E. (eds) 1988. *Consciousness in Contemporary Science*. Oxford: Clarendon Press, pp. 16–41.

Winograd, T. A. 1971. *Procedures as a Representation for Data in a Computer Program for Understanding Natural Language*. Cambridge, Mass.: MIT Project MAC.

Winograd, T. A. 1972. *Understanding Natural Language*. New York: Academic Press.

Winograd, T. A. 1975. 'Breaking the Complexity Barrier Again'. *SIGPLAN Notices*, 10, pp. 13–22.

Winograd, T. A. 1980. 'What Does it Mean to Understand Language?' *Cognitive Science*, 4, pp. 209–41.

Winograd, T. A. 1981. *Artificial Intelligence and Language Comprehension*. Reading, Mass.: Addison-Wesley.

Winograd, T. A., Flores, F. 1986. *Understanding Computers and Cognition*. Norwood, N.J.: Ablex.

Winston, P. H. (ed.) 1975a. *The Psychology of Computer Vision*. New York: McGraw-Hill.

Winston, P. H. 1975b. 'Learning Structural Descriptions from Examples'. In Winston, P. H. (ed.) 1975a. *The Psychology of Computer Vision*. New York: McGraw-Hill, pp. 157–209.

Wittgenstein, L. 1953. *Philosophical Investigations*. Oxford: Basil Blackwell.

Wood, C. C. 1978. 'Variations on a Theme by Lashley: Lesion Experiments on the Neural Model of Anderson, Silverstein, Ritz and Jones'. *Psychological Review*, 85, pp. 582–91.

Wooldridge, D. 1963. *The Machinery of the Brain*. New York: McGraw Hill.

Woolf, V. 1927. *To The Lighthouse*. London: Hogarth.

Young, J. Z. 1987. *Philosophy and the Brain*. Oxford: Oxford University Press.

Zuse, K. 1980. 'Some Remarks on the History of Computing in Germany'. In Metropolis, N., Howlett, J., Rota, G. C. (eds) 1980. *A History of Computing in the Twentieth Century*. New York: Academic Press, pp. 611–27.

Index

302   Index

consciousness
  baseline sense 164–6, 170, 270, 271;
  behaviourism and 163; blindsight and 35,
  166; brain science has little to say about
  163–4; Broadbent filtering effect and
  35–6; car driver example 165, 166, 271;
  confabulation and 167–70; free will and
  141–2; in other animals 166, 174–6; in
  other people 48, 170–1, 174–6, 178–9;
  internal monitoring and 166–70, 171, 270,
  271; language of thought and 181, 196;
  machine consciousness 2, 140, 164, 165–6,
  170–1, 179, 257; meaning of term 164,
  270; not necessary for thought 33–7, 54;
  physicalism and 173–9, 249, 272; qualia
  and 170–9, 272, 273; of self 164, 166,
  168–70, 271; split-brain operation and
  166–9, 271; taxonomy of 164–6, 170, 171;
  Turing Test and 272; word recognition
  and 34, 35–6, 218; see also physicalism;
  qualia
consistency 106, 112, 117–20, 198, 264, 265;
  consistency check 118
content-addressability see memory
context
  classification problem and 218; relevance
  and 115
contingent 155, 157
contradiction see inconsistency
contrapositive 227–8
Corballis, M. 277
corpus callosum 167; see also
  commissurotomy
cortex 35, 56, 129, 166–9, 173, 189–92,
  275, 279, 282; see also brain
counterfactual 108–9, 110–11, 137, 148,
  151–2
CPU see central processing unit
Craik, K. 202, 276
Cray 79, 232
Crick, F. 223
Culbertson, J. 163, 257, 270
Cullingford, R. 27
CYC 102–20, 261–5; description of 102–4;
  Horn clauses and 264, 265; inconsistency
  and 117–20, 264, 265; inference in 105–6,
  109–14, 117–20; ontology and 107–9;
  philosophy and 104–6; predictions
  concerning 103, 106–7, 111; relevance
  axioms of 114–17; representation of
  causality in 109–11, 112–14, 263, 264;

  temporal projection problem and 111–14,
  263, 264

Darrach, B. 95, 96, 260
Dartmouth Conference 8–9, 10, 24, 207,
  253, 255
data model see knowledge, data model of
Davidson, D. 262
decidability 233–41, 280, 281; algorithmic
  calculability and 236–8, 281; brain and
  237–8; characterization of 233–4;
  first- and second-order logic and 118,
  235–6, 265; halting problem and 281;
  lookup and 234, 238; nonsemidecidability
  23–8; recursive approximability and 281;
  semidecidability 235–7, 240; of set of
  infinite sequences 240; Turing machines
  and 238–40, 281; wave equation and
  280–1
decision 54, 57, 140–62; consciousness and
  165; see also choice; determinism; free will
decision problem see decidability
decision procedure 233–40; see also
  decidability
declarative paradigm see knowledge, data
  model of; symbol system hypothesis
decomposition tree 63–4
deduction see entailment; inference; logic;
  validity
Deep Thought 23, 83
DeJong, G. 28
Dendral 30, 94
dendrite see neuron
Dennett, D. 161, 257, 269, 271, 272
Descartes, R. 38–9, 182, 249, 272
desire
  compulsive 149–51; free will and 148–53,
  160; internal monitoring and 170; as
  involving representations 195; language of
  thought and 198–9, 200–1, 204;
  paradoxes of intentionality and 198–9,
  200–1, 204; second-order 150–1
determinism
  chaos theory and 154–7, 161;
  characterization of 143; compatibilism and
  147–9, 157–62; inevitability of future and
  157–62; libertarianism and 151–4; logic
  and 159–60; moral responsibility and
  146–7, 154; neurophysiological
  determinism 142, 143–4, 145, 146, 148–9,
  152, 155, 157, 158; of programmed device

Hitech 23, 83
Hobbes, T. 257, 269
Hodges, A. 254, 280
Hofstadter, D. 34, 188–9, 217, 257, 275
hologram 190–1, 275
Honderich, T. 161, 270
Honeywell 6, 251
Horn clause 264; inconsistent data and 265
Hospers, J. 149
Hsiung Hsu 23
human AI 26, 51, 255
human dignity 1, 2, 95–6, 140–1, 249, 250
human nature 2, 140–1, 144, 174, 180, 249, 250
Hume, D. 262, 269
hundred step limitation 186–7, 274
Huxley, T. 172
hypothalamus 56, 173

IBM 21, 22, 71, 180, 219, 251
IBM-701 253
identity conditions 52–3, 104, 108–9
imagery 196, 276; *see also* analogue
implementation level 246–7; *see also* hardware; multiple realizability
implication, material
  inference and 7, 118, 159–60; paradox of 110; representation of causality and 109–13, 263, 264; truth table for 263; *see also* conditional; logic
inconsistency
  classical logic and 117–20, 264, 265; frame problem and 112; Horn clauses and 265; intuitionism and 119; management of in data base 106, 117–20; paradox of intentionality and 198
inference
  causal 109–14, 118; constructive 119; frame problem and 111–14; Horn clauses and 264, 265; inconsistency and 117–20, 264, 265; length of 118–19, 265; massive adaptability and 55; nonmonotonic 105–6; paradoxes concerning 110, 117–20, 264, 265; PDP and 245–6, 247; programs for drawing 7–8, 15–18, 25, 26–8, 105–6, 109–20, 241; relevance and 114–17; scripts and 28–30; simulation and 227–9; *see also* counterfactual; entailment; implication, material; inference rule; logic; reasoning; truth tables; validity

inference rule
  contraposition 227–8; CYC and 109–20, 241; data model of knowledge and 100–1; examples of 7, 31–2, 119; in expert systems 31–2, 101, 243; Horn clauses and 264, 265; inconsistent data and 117–20, 264, 265; material implication and 110–11, 118, 224; modal 159–60; nonmonotonicity and 105–6
infinite
  capacities 199–200, 237–8; number of internal states 237–8, 280; resources 134–5, 231–2, 237, 238, 239, 254, 259, 280, 281; sets 80, 234–40, 259, 280, 281
information-processor 86, 205–6
inhibition 209–10, 213, 214, 222–3, 226
intelligence
  algorithmic calculability and 233; of artefact 1, 2, 7, 8, 15, 22, 24, 86, 87, 90, 95–7, 100, 102, 106, 107, 109, 119, 120, 124, 208, 214, 242, 250, 257; duplication versus simulation 2; human 1, 2, 7, 26, 102, 109, 124, 250, 257; superhuman 250; *see also* inference; knowledge; reasoning; search; symbol system hypothesis; strong symbol system hypothesis; thinking; Turing Test; understanding
intentional explanation 56–7, 257
intentionality, paradoxes of 198–9, 200–1, 204, 276
intuitionism 119
inversion task 212–14, 219
IPL-V 90
isomorphism 136–7, 267

Jackendoff, R. 256
Jackson, F. 174, 176–9, 273
Japan 95, 97
Jaynes, J. 163, 164–5, 270, 271
Jefferson, G. 9–10
JOHNNIAC 7, 9 252, 255
Johnson, Dr Samuel 141–2
Johnson-Laird, P. 201, 271

Kant, I. 149, 189
Kasparov, G. 23
Kilburn, T. 5
know-how 100–2, 222
knowledge 90–2, 98–107; in absence of conscious belief 35; by acquaintance 177–9, 273; data model of 100–2, 106,